JUSTICE

Interdisciplinary and Global Perspectives

/ 8

99 2

Edited by

T.M. Thomas
Jesse Levitt

University of Bridgeport

UNIVERSITY
PRESS OF
AMERICA

Lanham • New York • London

British Cataloging in Publication Information Available

Library of Congress Cataloging-in-Publication Data

Justice : interdisciplinary and global perspectives.

1. Justice. I. Thomas, T.M., 1933–
II. Levitt, Jesse.
JC578.J884   1988   320'.01'1   88–17320
ISBN 0–8191–7093–3 (pbk. : alk. paper)

Dedicated

to the

STUDENTS

in the

Capstone Senior Seminar

at the

University of Bridgeport

PREFACE

The need for suitable readings on justice to be used by students in the senior seminar at the University of Bridgeport has resulted in the publication of this book. The distinctive features of this book are its interdisciplinary and global perspectives, something not found in the abundant materials on justice. Hence a broad and comprehensive study of justice is offered in this book.

There is a pioneering program at the University of Bridgeport which deserves national attention. As part of the revised core curriculum, all students are required to take a seminar during their senior year. A theme is selected for one or two years to be studied as a "capstone" experience. It may be of interest to note that at our university the seminar is simply called "capstone"; it brings together senior students in different majors (arts, humanities, social sciences, physical sciences, health sciences, engineering, business, human services and others). The theme presently studied is "justice" following two other topics in previous years, "war and society" and "the future" (the program started in 1983). This year about a dozen sections are offered on justice, each with its own focus depending upon the interest and background of the professor. Classes are small, with 15 to 20 students, to encourage discussion and common exploration of ideas. Among the several paperbacks used in the classes, one or two books are common reading in all classes. It is the lack of such suitable common readings for undergraduate seniors that resulted in this publication.

Faculty members teaching the capstone seminar planned this book at their meetings, and many of them wrote a chapter each. We also received the cooperation of a few selected professors teaching at this university (not teaching the capstone), as well as some professors from outside this university -- Princeton, Yale and the University of Vermont. All those who wrote the fourteen chapters did their work in a planned scheme, according to an outline formulated by the capstone faculty. We are happy to note that all essays in this book are original except one. This one article written by Charles C. West has been revised by the author for this volume.

Substantial portions of this chapter appeared first in
The Ecumenical Review, Vol. XXVII No. 1 and we thank
that journal for allowing us to use the article. All
the twelve authors are competent to write on the
subject of justice, and they took their assignment
seriously to produce quality articles.

Every author was given full latitude to express
his or her own views on a chosen theme. No attempt
has been made to impose any overall philosophical,
social or political stand. Thus articles dealing with
similar themes may vary in their approach, their
content and their conclusions. The theme of justice
may be interpreted in various ways, and we have left
it to each contributor to interpret the theme as he or
she sees fit. Each individual author therefore bears
full responsibility for his or her own views and
conclusions. It was felt by the editors and
participants in this project that a variety of views,
sometimes conflicting with each other, would make for
more stimulating class discussion and debate.

Along with the contributions of the authors, we
secured the support of several distinguished
administrators for the completion of this book.
Professor Thomas Julisburger, Chairman of Capstone,
stood with us in moments of frustration and showed us
the way to move forward with the publication plans.
Dean J. Russell Nazzaro of the College of Arts and
Humanities has been supportive of capstone seminars
along with their special projects such as this book.
Vice President Edwin C. Eigel was generous enough to
give us a grant to meet part of the expenses for
manuscript preparation. The efficient typing of Mrs.
Jerri Brown and Mrs. Betty Jean Chandler enabled us to
complete the manuscript within a short time.
Different from most other publishers, University Press
of America has special arrangements to supply the book
for use in the fall semester though the manuscript was
submitted only in the spring. We are extremely
thankful to all these people for their valuable help
in publishing this book.

We trust that readers interested in the study of
justice from interdisciplinary and global perspectives
will learn much from this book. However, the book is
geared to the needs of capstone students who study the
theme of justice, to whom this book is dedicated.

Spring 1988   T.M.T.
                                               J.L.

TABLE OF CONTENTS

vii

1.

INTRODUCTION:

AN INTERDISCIPLINARY AND GLOBAL STUDY OF JUSTICE

T. M. Thomas

"It was the best of times, it was the worst of times,...it was the spring of hope, it was the winter of despair." Charles Dickens' observation, stated more than a century ago, seems quite appropriate today as a characterization of our own times. On the one hand, we live at the most exciting and promising time in human history. Advances in science and technology and abundance of knowledge have brought us to this fascinating age. On the other hand, we live at the most dangerous and depressing time in the history of the world. The threat of war, the oppression of the poor, and other such disturbing realities of today confront people everywhere. The Chinese proverb has come true in our time, "I curse you to live in an age of change."

These two types of descriptions of our age with their optimistic and pessimistic orientations seem simplistic because they do not try to resolve the dialectic nature of our modern world. What we need is confidence and hope in the midst of desperate events and trends. The upheavals and struggles of people everywhere can be seen as "birth pain" for the rise of a new global order, a world of peace with justice.

Our contemporary world is characterized by a greater longing for justice and equality. In newly independent nations of Asia and Africa, as well as in other Third World countries, the cry for justice is becoming louder and stronger. Poor and oppressed peoples everywhere have a different awareness about their social position compared to the past, when they accepted their sad lot for the most part. Today, they challenge the social system by demanding greater justice. To some extent, society recognizes their demand and treats poor people differently. In the past, the problem of the poor was left to the generosity of the rich for charitable outreach. Today, this charity approach has proved to be inadequate, and poverty is treated as a social problem to be solved by modifying the social structure. The

1

well-established political-economic systems of Capitalism and Communism in our present world are challenged from within, based on the idea of justice. Hence, problems of the homeless in one system and oppressed ethnic groups in the other have received special attention, as issues to be tackled by structural modification.

Following the struggle for political justice, which is mainly independence, modern nations have entered a struggle for social and economic justice. All oppressed groups challenge the well-established "peaceful" social practices of centuries. Today, peacemaking has started, not by keeping the system as such, but by modifying structures for greater justice. Oppressed people, such as racial groups, religious and other minorities, and women, work together for their rights in their own countries, and great achievements are being made. However, there is a growing realization that more needs to be done to establish a just society. Our modern age of science and technology that brings new ideas from other areas is characterized by a revolution of rising expectations.

We have achieved a more just society, but our expectations have also risen with new understandings of justice. The knowledge explosion and abundance of ideas demand new social structures on a global scale. We live in an interdependent world, and hence a just society should be conceived in global terms. The crucial issues of our times are not merely local in scope in this global village. A nuclear accident cannot be restricted to national boundaries. Race relations in South Africa, hunger in Ethiopia, conflict in the Middle East and other such problems transcend their national or regional character. The trouble spots of the world, whether in Central America or between superpowers, are immediately brought to the United Nations for discussion and resolution. The new economic order is conceived on a world scale. The bi-polar model of East and West is changing through the influence of the Third World. It is time to see these different worlds as one because major problems can be solved only on a global scale.

While admitting the interdependence of our modern world, we cannot ignore the reality of "gaps", the gap between rich and poor countries, the gap between capitalist and communist ideologies, as well as several others. In the global village, we still keep our tribal mentality of recognizing the members of our own tribe as real people while regarding others as enemies or non-people. Today, the tribe is called a "nation", which limits our loyalties and responsibilities to a particular group. It is high time we change our attitude in order to live successfully in a modern interdependent world. Structural changes in sociey should be simultaneous with changes in attitudes and values. In short, justice to be achieved on a global scale demands both social organization and values that are novel and different.

A divided world must seek unity within diversity; so also must its knowledge base. In our age of science and technology, knowledge has become fragmented or disciplinary. Though specialization of modern times has resulted in a knowledge explosion, the life-transforming nature of knowledge becomes weak because it is conceived as merely facts or information. With specialization knowledge becomes an end in itself, and it is accumulated to the maximum with scientific objectivity. Experts engage in the expansion of knowledge as their exclusive goal. The problem with this approach is the separation of knowledge from wisdom, a situation of modern times lamented by T.S. Eliot and some others. Also, social reality is distorted when viewed through the "tunnel vision" of specialization. The strict disciplinary approach ignores values and purpose; it results in not knowing the relative importance of social realities. Oscar Wilde's comment about an economist as "one who knows the price of everything and the value of nothing" may be true for every specialist.

In place of the present pursuit of the disciplinary approach in academic circles, we advocate an interdisciplinary perspective. Our main task is to bridge the gap between theory and practice, between empirical and normative aproaches and between academic and activist programs. Contemporary sociologist Immanuel Wallerstein's world-system approach offers an interdisciplinary model for macro-inquiry into the world historical process. John Cobb, a leading advocate of Alfred Whitehead's process theology, goes one step further by using the concept of "non-disciplinary", which transcends present disciplinary studies.

Any single discipline is not sufficient to study the major problems of our day. War, hunger, overpopulation, environmental pollution, and other

problems of today can only be understood fully when we
make use of several disciplines to see the problems
from various perspectives. The same is true with
great ideas--truth, goodness, beauty, liberty,
equality and justice, which are six great ideas that
Mortimer Adler discusses in one of his books. Among
them, justice occupies a central place and it can be
studied best by making use of the contributions of
many disciplines. Simply bringing together a few
subjects, however, is not enough for a comprehensive
understanding of any one great idea. Indeed, the "sum
of parts is not the same as the whole"-- the "whole"
has a reality of its own. The Eastern philosophic
approach recognizes the "whole" or synthesis of units
while the Western scientific approach relies on parts
or analysis of particular facts in the search for
truth. Indeed, truth is better understood if we gain
from both these approaches. Justice is studied in
this book from an interdisciplinary as well as from a
non-disciplinary perspective. This method enables us
to understand justice in relation to living in the
modern world. Accordingly, the book is divided into
four parts.

     Part I focuses on the nature and challenge of
justice. It begins with an exploration into the
meanings of justice. Thomas selects three cultural
settings: the Graeco-Roman culture, the Judeo-
Christian culture, and modern civilization. The
author shows that in modern times justice is explained
in terms of equality or fairness, liberty and human
rights. The next chapter by Charles West is on
justice and equality in modern American society. In
defining justice, the author focuses on the dialogue
between American democratic faith and Christian faith.
He shows the limitations of the former because this
democratic faith is interpreted in individualistic and
competitive terms. The sense of community and sharing
grounded in the Christian faith is presented as an
answer to the problem of injustice in society. The
author advocates a better distribution of economic
blessings in America for which both a change of heart
and structural modifications are necessary.

     In the last chapter of this part Robert Nash
discusses the idea of distributive justice in terms of
egalitarian, libertarian and utilitarian principles.
Various perspectives (liberationist, virtue and
caring) are also presented. Finally, the author
explores a post-liberal perspective which shows the

4

moral dimensions of our social problems. The goal is the common good, that which meets the needs of community existence. With illustrations and questions on justice, the author helps to make difficult principles and ideas more understandable.

Part II presents justice from the perspective of a few disciplines. We begin with the arts, the chapter written by David Conrad. The arts express revolutionary potential in the modern world by encouraging transformation into a more equal and humane social order. By focusing on the visual arts, the author shows how socially-conscious art contributes to the creation of a just world. Among the several artists discussed, two stand out prominently: Ben Shahn and Dorothea Lange. The author discusses the socially significant paintings of Shahn and explains the meaning of some of this art work, such as "The Lucky Dragon." Lange worked for social justice through her art, photography, by taking pictures of people often ignored and exploited by society.

The next two chapters are in the area of literature, one focusing on novels and the other on the film. Jesse Levitt selects two novels, The Stranger and The Plague of Camus. Many of us interested in reading novels get an opportunity to learn about justice from these two popular novels. After presenting the theme of these novels, Levitt shows Camus's concern for injustice in society. Meursault's case in The Stranger represents a gross miscarriage of justice, the author argues. In the other novel, the plague symbolizes evil, injustice, tyranny and fascism. It is Dr. Rieux who leads the battle against the enemy. The novel is an allegory of occupied Europe under Nazism. The next chapter by Leonard Bloom is on film perspectives of justice and the rich literary sources of films. Many films are discussed so that the interests of a wide audience are embraced. "Justice in Nuremberg" appeals to the conscience of our modern world. "Inherit The Wind" indicates that there is resistance to scientific advances even today. "Billy Budd" presents a trial in which true justice is overlooked. These and other films transcend time and teach us something about justice in various walks of life.

The essay that follows in this part is on economic justice by Charles Stokes. Economic justice is defined in terms of 1) how well the national economy performs (i.e. how much is produced), and 2) how equally the income of a nation or a world of nations is distributed. A surplus in production is necessary for the elimination of poverty. The impact of income distribution is shown upon Third World countries, as well as advanced nations. As an economist, the author examines a few issues, such as poverty and equality by making use of the central concepts of economics as a discipline.

Part III explores the issue of justice in selected parts of the world, a difficult task because of the numerous instances of injustice around the world. The two areas that are discussed here are the Soviet Union and the MIddle East. The serious situations in South Africa and Central America are left out, not because they are unimportant, but due to space limitation in the book. In his chapter on social justice in the USSR Albert Schmidt gives a clear picture of present-day life in the Soviet Union and its social dynamics under Secretary General Gorbachev. The concept of social justice is used for a penetrating analysis of the realities of Soviet life. Problems of poverty, privilege, housing, work conditions, health care and others are discussed to show the nature of social justice. The information provided on these topics is as contemporary as possible because of the author's regular visits to the Soviet Union and his contact with people there. The extensive notes at the end of the chapter are a valuable source for further studies on the subject.

Alfred Gerteiny discusses the condition of Palestinians as an instance of injustice in the contemporary world. He argues that the treatment of Palestinians by Israel can be considered genocide. Several arguments and proposals are made by the author on behalf of the Palestinians. In this well-documented paper, the author traces the history of the Arab-Israeli disputes since the inception of Israel. In the next chapter Jesse Levitt opposes the use of the term genocide to describe events in the Middle East and for this purpose he examines the meaning of this concept as explained by several authors and the UN Convention on genocide. Both authors, though presenting two sides of an issue, agree with the belief that a solution to the painful problems of this part of the world must not be sought in extreme demands which only divide the parties further. The bridge is to be found in mutual recognition and

toleration and in the abandonment of maximum demands
on both sides.

Part IV deals with selected issues of justice.
As before, selection is difficult because of the
numerous issues related to justice. In her article,
Kim Blankenship explains that gender inequality
persists in the United States, as well as in other
parts of the world, and the author gives several
instances of unequal treatment of women as evidence.
Why gender equality is viewed as a radical idea has
been discussed. Feminist scholars themselves have
different interpretations regarding the position of
women in society. Issues of public policy and laws on
the treatment of women are brought out.

Wesley Menzel's chapter on food and hunger
reminds us that though food production has reached a
level sufficient for feeding all people on earth,
millions are still starving; this situation is a
challenge to justice. The author traces the
techniques of producing food from early human history
to the present. The existence of hunger along with
abundance is a disturbing problem and the author
raises several questions in this context. The last
chapter by William Dunlap offers a critical
understanding of the United States Constitution. The
author shows that the U.S. Constitution is strong in
the realm of political justice, but weak in the area
of social justice. A variety of social and economic
rights appear in the French, German and Soviet
constitutions. By an analysis of Supreme Court
decisions and the discussions of doctrines such as
"separate but equal", the author broadens our
awareness of civil rights and related matters of
justice.

PART I.   NATURE AND CHALLENGE OF JUSTICE

2.

MEANINGS OF JUSTICE

T. M. Thomas
Acting Chairman,
Department of Education
University of Bridgeport

The quest for justice is so central in most past
and present human societies that we find various
meanings or interpretations given to this concept.
Though some of the meanings are very different from
one another, as we shall see in this chapter, there is
a core idea for justice. We begin with this central
idea which serves as a preliminary definition.

The basic idea of justice is giving people their
due, what they deserve or ought to have. The
definition of justice at the beginning of Justinian
codification of Roman Law was "the constant and
perpetual will to render to each what is his due."
In it justice is understood as 1) securing rights from
violation as well as 2) fair treatment. Both these
meanings are common in modern definitions of justice,
as we shall explain later.

From the above preliminary definition of justice,
we now proceed to a detailed discussion of the
meanings of justice by selecting three cultural
settings or periods in history. They are 1) the
Graeco-Roman culture, 2) the Judeo-Christian culture
(Biblical) and 3) the modern culture. We focus on
philosophy, religion, politics, and laws accepted in
the above cultures or historical periods so that we
can draw conclusions regarding the meanings of
justice.

I. The Idea of Justice Among the Greeks and Romans

The Greeks made valuable contributions to several
fields of study, among them philosophy. Greek culture
dominated the life of the Romans who made unique
contributions to institutional living and laws. A
systematic exploration of justice was undertaken by
Socrates and his disciples, Plato and Aristotle; we
will discuss these philosophers.

11

Socrates

Socrates discusses justice by opposing the views of Sophists who reached Athens by the fifth century B.C. In their emphasis on a reality of change, the Sophists deny the existence of objective truth and absolute justice. Being individualists and subjectivists, they teach that each man has his own way of seeing and knowing things. The statement of Protagoras, a leading Sophist, is famous: "Man is the measure of all things." Sophists pose the problem of justice by nature and justice by law. The issue is explored at length by later Greek thinkers as well as by modern jurists.[3]

"Know thyself" is the well-known motto of Socrates. He may be close to the Sophists in this emphasis on the study of man, but differs on fundamental beliefs. Socrates looks beyond the reality of a particular world to universality. Those who see only a variety of just things will not understand the nature of justice itself. As a philosopher, Socrates is concerned with the latter (justice by itself). "Beyond the contradictions of the empirical world, the object of opinion, lies the unity of an intelligible world, the object of wisdom. Philosophy is precisely love of wisdom."[4]

Socrates encourages people to respect laws. It is the duty of a person to obey the laws of the state. "The good citizen must obey even bad laws, in order not to encourage the bad citizens to violate the good ones."[5] Socrates himself puts this principle into practice when he serenely faces his death which he could have avoided by running away.

Plato

The question, "what is justice?", is repeatedly raised by Plato in the Republic and his other books. A clear and easy answer is not found because Plato gives many answers. Also, the exploration of justice is tied up closely with the core of his beliefs that are formulated over the years after much deliberation and deep thinking.

The substance of justice may be found in the idea of good. As philosopher Hans Kelsen explains, "Plato identified justice with the idea of the good which is his central belief." The question as to what is

12

justice coincides with the question as to what is good."[6]   The goal toward which Plato strives in his vast variety of subjects is absolute good.   The world of the good, which is also the world of Ideas, is contrasted with the material world.   The former is known by pure thinking and hence real, while the latter, known by the senses, is transitory and hence not real.   In the dualism of Plato, the world of the good is accepted as real over the unreal or changing world.   Plato believes that the soul of man will be punished for evil and rewarded for the good.   This punishment and reward may be accomplished in another world or by means of reincarnation in this world.[7]

In this exploration of justice Plato presents an ideal state with its tripartite division.   The three classes are philosopher-kings, warriors and workers. Leadership lies with the philosopher-king or guardian who is characterized by the quality of wisdom.   To Plato, a wise person is not only knowledgeable but also virtuous or good.   The knowledge-virtue relationship is assumed by Plato while discussing the qualities of a leader or an educated person.   A just society is achieved when the philosopher-king, assisted by the warrior, rules over the working class. An individual arrives at just action by governing his passions with the rational part of the soul.   "Just action thus results from activity which is directed by reason.   The question of the substance of justice is referred to the substance of reason.",[8]   Kelsen interprets.

The state dominates human activity in all its manifestations.   Upon it rests the duty to promote good in every form.   The idea that the individual has certain fundamental rights is not admitted by Plato, especially in his early writings.   The state is compared to a perfect organism which consists of several organs or parts.   There should be harmony in the workings of different parts and it is obtained through virtue.   Justice is the virtue par excellence, insofar as it consists in a harmonic relation between the various parts of a whole.   Through the medium of this virtue, namely justice, the goal of the state is achieved and this purpose is the happiness of all.[9]

Aristotle

While Plato prefers to raise justice to a higher level of the good by treating it as a mystery,

13

Aristotle's interest is to present justice at the level of "is" where human beings live their everyday lives. A famous painting of these two philosophers found in Rome depicts two different approaches to the understanding of reality and value: Plato looking up and pointing his finger to the horizon while Aristotle looking to the world and pointing his finger to his surroundings. Each approach by itself may be incomplete without the other.

Aristotle presents justice as the "chief of the virtues", the perfect virtue.[10] His well-known book, Ethics, discusses a system of human virtues, the totality of which is found in justice. One of the chapters of Ethics (Book V) is devoted to the problem of justice which is explained in terms of "Lawfulness" and "equality". To Aristotle justice means that which is lawful and that which is equal or fair.

If justice is the chief of virtues, the question to be raised is "what are virtues?" Aristotle answers it in terms of the "doctrine of the mean" which says "that excess and deficiency destroy perfection, whereas adherence to the mean preserves it".[11] Virtue is a mean state between two extremes and these extremes are vices, either as excess or as deficiency. For example, a person who exceeds in confidence is rash while another who exceeds in fear is cowardly. The mean of confidence and fear is courage. Instead of rashness which is the vice of excess or cowardice which is the vice of deficiency, Aristotle stands for the virtue of courage which is the mean.[12]

Aristotle associates virtues with happiness which is a final end, something "for the sake of which everything else is done".[13] Happiness is conceived of as a consequence or reward of virtue. If you are virtuous, that is to say, if you behave as you ought to behave, you will be happy. Aristotle defines happiness as "a certain activity of the soul in conformity with perfect virtue".[14] We all desire happiness and the best way to achieve it is by adhering to a virtuous life.

As noted earlier, Aristotle explains justice in terms of lawfulness and equality in a chapter in Ethics. Lawfulness is explored in a general sense while equality is discussed in a particular sense. Equality is related to lawfulness "as part to whole". Consequently justice in the sense of lawfulness is "not part of virtue but the whole of virtue".[15] Since it is displayed toward others, lawfulness is considered as a social virtue. Aristotle defines lawfulness as conformity to positive law enacted by the legislature. Thus he identifies positive law or lawfulness with justice.[16]

Now let us examine equality which is justice in its particular sense. It has two aspects, one distributive and the other corrective justice. "Distributive justice is exercised in the distribution of honor, wealth and the other divisible assets of the community which may be alloted among its members in equal or unequal shares by the legislators."[17] The principle of distributive justice is proportional equality and it raises the question: which differences are relevant or irrelevant? This issue is not discussed now because it comes later when we explore the modern idea of justice.

Corrective justice is that which supplies a corrective principle in private transactions. It is "exercised by the judge in settling disputes and inflicting punishments upon delinquents."[18] To go to a judge is to go to justice, for the ideal judge is justice personified. Aristotle mentions several acts of transactions (both voluntary and involuntary) which are punishable because they are violations of law. When a person commits a crime injuring another, equality is destroyed and the judge restores equality by the penalty or loss he imposes, thus taking away the gain secured by crime.[19]

In short, Aristotle presents equality and lawfulness as two key aspects of justice. As already noted, equality is related to lawfulness as part to the whole. Aristotle summarizes his belief in the centrality of law in his book Politics: "Justice is a function of the state. For the law is the order of the political community; and the law determines what is just."[20] If the law determines what is just, justice is lawfulness. If justice is equality, it is only equality before the law. This explanation of justice as equality before the law has been much debated over all these centuries in every effort to form a just society.

We shall conclude this discussion of Aristotle and the Greeks with a reference to the Stoic philosophy which serves as a bridge to the Romans. Stoicism flourished first in Greece and later in Rome from about 300 B.C. to 300 A.D. The stoics conceived the ideal of a wise man who controls his passions. Each man has within himself reason which relates him to all other men (universal reason). It enables people to be cosmopolitan, the idea that they are citizens of the world rather than a single nation. Another central belief of this philosophy is its explanation of nature. To the Stoics, the supreme precept of ethics is "to live according to nature." The natural law dominates the world and is reflected in the individual conscience. By nature people participate in the law.[21] Zeno is the founder of Stoic philosophy, followed by the slave Epictetus, the Roman Emperor Marcus Aurelius, and many others.

Romans

One of the great Roman contributions to Western civilization is law. It forms the basis for the civil law of many countries in Europe and America. One of the principles of Roman law is "universality" which has its basis in the common nature of all human beings. Another principle is the idea of "equity" as expressed in the saying "circumstances alter cases". The Romans believed that laws should be flexible enough to fit particular cases.

Codification or classification of many laws is one the great achievements of the Roman legal system. The "body of civil law", known as the "Justinian code", is the accomplishment of Justinian, ruler of the Eastern Roman Empire in the sixth century A.D. He commanded ten of his wisest men to draw up a collection of the Roman laws. The Justinian code is a compilation of early Roman law (published on twelve tablets in 450 B.C.) and new laws which are explained and illustrated by cases.

Progress is made in Roman law due to its adherence to the above mentioned guiding factors: one, natural law and another, the idea of equity. We have noted in the previous section that Stoic philosophy admits the existence of natural law and universal reasons. Among all systems of Greek philosophies, the Romans seem to be more influenced by Stoicism than any other system of philosophy. Accordingly, The Romans find the basis of Law in the very nature of things. "Natural law remains the highest theoretical criterion. From it are deduced the most general maxims, for example, that, by nature, all men are equal and free according to the teaching of Stoic philosophy. The Roman jurists thus recognize expressly that slavery is contrary to natural law."[22]

The concept of "jus naturale" is connected with that of "aequitas" or equity. "Aequitas, properly speaking, indicates an equalizing, an equal treatment of things and relationships which are equal."[23] Though slavery is contrary to natural law, it is justified because of the common practice. In this case, an unequal treatment finds justification in the Roman law. In the administration of law, circumstances and the special nature of cases are taken into account. Hence, a Roman magistrate had much more extensive power than does his modern counterpart.[24]

II. Biblical Understanding of Justice

While the Graeco-Roman tradition relies on reason for knowing the essence of justice, the Judeo-Christian tradition does not study justice in the abstract by resorting to a rational approach. Theologian Donahue agrees: "The Bible proclaims what it means to be just and do justice; it is less interested in what justice is in the abstract. It gives concrete instances of justice and injustice in the lives of people."[25] By looking at the lives of people, their social, economic, political or religious life, we get an idea of justice conveyed in the Bible.

Political understanding of justice differs also from that of modern times, known for its individualistic approach. "In contrast to modern individualism the Israelite is in a world where 'to live' is to be united with others in a social context either by bonds of family or by covenant relationships."[26] The web of relationships in the life of the community is central in understanding the Biblical notion of justice. The relationship is rooted in a personal God who takes interest in the day to day life of people. Indeed, the Israelites as a community, entered into a covenant relationship with God and all people in the community have a special relationship to one another based on the principle of justice.

17

Biblical Definition

Now we can define the Biblical idea of justice since we have recognized the centrality of relationships among people. Justice may be defined as faithfulness or loyalty to the demands of a relationship. In relating with one another, people are guided by principles or laws given by God. Indeed, the laws convey, in practical terms, the demands of this relationship. People are expected to regulate their every day life in accordance with the laws on commandments because they are in a "covenant relationship" which should not be broken. Leaders can enforce the commandments upon people because they are given by God. The famous Ten Commandments are written by God, not by Moses who only takes the two tablets inscribed by God to the people.

Faithfulness to the demands of a relationship (justice) implies a concern for the marginal people in society and they include the widow, the alien and the poor. "This concern for the defenseless in society is not a command designed simply to promote social harmony, but is rooted in the nature of Yahweh himself, who is the defender of the oppressed." A compassionate God delivers the people (Israelites) from bondage and the memory of this liberation is kept alive. When the Israelites resort to oppression and exploitation, their leaders such as Amos, the prophet of justice, step forward to admonish people and bring them back to the path of justice.

The demands of a relationship (justice) bring prosperity, peace and wholeness to the community. Injustice is not simply a bad moral attitude but a social cancer which destroys society. On the other hand, when justice prevails in society it bears the fruits of peace and harmony. "From justice flows peace and prosperity to the land and to all in the community." Jesus proclaims God's Kingdom and identifies it with God's justice: "Seek first the Kingdom of God and His righteousness." While working for justice a new social order or community is built. Such a new community of God's kingdom is not completed on earth, but begins here. People participate in the building of such a new community to be fully realized with the coming or second coming of a Messiah. According to the Bible, there is something to look forward to or hope for in the culmination of human history.

18

Laws for Community Living

The new community in which people participate to build is directed by rules and laws. Faithfulness to the demands of a relationship is the substance of this community. It does not simply happen; rather, justice is made when a community adheres to the laws of living. It is the living or community life that is significant, not laws by themselves. Though life (in community) or living is prior to the rules of living, there is a special place for laws or rules.

Mosaic Laws clearly conveyed the demands of a relationship to the Israelites who were transformed into a community by adhering to the laws. Not only Moses, but most other leaders including kings and prophets took the laws seriously by enforcing them upon people. Since the laws were given by God, people were obliged to obey them. The dominant character of God was righteousness and obedience to such a God would result in the formation of a just society. Jesus summarized all the laws into two: one is to love God and the other is to love one's neighbor. An integration of justice and love, two dominant characteristics of God, is achieved through the teachings of Jesus. St. Paul, known as the "apostle to the Gentiles" who brought Christianity to the Western world, accepted the kind and quality of life that Jesus lived and taught. With Paul and early Christian fathers, faith became the center of living because "justice comes through faith." "Faith is the obedient surrender to the love of God manifest in Christ."[30] Paul, along with early Biblical leaders, sees peace and harmony in the community as effects of justice. To Paul, "the kingdom of God is not food and drink, but justice, peace and joy in the Holy Spirit."[31]

Thus, the relationship between justice and law is an interesting issue. As already indicated, the demands of relationships (or justice) are made known to people by a system of laws or commandments in the Bible. The problem with this codification is that the laws may continue even when the justice is evaporated from laws. In other words, laws intended to establish justice in society will remain, even when injustice is done through laws. Some laws even may degenerate as injustice. Most leaders in the Bible are aware of this danger and hence they admonish people, including other leaders, for the just administration of laws. Jesus rebuked other religious leaders of his time for

19

their neglect of justice while enforcing laws.   Jesus
showed   justice,   mercy   and   faithfulness   as   "the
weightier matters of the law".[32]

Justice and Love

        The   God presented in the Bible is a God of   both
justice   and   love.   One of the purposes of justice is
retribution   and   God punishes people for   their   evil
behavior.   Social   events,   such   as   the   exile   of
Israelites   to Babylonia,   are explained in   terms   of
punishment   by   a righteous God.   Repentance   enables
people   to   receive blessings from a   loving   God   who
restores and saves people from sin.   Our understanding
of   justice   is enriched by seeing it in   relation   to
love.   Paul   Tillich,   the   leading   theologian   who
studied   the relationship between these two qualities,
concludes   that   "love is the   ultimate   principle   of
justice".   He   continues: "Love reunites;   justice
preserves   what   is to be united.   It is the form   in
which and through which love performs its work."[33]

        A   balance   between   love and justice   is   to   be
maintained.   In my view, the Bible seems to keep this
balance   though   some   people   argue   that   the   Old
Testament   and   New Testament can be divided into   two
parts in terms of their emphasis on justice and   love.
Others   believe   that the shift from justice   to   love
took   place   when   Christianity   grew   as   a   separate
religion   and that the shift happened in modern   times
beginning with Martin Luther.   If there is an emphasis
on the God of love over the God of justice,   "the task
of   our age may well be the reverse,   to translate the
love   of God into the doing of justice."[34]   Hence,   I
would argue that the Bible enriches our   understanding
of   justice   by integrating it with love,   instead   of
dividing them.   By focusing on a loving and just God,
the   Bible   encourages   people   to   strengthen   their
relationship based on justice and love.

        In   short,   the Biblical idea of justice is found
in   the community life of people who recognized   their
relationship to one another and to God.   The role of a
relationship   was   well   established   by   laws   or
commandments.   People admitted that the   relationship
was a covenant which they should not break.   The kind
of   life   to be lived through these relationships   was
conveyed   in the idea of justice.   In modern times we
have   changed the above emphasis on relationship   and
community   life by giving priority to individualism in

which the human bonds are weak. Now we move to modern times to study the idea of justice in a different setting.

III. Modern Interpretations of Justice

Following the Renaissance and the Reformation as well as the new developments in science associated with the names of Bacon, Galileo, and Newton, a new age had emerged in Europe, an age the essential feature of which is "enlightenment". It was "a conviction that Europeans now knew the secret of knowledge and therefore the secret of mastery over the world".[35] The central thrust of Western culture became reason and knowing, or using Kant's phrase, "dare to know". The enlightenment thinkers interpreted reason as those analytical and mathematical powers by which human beings could attain full understanding and mastery of nature. In place of submitting to an authoritarian church or empire, each individual began to assert himself or herself and used scientific method to gather necessary knowledge.

The revolutions of the eighteenth century, the French and the American, brought new ideas which shaped the modern world and they include liberty, equality and happiness. The idea of human rights, for which there was no suitable term in classical or medieval times, was used in society with a special meaning and significance.[36] An understanding of such new ideas in society is necessary in explaining the meaning of justice. First, we look at a few thinkers who shaped modern culture.

Early Thinkers

Laws and customs which were dictated by an authoritarian church or empire, found a new basis in the rational and human approach of people during modern times. Law asserted substantial independence from theology. The initiator of this new trend was Hugo Grotius (1583-1645), the founder of modern philosophy of law.[37] Grotius promoted the development of International Law at a time when states of law in the relationship between states and argued that treaties had judicial value and were obligatory by natural Law.[38] From Aristotle he accepted the fundamental theory that man is a social being and he is destined to a certain form of society, the

21

political form. Law is something presented by reason,
to be adapted for living together in society. Among
the conditions of sociableness which bring out law,
Grotius points out one in particular; it is "the
inviolability of pacts".[39]

    There are many other thinkers who shaped modern
life and we select a few of them belonging to the 17th
and 18th centuries. Hobbes, in contrast to Grotius,
argues that man is not social by nature. Being
egoistic man seeks only his own good and lives in a
permanent state of war. In this situation the
individual right is unlimited. However, Hobbes
advocates that people should leave this state of
nature and enter into a contract which has for its
content the renunciation of liberty by every
individual. While Grotius stands for free choice,
Hobbes wants the contract to be imposed upon
individuals who are expected to surrender their
rights.[40]

    John Locke (England, 1632-1704) is known as a
philosopher, educator, and a political theoretician.
His popular statement, that the mind at birth is a
blank slate on white paper on which nothing has been
written, gave a philosophical basis for the growth of
science using the senses as a way of obtaining
knowledge.[41] Locke influenced the founding fathers of
the United States, especially Jefferson, Franklin, and
Madison, in their drafting of the Constitution.
Locke's influence is shown best in guaranteeing
"individual" rights, which are both a promise and a
problem for the U.S. Constitution. Also, Locke
asserts that the popular will is sovereign and hence
the legitimacy of a government to rule has to derive
from the consent of the people. Such principles are so
ingrained in American life that people always claim to
cherish the values of democracy, freedom and equality.
Indeed these values become the meaning of justice in
America, and we shall discuss it in the next section.

    Jean Jacques Rousseau (French philosopher, 1712-
1778) is called a prophet of modern times. His
theories had great impact upon philosophy, education
and political systems. The French revolution of 1789
was influenced by the political beliefs of this
eminent thinker. Rousseau presented his views on
government and the rights of citizens in his book The
Social Contract.[42] People who place freedom in high
priority usually look to Rousseau and this book which
begins: "Man is born free; but everywhere he is in

22

chains." As noted in Émile, everything is good in
nature, but degenerates with civilization.[43] In order
to preserve the natural goodness and the primitive
happiness of freedom and equality, Rousseau advocated
the social contract, an ideal form of association.
The Rights of freedom and equality are assured in this
contract when justice prevails in society.

The ideas of Rousseau as well as a few others,
notably Voltaire, found expression in the French
Revolution. In spite of the apparent failure of this
revolution, its ideals of liberty, equality, and
fraternity became guidelines to many revolutions or
social upheavals of our contemporary world. It is an
indication of a sense of justice that is growing in
our age in every part of "the global village".

As part of the French Revolution the National
Assembly of France accepted a famous document in 1789,
the Declaration of the Rights of Man. It is not the
first document of its kind as there are other such
forceful documents, one being the Bill of Rights of
1688 in England. The famous Magna Carta goes back to
the 13th century when the king of England was placed
under the rule of law. All these documents, or more
correctly, the efforts and commitments in producing
these materials, deepened our awareness of freedom,
equality and the rights of all human beings.

Justice as Equality and Fairness

As noted before, equality is an important aspect
of justice to Aristotle. To him justice consists in
treating equals equally and unequals unequally. The
creation of a just society is an ongoing concern of
people throughout history. However, the idea of
equality has received greater emphasis in modern times
when the hierarchical order of a traditional society
has been weakened. There is a growing sense of
equality and fairness found in all different parts of
our contemporary world. Our discussion of this
concept in the present section helps us to understand
an important meaning of justice.

Equality of opportunity is the term that is
widely used in our modern times. 17th and 18th century
liberalism brought this idea to the forefront.
Political and some social equalities are demanded
followed by economic opportunity in the 20th century.
People begin to look to education to achieve equality

23

in other walks of life. Equal educational opportunity
does not mean the same opportunity for all, but one
that is fair. The issue of racial equality received
wide attention during the 1960's following the
landmark decision of the United States Supreme Court
in 1954. The Brown vs Board of Education decision
represents a fundamental shift in the thinking about
equality of educational opportunity; with it, the
"separate but equal doctrine" is declared
unconstitutional.[44]

Today the idea of equal results, over
opportunity, receives more attention. Accordingly,
preferential treatment has become an issue. The Bakke
case and other decisions show that the United States
has not fully accepted the principle of affirmative
action. In some countries, such as India, this
principle is incorporated into the constitution so
that it can be enforced. In India, there is
constitutional provision for the former "untouchables"
to receive preferential treatment for education and
jobs. Accordingly, youngsters belonging to the lower
castes (scheduled castes) are admitted for the study
of medicine, engineering and other professional fields
even when their grade point average is below the usual
cut-off point. This compensation is meant to offset
the discrimination that the lower castes experienced
for generations. John Rawls supports this view of
moving beyond equal opportunity "to a system that
compensates or corrects for at least social and
cultural disadvantages".[45]

A new understanding of the idea of equality is
provided by John Rawls through his widely discussed
book, A Theory of Justice (1971). He explains the
meaning of justice in terms of fairness or equality.
Central to Rawls' theory is the idea of the "original
position" which describes a hypothetical situation of
fairness when people must choose the principle of
justice. In Rawls' words, "The idea of the original
position is to set up a fair procedure so that any
principle agreed to will be just. The aim is to use
the notion of procedural justice as a basis of
theory."[46] The parties in the original position do
not know many things, being in a "veil of ignorance"
and they include the knowledge of social position (for
example their class, income, status, race, or sex) as
well as natural talents and abilities (Eg. strength or
intelligence). Rawls believes that people should not
be rewarded for characteristics that are accidents of
birth. In the veil of ignorance, Rawls assumes,

people will choose the principles of justice. This pure procedural justice is criticized on the ground that "there exists no independent criterion of justice; what is just is defined by the outcome of the procedure itself."[47]

Rawls advocates two principles which result from the above procedure. The first, each person is to have an equal right to "basic liberties" which include freedom of speech and assembly, freedom to hold private property, freedom from arbitary arrest and others. Rawls believes that limits can be placed on freedom in order to make everyone equally free. The second principle says that social and economic inequalities are to be arranged so that they are 1) to the greatest benefit of the least advantaged and 2) attached to offices and positions open to all under conditions of fair equality of opportunity.

These two principles are instrumental in changing the basic structure of society which, to Rawls, is the primary problem of justice. The "principle of greatest equal liberty", the first one, demands a change in "the basic structure of society" even in systems claiming to be democratic. Democratic claims are made by most modern nations, both capitalist and communist. The second principle known as the "difference principle" is widely debated because it says that "social and economic inequalities" are to be arranged so as to be of greatest benefit to the least advantaged. This principle is hard to accept in systems that advocate a "trickle down theory" where most economic advantages will benefit the upper five or ten percent of the population. The second principle also includes the idea of fair equality of opportunity which goes beyond the formal equality of opportunity advocated by the liberals. As noted before, Rawls is concerned with "equality of result."[48]

We will conclude this discussion of Rawls with an evaluation of his theory. Rawls shows respect for people by recognizing a place for the poorest member in society. It is good that he wants to overcome the vested interests as expressed through class, race, sex, personal temperaments, and abilities. Rawls draws our attention from the widely discussed liberalist topic of equal opportunity (see the next section when Nozick is presented) to the idea of equality of result or equality of outcomes. While the former is associated with capitalism, the latter

25

adheres to socialism. Rawls' explanation of distributive justice agrees with the assumptions followed in a socialist state.

Another person who has contributed to our understanding of justice as equality is Michael Walzer at the Institute for Advanced Study, Princeton. He shows how society distributes not only wealth or power, but also other social "goods" such as honor, education, work, leisure, and even love. Walzer speaks of justice: "A given society is just if its substantive life is lived in a certain way--that is, in a way faithful to the shared understanding of its members."[49] The theory of "complex equality" which he advances says that resources must be distributed in accordance with the principles appropriate to their "spheres" and that the success of one sphere must not be allowed to have an influence in another sphere. For example, success in making money should not result in buying votes. Walzer advocates that we look to the existing social conventions to find out the appropriate principles for the distribution of specific goods."[50]

Justice as Liberty

Another meaning of justice given by a contemporary theorist is that of liberty. The leading advocate of this view is Robert Nozick who is contrasted with John Rawls with his explanation of justice as equality or fairness. Nozick and other liberalists support equal opportunity over equality of outcome. In this context liberalism adheres to three basic assumptions; they are the principle of merit, equality of life chances and the idea of fair competition. Liberalists strongly advocate that "there should be fair competition among individuals for unequal positions in society."[51] To the liberalists, it is the way in which competition is carried out, not its result, that counts.

Nozick attacks Rawls' notion of sharing and argues that there is another way of looking at talents and ability. Even though an individual may not "deserve" his or her talents, he or she nonetheless "has" them and is entitled to benefit from them. This is referred to as the "entitlement" theory of benefits. Talents and abilities cannot be separated from an individual who has them. What is most important, explains Nozick, is the way the benefits

26

came about and individuals are entitled to hold them.[52] Thus, Nozick draws our attention from the "end distribution" to the "process" by which holdings are acquired. He explains the legitimacy of this process. He contends that the "end-state" can be maintained only by continuous interference with people's lives and hence opposes it. Nozick's entitlement theory is concerned with the subject of justice in holdings.[53]

The just society that Nozick advocates can be maintained only by adhering to a system of rewards or incentives. Talented people receive merit rewards for the best work they do. Competition forms the cornerstone of the social system. Capitalism as an ideology subscribes to this social system. Hence, Nozick presents justification for the American capitalist system while discussing his liberal views on justice. Freedom to compete with others and secure rewards to the maximum lies at the heart of Nozick's idea of justice. He agrees with Aristotle in recognizing merits for the administration of rewards. The principle of distributive justice, according to Aristotle, is proportionate equality. He wants goods to be distributed in proportion to the merit of a person.

There are problems with the theory of Nozick. His entitlement theory has the shortcoming of not adequately addressing the question of what constitutes an "originally" just holding. Though he briefly mentions Locke's theory of original acquisition, Nozick does not explain enough the issue of how property rights arise and how they should be allotted. He defends any distribution of wealth so long as it has resulted from voluntary or contractual agreements. A minimum of life's necessities, such as food and shelter, must be available to all people and Nozick is not making any provision for the least powerful groups in society.[54] This can be seen in as inherent weakness of capitalism itself. In spite of all the wealth in the United States, many people are malnourished or are homeless. Justice demands that such problems be solved.

Though there are many supporters of Nozick's theory of justice as liberty, we will not discuss any one of them. However, we shall conclude this section by referring to a person who builds a bridge between the ideas of liberty and human rights, discussed in the next section. This bridge is found in the theory

27

of Alan Gewirth who is able to synthesize the views of several sociologists including Max Weber and Talcott Parsons. The theory of Gewirth focuses on two moral rights; they are freedom and human well-being and the obligations that are correlative with such rights. Gewirth concludes that these two generic rights constitute the moral "first principles" and they regulate the just social order.[55]

Human Rights as the Core of Justice

A third meaning of justice is found in the idea of human rights which is tied up with the two meanings already discussed. Human rights encompass both equality and freedom as two central pillars. Recently, during the Carter administration, the issue of human rights became a professed policy of the United States in its relationship with foreign countries. Also, in the Soviet Union today there is renewed emphasis on human rights as shown in the revised Soviet Constitution of 1977. Third World countries, in general, place much significance on human rights, understood differently in the emerging socio-political conditions of these new nations. Globally, all kinds of discrimination, whether directed against skin color (racism), women (sexism), or other such factors, are regarded with greater seriousness, manifesting a growing sense of justice.

"A right may be defined as a claim that is or can be justly made by or on behalf of an individual or group to some condition or power. The moral justification of the claim is that the condition or power is an element of well-being or a means to it."[56] This definition presents human rights in terms of claims we make for human well-being.

The modern understanding of justice as human rights began to take a definite shape by the eighteenth century with the famous French and American revolutions as well as the "declarations" associated with these revolutions. They declared the rights of individuals to life, liberty, the pursuit of happiness and others. The early awareness of human rights was limited to the political rights of people followed by the social. Only during the 20th century do we find a real recognition of economic rights. A comprehensive meaning of human rights has developed in recent years following the Second World War. The cry for justice as human rights is rising from all people, especially

28

those who are discriminated against.   Radical changes
are taking place in attitudes and structures.

The Universal Declaration of Human Rights adopted
by the General Assembly of the United Nations in 1948,
may be regarded "as a common standard of achievement
for all peoples and all nations." The rights in the
Universal Declaration can be divided into two parts.
The first refers to civil and political rights which
include the right to life, liberty, security of
person, property, political participation, freedom of
expression and others.   The second includes economic,
social and cultural rights which relate to work, a
reasonable standard of living, education and so forth.
Also, this Declaration expresses the universality of
rights in terms of the equality of human dignity.[57]

The idea of universality recognizes the rights of
people everywhere, irrespective of their nation or
region. First it was noted in the "natural" rights of
people.   In the section on the Romans we have shown
the place of natural law among the Romans and the
Stoics.   Though the 18th century revolutions were
fought on such claims, this doctrine of natural rights
was questioned by Karl Marx and others in the 19th
century.   Karl Marx considered natural rights
ideological statements intended to preserve wealth by
the rich.   So the term "natural" faded giving rise to
"positive" rights based on man-made laws.   Also, Marx
argues against the individualist stress of human
rights in favor of communal emphasis.[58]

This individual stress permeates modern Western
society.   Individualism as it dominates American life
is well described by Robert Bellah and others.[59]   Both
the strength and weakness of the United States
Constitution may be noted in its focus upon an
individualistic approach. The rights of an <u>individual</u>
are well guaranteed in the Constitution while it
ignores the <u>social</u> rights. Recently, a noted American
Indian lawyer mentioned that his house, the private
property in Washington, is secure as no one will take
it away from him, while his land owned by the
community can be lost any time.[60]   Human rights should
include both individual and social claims. Justice is
achieved by keeping a balance between these two types
of claims.

Justice in the sense of human rights or the claim
people make in the name of human dignity rests upon
two foundations, one legal and the other moral.[61]   The

29

legal basis of social arrangements or equality before law has already been discusseed. People come together and make contracts which consist of laws that are binding on all. Their approval or consent of the government which is the most important aspect of the law earns greater recognition in modern times. Also, there is wider acceptance regarding the flexibility of laws, instead of treating laws as rigid. Piaget, Kohlberg and other psychologists argue that the morality of laws at a higher stage lies in regarding laws as flexible. Gandhi, King and other social reformers of this century have constantly fought for changing laws while admitting the "sacred" place of laws in society. Their aim is to modify laws which discriminate against some people or laws that are unjust.

The moral basis of human rights, the second foundation, is vigorously debated by moral theorists at all times. Among the several moral theories, the two that are most influential in the Western world are formalism and utilitarianism. The former advocates fixed moral principles that are not altered by circumstances. Kant, the leading formalist, places duty at the center of morality, which can be known by the use of reason. The intention or motive behind an action makes it moral. He believes in categorical imperatives: when the will or motive is governed by reason and not desire, it is absolute and unconditional and to obey this will is one's duty. His central message is to treat human beings as ends and not as means. When people are seen as ends, we admit their worth or dignity, which is the core of human rights.

The other theory, utilitarianism, has been most popular in the Western world for more than a century after its formulation by Bentham, J. S. Mill and others. Utilitarians argue that we consider the consequences of our action and try to maximize our happiness. "The basic principle of utility required us to weigh up the consequences, in terms of happiness and unhappiness, of various alternative actions, and choose that action which would, on balance, have the best consequences, in the sense of producing the largest net balance of happiness."[62] Several contemporary theoreticians of justice, such as Rawls and Dworkin, disagree with this utilitarian approach to rights.

Ronald Dworkin is one of the leading theoreticians of justice in our contemporary world along with Rawls or Nozick discussed already. Dworkin argues for a logical connection between justice and morality. He rejects the traditional positivist separation of justice from morality. Also, he opposes the utilitarian explanation of a right; if someone has a right to something, it is morally wrong for the government to deny this right to a citizen even when it maximizes general happiness. Dworkin makes a strong plea for "taking rights seriously." He remarks that in the United States citizens "have certain fundamental rights against their Government, certain moral rights[63] made into legal rights by the Constitution".[63] He continues, "Our constitutional system rests on a particular moral theory, namely that men have moral rights against the state".[64] Dworkin gives a key position to judges who should be guided by principles, not policies. "A principle defines and protects an individual right, whereas a policy stimulates a collective good.... Rights are individual claims which operate as 'trumps' over collective goals".[65]

We conclude this section with a remark that the idea of human rights explained as the core of justice is to be seen as one of the greatest or most explosive ideas of our times. The poor and oppressed people all over the world make claims based on an increased awareness of their rights and this results in social upheavals. The new social structures to be built should be conceived in global terms to make them strong and stable. Also, we have to keep in mind that rights and claims are to be balanced with duties and responsibilities. Rights have both a legal and a moral basis. The tendency to contrast rights with the good is strong and in that regard we advocate that they are complementary. Rights can be better realized in a caring and humane world which subscribes to the idea of good.

Summary and Conclusion

We started with the preliminary definition that the basic idea of justice is giving people their due, what they deserve or ought to have. In order to study the Greek and Roman idea of justice we selected some philosophers. They explained justice in terms of the highest good or final end which is happiness. Two other central questions that they raised were explored throughout all these centuries; these questions are related to the place of law and equality in social life. Aristotle concludes that justice is lawfulness; it is equality before the law. The Romans established or codified a system of law which was used throughout history. The central questions that the Greeks and Romans raised on justice are alive today and hence we still struggle with the ideas of equality to be established in society based on appropriate laws. Perhaps "equality and excellence" is the latest issue in a long debate over equality throughout all these centuries. Can we achieve excellence while committed to equality?

In the Biblical understanding, justice is explained as faithfulness or loyalty to the demands of a relationship. A covenant relationship already exists between God and human beings, the discovery of which enables people to strengthen the bonds between them. The Bible presents a God of both love and righteousness (justice) and this God expects people to live as a community by obeying His commandments in their everyday community living. Marginal people, such as the widow, the alien or the poor are given a special recognition in the Biblical idea of justice. A question that emerges from this Biblical idea of justice is whether faith in God deepens human relationships. Modern individualism ignores a sense of community and in this context it makes sense to look at the Biblical explanation of justice which focuses on the community.

With the rise of the modern period, fundamental changes took place in people's attitudes toward institutional life. In place of the authoritarian rule of a church or an empire there emerged a new political and social system in which the agreement of the people or the consent that they gave to the ruler, became the guiding principles for political and other organizational living. The contributions of Hobbes, Locke and Rousseau are noteworthy in this context. Grotius established the place of law, especially international law, in the modern setting. The French and American revolutions spread a new mode of thinking among more people. Liberty and equality became two central values which transformed, or at least questioned, the existing political and social life. Eventually economic equality received greater attention. People were aware of their rights and they made new claims for a greater share in all different aspects of living. The revolution of rising expectations of the masses is becoming an issue in every part of the world today.

So the modern understanding of justice focused upon three emerging realities or values of our times. They are equality, liberty and human rights. All modern nations subscribe to these values and try to change their political, social and economic lives in various degrees. Some nations place more importance on certain values and give their own interpretations. In America, freedom has a special meaning and significance just as equality in the Soviet Union. Instead of discussing social life in these countries, we selected two theoreticians, one explaining equality and the other liberty. The concept of justice can be interpreted as equality as well as liberty.

The two theoreticians are Rawls and Nozick, the former explaining justice as equality or fairness and the latter as liberty. Nozick presents his beliefs by attacking the theory of Rawls and in adhering to the assumptions of a capitalist system. To Rawls, the primary subject of justice is the basic structure of society. In order to change the structure he advocates two principles to be recognized in the original position. Rawls stands for equality of results and not merely equality of opportunity. On the other hand, Nozick advocates a system of incentives based upon the merits of people. Followers of these two theoreticians are sharply divided on many practical issues. For example, Nozick's supporters would vote for merit pay while Rawls' supporters want to distribute the money to all equally (perhaps unequally, if there are some paid lower than the accepted minimum; they are compensated by special payment.) In several schools and colleges salary negotiations are divided on the issue of merit pay.

At the end of this chapter the issue of human rights is discussed as the core of justice. Rights only exist where there is a legal and social structure that defines them. Such a structure has emerged in modern times with the rise of the eighteenth century nation-state when people look to the nation-state for the realization of their rights. The United States Constitution is a forceful document in terms of human rights, especially for the individual. Many countries that achieved independence in recent years have drafted their constitutions by guaranteeing rights to the people. They are an expression of a growing sense of equality, freedom and justice all over the world. The revolution of rising expectations brings upheavels in many countries. In this context, creation of a just society is one of the greatest tasks of all these countries.

The creation of a just society is to be achieved on a global scale because many of the problems we face today, such as war, hunger, poverty, illiteracy, overpopulation and environmental pollution, are really worldwide and need to be tackled beyond the national level. On such matters, namely tackling our problems on a global scale, we are still in the "dark ages" and we need an "enlightenment." The Universal Declaration of Human Rights is a guiding light and we should build new social structures to meet the demands of this Declaration. We conclude by stressing the need for "a just world order".

NOTES

1.

Brian Wren, _Education for Justice_ (Orbis Books, 1977), p. 32.

2.

Mortimer Adler, _Six Great Ideas_ (Collier Books 1981), p. 192.

3.

Giorgio Del Vecchio, _Philosophy of Law_ (Washington, D.C. The Catholic University of America Press, 1953) pp. 25-27.

4.

Ibid p. 28.

5.

Ibid p. 28.

6.

Hans Kelsen, _What is Justice?_ (University of California Press, 1957) p. 11.

7.

Ibid pp. 99-103.

8.

Ibid p. 104.

9.

Del Vecchio, _Philosophy of Law_, _op. cit_ pp. 29-30.

10.

Kelson _op. cit._ p. 107.

11.

Aristotle, _The Nicomachean Ethics_, Transl. by H. Rackham (Loeb Classical Library 1926) p. 1106b.

12.

Ibid 1107b.

13.

Ibid 1102a.

14.
   Ibid 1102a.

15.
   Ibid 1130a.

16.
   Kelsen, *op. cit*. p. 126.

17.
   Ibid p. 126.

18.
   Ibid p. 126.

19.
   Ibid p. 1929.

20.
   Aristotle, *Politics* p. 1253a.

21.
   Del Vecchio, *Philosophy of Law*, op. cit, 38-89.

22.
   Ibid p. 44.

23.
   Ibid p. 43.

24.
   Ibid p. 44.

25.
   John   R.   Donahue   "Biblical   Perspectives   on Justice",   in John C. Haughey *The Faith That Does Justice* (New York: Paulist Press 1977), p. 108.

26.
   Ibid p. 69.

27.
   Ibid p. 73.

28.
   Ibid p. 70.

29.
   Matthew 6:33.

30.
Ibid p. 103.

31.
Romans 14:17.

32.
A. J. Kerr Law and Justice: A Christian Exposition (South Africa, Grahamtown: Grocott and Sherry, 1963), p. 28.

33.
Paul Tillich, Love, Power, and Justice (Oxford University Press, 1954), p. 71.

34.
Donahue, Biblical Perspective, p. 108.

35.
Leslie Newbigin Foolishness to the Greeks (William Eerdman Pub. Co. 1986), p. 23.

36.
Alasdair MacIntyre, After Virtue (London: Duckworth 1981), p. 123.

37.
Del Vecchio Philosophy of Law, op. cit. p. 64.

38.
Ibid p. 72.

39.
Ibid p. 69.

40.
Ibid p. 75.

41.
John Locke, An Essay Concerning Human Understanding (New York-Dutton 1947).

42.
Jean Jacques Rousseau, Social Contract (New York: Hafner Publishing Co. 1947).

43.
Jean Jacque Rousseau, Emile (Teachers College Press 1956).

44.
Edward Stevans and George Wook, _Justice, Ideology and Education_ (Random House 1987), p. 6.

45.
Ibid p. 7.

46.
John Rawls, _A Theory of Justice_ (Harvard University Press, 1971) p. 136.

47.
Derek L. Phillips, _Toward a Just Social Order_ (Princeton University Press, 1986), p. 61.

48.
H. Gene Blocker and Elizabeth Smith. _John Rawls Theory of Social Justice_ (Ohio University Press, 480), pp. 8-12.

49.
Michael Walzer, _Spheres of Justice_ (Basic Books, 1983), p. 313.

50.
D. Phillips _op. cit._ p. 112.

51.
James Fishkin, _Justice, Equal Opportunity, and the Family_ (Yale University Press, 1983), p. 5.

52.
E. Stevens and G. Wood, _Justice, Ideology and Education op. cit._ p 7.

53.
D. Phillips, _Toward a Just Social Order op. cit._ pp. 67-69.

54.
Ibid pp. 69-71.

55.
Ibid pp. 88-115.

56.
Morris Ginsber, _On Justice in Society_ (Cornell University Press, 1965), p. 74.

57.
Leal Levin, Human Rights: Questions and Answers
(The Unesco Press, 1981), p. 15.

58.
Walter Laqueur and Barry Rubin, (ed) Human Rights
(New American Librry, 1979), pp. 10-14.

59.
Robert Bellah et al, Habits of the Heart.

60.
Capstone lecture at the University of Bridgeport
in Nov. 87.

61.
L. Levin, Human Rights op. cit. p. 11.

62.
N.E. Simmonds, Central Issues in Jurisprudence:
Justice, Law and Rights (London: Sweet and
Maxwell, 1986), p. 15.

63.
Ronald Dworkin, Taking Rights Seriously (Harvard
University Press, 1977), p. 190.

64.
Ibid p. 147.

65.
N.E. Simmonds, Central Issues in Jurisprudence
op. cit. p. 105.

JUSTICE AND EQUALITY IN MODERN AMERICAN SOCIETY: A THEOLOGICAL VIEW

Charles C. West
Stephen Colwell Professor of
Christian Ethics
Princeton Theological Seminary

"We hold these truths to be self-evident: that all men are created equal,that they are endowed by their Creator with certain inalienable rights, that among these rights are life, liberty, and the pursuit of happiness. To secure these rights, Governments are instituted among men, deriving their just powers from the consent of governed."

It has been more than 200 years since these words became the Credo of the American Revolution. What has happened since that time to liberty, equality, and to the justice which undergirds them? Let me start with a thesis. We have lived for two centuries in America and in the Anglo-Saxon world as a whole with a secular political faith. This faith was belief in the power of free individuals competing with each other to solve all the problems of justice and to create an ever-better life for everyone. Today this faith is being challenged from without and is breaking down within. Can free enterprise solve the problems of justice and equal opportunity for the poor? Can democracy curb the powers of world finance and business on the right and ideological dictatorship on the left? Are private interests and the public welfare really compatible and are human beings really capable of valuing the good of their neighbors as equal to their own? Our confidence in all of this is breaking down. Will its collapse drag down with it the _values_ of equality, justice and of human fellowship?

This American democratic faith is indirectly related to the Christian heritage with its Jewish roots, out of which it came. It is not, however, the same. Despite much talk about civil religion in America with its biblical background and references, the community of Christian faith has a different base from that of America as a nation. On this base, from its own faith, this community must raise some of the same questions. What is equality among human beings before God and in Jesus Christ? What is human justice in the light of divine judgment? What do creation, judgment, and redemption as God's dealing with humanity have to do with American politics? This essay is a contribution to the dialogue between American democratic faith and Christian faith in our common effort to define justice and equality in American society going into its third century.

Let me say a word about the first part of this thesis. Politically, the United States of America is heir to the contract theory of human society. This is the underlying philosophy of the Declaration of Independence as it was expressed by Thomas Jefferson. The philosophy goes back to John Locke. Its assumption is that in a state of nature, individuals exist. It is society which needs to be explained. The bonds between human beings are formed by contract for certain definite purposes. Individuals surrender certain of their property in order to enhance the common good which comes out of contract arrangements. This is the basis of government and of civil society. The assumption is that an association of free individuals acting rationally in their self interest will solve the problems of the common life, will secure freedom, prosperity, and peace for themselves and for the world with a minimum of limitation on the liberty of each person to develop in the way he wishes. Government by consent of the governed is subject to constant revision as the majority of the people desire, and to the inalienable right of individuals over against all expressions of public coercion.

Economically, we have a similar heritage. It goes back this time to Adam Smith. The assumption is that there exists a free market into which everyone brings his labor and his products, where each seeks the highest reward for this labor, the highest price for his product, and therefore is moved to produce what those who buy demand. In this trading, each seeking his private gain, will contribute most to the public good. As long as the market is allowed to operate, and free competition is not interfered with, there will be an indefinite expansion of human productive capacities serving to meet the needs of those who buy. There will be inequality between rich and poor, but this will be overcome by the expansion of the economy as a whole.

Today, two things have happened to this political and economic faith in the immanent powers of human enterprise and the immanent rationality of human individuals. First, we have discovered that the democratic political systems which we have set up to secure the common good have excluded large groups of people. They are outside the contract which makes our society work. They cannot make their power felt to redress the injustices of the system. First, it was the black people who were slaves in our society. Then it was the Indians. More recently, it has been varios waves of immigrants until they have established themselves; and, most recently of all, it is the Chicano and the Spanish-speaking American. We find, furthermore, that new classes of people are being created who also do not participate. There has grown up in recent years a permanent culture of poverty in America, people who pass on from one generation to the next their role as victims and outcasts in an otherwise propserous society. The balancing of power with power and the assumption of free and equal individuals which underlies a contract theory of government have shown themselves to be false. They are experienced by these outcasts' groups as violence toward them. Small wonder that many of them respond to it in a violent way!

Secondly, we have discovered that the created environment puts limits on the expansion of our economy. We cannot go on indefinitely producing more and more. There are limited supplies of energy. There are limited resources which we can convert into products. There are unforeseen consequences of interfering with the ecological balance of our environment. The invisible balance of private greed and public welfare which the free enterprise system turns out to have been a two-century illusion. We are now waking up to the limits which God and His creation have placed upon the material expansion of human power and wealth.

So we face a double limit today: the other person and the environment. Within these limits, the question of justice to one another becomes acute once again.

Some people would say we are back to square one. After three centuries of expanding economy and

43

increasing domestication of the forces of nature, we are facing again the intractable problem of living within limits and trying to learn how to share those limits equitably and to discern the transcending promise of God in something else than an extension of our own powers. The two tasks go together: working out the form of distributive justice and discovering a new form of hope. The politics of bending human power to humane ends is a function of them. The newest statement of the human problem is classical in its outlines. Gone are the ideologies, revolutionary or developmental, which find the solution in the dynamics of change itself. We are thrown back into the realm of ethics, and therefore of theology, even when we talk the language of science and economics.

Is it really square one? Have we learned nothing in the period of greater elbow room for human enterprise which will stand us in good stead now? Is Heilbroner for instance right that democratic institutions will not stand the pressure of redistributing limited resources and curbing the ambitions of some? Were all the theories of tolerance and individual rights moral superstructure on an expanding material base? This writer assumes the contrary: that the ubiquity of human sin is not the only lesson to be learned from history and that something about the mercy of God and the sanctification of human relations has come into focus which will help us in the future. Let me suggest four levels of the situation.

1. Justice within Limits

We are back with the problem of distributive justice, unmitigated by the illusion that human avarice can be reconciled with social equality by the indefinite expansion of human productivity. For a while we thought we had transcended it. It was assumed by capitalists and socialists alike that there is no end to the expansion of man's capacity to harness nature to meet human needs and therefore to raise standards of living by expanding the economic product of the society. Justice was therefore understood only as sharing control of the process, of empowering the poor so that they might feed their needs and desires into the decision-making process and have a part in the promise. Today we have lost this promise. We face each other once again with the stark realization that in a finite world one man's wealth is another's poverty. One man's power is another's weakness. The economic question that faces us is also a spiritual question: how should the limited material gifts of God--the raw materials, the sources of energy, the water, air and fertile earth--be distributed among His creatures both now and in future generations?

This is an old question. It has been with us since the dawn of human conscience. It was the assumption behind Christian and Jewish economic ethics from the time of Moses until economics set itself up as an autonomous science based on commercial and industrial expansion, led by the French Physiocrats and Adam Smith. It was shared by John Calvin and those early Puritans who transformed the economic life of Britain and founded New England, though the fact is often obscured by a misunderstanding of the Max Weber thesis about the Calvinist roots of capitalism. Out of this heritage, certain basic guidelines have emerged. It might be well for us to remind ourselves of them.

First, material well-being, even prosperity, is a blessing from God. Economic asceticism has at best been a subordinate theme in Hebrew-Christian history. Where poverty has been accepted as a discipline or a virtue--St. Francis of Assisi is the shining example-- the goodness of God's material creation has not been thereby despised or denied, but only placed in its proper relation. Abraham becomes wealthy as a part of the promise to him. The people of Israel move into a land flowing with milk and honey. Jesus turned water to wine for a feast, distributed loaves and fishes, and promised to those who seek first the kingdom of heaven, that "all these things will be added unto you." There "was not a needy person" in the early church, as the book of Acts relates it. The suffering of want, hunger, or exploitation is not a Biblical virtue. The promise of God, also in Jesus Christ, has a material dimension.

Second, in the distribution of economic blessings, those in need have first call: "for as many as were possessors of lands or houses sold them, and brought the proceeds of what was sold and laid it at the apostle's feet, and distribution was made to each as any had need." (Acts 4:34-35.) "If you lend money to any of my people with you who is poor, you shall not be to him as a creditor." (Ex. 23:25.) Over and over again throughout Scripture the poor are described as the special objects of God's compassion, and the

45

cheating or oppression of the poor or defenseless as the major sin coupled with idolatry. The material dimensions of the promise of God have the poor especially in mind: "Ho, every one who thirsts, come to the waters; and he who has no money, come, buy and eat! Come, buy wine and milk without money and without price." (Is. 55:1) "Blessed are you poor, for yours is the kingdom of God. Blessed are you that hunger now, for you shall be satisfied." (Lk. 6:20-21) To "spiritualize" the exegesis of passages like this, is to miss the earthiness of the Gospel and the meaning of the incarnation. The material needs of the poor are God's special concern--at the cost, if need be, of the rich.

Third, material prosperity is a blessing from <u>God</u>. It is not a right by which His creatures can hold and measure His faithfulness or justice. It is absolutely dependent on the primary convenantal relation, on faithful obedience to the divine calling, and on the realization of love and justice in the convenant of human society. Whenever the order is reversed, whenever the search for material security is the primary goal, the result is idolatry and material goods become a curse. "You cannot serve God and Mammon." This is the lesson of the manna in the wilderness for the Hebrew people, and of Jesus' admonition to "be not anxious for the morrow, what you shall eat, and what you shall drink." Material prosperity is a by-product, not a goal of human purposive activity in this time which prepares the way for the coming of Christ. Human relations and human needs have absolute priority over economic calculations. Jesus had vivid ways of demonstrating this fact throughout his ministry: 2,000 pigs plunged into the sea to save the sanity of one man, Zacchaeus' fourfold restitution as a sign of salvatin, praise of the steward who wrote down his master's credits, the pearl of great price, or the command to the rich young man to "sell all you have and give it to the poor, and come, follow me."

It follows from this that both the Biblical history and the ethics of the church down into the eighteenth century, show a profound suspicion of the temptations of the rich and of the spirit of economic calculation. The Gospel parables of the man who built many barns, and of the rich man and Lazarus, not to mention the fate of Ananias and Sapphira, haunt Christian history with a dire warning. The vocation of merchant was suspect in the early church because of

46

its temptations to avarice. Clement of Alexandria tried to soften the stern warning concerning the rich man and the kingdom of heaven by suggesting that one could hold riches if one were spiritually free from them, but the whole monastic movement of his time thought otherwise. Medieval moral theology spent much effort carefully defining justice in the economic realm, including every step in the transactions of manufacture and trade: Just price, just wage, just return for non-productive services performed, and the like. Calvin and the Puritans followed this tradition and elaborated it in a herculean effort to bring the energies of emerging capitalism under moral and spiritual control. They believed that productive work was a divine calling, to organize the substance of this world for the glory of God, but at every point they too set limits on prices, profits, market-cornering, interest rates on loans and the like with an eye both to the needs of the whole society and the control of avarice among the rich, and powerful. It is the faithfulness, not the economic success of the steward of God's blessings, which is a sign of his sanctification.

Fourth, human beings are called to be stewards, not owners, of the material gifts of creation. The image of the steward in the New Testament negates every absolute right to private property, while it empowers and encourages us to economic activity. The New Testament steward (<u>oikonomos</u> in the Greek) was responsible for the management of the estate, both its material production and the people on it, but the estate was not his. The owner might be present or absent, but the steward was at any moment accountable--not for the profits be turned for his master, but for the faithfulness of his dealings with the servants as well as with the goods (Lk. 12:41ff). This steward image was broadened by Paul to apply to the whole calling of the Christian--"Servants of Christ, and stewards of the mysteries of God" (I Cor. 4:1), but the material dimension was not lost from it. The mysteries of God, the plan (oikonomia) of God "for the fullness of time, to unite all things in him, things in heaven and things on earth," (Eph. 1:10) includes the whole of creation in such a way that economic activity--production and distribution of earthly wares--of human beings becomes part of the harmony of the whole, a channel of grace by which all things are fulfilled. The Christian, says Paul, is a steward of this whole process: "to preach to the nations the unsearchable riches of Christ, and to make

47

all men see what is economy of the mystery hidden for
ages in God who created all things, that through the
church the manifold wisdom of God might be made known
to the principalities and powers in heavenly places."
(Eph. 3:8-10.) This supra-social cosmic economy
determines the distribution of goods in this age,
bearing witness to the age to come. Of it human
beings are called to be stewards.

A footnote: in the light of the distortions of
the Christian doctrine of stewardship one must add
that stewards are accountable for their divine
vocation also to human colleagues--to the persons
affected by them, to the church as the body of Christ.
The line to God is not private. Only in modern times
has the church tended to forget this fact, and to
leave economic accounting out of its discipline, for
its members. Those who have influence and power over
the distribution of material wealth, are accountable
to society and the church.

II. Justice and Justification

So far, we have dealt only with the lowest level
of justice in Christian understanding. We have
accepted the limits of material creation and asked
about the theology of sharing them. We could not do
even this, however, without sounding the dominant
chord in Biblical history--the open-ended promise
of God who "in Christ, was reconciling the world to
himself." There is more to justice than equal
distribution of things; there is an affirmation of
persons which responds to and reflects the love of
God.

This becomes clear when we look at the Biblical
use of the word. In contrast to the Greek
philosophical concept of a duly proportioned harmony
in which each will receive his due according to his
character, justice in the Bible is power-related. Its
basic meaning is to be straight, effective, to fulfill
one's nature in action, therefore not to be devious or
double-minded in character or frustrated or oppressed
in society. The just man is one of inner integrity
and outward success. This sometimes carried no moral
connotation at all. When Pharaoh said to Moses, after
the seventh plague on Egypt, "The Lord is in the
right, and I and my people are wrong," he was simply
acknowledging his people's misery and the Lord's
power, not undergoing a moral conversion. Sometimes
it referred, and still refers, to outward success

48

which claims to be the result of inner integrity. When Jesus spoke of the righteousness of those who need no repentance, or of the righteousness of the scribes and Pharisees, he was using the word in its conventional meaning at the time. When my grandfather showed me the silver beaver on his watch chain (the award for distinguished service to the Boy Scouts of America) and told me without a hint of embarrassment that this is the reward of a life of service to the public good, he reflected the same spirit. Power, honor, success and integrity go together in the just or righteous man. When one of these ingredients was missing, the people of the Bible, like people today, felt that their justice was incomplete and they cried out to the Lord in protest: "Hear a just cause, O Lord, attend to my cry! Give ear to my prayer from lips free from deceit. From thee let my vindication come. Let thy eyes see the right." (Ps. 17:1-2)

There is a paradox in this and throughout the Psalms; on the one hand, the Psalmist proclaims his righteousness, his inward integrity, his faithfulness to the covenant both in sacrifice to his God and just dealings with his neighbors. On the other hand, he recognizes that he is suffering and oppressed, and he cries to be vindicated by the destruction of his enemies. In some of the Psalms this drives him to self-examination and personal repentance: "Enter not into judgment with thy servant, for no man living is righteous before thee." (143:1) The burden of this paradox is that justice in the Biblical history is revealed to be neither individual integrity nor social power or respect, but a demand of human relations with its roots in God's relation to humankind. It is, not "a quality of a person or action but a personal contribution made within a concrete relationship. It is directed towards maintaining the security and right of the parties involved, and toward rectifying the relationship where it has been damaged or broken." (Sohrey, Walz & Whitehouse, The Biblical Doctrine of Justice and Law.) It is that which, in human relations, reflects the balance and intention of God's convenant and purpose.

To know what is just, then, one must reflect on God's dealings with Israel, and the work of Christ in the world. Righteousness is first of all a description of God, and gets its redefinition from Him. It is therefore a concept, the meaning of which is never exhausted but about which, with fear and trembling, we can say certain things.

First, God's righteousness showed itself first of all in choosing a people and delivering them from bondage, for covenant with him. There was nothng in Israel that deserved this election; they were oppressed, poor and needy. God in his justice sought them out there, called them, rescued and established them. He gave them a new humanity. This event was the parable of his dealings with all mankind. Continually the Psalms and the prophets define his justice in these terms: "With righteousness he shall judge the poor, and decide with equity for the meek of the earth." (Is. 11:4) So also with human justice. It has meant, in the Hebrew-Christian tradition, not the balance of civil claims or the enforcement of contracts but outrageous partisanship for the poor and helpless, a concern to lift them up, to _empower_ _them_ as equal members of the community, to give them their humanity in the convenant. One of its most moving expressions is in the book of Job:

"When the ear heard, it called me blessed, and when the eye saw, it approved; because I delivered the poor who cried, and the fatherless who had none to help him. The blessing of him who was about the perish came upon me, and I caused the widow' heart to sing for joy. I put on justice and it clothed me; my judgment was like a robe and a turban. I was eyes to the blind, and feet to the lame. I was a father to the poor, and I searched out the cause of him whom I did not know. I broke the fangs of the unrighteous, and made him drop his prey from his teeth." (29:22-17)

The poor and helpless have a just claim on the rich and powerful. Justice is the business of vindicating them. The struggle of the poor and oppressed for justice has in it a reminder of the judgment and grace of God. It is an open-ended process which aims at the quality of covenant community God intends in his kingdom.

Second, the crime of injustice is disobedience to God's justice, the misuse of power, the denial of covenant, the spoiling of community and hardening of heart toward the poor. It is to shift the focus from what the promise of the community calls for to my rights, my security and my power in the society. This shift can be given very specific names--murder, adultery, stealing, deceiving, coveting, to name only the ten commandments--but the underlying orientation is the basic injustice. The rich and powerful are more guilty because they have more opportunity, but the lesson of Israel's history and the experience of the church is that all people are tempted. The imprecatory Psalms are evidence of this temptation. The need even of the poor, oppressed Israel is for both inner and outer justification.

Third, God's supreme justice is expressed in his justification of the unrighteous. He creates a new covenant when the old one has been broken. He renews the heart and transforms the society that has broken down. "In his days Judah will be saved, and Israel will dwell securely. And this is the name by which he will be called: 'The Lord is our righteousness'." (Jer. 23:6) "By his knowledge" the suffering servant, "the righteous one" will "make many to be accounted righteous" (Is. 53:11). This is of course what happened in Jesus Christ. Justice is not a human possession. It is God's forgiving action which creates a new relation with us all. To claim to be just in the sense of needing no repentance or reconciliation is the greatest sin of all. To share his transforming and reconciling mission is to "become the righteousness of God."

For the human struggle for justice this has a double implication: first that justice is liberation, or better, humanization. It is the open-ended movement toward the vindication and establishment of the poor and the meek in the community of the covenant which has its end only in the kingdom of God. This means it is a struggle against the powers of self-sufficient domination which lasts just as long. Second, justice is transformation of the conflict itself. It is forgiveness of us all; it is reconciliation which creates new community beyond our self-assertions. Never in this world does this process stop. In every new age it must be recast. Here is the dimension which transcends material creation and the limits of distributive justice. There is no limit on the sensitive imagination discovering new forms of liberation, ways of repentance and new community, and no limit on the possibilities of embodying these in social and personal policy.

III. Justice and Hope

This leads to the dimension of hope in human affairs. The Christian message is in no small degree responsible for the linear view of history and the confidence of a better future which was built into modern economic theory, even though the latter was a distortion of it. Scientific discovery and technological invention have bred a false confidence in human power. But they have also borne witness to a dimension of God's promise present in Scripture and in the Gospel itself: the world will be transformed, the new will come, the whole creation "waits with eager longing for the revealing of the son of God" (Rom. 8:19), and will be reconciled in Christ who is the head of the church (Col. 1:18-20). Creation is not static. It participates in the history of God with his people, both in sin and judgment, and in the promise of the new life which begins now in Christ and will come to its completion in the new heaven and the new earth. God, not material nature, sets the limits and opens the horizons in which we are to live. To this the amazing expansion of science, technology and economic life have borne indirect witness during the past two centuries. The search for justice in a time of new awareness of limits cannot forget this; it must be a search for the present form of the promise of God, the present style of Christian stewardship of all the mysteries of Christ and the economy of God, to fulfill all things.

This means concretely that we have the task of recasting human hope in terms that guide, not undercut, technological invention and scientific research, and which will give the proper economic value to humanizing work in a world of limited resources. It means that when we embody this hope, we must be responders, not masters in both the divine-human and the human-human encounter, stewards, not lords. If we take this seriously, it casts two other relations in a new light. We will understand non-human creation neither as some divine mystery with its own rights even if human beings perish, nor as material to be used and used up to satisfy human desire. It is rather the provision of God for human life, whose beauty is to be enhanced by being cultivated and drawn into the movement of human history, which is to be respected and cared for as a reflection of our faithfulness to its maker.

52

Second, we will understand future generations as a projection of God's grace into the times to come, witness either to our faithfulness or our disobedience to the heavenly vision, before the throne of grace. They will not be more important than our fellow humans who are living now, not an excuse for inhuman acts today, not population statistics, but part of the cloud of witnesses in whose community we will be judged and with whom we hope for the consummation of all things.

IV. The Politics of Justice and Hope

In conclusion, then, let met suggest just a few lines of policy which, it seems to me, all this implies:

1. In technological and economic policy, the Christian church should seek that the public good be given priority over private goods, the general welfare over private property or contract rights, and planning for the whole society over the pull and haul of group and personal interests. This does not necessarily mean socialism; the form of ownership and management of production and distribution remains an open question. But our society has lived too long with the illusion justice is only individual rights and that liberation is only individual freedom. In this context, private powers have been allowed to grow to the point where they dominate our economy and can only be called to account by a responsible public planning and enforcing agency. When our public responsibility for decision and execution of policy for our society is properly focussed, the issue of covenantal responsibility can at least be raised and the victims of social change breakdown can make their voice heard.

2. The church can help the nation and the world in a fundamental reassessment of the values by which we live and the goals we set. We can and must redefine "the pursuit of happiness" in such a way that it aims at new and more promising human relationships rather than an over-expanding control over material things for private enjoyment. This is the direction of the promise of God. It is the basis for the creative asceticism which has always been part of the Christian tradition, and which is now being forced on us all by limiting circumstances.

3. In our planning for the future, the relation of public policy to the poor is the touchstone of its

faithfulness to the divine promise. This is true in a
double way. The reduction in material "standard of
living," in order to create community with the poor is
to open new possibilities for human development. It
is the way of promise. To neglect or exploit the poor
and not to put them first in planning, is to court the
destruction not only of our souls but finally of
society.

4. It may be that our policies will not avoid an
ecological catastrophe, that the political power of
human sin--greed, selfishness, short-sightedness and
the like--will make an intelligent environmental
policy impossible in time to avoid at least a relative
apocalypse. Our hope however is not in the success of
human policies. We do not hold up the world like a
weary Atlas. Rather we find signs of hope, signs of
the inbreaking of the kingdom of God, in the midst of
the world, signs which may take the form of redemptive
suffering or of repentance forced by events
themselves. It is this faith in the new reality
created by God in Jesus Christ that gives us courage
and confidence to work for very relative political and
economic goals, for small improvements, reforms and
revolutions, without setting our total hope upon them,
while we discern the judgment--and therefore the
promise--of God, in such catastrophes as befall us.
Christians are called to be the guardians both of hope
and realism in the face of where human sin is taking
us today. We are called to take absolute risks at
times, for very relative policies.

5. Finally, Christians can be creators of new
life styles, and discerners of these styles when they
appear elsewhere, which liberate human beings from the
social imprisonment of a consumer product centered
society, and therefore from the grip of greed. The
problem of justice in the face of environmental limits
will not be solved by public policy alone, any more
than by individual changes of heart. But communities
of a renewed covenant, signs of the promise of God for
us all, may be a dynamic and redeeming force. The
church should discern, form, and be such communities.

4.

PHILOSOPHIC AND MORAL PERSPECTIVES ON JUSTICE

Robert J. Nash
University of Vermont

A Modern Fable

Once upon a time, in a Northeastern State, there lived a young man named Patrick O'Brien. Patrick was raised by working class, Irish Catholic parents in West Hartford, Connecticut. Patrick's parents tried very hard to live a peaceful and just life, and they appeared to be free of much of the racism and sexism that plagued so many of their neighbors. Patrick's father and mother on many occasions participated in peace and justice projects--sponsored by their church--and they had spent several weekends volunteering to assist the down-and-out in the inner city.

Patrick himself, inspired by his parents' benevolence, was an active member of the National Association for the Advancement of Colored People, the National Organization for Women, and the National Association for Hispanic Rights. Patrick wanted to become a doctor in order to help those people in society who had been victimized by racism and sexism. Somehow, when Patrick claimed that his main motive was to help the oppressed, he was believable.

Patrick was a good undergraduate student at the State University but not an excellent one. His application to the State University's School of Medicine placed him in the 75th percentile of those who applied in 1987. He was in that percentage of candidates who were more than marginally qualified but where few were accepted. Sadly, Patrick was rejected in favor of a black woman, Rachael, who was in the 50th percentile of applicants. A family friend in the University admissions office consoled Patrick that he had been "hurt" by affirmative action requirements. The friend conjectured that if only Patrick had been a black, or a black woman, or a black woman with one Hispanic parent, then he would have been admitted.

Patrick was a realist and he quickly surmised that rejection from his own state medical school (which gave preferential treatment to state residents) was tantamount to rejection elsewhere. He would not be a doctor. And so Patrick, with little trace of bitterness, dealt with the rejection admirably, and he applied to the local State College's graduate program in teacher education. He was accepted, studied for a high school teaching degree in science, and lived somewhat happily ever after.[1]

Introduction

American traditions encourage us to think of justice as the fair treatment of every individual, regardless of race, class, creed, color, or gender. We believe that each individual ought to be accorded an equal opportunity to pursue goals in line with unique individual talents, interests, and needs. In fact, equal opportunity laws have been instituted to guarantee that each person will get his due. Lately, however, it is becoming painfully apparent that important resources are scarce. For example, there appear to be many more qualified applicants than openings for those who wish to attend this country's medical, business, and engineering schools.

It is also becoming increasingly obvious that equal opportunity policies in admissions procedures are not enough to assure justice because many of the educationally disadvantaged are left well short of the starting line due to a lifetime of subtle (and explicit) discrimination. Thus, the purpose of affirmative action policies in admissions (and in hiring) procedures has been precisely to correct present discriminatory patterns in these procedures so that discrimination will not recur. Systematic preferential affirmative action policies involve positive steps to include those previously excluded groups who historically have not been able to make it to the starting line to compete equally with the more socially privileged groups. However well meaning, though, simple procedural solutions (rules of fairness under which a society operates and disputes are adjudicated) to social justice problems raise a series of perplexing moral questions.

Is it right that a relatively few people have access to inordinate rewards? Can injustice be adjudicated out of existence? More specifically, was Patrick treated justly in the above fable? Was Rachael treated justly? Is preferential affirmative action as one type of fairness rule an equitable way of redressing current injustices? How should scarce resources--e.g., admission to Ivy League Schools, seats in medical schools, kidneys, livers, appointments to prestigious law firms, etc.--be distributed by a just society? What would a truly just society look like, and why would a truly just society be a desirable one?

To answer such questions we need to think about more than fair legal procedures (although these procedures are highly essential in the pursuit of a just society). We need to understand some representative moral and philosophical thinking about distributive justice. The following section of this essay will briefly explore three historically important ideas about distributive justice in order that we might determine whether Patrick's rejection from medical school was fair or unfair. Was his rejection a matter of justice, or was it a classical case of using an unjust means to achieve a just end?

Distributive Justice

What is society's most just system of rewards, its most fair distribution of goods and opportunities? In the best of all possible systems of justice, how would Patrick and Rachael be treated most fairly? Aristotle, in the Nichomachean Ethics, points out that justice can be understood as "fairness in distribution," as the ethically appropriate way to spread limited resources throughout the moral community.[2] One of the essential moral tasks of a peaceable, democratic society is to articulate and implement a principle of distributive justice. While Americans generally agree with Aristotle that equals ought to be treated equally, and each ought to get his due, the more difficult problem is to specify the material properties of justice--the relevant respects by which people are to be treated equally.

Who is equal and who is unequal? Is it just for some to have more freedom, benefits, or opportunities than others? Is it right for one person to gain an economic advantage over another? Is it the just course of action that Patrick's right to pursue a medical degree should be overriden by what appears to be a retributive policy of preferential affirmative action? The following is a brief overview of three principles of distributive justice, each of which specifies a morally relevant property on the basis of which burdens and benefits should be distributed.

Egalitarian Principle

In its radical form, egalitarianism is the thesis that distributions of burdens and benefits in a society are fair to the extent that they are equal.[3] Any deviation from absolute equality in distribution is _ipso_ _facto_ unjust regardless of the respects in which individuals in society may differ. Egalitarianism so construed is tied to the material principle of basic need. Thus, in the aforementioned fable, neither Patrick nor Rachael deserve anything less than the satisfaction of their fundamental need for admission to their State Medical School. If their need is unmet, then according to the radical egalitarian thesis, they are being treated unjustly. Radical egalitarians do not permit even minimal inequalities in income, wealth, and power (and access to preferred graduate school placements) if these are what people genuinely need, because just desert cannot be judged unless every individual need is met.

For the strictest egalitarians, the fact that all people share a common humanity ought to be the sole respect in which people are to be compared in the distribution of scarce resources. For more moderate and qualified egalitarians, however, what is fundamentally required is a basic equality of opportunity. Patrick and Rachael are to be given only an equal opportunity to be admitted to medical school. However, egalitarian supporters of affirmative action programs maintain that genuine equality of economic opportunity is possible only if the government intervenes directly to promote the admission (and hiring) of women, blacks, and other minorities.

Radical egalitarianism is untenable because it ignores the significant respects in which people differ, and rejects outright the resultant unequal distribution of goods based on those differences. John Rawls, a more moderate egalitarian, has constructed a "maxi-min" principle concerning the just distribution of benefits and burdens. Rawls permits inequalities only if they benefit the most disadvantaged in the society. In his own words, Rawls argues that, in addition to a principle of equal liberty for all, "social and economic inequalities are to be arranged so that they are both: a) to the greatest benefit of the least advantaged, consistent with the just savings principle [a concern for the good of future generations], and b) attached to offices and positions open to all under conditions of fair equality of opportunity."[4] What Rawls calls the "difference principle" would permit inequalities of distribution so long as they are consistent with equal liberty and fair opportunity.

Thus, Rawls might argue that if Patrick were more qualified than Rachael to be admitted to medical school (by virtue of the fortuitous distribution of social advantages and personality characteristics), then the difference principle would allow for this extraordinary benefit as long as it were to produce advantages for a student like Rachael (who has been denied benefits based on undeserved inequalities of birth, race, historical condition, and even natural endowment). Admit Patrick, Rawls might argue, if he is qualified; but also find a way to benefit the less qualified Rachael. Maybe Patrick's tuition could include a subsidy for Rachael to undertake a rigorous and compensatory pre-medical course of study in order to make up for previous academic deficiencies. The moderate egalitarian thus provides a standard for justice: equal rights as the sine qua non, and only those social and economic inequalities that make the least advantaged better off than they would have been otherwise.

Libertarian Principle

In its radical form, libertarianism is the thesis that distributions of burdens and benefits in a society are fair to the extent that they are chosen by self-interested agents who freely enter into, and withdraw from, economic arrangements. In Adam Smith's view, people ought to receive economic benefits in proportion to their contributions to production.[5] Libertarians believe that it would be a direct violation of the principle of justice to assume that need a priori necessitates equality of opportunity and outcome. Rather, for the libertarian, individuals are fundamentally different

59

(unequal) in that skills, knowledge, and personality characteristics are unevenly distributed throughout the society. Further, individuals have fundamental rights to life, liberty, and property, including the right to own and dispense with the products of their labor, if they wish.

For many libertarians, this last fundamental right must be respected even if it leads to extraordinary inqualities of wealth within a single society. And it is a violation of the principle of justice to impose a public policy of distribution on individuals which infringes their economic rights. By extension, the libertarian might argue that it is a violation of the principle of justice to impose a policy of preferential affirmative action on individuals which infringes their right to an appropriate level of education, health, and welfare. For the libertarian, this would constitute an act of reverse discrimination.

In _Anarchy, State, and Utopia_, Robert Nozick argues that an individual is entitled to what he possesses, provided that it has been acquired justly.[6] An individual is free to use his natural and social endowments to pursue benefits whenever possible. The state's role is simply to protect itself against unjust appropriation. Nozick argues that the state should not attempt to compensate for individual advantages resulting from natural and social contingencies by promoting policies that redistribute benefits and burdens. For Nozick, Patrick has a right to a scarce medical school placement because he earned it. Social benefits are never given to individuals like "manna"; rather, individuals are entitled to them because they deserve them. In Nozick's own words: "From each according to what he chooses to do, to each according to what he makes for himself..."[7]

From a libertarian perspective, Nozick might argue that when the state is permitted to interfere in college admissions policies, in a way that individual rights are violated, then injustices result. Patrick is de jure discriminated against in the well-meaning attempt to correct patterns of discrimination. His individual right to admission based on merit is overridden by a criterion of minority group membership. Rachael's membership in an oppressed minority group trumps Patrick's individual right to meet the requirements of admission based on maximal competence.

By extension, Nozick would correctly observe that preferential affirmative action policies are in conflict with three principles that exist in uneasy tension in this society: merit, equality of opportunity, and individual autonomy. If liberty is held to be the primary principle, then equality may have to be sacrificed. If merit is held to be the primary principle, as in the case with Patrick, then liberty and equality may have to be sacrificed. If equality is upheld, as in the case with Rachael, then there will be violations of merit and liberty. The basic weakness of Nozick's libertarian view, however, is its one-dimensional emphasis on claims of negative entitlements based on free choice. Other justifiable entitlements based on need, desert, and discrmination are virtually ignored by Nozick.

Utilitarian Principle

In its classic formulation, utilitarianism is the theory which advocates the greatest good for the greatest number; it is also a currently popular costs-benefits method of resolving conflicting claims over limited resources--a favorite strategy of economists, health care professionals, educators, and politicians. Because individuals cannot gain every good that they need (e.g., prestigious college admissions, access to kidney and liver transplants, expensive computer technology in public schools) then they must carefully calculate the benefits and costs of the alternatives and choose the course of action that maximizes the benefit-cost ratio, or that maximizes the net benefits over costs. This is an updated version of the utilitarianism of John Stuart Mill and Jeremy Bentham who argue that the right action is what will produce the most good overall for the greatest number.[8]

Thus, justice in the narrow sense of the honoring of individual claims might have to be sacrificed for "utility" in the sense of the greatest good for all. Justice, according to the utilitarians, requires attention both to individual fairness and to social utility. Both equality and utility are required for justice in the sense that systems that distribute income and other benefits equally must also somehow provide the maximum incentive for production and consequently provide for the maximum increase of the benefits available to all.

The strength of the utilitarian principle of justice is that it provides a concrete method for making difficult decisions, and it admits the importance of producing benefits for the general good. Hence, Rachael's admission to medical school can be justified by utilitarians on the grounds that when all the entailed short- and long-term costs and benefits of preferential affirmative action are considered, a larger social good is produced: the medical profession is enriched by the presence of black culture and perspectives; the white medical monopoly is broken; black empowerment is encouraged; and black people finally get their due, thereby fulfilling the promise of the equal protection clause of the Fourteenth Amendment, which serves to end the hostile pattern of discrimination against minorities.

The weakness of the utilitarian principle of justice is that it does not take seriously enough the possibility that the rights of individuals can be violated. The preferential admissions policy that produces the greatest good for society in the long run can also bring about an unjustified harm to individuals like Patrick. To the extent that utilitarianism requires that the good of an individual be surrendered in the interests of the majority, the principle seems unjust.

Substantive Perspectives on Justice

Each of the above theories of justice is good as far as it goes. Justice is most certainly a matter of treating individuals equally and of improving the lot of the least advantaged. Justice is also most definitely a matter of accepting the consequences of individual choices based on merit and effort that give people certain rightful entitlements to scarce goods. And finally justice is most certainly a matter of maximizing social utility even though some individual entitlements may be abridged. On the surface, what all three theories of justice appear to have in common is their implied support for a market-centered, capitalist economic system based on egalitarian "trickle-down" notions of a just economy, utilitarian notions of trade-offs and greatest net goods, and libertarian notions of the right of

62

private property and individual entitlements based on productivity.

However, what is troublesome about the three theories is that in spite of what they have in common, there is no solid agreement on how to resolve such conflicting justice claims as appear in the above fable. What we are left with are major differences of opinion over what ought to constitute the just order of a society as a whole. There is little agreement among the three positions regarding the desired purposes or ends of life.

Thus, we are left with two undemonstrated assumptions: that a market-based, capitalist economic system is desirable, and that procedural policies like preferential affirmative action are the only fair way to adjudicate disputes over justice. The three theories need some sense of substantive goals, some ways to ground their thinking about distributive justice. While it is not possible to work out a full theory of justice here, what follows are four substantive perspectives on justice, each of which presents a compelling challenge to the distributive justice principles elucidated above. Included in each perspective are concerns about distributive justice, but more importantly speculations about the basic structures of society, about the purposes of life. The issue is not merely: "who gets how much of the pie, and how?" but" what kind of pie is it to be, and why?"

A Liberationist Perspective

Paulo Freire is an important secular representative of the liberationist perspective on justice.[9] As a democratic humanist, with revisionist Marxist tendencies, he clearly opposes what the three theories above assume to be a good--the free market forces of a capitalist economy. Freire believes that such a system is unjust because it leads to excessive concentrations of wealth in the hands of a few, and to domination of the individual who is considered significant only as a part of the calculus of profits.

For Freire, economic domination results in the cruelest form of injustice: it limits the consciousness of individuals and makes them mere passive observers of their existence. People take on the language of their oppressors that both reinforces

63

their exploitation and prevents them from thinking about how human beings ought to live. To be human, for Freire, is to be free in a just society, to be able to engage in a dialogue with others that enables individuals to name the world and to change it. Dialogue is liberating because it leads to critical reflection on the conditions of oppression and exploitation.

Freire's liberationist perspective on justice is less concerned with specific principles of distributive justice than it is with separating the forces of good from the forces of evil, and with articulating the nature of the just social order. The just society is one where oppressed human beings engage in an open, trusting, critical dialogue with each other as a way to understand their world and to transform it. For Freire, education becomes a source for social change because it represents a struggle for justice, a struggle for meaning and empowerment. Education is the terrain where the dialogue is carried out, where justice, power, and politics are given a fundamental expression because it is where people contemplate what it is to be human, to dream, and to name and fight for a just society.

From a biblical perspective, justice involves the liberation of those who lack power to correct imbalances in society. The jubilee concept of justice releases people from bondage through deliverance, through achievement of equal rights and justice, and through personal freedom. (In ancient Israel, every fiftieth year was proclaimed the Year of Jubilees. All those poor who had been forced to sell themselves into servitude were freed so that the poor might be returned to their own productive capacities. The intention of the Year of Jubilees was to prevent the partitioning of society into the haves and the have-nots.)

More recently, a group of Christian theologians has produced a "liberation theology" that is a systematic interpretation of Christian faith out of the experience of the poor.[10] Liberation theology is an attempt to read the Bible and key Christian doctrines through the eyes of the poor; it is a critique of unjust economic structures that permit massive inequalities, especially in Latin America.

Influenced by Freire's method of <u>conscientization</u> (critical consciousness raising about the economic and political injustices in a society), liberation theologians teach peasants how to read by using a dialectical technique: start with the peasants' own experience and move them from a consideration of effects (their own poverty) to causes (unjust power arrangements in society). Thus, in the words of Gustavo Gutiérrez, a pioneer liberationist, conscientization is "a commitment of solidarity with the poor, with those who suffer misery and injustice. The commitment is to witness to the evil which has resulted from sin and is a breach of communion. It is not a question of idealizing poverty, but rather of taking it on as it is--an evil--to protest against it and to struggle to abolish it."11

It is the expansiveness of the liberationist understanding of justice that is its major contribution. Justice for the liberationist is far more than simply giving individuals their due, or treating equals equally, or distributing scarce resources fairly, within established capitalist structures. Rather, the liberationist perspective challenges those structures in its understanding that justice encompasses every dimension of human living; justice has to do with the fullness of right relationships in non-oppressive economic systems.

For Freire, every individual is equal in the sense that each is a rational, political human being who has the capacity to enjoy and exercise freedom. The just society is one whereby the people themselves, through dialogue, become the agents of their own transformation. And, for liberation theologians, justice for the poor is summed up in God's liberating activity in the Exodus. God is a God of justice above all, and God is known primarily in the doing of justice. There can be no sharp divisions of economic and political spheres, for the doing of justice is biblically required of all, as an all-embracing commandment.

A Virtue Perspective

Plato and Aristotle represent a virtue perspective on justice that is fundamentally at odds with a distributive approach. The Greeks are less concerned with accounts of what individuals ought to do by way of just action than they are with what persons ought to be if they are to be considered of just character. For all their differences,

65

egalitarian, libertarian, and utilitarian thinkers on justice agree that distributive systems are basically moral systems in that they provide general guides to action in the form of certain principles and rules of just behavior.

Yet just choices made from a proper sense of distributive duty do not necessarily indicate that a person is just; it is possible that Patrick, perceiving himself as unjustly preempted from medical school by Rachael, could despise and only grudgingly comply with preferential affirmative action policies. He could even attempt to subvert these policies through various types of non-compliance: litigation, covert political action, gossip, slander, lying, or even physical violence.

In contrast, Plato and Aristotle believe that the cultivation of particular virtues is the primary function of morality because the life-long development of fixed dispositions, habits, and character traits produces a people who by nature are motivated to do what is morally commendable, that is to pursue just ends.[12] The function of a virtue perspective for the classical thinkers is to train people from birth to death in how to live justly. In Aristotle's words: "The virtuous man will act often in the interest of his friends and of his country, and, if need be, will even die for them. He will surrender money, honor, and all the goods for which the world contends...."[13]

However quixotic the above quote sounds to the modern ear, a virtue perspective reminds us that the achievement of justice is not simply a question of distributive principles and formal procedures. Rather, the ways that we understand and confront situations of injustice have more to do with the kind of people we are than the kinds of rules we comply with. For virtue thinkers, to be just people, therefore, involves a life-long training in such qualities of character as compassion, courage, conscientiousness, caring, sacrifice, fairness, hope, and patience.

The difficulty with this prescription though is that this kind of training can only occur in the presence of a shared conception of a just society. In this society, in the absence of any consensual agreement about what would constitute a just society--beyond a willingness to comply with certain procedural rules of justice, e.g., due process, preferential affirmative action--judgments about virtues and actions will always be logically independent of each other. Who after all is qualified to determine what virtues ought to be normative in the pursuit of justice in a liberal, pluralistic society?

According to some virtue thinkers, the ideal of liberalism seems inevitably to lead to the disintegration of any moral consensus on the virtues. Consequently, we have failed in this society to show, for ourselves and others, why discrimination and injustice are an affront to our most basic convictions about what makes life purposeful and worthwhile. And so, in Patrick's case, we are left only with the hope that he is a rational and fair man who is willing to accept his fate agreeably, peaceably, and graciously.

A Caring Perspective

Some feminist writers argue that generally women do not approach moral problems merely as problems of abstract principle, objective reasoning, and legal judgment.[15] For these writers, a regard for caring is paramount; a heightening of moral perception and sensitivity is considered more important than a concern for universal principles of distributive justice. This ethic of caring considers acts in their full human context: an assessment of concrete events and intentions is necessary. Moral dilemmas are not problems to be solved only by formal legal reasoning; they are flesh-and-blood problems to be lived, and solved by resorting to feelings, needs, and personal ideals.

Individuals like Patrick and Rachael must be experienced as persons to be cared for; they must be met in genuinely human encounters. What each thinks and feels about a policy of preferential affirmative action is not to be dismissed as beside the point; each needs to be listened to intensely. Each of them as persons is infinitely more important than any formal system of distributive justice. What matters most to advocates of caring are Patrick and Rachael, and how each will approach the dilemma of preferential admissions in the future. Will they reach out to each other from an ethic of caring or from an ethic of rules and the likelihood of forced legal compliance? Will each ever be able to ask what preferential affirmative action means in terms of the feelings, needs, and hopes of the other?

Authors who advocate an ethic of caring invite us to consider justice issues through dialogue. They maintain that, in the long run, hierarchy, specialization, separation, objectification, and the loss of relation in decision making are enemies to individual and social justice. For these authors, justice is achievable mainly through encounters between equal men and women who engage each other within a web of complex and interdependent relationships, instead of through the usual masculine hierarchical order. It is time, say these writers, for the feminine voice of caring to be heard in discussions of justice.

From this perspective, individual responsibility for just social structures will occur only when men and women meet each other in caring, and only when conversation is grounded in a concern for mutual support and not for power and domination. The truth in the caring perspective is that legal and moral judgments concerning justice will remain false and hollow unless they are informed by compassion and sensitivity. And the logic underlying an ethic of caring is a logic of relationships which must somehow complement the formal logic of fairness that informs so much current philosophical and legal thinking about justice.

A Post-Liberal Perspective

Post-liberal writers attempt to promote the importance of tradition, community, transcendence, and sacrifice in their contributions to contemporary political thinking.[16] They are largely skeptical of the Enlightenment tendency to repudiate tradition in favor of rational and scientific authority, and to separate the individual from community and religious ties in favor of independence and secularism. These writers believe that the canons of modern liberalism lead to a view of social justice that could threaten the very civil liberties that are part of the liberal tradition itself. The rise of science, rationalism, and atomistic individualism has led to a secularized world where there is no consensual grounding for a coherent set of moral assumptions about such principles as justice. Thus, the individual is seen to be the autonomous and self-sufficient source of fulfillment as all external forms of authority, responsibility, and belonging to a community are stripped away.

For the post-liberal thinker, moral consensus has disintegrated in that we no longer are able to agree on the value of human life, on what we owe to each other, on the significance of marriage and the family, and on the meaning of being human. And so it is left to liberalism to provide us with an account of morality divorced from any substantive commitments about what kind of people we are or should be--except to the extent that we should be rational or fair or support due process procedures.

Daniel C. Maguire argues, in contrast, that human life is a shared life.[17]Our languages, liturgies, friendships, families, and sexual relationships are all manifestations of our social nature. We are not detached individuals who are without debts to the rest of humanity. On the contrary, we are sharing animals and we would cease to exist without the state's willingness to meet our most indispensable health, educational, and welfare needs. For Maguire, distributive justice is entailed by the fact that people are sharing animals. In fact, human life is enriched as public and private sharing patterns do more and more justice to persons.

Furthermore, we attack our own good when we do not pay our debts to the common good. For Maguire, the common good is not "the greatest good of the greatest number" as the utilitarians would have it. The principle of utility is expedient in that it dangerously allows for a tyranny of the majority, and excludes significant minorities. Neither is the common good the maximization of individual liberty, as the libertarians would have it. In Maguire's words, "we cannot realistically believe any longer that the more self-made individuals gobble up, the better for the common good."[18] And the common good is not synonymous with egalitarianism; at times justice may require inequality, equality may be unjust, and equal opportunity is not always fair opportunity.

For Maguire, the concept of a common good describes that which meets the needs of community existence, and it implies that we ought to think of these needs when we assess our private goals. It is obvious, moreover, that, at times, the sharing

69

required by social justice will require sacrifice, and relative to preferential affirmative action, individual rights may have to be sacrificed for the common good. Inequalities may be required to produce justice for minorities. In fact, historically, the common good has commanded sacrifice from all of us in the name of "the national interest," or in "the public domain." And, furthermore, each of us is in debt to the common good and to the sacrifice of other citizens to the common good.

Does it then make any sense to say that a person like Patrick who has done no wrong and assumed no contractual obligations, should be required in a just society to sacrifice his entitlements, rights, and career goals for the common good? Maguire's answer to this question is yes, or even fortunately yes, since, without such a sacrifice, the common good is injured. According to Maguire, we ought to empathize with, and celebrate, the pains that Patrick experiences when he is excluded from what appears to be his rightful due because Patrick's sacrifice is but one more stunning example of how a society is fortified by such a commitment. In matters of social justice, Maguire does not settle only for the libertarian axiom "Give to each according to merit"; he adds the post-liberal axiom: "When appropriate, sacrifice rights, opportunities, and even life for the common good."[19]

Conclusion

What conclusions can we reach regarding the above brief overview of current philosophical thinking on justice? The egalitarian perspective offers a standard for justice based on equal rights and liberty for all, and it allows for some social and economic inequalities only if they benefit the least advantaged. The libertarian perspective rejects any all-encompassing principle of egalitarianism as the basis for justice. Instead, justice becomes the product of individual initiative, personal freedom, risk ventures, and unhindered exchange. Thus, individual liberty and not equality comprises the core of justice. And the utilitarian perspective argues that equality and liberty might sometimes have to be sacrificed for utility in the sense that systems that distribute income and benefits equally must also somehow provide the maximum incentive for production, and thereby provide for the maximum increase of the benefits available to all.

In some very basic senses, all three perspectives are necessary for the just social order. Each checks and corrects the excesses and omissions of the others. Thus, a society can be said to achieve justice when liberty and equality are insured to each and every person, when those social and individual inequities that do rightfully exist (e.g., because of outstanding effort) benefit the least advantaged, when individual merit and hard work result in deserved entitlements, and when the common good is enhanced through maximum incentives for production.

But are distributive schemes of justice enough to insure that individuals and groups will be treated fairly? What happens when distributive justice schemes are in irremediable conflict? I believe that for all their promise, such schemes require something more fundamental, if they are to inspire a "thick consensus" (agreement on both just procedures and on the purposes or ends of a just life). The four substantive perspectives above offer speculations about the essential structures of society, about the purposes of life, as well as distributive concerns about who should get how much and how.

The liberationist perspective reminds us that justice encompasses every aspect of human living. It has to do with the fullness of right relationships and personal empowerment. Throughout their lives, people must be encouraged and assisted to participate in self-critical dialogue as a way to understand the systemic disparagement in their lives, and to transform their worlds.

The virtue perspective realistically warns us that people need to cultivate a certain kind of character throughout their lives, if they are to live justly. How we concretely confront instances of injustice in our institutions has more to do with the qualities of compassion, courage, conscientiousness, hope, and patience that we possess than the laws we are forced to obey.

The caring perspective challenges dominant masculine thinking about justice; the feminine perception of justice is that it is a problem of care and mutual responsibility in relationships. This contrasts with (but does not preclude) the formal

71

logic of fairness that informs masculine thinking about justice. Individual lives are connected and enmeshed in a context of relationships. Hence, responsibility toward others begins with an awareness that self and other are different but connected, rather than separate and opposed.

And the post-liberal perspective inspires us to realize that our social problems are not just political. They are profoundly moral and have to do with our need for shared meanings and sacrifices. Our common life together requires enduring faithfulness to those we love, and civic responsibility toward all of our fellow citizens, toward those who are well off and those who are not. Our common life demands more from us than a preoccupation with individual success. In the interests of achieving genuine peace and justice, it would be well for us to rejoin the human community, to accept our mutual interdependency as a gift, and to share our material plenty with those in need.

1

I am indebted to Daniel C. Maguire, A New
American Justice (Minneapolis, Minnesota: Winston
Press, 1980) pgs. 55-56, for the idea of the
fable. I have modified his version
substantially. I am also grateful to Maguire for
provoking my thinking on the topic of
preferential affirmative action.

2

See Aristotle, Politics Book III, Chapter 9.
Benjamin Jowett, trans. in The Works of Aristotle
vol. 2 (Chicago: Encyclopedia Britannica, Inc.,
1952), p. 477.

3

Actually there are few radical egalitarians
writing today. Most egalitarian accounts of
justice are more heavily qualified and carefully
formulated than the radical position presented
above. See Tom L. Beauchamp, Philosophical
Ethics (New York: McGraw-Hill, Inc., 1982) pgs.
219-258 for an excellent moral analysis of the
three distributive principles of justice. Also,
see Karen Lebacqz, Six Theories of Justice
(Minneapolis, Minnesota: Augsburg, 1986) for an
excellent philosophical and theological overview
of theories of distributive justice.

4

John Rawls, A Theory of Justice (Cambridge,
Mass.: Harvard University Press, 1971), p. 83.

5

See Adam Smith, An Inquiry into the Nature and
Causes of the Wealth of Nations (New York: Modern
Library, 1937).

6

Robert Nozick, Anarchy, State and Utopia (New
York: Basic Books, 1974).

7

R. Nozick, p. 168.

8

John Stuart Mill, Utilitarianism (New York: Bobbs-Merrill, 1966); Jeremy Bentham, An Introduction to the Principles of Morals and Legislation, ed. J.H. Burns and H.L.A. Hay (London: Metheun, 1982.

9

See, Paulo Freire, The Politics of Education (Massachusetts: Bergin and Garvey, 1985); also Pedagogy of the Oppressed (New York: Herder and Herder, 1975).

10

See Phillip Berryman, Liberation Theology (New York: Pantheon, 1987), for a fine overview of liberation theology's major thinkers and doers.

11

As quoted in P. Berryman, p. 33. For a representative classic work, see Gustavo Gutierrez, A Theology of Liberation (Maryknoll, New York: Orbis Books, 1973).

12

See Plato, Republic (New York: Oxford University Press, 1945); Aristotle, Nichomachean Ethics, W.D. Ross, ed. and trans., The Works of Aristotle (Oxford, England: Clarendon Press, 1925).

13

Aristotle, Bk. 9, Chap. 8.

14

See Alasdair MacIntyre, After Virtue 2nd edition (Notre Dame, Indiana: University of Notre Dame Press, 1984).

15

See Carol Gilligan, In a Different Voice (Cambridge, Mass.: Harvard University Press, 1982); also, Nell Noddings, Caring (Berkeley, Cal.: University of California Press, 1984).

16

For two excellent post-liberal critiques of contemporary sociopolitical thinking see Robert N. Bellah, et al., Habits of the Heart (Berkeley, Cal.: University of California Press, 1985); and C.A. Bowers, Elements of a Post-Liberal Theory of

Education (New York: Teachers College Press, 1987).

17

See D. Maguire, pp. 85-98.

18

D. Maguire, P. 21.

19

D. Maguire, p. 98.

PART II. INTERDISCIPLINARY APPROACHES TO JUSTICE

JUSTICE THROUGH THE ARTS:
THE POWER OF SOCIALLY CONSCIOUS ART

David R. Conrad
University of Vermont

Throughout human history artists have expressed
indignation toward injustice and enthusiasm for
justice in a wide range of media. In the twentieth
century alone visual artists have commented powerfully
upon problems of poverty, racism, and militarism.
Dramatists have made insightful statements about
alienation, genocide, and fear of nuclear
annihilation. Filmmakers have focused upon the evils
of apartheid in South Africa, repression in Chile, and
McCarthyism in the United States. Musicians have
stirred the conscience of Americans with songs about
suffering caused by war in Vietnam and cruelty
perpetrated by contras in Nicaragua.

Though this essay will concentrate on the visual
arts as they reveal the depth of commitment of many
artists to a more just and humane world, it is worth
taking a brief glimpse at the role of theater and
music in the struggle for a transformed world. A
number of socially-conscious plays were written and
performed in the United States in the 1930's, for
instance. Some were produced to fight fascism which
was threatening global peace. Others deplored racism
and the class society which fostered vast wealth for a
few and severe deprivation for many. Bertholt Brecht's
popular Threepenny Opera was an indictment of
Capitalist society and Of Thee I Sing was a biting
satire on American political life. One play with an
anti-war theme, Robert Sherwood's Idiot's Delight of
1936, accused weapons producers of starting a war but
also blamed patriotic citizens for paying for and
using the weapons. In spite of violence and
exploitation prevalent in society, Sherwood expressed
hope for the future in this play which ran for an
impressive 300 performances. Audiences watching
Idiot's Delight laughed but were also moved by
Sherwood's vision.[1]

In Third World countries, drama is an effective
tool to protest injustice and promote justice. In
South Africa, for example, drama has been used for

years by blacks to condemn the apartheid system. The play <u>King Kong</u> was produced intentionally for white audiences in the 1950's "to prod gently their consciences and touch their hearts."[2] Later the Black Consciousness movement was furthered by the play <u>Shanti</u> which protested cultural domination and supported liberation.[3] Black South African theater continues today to attack racial oppression in its multiple insidious forms.

Latin American scholar Augusto Boal argues that theater is a very efficient social weapon. The ruling classes make every effort to use theater as a tool for domination, but theater can also be a weapon for liberation, he insists. In order for liberation to occur change is necessary, and change is indeed happening in Latin America whenever the barrier between actors and spectators is removed. "All must act, all must be protagonists in the necessary transformations of society," Boal affirms.[4] The main objective of the new theater is "...to change the people--'spectators,' passive beings in the theatrical phenomenon--into subjects, into actors, transformers of the dramatic action."[5]

Helping people become subjects rather than objects through personal empowerment is also the goal of the great Brazilian educator Paulo Freire and countless Latin American advocates of liberation theology. Boal rejects the idea of the spectator delegating power to dramatic characters to think or act for himself or herself. Instead, "the spectator frees himself; he thinks and acts for himself! Theater in action! Perhaps the theater is not revolutionary in itself; but have no doubts, it is a rehearsal of revolution," Boal concludes.[6]

Social critics have long commented upon the use of music and song to help achieve social and political goals. In this century folk music has been used extensively to support freedom for oppressed blacks and nonviolent rather than violent conflict resolution. Folk singer Woody Guthrie wrote "This Machine Kills Fascists" on his guitar and Pete Seeger inscribed "This Machine Surrounds Hate and Forces It to Surrender" on his in order to express the depth of their commitment to justice though music.[7] Guthrie, Seeger, and folksingers like Kentucky's Aunt Molly Jackson, composer of "I Am Union Woman," were especially concerned about the unemployed, exploited, and rejected in society.

Labor struggles were a fertile field for folk musicians with Zilphia Horton of the Highlander Folk School in Tennessee herself collecting some 1300 songs on labor and Southern issues. Music has always played a central role at Highlander, a gathering place for blacks and whites to learn and organize together around common problems since its founding in 1932 by Myles Horton. The most famous song of the Civil Rights Movement, "We Shall Overcome," was revised at Highlander by Zilphia Horton, Guy Carawan, and Pete Seeger.

For many years Highlander was attacked for its work with labor organizers and civil rights activists. It was denounced as a "Communist training school" attended by Martin Luther King, Jr. and Rosa Parks and was forced to close by the state, only to re-open proudly in a different location with a new name: the Highlander Education and Research Center. Pete Seeger and other musicians connected or not connected with Highlander often experienced the sting of Red-baiting. But Seeger, like others, became aware of social injustice at an early age and was not dissuaded by controversy or harrassment. One time he heard the painter Rockwell Kent urge artists to join the fight against fascism and he commented on a radio broadcast, "...it seemed to me natural that music should be a part of this."[8]

After singing with the Almanac Singers and the Weavers for a number of years, Seeger and fellow musicians were blacklisted by major media and concert halls. After 17 years of blacklisting, Seeger appeared on "The Smothers Brothers Comedy Hour" in 1967 to sing "Waist Deep in the Big Muddy," a song critical of US involvement in Vietnam. Following a letter-writing campaign by right-wing groups, CBS refused to allow the final verse to be sung on the air. Seeger strongly protested this censorship and the whole song was dropped. However, a year later Seeger did get to sing the entire controversial song on the same show.[9]

During the Civil Rights Movement in the 1960's folk singers from the North travelled south to aid the movement. They brought back freedom songs, and in 1963 the Freedom Singers, four teenagers who sang for the Student Non-Violent Coordinating Committee (SNCC), came north to perform. Joan Baez, Odetta, Bob Dylan, Peter, Paul and Mary, and others sang in Washington at the huge August 1963 rally when Martin Luther King,

Jr. delivered his gripping "I Have a Dream" Speech.
These and many other musicians played a central part
in the Civil Rights and anti-Vietnam war movements.
Their music helped develop a sense of solidarity,
attracted new members to the cause, and raised the
consciousness of thousands of listeners who were moved
by their compelling message in song.

The Roots of Socially Conscious Art

It is clear that all of the arts have been alive
with protest and dissent in this century. Though
sometimes overshadowed by art with no explicit social
message, socially-conscious art has made a deep
imprint. Whatever form it takes, such art helps men,
women, and children in all cultures gain a more solid
understanding of justice issues which confront the
world. The "art of social conscience," as humanities
scholar Paul Von Blum calls it, is "art which in its
content sheds important critical insights on such
broad concerns as society and its institutions and
ethics, and perhaps even more broadly on the human
experience and condition."[10]

Socially-conscious art which points the way to
personal and cultural transformation not only attacks
injustice and supports justice but also reveals vast
human creativity, stirs emotional as well as
intellectual responses, and inspires deeper analysis.
Von Blum speaks of the "art of negativity," a
dialectical perspective with a major assumption that
"a critical or negative view of reality--the
dialectical antithesis represented by the content of
their art--is the beginning of a process in which
qualitative change in the status quo may be effected."
In this dialectical context, "...artistic content that
initially negates a social reality is ultimately a
higher form of affirmation."[11]

Socially-conscious art, therefore, may sometimes
seem depressing to view or experience, but out of this
critical or negative framework may grow a willingness
to act positively to right a wrong or overcome an
evil. The significance of this art is that beauty
associated with artistic achievement is appreciated on
a much deeper level. Beauty is seen in the
possibility of social change embedded in the work of
art rather than in the surface treatment of the work
itself. This is not to say that the particular
artistic creation cannot be appreciated for its

intrinsic beauty, but that the greatest meaning of the art work lies beneath the surface in its ability to persuade and its power to move the viewer to action.

Art has served many functions throughout human history: educational, utilitarian, religious, purely enjoyable, and socially beneficial. Art as an instrument for social change has a long history in Europe and the United States. Sympathy for the peasant can be traced as far back as 15th century Germany. The theme of class struggle has stimulated protest art for almost as long, art critic Ralph Shikes demonstrates in a well-documented and finely illustrated book called The Indignant Eye: The Artist as Social Critic.[12]

Eighteenth century French editor and critic, Denis Diderot, believed that art had an important educational and social role in improving society. Following his belief that art could be an instrument for social change, leaders of the French Revolution thought that artistic works of the past should be destroyed and replaced with works supporting the revolution. Valuable art works were intended to be saved during the first years of the revolution, but many symbols of the past were obliterated nevertheless. A statue of Louis XIV with four slaves in chains at the base was ordered destroyed, but artists asked that it be moved instead to another location after the chained slaves were taken off.[13]

Almost one hundred years later Pierre Joseph Proudhon defined the role of art in a socialist society. Writing in The Principles of Art and Its Social Function, Proudhon argued that the socialist revolution needed the cooperation of artists, and it was the artist's responsibility to participate in it. "We socialist revolutionaries," Proudhon wrote, "we tell our artists, as well as our writers, that our ideal is justice and truth. If you don't know how to make art in style, then we don't need you..."[14] Expressing the philosophy of Proudhon, the artist Gustave Courbet wished to create "living art," meaning the world as it is. He focused on social problems in his painting and furthered the ideas of the French Revolution.[15]

One of the greatest socially-aware artists of all times was Francisco Goya. Goya cried out for social justice and peace in his remarkable paintings. He harshly criticized Spanish royalty, intellectuals, the

Inquisition, and priests. The American philosopher
Lewis Mumford praises Goya and Brueghel, an earlier
Flemish painter, for expressing visions of heaven as
well as of hell:

> ...because they were honest enough to
> face every part of their experience, they
> both produced surrealist pictures of the most
> macabre kind, recording the horrors of war,
> the starvation and misery and torture they
> had witnessed and what is more, had agonized
> over. Fortunately...they knew heaven as well
> as Hell: the delights of erotic love, of
> parenthood, of honest labor in tune with
> nature, the joy of the hunter, and the
> plowman and the harvest hand. So, though
> they sensitively recorded the degradations of
> the day, they were still capable in their art
> of testifying to a fuller and better life."[16]

At the same time some artists bitingly criticize
the status quo and perversely degraded social forms,
they affirm humanity through the creative process.[17]
Especially in a world which emphasizes quantification
and abstraction over qualitative and personal
dimensions of life, art becomes a much-needed
stronghold of genuinely human values. Art critic
Adolfo Sánchez Vásquez argues that "man elevates and
affirms himself in the process of transforming and
humanizing reality, and art satisfies this need."[18]
Therefore, he claims, there is no such thing as "art
for art's sake" but only art by and for human beings.
Because humans are basically creative beings, they
create art to express their creativity and humanity.

American artist Ben Shahn is one of many artists
and critics who reject the concept of "art for art's
sake" and propose instead the idea of "art for life's
sake" because they believe passionately that art must
serve the very real needs of people. Like the
philosopher-educator John Dewey, Shahn and other
socially-conscious artists want to take the fine arts
off their pedestal and make the arts relate to human
problems, hopes, and dreams. Shahn places the person
at the center of his value system and supports
whatever institutions or activities broaden or enrich
the human spirit.[19]

Mexican muralist Diego Rivera challenges the "art
for art's sake" theory because it implies that only a
few select individuals can appreciate art and this

makes art elitist, sacrosanct, and therefore inaccessible to the masses.[20] Artists like Rivera who are influenced by Marx stress the kinds of art most easily seen and understood by large numbers of people: murals, public sculpture, prints, cartoons, films, and drama. They reject the idea of art as an economic commodity with Marx himself stating that "capitalist production is hostile to certain branches of spiritual production, such as art and poetry."[21] The artist plays an important role in society, helping or hindering progress toward a classless society. In the Marxian view, artists have a responsibility to help educate and spur the masses to action since ends cannot be separated from means.[22]

The conflict between advocates of "art for art's sake" and a more social art has been brewing for years and no end is in sight. A strong defender of abstract art, Lloyd Goodrich, writes that "abstraction may serve as an escape from troubling realities into a world of aesthetic order where the artist is in full control."[23] In contrast, Ben Shahn observes that "we live in a time of turmoil, too susceptible to drastic and deplorable changes. I feel that the painter who can, under such circumstances, concern himself with a bowl of pansies (or a 'pure' abstraction) is dodging issues and is afraid to participate in the life around him."[24] Critic Willis Truitt is harsher than Shahn, charging that the tendency in art during the last seventy years is "toward aesthetic hedonism, subjectivism, reification, and mystification." He accuses distinguished art theorist Benedetto Croce of being an "exquisite snob" with an aesthetic attitude which is "typically bourgeois: individualistic, asocial, autonomous," leading to the "compartmentalization of aesthetic experience."[25] Truitt is worried that the revolutionary thrust of much art is lost when formal characteristics like line, color, and texture are emphasized.[26]

The issue of propaganda and art arises with a discussion of art which comments upon social and political ideas. The propaganda value of art has certainly been known for a long time. Napoleon, who became French emperor in 1804, wanted to be remembered as a great soldier and political leader. So he commissioned distinguished painters, including Jacques Louis David, to portray him as a friend of the people dressed in simple clothing. Few painters dealt with the harsh realities of life under Napoleon. Napoleon, his great victories, and his wife Josephine were the acceptable subject matter.[27]

In more modern times critics have attacked Marxian and other socially-radical artists for simply illustrating an economic theory or stacking the cards in the interest of a political game without independent and fresh exploration.[28] One scholar remarks that if political radicalism leads the artist to devote his or her art "entirely to fostering social aims so that the works of art are nothing but a means to nonartistic ends,[29] art then becomes nothing but a kind of propaganda."[29] Though a serious concern and one that deserves attention, much socially-conscious art goes far beyond propaganda in its profound message and even more profound impact on the viewer. The finest art of this nature stimulates the viewer to think, to question, to examine his or her values and belief system. High quality art with a social vision may focus on a particular social or political event, but will lead the person experiencing the artistic work to make connections between a specific incident and a universal truth or reality. This linking of the particular and the universal has been successful in much socially-responsible art, especially in a great deal of art produced in the United States during the 1930's.

Social Realists as Critics and Dreamers

Painter Max Weber, addressing the First American Artists' Congress, declared: "What we need today is an American art that will express the Whitmanesque spirit and conception of democracy, an art as heroic and prophetic as the undying Leaves of Grass in literature and philosophy of the new world."[30] A large number of painters and photographers struggled to create such an art which served as a catalyst for personal and social transformation. Photographers included Lewis Hine, Dorothea Lange, and Walker Evans. Painters included Edward Hopper, William Gropper, Jack Levine, and Ben Shahn. Though many artists paid little attention to social and political struggles swirling around them, others engaged themselves artistically in such struggles.

Some of the artists submitted works to The Masses, a magazine of social protest, or its successors, The Liberator and The New Masses. Many were influenced by the Mexican artists Rivera,

Siqueiros, and Orozco who were largely responsible for the exciting revival of mural painting in fresco. Ben Shahn, for instance, worked with Rivera on his Rockefeller Center mural expressing new human and economic possibilities, but Rivera was ordered to change the mural which included among other things a small picture of Lenin and some venereal disease germs floating above rich people playing cards. Rivera refused to strike out the offending images and the Rockefellers, finding it too dificult to move to the Museum of Modern Art, ordered the mural destroyed.[31]

So-called "protest artists" or "social realists" were idealists and reformers, sometimes even revolutionaries like Rivera, who expanded the meaning and function of art. They combined incisive social comment with personal vision as they grappled with momentous problems like poverty, fascism, and war. The movement known as "social realism" grew out of the Great Depression and is a genuine form of American art with roots in Europe. Social realists saw their art as a demand for social justice and a demonstration of the insidious social and economic problems confronting American society. Theirs was not an art of the studio, but an art which focused on significant moments in the lives of ordinary people. Often criticism was made of the capitalist system, and the seamier sides of North American life were emphasized. Social realists identified with the workers' cause, communicating through images the workers' concerns as insightfully as possible.[32] It was Rivera who wrote that "at present art has a very definite and important role to play in the class struggle. It is definitely useful to the proletariat...Art has the advantage of speaking a language that can easily be understood by the workers and peasants in all lands."[33] Though not as revolutionary in their language or goals as Rivera, social realists could relate well to Rivera's passion for social, economic, and political justice.

Social realists rejected the idea of a split between mind and body, a split between an artist's creation and the objective world. They saw this dualism as alienation in the Marxist sense. Their major goal[34] was to relate art and life more intimately. When most successful, social realism was not merely imitative but, as art historian David Shapiro points out, its unique perspective "...sometimes allowed it to transform objective reality into symbols of transcendent meaning...the artist saw the working class as the dynamic new force,

87

the bourgeoisie as broken, and the ruling class as wicked."[35]

The Depression times seemed good as well as bad to many artists. Hunger, unemployment, floods, the Dust Bowl, and rampant militarism abroad were dismal realities, but evidence abounded that capitalism was fading, the new Deal was working, and class consciousness was spreading. One scholar claimed that alongside the trenchant social criticism was an "ever-growing inclination to discover and celebrate some thing that could lead humans through the calamity and that would guide them past the destitution almost automatically."[36]

This hopeful side of socially-conscious art during the Depression years manifests itself in the expression of human spirit in Ben Shahn's paintings and Dorothea Lange's photographs. These--and other-- social artists combined criticism and compassion, attacks on the social system with implicit or explicit suggestions of what the social system might become. Viewers may need to search closely for possibilities of transcendence in seemingly negative works of art, but the search can be rewarding. The process of making connections between the specific incident or person depicted and the broader, universal global meaning inherent in the art work is especially important. Moving from the particular to the universal is a process demanding patience, sensitivity, and a willingness to exercise imagination. Undergoing such a process can lead to a much greater understanding of and wider appreciation for socially-conscious photographs, paintings, and drawings.

The Compelling Art of Ben Shahn

An artist who based his art on particular people and events, Ben Shahn moved beyond the particular to encompass universal values of love, justice, and peace. In his book The Shape of Content, a series of lectures delivered at Harvard in the 1950's, Shahn analyzed a painting called "Allegory" which featured a gigantic red creature, its head surrounded by flames and four children crouching beneath. A New York critic, once friendly to the artist, saw signs of Communism in the brilliant red beast created by Shahn. But the artist explained in "The Biography of a Painting" that the actual source of the beast was a terrible Chicago fire in which a black man's four children had been killed. Many years earlier, as a child growing up in Lithuania in the early years of the century, Shahn remembered his grandfather's small village burning and recalled the excitement he felt as flames devoured the buildings. Another fire, this one after his family moved to New York, was much more terrifying. His father rescued the boy and his brothers and sisters from their burning house, suffering serious injuries as he did so.

Shahn read about the so-called "Hickman Story" in Chicago and was asked to do some drawings. The tragic story brought back old memories of fires and Shahn decided to develop a painting which somehow would express his feelings about the Chicago fire as well as touch on the universal human fear of suffering caused by fire. He used the image of a wolf, to Shahn a dreaded creature, as a symbol and his disconcerting recall of Romulus and Remus being suckled by the She-Wolf led him to decide that "...the stance of my imaginary beast was just that of the great Roman wolf, and that the children under its belly might almost be realization of my vague fears that, instead of suckling the children, the wolf would most certainly destroy them."[37] In creating and expressing such powerful symbols in "Allegory," Shahn was able to show great compassion for the victims of the "Hickman Story" while at the same time transcending the immediate incident. Shahn was aware of the universality of sorrow felt by everyone during such a tragic experience as well as of racial injustice which played a disturbing part in this lamentable event. The artist added that "...the relentless poverty which had pursued this man, and which dominated the story, had its own kind of universality."[38]

Shahn spent a lifetime devoted to socially-significant art. He became known as a social realist in the early 1930's with paintings focusing on the Sacco-Vanzetti case. Inspired by demonstrations in Europe supporting two Italian-American immigrants accused of murder, Shahn completed a series honoring the two men who became victims of cruel discrimination and oppression in the United States. Abuse of authority was symbolized in one painting showing a fraudulent investigating committee. The dignity of working-class women was expressed in another called "Six Witnesses Who Bought Eels from Vanzetti." Twenty-five years later Shahn produced a serigraph portraying the two condemned men and an inscription of

Vanzetti's eloquent words spoken during the trial. In 1965 Shahn selected the Sacco-Vanzetti theme for a mosaic at Syracuse University. He welcomed this opportunity to make a more accessible statement to the public about his hatred of injustice, whatever form it takes.[39]

During the 1930's Shahn was active as a photographer of urban street scenes while employed by the Public Works of Art Project in New York. Later he served as artist, designer, and photographer with the Farm Security Administration. In this position he worked on a giant mural at a community center in a New Deal housing development for garment workers. Commenting on dismal working conditions and totally inadequate housing, he also cited reforms evidenced by increased unionization, cooperative stores, and modern schools. At the end of the decade Shahn and his artist wife Bernarda Bryson painted fresco panels honoring factory workers and farmers in the lobby of a Bronx Post Office. A few years later Shahn completed murals in the corridor of the Social Security (now Federal Security) Building in Washington which depicted recipients of social security who were most needy: the elderly and handicapped, blacks, migrant workers, the young and poor.

Shahn wanted to reach the largest number of people he possibly could because he saw himself as an educator as well as an artist. Like other social realists, or "personal realist" as he called himself after the 1930's, he wanted to bring art to the people, to address real personalities and real situations in artistic, aesthetically satisfying ways. It was never beneath him to work on murals, posters, or magazine covers; in fact such commissions were seen as a welcome challenge because they afforded him an opportunity to reach an audience which might never set foot in a gallery or museum.

The Office of War Information where Shahn worked for almost a year during World War II published two of his posters, one of them expressing outrage at the Nazis who murdered the residents of a small village in Czechoslovakia. Another poster published by the Political Action Committee of the CIO made a powerful statement for racial integration at a time when prejudice among shipyard workers was rampant. A photograph showing two white workmen was the source of Shahn's poster "Welders," but the artist decided to make a strong antidiscrimination statement by painting a black and a white welder working side-by-side. Today this may seem obvious or even insignificant, but in the mid-1940's it was a bold step by an artist with a social conscience. "Welders" was reproduced for more than eight million newspaper readers and appeared in _Time_ and _Life_ magazines, eventually reaching some twenty-five million people.[40]

In the mid to late 1950's, Shahn completed portraits of Freud, Lenin, Adlai Stevenson, and Martin Luther King, Jr. for _Time_ magazine covers. In the sixties he was distressed to hear about the hapless Japanese trawler which sailed near the US Bikini nuclear test site. The "Lucky Dragon" was showered with radioactive debris. Many of the crew became ill and the radio operator subsequently died of radiation poisoning. Shahn was deeply troubled by this horrible event as well as by the larger issue of nuclear weapons testing and production. Included in his "Lucky Dragon" series of art works is one showing the radio operator holding a written statement describing his fate with a symbolic atomic cloud threatening in the background. Another shows the release of doves at the end of the funeral ceremony and still another called "We Did Not Know What Happened to Us" depicts the guiltless crew at the mercy of the nuclear monster. Ben Shahn demonstrated in this poignant and disturbing series his depth of concern for the "Lucky Dragon" crew as well as his disgust with nuclear policies which threaten all life on earth. The gross injustice of radioactively poisoning the Japanese fishermen and the even grosser injustice of potential poisoning of the global environment and its inhabitants were not lost on Shahn.

Before his death in 1969 Shahn concentrated on the civil rights movement. He expressed grief and anger over the murders of three civil rights workers in Mississippi in 1964 through a portfolio of prints done as a benefit for the Human Relations Council of Greater New Haven, Connecticut. His print titled "I Think Continually of Those Who Were Truly Great" was a tribute to ten civil rights activists who lost their lives in the struggle for racial justice. Several editions of prints of Martin Luther King, Jr. stressed King's extraordinary ability as an orator, and Shahn happily donated these editions to civil rights organizations. Even as Shahn himself was dying in the hospital less than a year after King's assassination, he personally signed editions of the King prints for a charity fund drive. None of this activity was surprising because Shahn's dedication to equality and justice was steady throughout his life. He was a remarkable artist and man who condemned intolerance and oppression but affirmed equality, social justice, and peace.[41]

The Vibrant Photography of Dorothea Lange

Dorothea Lange "made contributions comparable in stature to those of the finest socially-conscious painters and graphic artists."[42] An outstanding documentary photographer, Lange--like Shahn--spent a lifetime devoted to exposing social problems through her photography. At the same time she affirmed the basic human dignity of all human beings.

Lange was born in 1895 and lived as a child in Hoboken, New Jersey, but spent most of her time when not attending school exploring the Lower East Side of New York City. In high school she decided she wanted to be a photographer and soon after graduation began an apprenticeship with a well-known photographer at the time. Later she worked in a number of studios and studied with the famed teacher of photography Clarence H. White at Columbia University.

Moving to San Francisco was a big step in Lange's growth as a professional photographer. After the stock market crash of 1929, Lange turned increasingly toward photographing the unemployed and the exploited. Several years after the crash a woman called the "White Angel" organized a bread line near her studio and Lange decided to photograph it. In the foreground of her photograph, "White Angel Bread Line," was an unshaven man leaning on a railing with a tin can resting in his arms. Defiantly and bitterly, he turned away from other men in the background who were awaiting a handout. Commenting on the photograph, Lange's biographer Milton Meltzer observed that "now, some fifty years later, it has become one of the great images of the Depression era, of people in trouble."[43]

During the severe winter of 1934-35 California experienced a gigantic regional migration of desperately poor rural families who had left drought-stricken farms. University of California, Berkeley sociologist Paul Taylor was asked to do research to discover what could be done to alleviate this dire situation. He requested a photographer to help relief administrators actually see what rural conditions were

like. Though an unusual request at the time, Taylor's
request was granted and Lange was hired. This began a
long, productive relationship between Taylor and Lange
which later included marriage.

Lange learned to gain the confidence of migrants
in order to better photograph them and their struggle
to survive in hostile environments. Before long
Lange's and Taylor's base of operations was expanded,
and Lange became a staff member of the Resettlement
Administration (RA) created by President Roosevelt.
Driving home from her first field trip for the RA,
Lange passed a sign by the side of the road that read
"Pea-Pickers Camp." She debated whether or not to
turn back, but after twenty miles of agonizing she
made a U-turn to return to the camp. Lange wrote in
her jounal:

> I was following instinct, not reason; I drove
> into that wet and soggy camp and parked my
> car like a homing pigeon. I saw and
> approached the hungry and desperate mother as
> if drawn by a magnet. I do not remember how
> I explained my presence or my camera to her,
> but I do remember she asked me no
> questions...She had just sold the tires from
> her car to buy food. There she sat in that
> lean-to tent with her children huddled around
> her, and seemed to know that my pictures
> might help her and so she helped me. There
> was a sort of equality about it...The pea
> crop at Nipomo had frozen and there was no
> work for anybody.[44]

Lange was not aware of it at the time, but she
had made one of the great photographs of the century.
"Migrant Mother" was later reproduced in thousands of
magazines, newspapers, books, and pamphlets and was
shown in exhibitions around the world. Arriving home
with the film, she developed the negatives and rushed
to the San Francisco News to inform the city editor
that the pea pickers were starving. The United Press
was alerted and within days the News announced that
the federal government was sending thousands of pounds
of food to the pickers. Two of Lange's photographs
appeared next to the headline.[45] Her photos and quick
action brought almost immediate help to those
suffering from misery and deprivation, a direct result
of her creative effort that most socially-conscious
artists could not expect to achieve so promptly.

Travelling throughout the South a year later, Lange and Taylor photographed and wrote about the victims of rural poverty. They were appalled by the terrible treatment of tenant farmers: the exploitation of their labor, the shacks they lived in without plumbing or heating, and the malnutrition which dogged them constantly. According to Meltzer, "Dorothea's photographs of that time reveal a depth of poverty which, twenty years later, she would see matched only by conditions in the famine-stricken or war-torn lands of Asia."[46]

In 1937 the Resettlement Administration became the Farm Security Administration with a similar charge to help alleviate rural poverty. Lange continued on the staff with several other photographers like Ben Shahn and Walker Evans. In the late thirties she and Paul Taylor worked on a book titled An American Exodus which Von Blum claims "...is a remarkable accomplishment that can be viewed as a complement to John Steinbeck's The Grapes of Wrath. It is an invaluable document for anyone who wants to understand the spirit of the times."[47]

Hired by the War Relocation Authority after the start of World War II, Lange was told to photograph the internment of thousands of Japanese-Americans. All persons of Japanese ancestry were ordered to evacuate the West Coast military area in one of the most offensive violations of justice ever perpetrated by the United States government. Japanese-Americans were shocked by the decree, but were nevertheless forced to sell their household belongings and leave their farms or businesses behind. Lange photographed the processing centers and the proud people, young and old, who faced humiliation and despair. Her work resulted in a book and exhibition called Executive Order 9066 which recorded, in Paul Von Blum's words, "...the shame that should be felt by the architects of the policy and the millions who lent their active or passive support."[48]

One revealing photograph in the book shows a grandfather and his grandchildren awaiting the evacuation bus. The old man displays great dignity in spite of the shame of wearing a tag like luggage and in spite of the vicious racism inherent in the evacuation order itself. The humanity of this dignified grandfather is asserted even in the face of ugly dehumanization forced upon him. Another photo depicts the Manzanar Relocation Center where many

94

Japanese-Americans were taken. An American flag waves dramatically in the foreground as a duststorm partially obscures endless rows of dingy barracks lining both sides of the picture. A feeling of loneliness, grimness, oppression overcomes the viewer. The shock of seeing an American concentration camp with a flag in front center and picturesque snow-covered mountains as a backdrop is not easy for the viewer to forget.[49]

Dorothea Lange suffered from illness for many years, but maintained her work for social justice by assisting Edward Steichen and Wayne Miller with the "Family of Man" exhibition which later became a best-selling book. Her photography during the last years of her life concentrated on the role of the public defender in court cases and on the high price of progress resulting in destruction of the scenic Berryessa Valley in Californis. In her teaching Lange encouraged students to appreciate the interaction between life and art. She wanted them to explore and see more sharply, but also to persuade more skillfully. "Bring the viewer to your side," she urged, "include him in your thought. He is not a bystander. You have the power to increase his perceptions and conceptions."[50]

Conclusion

Like Ben Shahn, Dorothea Lange made a tremendous contribution to socially-conscious art. Like Shahn, she was bold about her convictions and never wavered in her commitment to justice. Both artists were exemplars of a long American tradition of commitment to equality and of repudiation of bigotry. Though American policy often promoted inequality or racism, as in the case of rounding up Japanese-Americans, some thoughtful, compassionate Americans like Lange and Shahn resisted the tide and, through their art, made positive strides toward freedom from oppression.

For far too long socially-conscious art of all kinds has taken a back seat to more abstract art or art which does not convey sociopolitical meanings. Art critics have focused on formal analysis at the expense of examining the social and political contexts of art. Public school and university instruction has failed to give adequate attention to socially-conscious drama and music, painting and photography. While many artists have expressed disgust with prejudice or shock at ill treatment of the poor, often their works have been pushed aside in favor of drawings, paintings, or plays which portray a prettier picture or a less controversial theme. Certainly not all socially-oriented art is worthy of exaltation or even of prolonged scrutiny, any more than all abstract or surrealist art is worthy of such consideration. But socially-responsible art does have an important role to play in understanding justice issues on a deeper level. It is high time that this art be recognized for its great value to humanity.

The art explored in this essay is art for all people. When at its best it touches on universal themes facing the human family while addressing the concerns of particular individuals. Many voices for justice must be heard and the voices of socially-conscious artists must be included among them. Sometimes the voices are quiet or muffled, sometimes louder or more direct, but they can be "heard" in the photography of Dorothea Lange, the theater of black South Africans, and the music of Pete Seeger. They can be seen and "heard" in the posters of Ben Shahn and the murals of Diego Rivera. Socially-conscious artists will continue to add their voices for justice as long as injustice exists in the world. They will do their part in the significant work of social, economic, and political transformation from a world bristling with injustice and cruelty to a world thriving upon justice and love for all.

NOTES

1

Morgan Y. Himelstein, Drama Was a Weapon: The Left Wing Theatre in New York, 1929-1941 (New Brunswick: Rutgers University Press, 1963), pp. 138-39.

2

Robert Mshengu Kavanagh, Theatre and Cultural Struggle in South Africa (London: Zed Books, 1985). p. 109.

3

Ibid., p. 181.

4

Augusto Boal, Theater of the Oppressed (London: Pluto Press, 1979), p. x.

5

Ibid., p. 122.

6

Ibid., p. 155.

7

R. Serge Denisoff, Great Day Coming: Folk Music and the American Left (Urbana: University of Illinois Press, 1971), p. 4.

8

Pete Seeger, quoted in Denisoff, Great Day Coming, p. 80.

9

Denisoff, Great Day Coming, pp. 159-60.

10

Paul Von Blum, The Art of Social Conscience (New York: Universe Books, 1976), p. 1.

11

Ibid., p. 2.

12

Ralph E. Shikes, The Indignant Eye: The Artist
As Social Critic in Prints and Drawings from the
Fifteenth Century to Picasso (Boston: Beacon
Press, 1969), p. 4.

13

Moshe Carmilly-Weinberger, Fear of Art:
Censorship and Freedom of Expression in Art (New
York: R.R. Bowker, 1986), pp. 58-59.

14

Pierre Joseph Proudhon, quoted in Carmilly-
Weinberger, Fear of Art, p. 66.

15

Carmilly-Weinberger, Fear of Art, p. 67

16

Lewis Mumford, Art and Technics (New York:
Columbia University Press, 1952), p. 147.

17

Melvin Roman, "Art and Social Change," Americas,
22 (February, 1970), p. 17.

18

Adolfo Sanchez Vasquez, Art and Society: Essays
in Marxist Aesthetics (New York: Monthly Review
Press, 1973), pp. 43-4.

19

Ben Shahn, "How an Artist Looks at Aesthetics,"
in Social Realism: Art as a Weapon, ed. by David
Shapiro (New York: Frederick Ungar, 1973), p.
287.

20

Diego Rivera, "The Revolutionary Spirit in Modern
Art" in Social Realism, ed. by David Shapiro, p.
56.

21

Karl Marx, quoted in Social Radicalism and the
Arts by Donald Drew Egbert (New York: Alfred A.
Knopf, 1970), p. 20.

22

Egbert, Social Radicalism and the Arts, p. 28.

23

John I.H. Baur, Revolution and Tradition in Modern American Art (Cambridge: Harvard University Press, 1951), p. 139.

24

Ben Shahn, quoted in Portrait of the Artist as an American, by Selden Rodman (New York: Harper and Brothers, 1951), p. 28.

25

Willis Truitt, "Art for the People" in The Arts in a Democratic Society, ed. by Dennis Alan Mann (Bowling Green, Ohio: Popular Press, 1977), pp. 59-60.

26.

Ibid., pp. 64-65.

27

Carmilly-Weinberger, Fear of Art, p. 52.

28

Thomas Craven, "Art and Propaganda," in Shapiro, Social Realism, pp. 88-91

29

Donald Drew Egbert, Socialism and American Art (Princeton: Princeton University Press, 1967), p. 129.

30

Max Weber, quoted in Artists Against War and Fascism: Papers of the First American Artists' Congress, ed. by Matthew Baigell and Julia Williams (New Brunswick: Rutgers University Press, 1986), pp. 37-38.

31

Carol Herselle Krinsky, "Rockefeller Center: The Success of the Architecture and the Failure of the Art Program," in Artistic Strategy and the Rhetoric of Power: Political Uses of Art from Antiquity to the Present, ed. by David Castriota (Carbondale: Southern Illinois University Press, 1986), pp. 155-156.

32

Shapiro, Social Realism, pp. 13-17.

33

Rivera, "The Revolutionary Spirit," p. 57.

34

David P. Peeler, Hope Among Us Yet: Social Criticism and Social Solace in Depression America (Athens: University of Georgia Press, 1987), p. 269.

35

Shapiro, Social Realism, p. 15.

36

Peeler, Hope Among Us Yet, p. 2

37

Ben Shahn, The Shape of Content (Cambridge: Harvard University Press, 1957), p. 33.

38

Ibid., p. 28.

39

David R. Conrad, "Ben Shahn as Aesthetic Educator," The Journal of Aesthetic Education, XV (April, 1981), p. 74.

40

Ibid., pp. 76-77.

41

Ibid., pp. 77-80.

42

Paul Von Blum, The Critical Vision: A History of Social and Political Art in the US (Boston: South End Press, 1982), p. 44.

43

Milton Meltzer, Dorothea Lange: A Photographer's Life (New York: Farrar Strauss Giroux, 1978), pp. 71-72.

44

Dorothea Lange, quoted in Meltzer, Dorothea Lange, p. 133.

45

Meltzer, Dorothea Lange, pp. 133-134.

46
Ibid., p. 147.

47
Von Blum, The Art of Social Conscience, p. 204.

48
Ibid., p. 207.

49
See Von Blum, The Art of Social Conscience. p. 204

50
Dorothea Lange, quoted in Meltzer, Dorothea Lange, p. 306.

JUSTICE IN TWO NOVELS:
THE STRANGER AND THE PLAGUE BY CAMUS

Jesse Levitt
Prof. of Modern Languages
University of Bridgeport

"The passion for justice animated all of Camus's works...," says French critic Jacqueline Levi-Valensi. "It protests against the injustice done to man, as Martha says (in The Misunderstanding), but also against that which prevails among men..." (Lévi-Valensi, p. 8). Germaine Brée and Margaret Guiton consider "the fundamental theme of Camus's writings" to be "at once a bitter protest against man's position in the universe and an examination of the ethical problems which this implies" (Brée-Guiton, p. 219). Camus's protest against injustice is directed against both divine and human injustice, which are strangely interwoven. "It is shocking to realize that nature can imitate the cold-blooded procedures of a modern bureaucrat, it is still more shocking to realize that human societies can imitate the inhuman laws of nature." In L'Étranger (The Stranger) the symbol of human justice points to the divine injustice of the universe; in Camus's second novel the divine injustice of the plague points to the arbitrary, wholesale slaughter of modern war" (Brée-Guiton, pp. 223-224).

Albert Camus (1913-1960) is one of the foremost men of letters of twentieth century France. He was born at Mondovi, department of Constantine in Algeria, then considered part of France. His father, a cellarman for a winery, who was of Alsatian origin, was killed in 1914 at the battle of the Marne at the beginning of the First World War. His mother, Catherine Sintès, was of Spanish origin, and Camus always considered Spain his second native land. She was a humble, illiterate woman who did washing and house cleaning in the proletarian Belcourt section of Algiers.

Between 1923 and 1930, Camus attended the Algiers lycée as a scholarship student. In 1930 he felt the first attack of tuberculosis. But in 1933 he entered the University of Algiers, with a major in philosophy. He was briefly married in 1934, but divorced in 1935.

In 1937 he was unable to take the agrégation examination for a teaching post because of ill health. The following year, together with Pascal Pia, he founded the newspaper Alger Républicain. In 1940 he married Francine Faure, of Oran, who would later give birth to twins. Alger Républicain was suppressed by censorship, and Camus then went to work for Paris-Soir, but returned to Oran in 1941, taking a teaching post. In 1942, his first novel, The Stranger (L'Étranger), was published, followed the next year by his philosophical essay, The Myth of Sisyphus (Le Mythe de Sisyphe). In 1944, together with Pascal Pia, he assumed direction of the underground newspaper Combat. His play, The Misunderstanding (Le Malentendu) was first staged in 1944; Caligula followed on the stage in 1945.

In 1947 Camus published The Plague (La Peste), his greatest novel. Two plays followed--State of Siege (État de Siège) in 1948 and The Just Assassins (Les Justes) in 1949. In 1951 Camus published a philosophical work, The Rebel (L'Homme révolté), in 1954 Summer (Été), in 1956 The Fall (La Chute) and in 1957 The Exile and the Kingdom (L'Exil et le Royaume). He adapted and staged Faulkner's Requiem for a Nun (Requiem pour une Nonne) in 1956. In 1957 Camus was awarded the Nobel Prize for Literature in Stockholm. He died in an automobile accident in 1960 on his way to Paris from his home.

Much of Camus's ethics can be traced to the notions of the absurd and of philosophical revolt. "The absurd is born of this confrontation between the human need and the unreasonable silence of the world" (Camus, Myth, p. 21). The absurd "is that divorce between the mind that desires and the world that disappoints, my nostalgia for unity, this fragmented universe and the contradiction that binds them together" (Camus, Myth, p. 37). The absurd can be seen in "my appetite for the absolute and for unity and the impossibility of reducing this world to a rational and reasonable principle" (Camus, Myth, p. 38).

Henri Peyre in his Contemporary French Novel offers a clear and succinct summary of the notion of the absurd, according to Camus, and of its logical consequences. "Man wants rationality, and he is faced everywhere by the irrational. He is impelled by the will to control and steer his fate, but he is chained by blind and evil forces. He is athirst for freedom, fraternity, solidarity, and everywhere he encounters a selfish social order, a dried-up bureaucracy, a mechanized world readied for the impersonal slaughter of modern war. Man waits for a voice from Heaven, but receives only the answer of eternal silence. He feels dissonant in this cruel world (dissonance is the original meaning of absurdity), de trop, unwanted and insignificant, and the temptation of suicide follows fast upon the realization of such all pervading absurdity."

But Camus decided against suicide, which suppresses conscious revolt, silences the voice protesting against absurdity and actually contributes to absurdity. Not suicide, but revolt is the answer to absurdity (Peyre, p. 242).

Camus concludes his essay with the ancient Greek myth of Sisyphus, condemned by the gods after his death to roll a stone up to the top of a mountain, from which it would then fall down of its own weight. "His scorn of the gods, his passion for life won him that unspeakable penalty in which the whole being is exerted toward accomplishing nothing." The myth is tragic because the hero is conscious. "Sisyphus, proletarian of the gods, powerless and rebellious, knows the whole extent of his wretched condition." But, Camus concludes, "the struggle itself toward the heights is enough to fill a man's heart. One must imagine Sisyphus happy" (Camus, Myth, pp. 88-91). For Camus, therefore, man's dignity consists in fighting against the absurd for a victory that will nevertheless be only temporary.

The Stranger (L'Étranger), published in 1942, was Camus's first literary success, though not his first literary work. It "provides not the demonstration but the feel of the absurd, as Camus conceives it" (Peyre, p. 243). Meursault, an office clerk in Algiers who leads an apparently drab and meaningless existence, is informed by telegram that his mother has died in the old age home at Marengo, fifty miles from Algiers. Meursault takes a bus on a very hot day and reaches the home, where he shows apparent indifference to his mother's death. He refuses to take one last look at the body and later drinks coffee with milk with the janitor, smokes a cigarette and dozes. The next day, after an all night vigil, he follows the funeral convoy to the cemetary, in blazing sunshine that gives him a feeling of dazed fatigue. Numerous details in the novel continually stress Meursault's inability to withstand strong light and sunshine, which completely upset his mental balance. At the end of the funeral, his only thought is to get back home as soon as possible and get to bed.

The next day, which is a Saturday, he goes to the beach, where he meets a former secretary from his office, Marie Cardona. Later, he takes her to the cinema to see a comic film starring Fernandel, and Marie spends the night with him in his apartment. On Monday, after he returns from work, his neighbor, Raymond Sintes, a pimp, invites him into his apartment for refreshments and asks him to write a letter to one of Raymond's former mistresses, an Arab woman who, Raymond says, had not earned her keep and had been unfaithful to him. Raymond's purpose is to entice her back and give her the beating he thinks she deserves. Meursault obligingly writes the letter. The following Saturday, Meursault again goes to the beach, spending the day with Marie, who then comes back to his apartment. On Sunday Meursault and Marie hear the screams of a woman in Raymond's apartment. Meursault refuses to call the police, but other neighbors do and Raymond is sharply warned by the police. Raymond asks Meursault to serve at a later date as a character witness for him, and Meursault agrees. Raymond then invites Meursault and Marie to spend the following Saturday at the beach home of his friend Masson. But as they leave, they are observed by a group of Arabs that includes the brother of Meursault's mistress, and the Arabs later turn up at the beach. Raymond confronts the mistress's brother and is slashed with a knife. Meursault does not take part in the fight; he accompanies Raymond back to the cabin and takes away his revolver as a precaution. Then Meursault goes out along along the beach at high noon, when the sun is most oppressive. He heads toward a small stream, but finds the brother of Raymond's mistress already there. Anxious to get out of the blazing sun, Meursault approaches; the Arab then pulls out a knife and Meursault fires first one, then four more shots into the Arab, killing him.

In the second part of the novel, Meursault is interrogated by his court appointed attorney, who is annoyed at Meursault's seeming indifference to the death of his mother. Next he is questioned by the examining magistrate, in the absence of his attorney, but with Meursault's consent. The magistrate in an emotional tone asks why Meursault fired four additional shots after the first, but Meursault

remains silent. The magistrate dangles a silver
crucifix before Meursault, adding that even the worst
of sinners could obtain forgiveness by first
repenting. But Meursault replies that he does not
believe in God. The magistrate then says: "Never in
all my experience have I known a soul so case-hardened
as yours...All the criminals who have come before
me until now wept when they saw this symbol of our
Lord's sufferings" (Peyre, p. 243). Thereafter,
Meursault becomes Mr. Antichrist to the magistrate.

At Meursault's trial, the janitor of the Marengo
old age home testifies that Meursault did not shed a
single tear for his mother and left immediately after
the funeral, without lingering at the grave. One of
the undertaker's men says Meursault did not know his
mother's age, while the janitor refers to Meursault's
taking coffee with milk and a smoking cigarette.
After the testimony of Marie and Raymond, the
prosecutor in his self-righteousness declares: "Not
only did the man before you in the dock indulge in
the most shameful orgies on the day following his
mother's death. He killed a man cold-bloodedly, in
pursuance of some sordid vendetta in the underworld of
prostitutes and pimps" (Camus, Stranger, p. 121).
When the defense attorney asks: "Is my client on
trial for having buried his mother, or for killing a
man?" the prosecutor answers: "I accuse the prisoner
of behaving at his mother's funeral in a way that
showed he was already a criminal at heart" (Camus,
Stranger, p. 122).

Following Meursault's trial, the court was to try
a parricide, and the prosecutor, referring to
Meursault, declares: "This man, who is morally
guilty of his mother's death, is no less unfit to have
a place in the community than that other man, who did
to death the father that begat him...Yes, gentlemen, I
am convinced...that you will not find I am
exaggerating the case against the prisoner when I say
that he is also guilty of the murder to be tried
tomorrow in this court" (Camus, Stranger, p. 128). In
his defense, Meursault can say only that he killed the
Arab because of the sun. That is, of course, the
truth, but it makes no impression on the jury, which
prefers the prosecutor's fantasy and sentences
Meursault to execution by the guillotine.

Back in his cell, Meursault refuses to receive
the chaplain; but the latter comes anyway, and there
is a violent scene in which Meursault says he has very

little time left and is not "going to waste it on God" (Camus, Stranger, p. 150). The novel ends with Meursault's wish, in order to feel less lonely, "that on the day of my execution there should be a huge crowd of spectators and that they should greet me with howls of execration" (Camus, Stranger, p. 154).

Even the most superficial reading of The Stranger must forcefully bring out the fact that Meursault's trial and sentence represent a gross miscarriage of justice, strongly influenced by society's disapproval of those it considers eccentrics. As Jean-Paul Sartre comments, "the stranger he (Camus) wants to portray is precisely one of those terrible innocents who shock society by not accepting the rules of its game. That is why some people like him--for example his mistress, Marie, who is fond of him 'because he's odd.' Others, like the courtroom whose hatred he suddenly feels mounting towards him, hate him for the same reason" (Brée, Collection, p. 111).

Camus himself, concerned about misinterpretations of his work confirms Sartre's judgment in an introduction to the American student edition of his work. "I summed up The Stranger a long time ago with a sentence that I recognize is very paradoxical: °In our society any man who does not weep at his mother's burial runs the risk of being sentenced to death.' I merely meant that the hero of the book is sentenced to death because he does not play the game. In that sense, he is a stranger to the society in which he lives, he wanders, at its edge, in the outskirts of private, solitary, sensual life." But, Camus adds, Meursault is not a derelict; "he refueses to lie." Lying also involves exaggerating one's feelings. Meursault is asked to say that he regrets his crime, "according to the consecrated formula," but he refuses. Meursault is not insensitive, but is animated by a deep passion for truth; his story is that of "a man who without any heroic attitude, consents to dying for the truth," "the only Christ that we deserve" (Camus, L'Etranger, pp. VII-VIII).

A similar view is taken by many commentators. Thus Rachel Bespaloff says: "Though he (Meursault) does not condemn social oppression, nor tries to fight it, he denounces it through his quiet refusal to conform to the defiant attitudes one expects of him. One realizes that this indifferent man is intractable in his respect for truth. On this point he exhibits

108

an even heroic firmness since in the end it will cost him his life" (O'Brien, p. 20).

Nevertheless, as Conor Cruise O'Brien notes, one may have some serious reservations as to the extent to which Meursault fights for truth. He composes a letter for Raymond to entice the latter's Arab mistress to return so that Raymond can beat her up as he sees fit. When Marie, hearing the screams of the woman, suggests calling the police, Meursault refuses. It is left for other neighbors to do so. Besides, Meursault is willing to serve as a character witness for Raymond the pimp. "These episodes," says O'Brien, "show him as indifferent to truth as he is to cruelty. And his consent to these actions sets in motion the chain of events which leads to the killing of the Arab on the beach...There is just one category of phenomena about which Meursault will not lie, and that is his own feelings. Neither to give pleasure to others nor to save them pain nor to save his own skin will he pretend that he feels something that he does not feel...He dislikes the idea of the police. He is indifferent to the beating up of the woman" (O'Brien, pp. 21-22).

Furthermore, O'Brien doubts that a French court in Algeria would have condemned to death a European for shooting an Arab who had drawn a knife on him and had previously stabbed another European. The suggestion that the court is impartial between Arab and Frenchman, says O'Brien, "implicitly denies the colonial reality and sustains the colonial fiction" (O'Brien, p. 23). He wonders at the readiness of commentators, including Camus himself, "to canonize Meursault." Besides, the killing of the Arab is made to seem irrelevant because while the European characters in the novel all have names, i.e. are individualized, "the man who is shot has no name, and his relation to the narrator and his friends is not that of one human being to another" (O'Brien, p. 25). (Obviously, this is not Camus's interpretation of his novel.)

Another commentator, Pierre Nora, finds that Camus, like other Europeans of Algeria were unable to confront the problem of European-Arab relations; the trial scene is "a disturbing admission of historical guilt and takes on the aspect of a tragic anticipation" (O'Brien, p. 26).

O'Brien concludes that Camus's work is "a notable expression of the Western moral conscience. But we should not ignore the fact that it also registers the hesitations and limitations of that conscience and that one of the great limitations lies along the cultural frontier, in the colony" (O'Brien, p. 28).

Personally, I am unconvinced by these arguments of Conor Cruise O'Brien and Pierre Nora. The essential elements of the novel could have taken place unchanged even if Raymond's mistress and Meursault's victim had been Europeans. Raymond does not beat the woman because she is Arab but because he considers that she "betrayed" him, and Meursault kills the woman's brother not because he is an Arab, but because of the sun. Raymond the pimp probably did have Europeans in his employ, and a European brother whose sister had been mercilessly beaten might well have reacted in a similar way. Besides, the point of the story is that Meursault is tried not so much for having killed a man, but because he did not weep at his mother's funeral. Nowhere in the trial proceedings is there any emphasis on the fact that the dead man was an Arab; had he been a European, the trial would have proceeded the same way. Meursault is portrayed as a victim of society's prejudices, and Camus suggests a comparison with the victimization of Jesus.

In no way is Meursault being offered by Camus as a role model. The most "normal" character in the story seems to be Marie Cardona, who loves Meursault precisely because he is "strange." There is no question of the "canonization" of Meursault, who thinks that nothing matters and whose constant refrain is "That makes no difference." Raymond's victim and her brother are not given any names, but the funeral director, the janitor at the old age home, the examining magistrate, the judge and the journalists present at the trial have no names either. I therefore fail to see any implications of racism or even ethnic snobbery in the novel.

Germaine Brée finds similarities with Coleridge's Ancient Mariner. Meursault has killed the Arab the way the mariner killed the albatross. "Like the ancient mariner, Meursault has transgressed a natural, not a human law. Eventually, what frees Meursault (as it frees the ancient mariner) is the awareness of the beauty and, therefore, the sacredness of all living things" (Brée, Camus, p. 115). Camus, she adds, "suggests that in the face of the absurd no man can afford passively just to exist. To fail to question the meaning of the spectacle of life is to condemn both ourselves, as individuals, and the whole world to nothingness" (Brée, Camus, p. 117).

Pierre-Louis Rey considers Meursault as having "the pre-moral mentality of a four or five year old child, who knows what one must do or not do but without really understanding why." He is always ready with excuses but not at all anxious to analyze himself. (Rey, p. 41)

The Stranger, in addition to the more obvious question of the guilt or innocence of Meursault, poses the more general question of the justice of the death sentence. Meursault remembers his mother having told him how his father had gone to see a criminal executed. "The mere thought of it turned his stomach. But he'd seen it through and on coming home, was violently sick. I found my father's conduct rather disgusting. But now I understood, it was so natural" (Camus, Stranger, p. 138). In fact, Camus's own father had had the same reactions after witnessing an execution.

In his Reflections on the Guillotine, Camus condemns capital punishment, considering it a new crime added to the one committed by the murderer. "The survival of such a primitive rite," he says, "has been made possible among us only by he thought-lessness or ignorance of the public, which reacts only with the ceremonial phrases that have been drilled into it" (Camus, Resistance, p. 177). "The death penalty besmirches our society, and its upholders cannot reasonably defend it" (Camus, Resistance, p. 179).

The death penalty, he adds, cannot be exemplary. If it were, not only "should the photographs be multiplied, but the machine should even be set on a platform in Place de la Concorde at two p.m., the entire population should be invited and the ceremony should be put on television for those who couldn't attend. How can a furtive assassination committed at night in a prison courtyard be exemplary?" (Camus, Resistance, p. 181). Camus then gives the lurid details of what an execution actually entails. According to statistics drawn up in England at the beginning of the century, he adds, out of 250 criminals who were hanged, 170 had previously attended one or more executions. The victim has a family and relatives who are punished beyond all justice. Camus also objects to government encouragement of the alcoholic drinks industry, since alcholism contributes significantly to crime.

He wonders whether any of those executed might be innocent, and he cites the execution of Burton Abbott in California, March 15, 1957. Abbott went to the gas chamber maintaining his innocence. The Committee on Reprieves was a few minutes too late telephoning the prison to halt the execution" (Camus, Resistance, p. 212). A large element of chance enters into any sentence. "The look of the accused, his antecedents (adultery is often looked upon as an aggravating circumstance by jurors who may or may not have always been faithful), his manner (which is in his favor only if it is conventional--in other words, play acting most of the time), his very elocution (the old hands know that one must neither stammer nor be too eloquent), the mishaps of the trial enjoyed in a sentimental key (and the truth, alas, is not always emotionally effective): so many flukes that influence the final decision of the jury" (Camus, Resistance, pp. 214-215).

"Capital judgment upsets the only indisputable human solidarity--our solidarity against death--and it can be legitimized only by a truth or a principle that is superior to man." The Catholic Church through the centuries has often inflicted the death penalty, and Camus comments: "The unbeliever cannot keep from thinking that men who have set at the center of their faith the staggering victim of a judicial error ought at least to hesitate before committing legal murder" (Camus, Resistance, p. 224).

Forbidding executions "would amount to proclaiming publicly that society and the state are not absolute values, that nothing authorizes them to legislate definitively or to bring about the irreparable" (Camus, Resistance, p. 228). In the unified Europe of the future the abolition of the death penalty should be the first article of the European code.

The Plague (La Peste), published in 1947, is without doubt Camus's best novel. It probably was most influential in the decision of the Nobel Prize jury in 1957 to award the prize for literature to Camus for "his important literary production, which with clear-sighted earnestness illuminates the problems of the human conscience of our time" (Brée, Camus, p. 5).

The novel starts with a quotation from Daniel Defoe in 1721, taken from the third volume of Robinson Crusoe: "It is as reasonable to represent one kind of imprisonment by another, as it is to represent anything that really exists by that which exists not." The first sentence of the novel says: "The unusual events described in this chronicle occurred in 194_ at Oran." In a preliminary draft Camus had written: "...in 1941 during the Second World War in our little town of Oran" (Camus, Théàtre, p. 1967). No plague epidemic ever occurred at Oran in the forties, although there was a smaller typhus epidemic. The epidemic in the novel is mainly a symbol of something else--the brown plague of Nazism.

The novel, in fact, must be read at several levels simultaneously. Camus has made every effort to provide a realistic description of a plague, its ravages and its effects on a city. But at a deeper level, the plague is the symbol of evil, totalitarianism, war and oppression, and the city of Oran represents occupied France, and more generally Nazi-dominated Europe. The sudden outbreak of the plague in the first chapter, which lasts only two weeks, suggests the rapidity of the events that unleashed the war. The official declaration of a state of siege and the closing of the gates of the city suggest the defeat of the French and the armistice of 1940. The draconian measures taken by the authorities to guarantee order, the curfew and the incineration of the victims of the plague suggest the worst oppression of the Nazi occupation. The energetic work of the health squads suggests the development of the Resistance, and the jubilant celebration of the departure of the plague suggests the final victory.

At the end of the novel, as the populace celebrates the defeat of the plague, they want to put the horrors of the past behind them. "Calmly they denied, in the teeth of the evidence, that we had ever known a crazy world in which men were killed off like flies, or that precise savagery, that calculated frenzy of the plague, which instilled an odious freedom as to all that was not the here and now; or those charnel house stenches which stupefied whom they did not kill. In short they denied that we had ever been that hag-ridden populace a part of which was daily fed into a furnace and went up in oily fumes, while the rest, in shackled impotence, waited their turn" (Camus, _Plague_, p. 268). The last sentence of the passage in particular recalls a famous statement by the seventeenth century moralist Pascal. But for readers who themselves had survived the ordeals of the Nazi occupation and the Second World War, this passage could not fail to evoke images of Auschwitz, Buchenwald and Dachau.

At the end of the novel, Dr. Rieux, the leader in the fight against the plague, reveals that he is the narrator. The plague is assimilated with a crime, and Dr. Rieux considers himself a witness. "Summoned to give evidence regarding what was a sort of crime, he has exercised the restraint that behooves a conscientious witness. All the same, following the dictates of his heart, he has deliberately taken the victims' side and tried to share with his fellow citizens the only certitudes they had in common--love, exile and suffering" (Camus, _Plague_, p. 272).

Despite the enormous success of _The Plague_, with most critics and the public, there were strong criticisms, particularly from Jean-Paul Sartre and his associates in the existentialist movement. They saw in _The Plague_ merely a "Red Cross morality," and asked Camus: What would your characters do if they were fighting not a natural disaster, but one caused by humans? Camus replied that he had used the symbolism of the plague precisely because he wanted to deal not merely with Nazism, but with all oppression, all tyrannies. "What those fighters did, whose experience I translated a little, they did precisely against men, and at a price that you know. They will doubtless do it again in the face of any terror, whatever its face, for terror has several faces, which further justifies the fact that I did not exactly name any in order to be able better to strike them all" (Gaillard, pp. 29-30).

As an active member of the Resistance during the Second World War, Camus evidently must have had occasion to kill some of the enemies of his country. In his _Letters to a German Friend_, he writes: "...Contrary to what we sometimes used to think, the spirit is of no avail against the sword, but...the spirit together with the sword will always win out against the sword alone" (Camus, _Resistance_, p. 9). "We know now that the weapons of happiness cannot be

forged without considerable time and too much blood"
(Camus, Resistance, p. 29).

Nevertheless, one of Camus's main characters in
the novel, Tarrou, who is mistakenly identified with
Camus himself, appears to argue against the death
sentences in any form or shape. Tarrou tells Dr.
Rieux about his father, who had been a prosecutor and
whose work required him to demand death sentences and
witness executions. Tarrou goes to a trial one day
and looks at the man in the dock. "That little man of
about thirty, with sparse, sandy hair, seemed so eager
to confess everything, so genuinely horrified at what
he'd done and what was going to be done with him, that
after a few minutes I had eyes for nothing and nobody
else. He looked like a yellow owl scared blind by
too much light. His tie was slightly awry, he kept
biting his nails, those of one hand only, his
right..." (Camus, Plague, p. 224).

Evidently, the man in the dock is Meursault.
Tarrou, horrified by his father's profession leaves
home. "...My real interest in life was the death
penalty; I wanted to square accounts with that poor
blind owl in the dock. So I became an agitator, as
they say. I didn't want to be pestiferous, that's
all. To my mind the social order around me was based
on the death sentence, and by fighting the established
order, I'd be fighting against murder" (Camus, Plague,
p. 226).

For Tarrou, as for Camus, the plague becomes the
ultimate symbol of injustice, murder and oppression.
Tarrou, however, goes further, declaring that he is
"resolved to have no truck with anything which,
directly or indirectly, for good reasons or for bad,
brings death to anyone or justifies others' putting
him to death" (Camus, Plague, p. 228-229). His
concern is "with the poor owl; with that foul
procedure whereby dirty mouths stinking of plague told
a fettered man that he was going to die, after nights
and nights of mental torture while he waited to be
murdered in cold blood" (Camus, Plague, p. 228).

The ultimate question for Tarrou--who is an
atheist--is: "Can one be a saint without god?" (Camus,
Plague, p. 230)

Obviously, Tarrou cannot be a real Resistance
fighter, he can only work with the Red Cross. But
does he really represent Camus's thought? French

critic Serge Doubrovsky summarizes as follows Camus's attitude toward violence: "Camus never denied that, in certain exceptional cases, violence must be an arm, but he always refused to accept it as a policy" (Gaillard, p. 70). In his _Actuelles_, Camus writes: "Complete pacifism appears to us badly thought out, and we know henceforth that there always comes a time when it is no longer tenable" (Camus, _Essais_, p. 289). "Refuting non-violence is not refuting _me_. I have never argued for it. That is an attitude that is attributed to me for the convenience of a polemic. I don't think that one must answer blows with benediction" (Camus, _Essais_, p. 355).

The narrator of the novel, Dr. Rieux is obviously the character who appears to speak most directly for Camus's point of view. For Camus, the plague is the symbol of the most absolute evil and injustice, and it is Dr. Rieux who leads the battle against the enemy. Interviewed by a journalist at the beginning of the novel, Rieux is described as "a man who was sick and tired of the world he lived in--though he had much liking for his fellow men--and had resolved, for his part, to have no truck with injustice and compromises with the truth" (Camus, _Plague_, p. 12-13). He rejects the view of the Jesuit Paneloux, who preached that the plague was God's punishment for the sins of man. "What's true of all the evils of the world is true of the plague as well. It helps men to rise above themselves. All the same, when you see the misery it brings, you'd need to be a madman, or a coward, or stone blind, to give in tamely to the plague" (Camus, _Plague_, p. 115). The doctor "believed himself on the right road--in fighting creation as he found it" (Camus, _Plague_, p. 116). Rieux is an atheist who considers creation evil and refuses to believe in God. "...Since the order of the world is shaped by death, mightn't it be better for God if we refuse to believe in Him and struggle with all our might against death, without raising our eyes toward the heaven where he sits in silence." Tarrou then says: "But your victories will never be lasting"; Rieux replies: "Yes, I know that. But it's no reason for giving up the struggle" (Camus, _Plague_, p. 117-118).

The conversation between Rieux and Tarrau thus echoes some of the essential arguments of the _Myth of Sisyphus_. Man can never hope to conquer the absurd because death itself is an integral part of the absurd. But man's dignity consists precisely in the struggle against the absurd for a temporary victory.

116

Sisyphus pursues his absurd task of rolling the stone up the hill, knowing that it will only roll down again. But as he rolls the stone up the hill, his heart is filled with joy and he proclaims his hatred of the gods. His is a temporary victory over the absurd. So it is with the plague. Dr. Rieux and his colleagues at the end of the novel have achieved victory over the plague, and the joyous population comes forth to celebrate. But Rieux knows what the jubilant crowds do not understand: "that the plague bacillus never dies or disappears for good; that it can lie dormant for years and years in furniture and linen-chests; that it bides its time in bedrooms, cellars, trunks and bookshelves; and that perhaps the day would come when, for the bane and enlightening of men, it would rouse up its rats again and send them forth to die in a happy city" (Camus, Plague, p. 278). These are, in fact, the last lines and in a sense the conclusion of the novel.

For Camus, the war against injustice, oppression, totalitarianism is never completely won. A battle may be won, but the fight will inevitably resume and be renewed elsewhere at another time. Still, one must not give in tamely to the plague. The dignity of man consists in fighting injustice and evil, even though the victory can only be temporary.

For Rieux, as for Camus, religion has no role to play in the fight for justice. Rieux adamantly rejects the notion that the plague is God's punishment for man's sins. At the bedside of a dying child, he meets Paneloux and angrily tells him: "Ah! That child, anyhow, was innocent, and you know it as well as I do." Paneloux answers: "Perhaps we should love what we cannot understand." But Rieux replies: "No, Father. I've a very different idea of love. And until my dying day I shall refuse to love a scheme of things in which children are put to torture." Nevertheless, Rieux looks for support from Paneloux in a common struggle against death and disease. Paneloux, deeply affected by the child's agony, preaches a second sermon, in which he no longer speaks of God's punishment. He concludes: "We must believe everything or deny everything. And who among you, I ask, would dare to deny everything?" (Camus, Plague, pp. 196-197, 202)

This is obviously not Camus's message. In fact the arguments in Paneloux's first sermon, in which he considers the plague God's punishment, have been

117

compared to the propaganda of those priests who supported the Vichy regime in its efforts to depict the French defeat as a result of the sins of the politicians of the Third Republic.

Camus's anti-Christian message is repeated constantly in essays and interviews. On September 8, 1944 he wrote: "Christianity in its essence (and that is its paradoxical greatness) is a doctrine of injustice. It is based on the sacrifice of an innocent and the acceptance of this sacrifice. Justice, on the contrary—and Paris has just proved it in its nights illuminated by the flames of insurrection—does not proceed without revolt" (Camus, Essais, p. 272-273).

On December 26, 1944 he noted that the Pope had just addressed a message to the world openly espousing democracy. "We would have wanted the Pope to take sides, in the very heart of those shameful years and to denounce what should have been denounced. It is hard to think that the Church left this task to others, more obscure, who did not have its authority, some of whom lacked the invincible hope on which it lives" (Camus, Essais, p. 284-285). In a talk to the Dominicans he denounced certain political priests. "When a Spanish bishop blesses public executions, he is no longer a bishop nor a Christian and not even a man; he is a dog..." (Camus, Essais, p. 375).

Christian commentators have had some difficulty evaluating Camus. Jean Onimus in his study Camus devant Dieu (Camus Before God) wonders whether Camus's spiritual life was that of "a great love that was missed" (Gaillard, p. 67).

Thomas Hanna, after analyzing The Plague, says that this novel "should leave us no doubt that Albert Camus is a Christian philosopher, and, at least in this novel, there are grounds for the statement made by Rachel Bespaloff that Camus is proposing a 'dechristianized Christianity" (Hanna, p. 202). Peyre notes that some victims of the plague respond to the epidemic like the seekers of "diversion," condemned by Pascal, who concentrate on endless repetition of some meaningless gesture. One spits from his balcony on cats, another pores over railroad time tables and imagines travels that never take place, a third, aspiring to be a writer, polishes the same sentence endlessly and makes no further progress. Pascal had described such men as "prisoners sentenced to death

118

who weave straw in the courtyard of their prison in order to forget" (Peyre, p. 247).

Obviously there are convergences between the thought of Camus and that of some Christian thinkers, particularly Pascal. Nevertheless, it seems to me that such efforts to metamorphose Camus into a Christian are highly distorted and deliberately over-look explicit statements repeated over many years to the very end of his life in which Camus constantly rejects Christianity and its basic teachings. Paneloux's arguments are rejected, and while Tarrou wonders about sainthood, it is a sainthood without God, if that is possible. In an interview Camus stated: "The closest to myself is not Tarrou the saint, but Rieux the doctor" (Peyre, p. 249).

At his news conference in Stockholm in 1957, at the time he was awarded the Nobel Prize for Literature, Camus told correspondents that he had written with warmth about Jesus and that he had respect and veneration for his teachings, but that he did not believe in the Resurrection" (Lottman, p. 615). In view of Camus's constant and specific repudiation of Christianity, it seems to me that we should take Camus at his word and not try to convert him posthumously to a religion that he did not accept.

The Plague is a symbolic interpretation of the struggle against evil, and the greatest evil in the first half of the forties was obviously Nazism, which produced the Second World War and the terror that gripped all Europe. For Camus, there was never any question that Nazism represented evil and had to be destroyed. These views are presented very clearly in Camus's four Letters to a German Friend. Written between July 1943 and July 1944 they form an indictment of Nazi Germany as the symbol of injustice, as compared to France, fighting for justice.

In a post-war preface, Camus specifies that "you" means not "you Germans," but "you Nazis," and that "we" means not always "we Frenchmen," but sometimes "we Europeans." "For a long time," he writes, "we both thought that this world had no ultimate meaning...You supposed that in the absence of any human or divine code the only values were those of the animal world--in other words violence and cunning...I, believing I thought as you did, saw no valid argument to anwer you except a fierce love of justice which,

119

after all seemed to me as unreasonable as the most sudden passion.

"Where lay the difference? Simply that you readily accepted despair and I never yielded to it. Simply that you saw the injustice of our condition to the point of being willing to add to it, whereas it seemed to me that man must exalt justice in order to fight against eternal injustice, create happiness in order to protest against the universe of unhappiness...

"I, on the contrary chose justice in order to remain faithful to the world. I continue to believe that this world has no ultimate meaning, but I know that something in it has a meaning and that is man, because he is the only creature to insist on having one. This world has at least the truth of man, and our task is to provide its justifications against fate itself."

Camus implies that justice had to defend itself against the Nazis with violence. "...We know now that the weapons of happiness cannot be forged without considerable time and too much blood...We were forced to imitate you in order not to die....I am fighting you because your logic is as criminal as your heart. And in the horror you have lavished upon us for four years, your reason plays as large a part as your instinct. This is why my condemnation will be sweeping; you are already dead as far as I am concerned" (Camus, Resistance, pp. 4, 28-30).

Camus's revulsion against Nazism and his total rejection of Hitler is again forcefully brought out in his philosophical essay, The Rebel (L'Homme révolté), published in 1951. "The crimes of the Hitler regime," he writes, "among them the massacre of the Jews, are without precedent in history because history gives no other example of a doctrine of such total destruction being able to seize the levers of command of a civilized nation. But above all, for the first time in history, the rulers of a country have used their immense power to establish a mystique beyond the bounds of any ethical considerations. This first attempt to found a Church on nihilism was paid for by complete annihilation."

"Seven million Jews assassinated, seven million Europeans deported or killed, ten million war victims, are perhaps not sufficient to allow history to pass judgment: history is accustomed to murderers." But, Camus adds, Hitler, having suffered defeat, decided to drag the whole German nation with him to the grave "and to make their destruction his apotheosis." The destruction of his final justification, the German nation, "henceforth makes this man, whose presence in history for years on end haunted the minds of millions of men, into an inconsistent and contemptible phantom" (Camus, Rebel, pp. 184-185).

Camus's wife, the former Francine Faure, was partly of Jewish origin; her mother had a maternal grandfather who was a Berber Jew and who had married a Turkish Jew (Lottman, p. 183). When the anti-Semantic laws of the Nazi-inspired Vichy government drove Jews out of the public schools, Camus and his wife Fancine both taught in Oran at a Jewish institute directed by André Benichou, himself driven out of the public school system by the anti-Jewish laws of Vichy. Camus's teaching in the French Studies program at the institute left him enough time to work on The Plague (Kellman, Approaches, p. 102).

Despite Camus's loathing of Nazism, Camus's opposition to the death sentence led him to oppose the execution even of wartime collaborators in the post-war years. Thus he signed a petition for clemency for Robert Brasillac, a pro-Nazi writer whom he despised and who had described Fascism as "the very poetry of the twentieth century." Brasillach's anti-Semitic and pro-Nazi denunciations had encouraged the beatings and mutilations of Camus's friends; but Camus signed the petition because of his opposition to the death penalty in all circumstances. Although he first called for "pitiless justice" for Marshal Petain, the head of the collaborationist Vichy government, he opposed a death sentence, which "would give this vain old man the reputation of a martyr..." (Lottman, p. 349).

Camus condemned the atomic bombing of Hiroshima, stating that "mechanical civilization has just reached the last degree of savagery. It will be necessary to choose between collective suicide or the intelligent utilization of scientific conquests." He added that if the Japanese surrendered, he would be delighted, but the news of the bombing led him to "plead still more energetically in favor of a veritable inter-national society" (Lottman, pp. 362-363).

121

The scene of the Plague is the Algerian city of Oran, which in the novel symbolizes France and occupied Europe in general. Oran was not in metropolitan France, but North Africa; yet there is virtually no mention of Arabs in the novel. It is true that in the forties Oran was 74 percent European in population, the most European city in Algeria; the Arabs, representing 23.7 percent of the population did not have citizenship or voting rights (Kellman, Approaches, p. 108). In that respect, Camus was perhaps justified in regarding Oran as a French city. But the absence of Arabs, who were after all the majority in Algeria, has been taken by some as an indication of insensitivity on the part of Camus to the issue of justice for the Arab population.

At the beginning of the novel the journalist Rambert inquires about the health situation of the Arabs, and he later accompanies Rieux on a trip to a downtown dispensary, the trip taking them through the Arab quarter known as the village nègre. But then the Arabs disappear completely. Conor Cruise O'Brien, a noted Irish writer and diplomat, points out that Camus wanted to situate his tale in a city that he knew; he therefore had to remove the Arabs. But the possibility exists, O'Brien notes, of looking at things differently. "There were Arabs for whom 'French Algeria' was a fiction as repugnant as the fiction of Hitler's new European order was for Camus and his friends. For such Arabs the French were in Algeria by virtue of the same right by which the Germans were in France: the right of conquest...From this point of view, Rieux, Tarrou and Grand were not devoted fighters against the plague; they were the plague itself" (O'Brien, pp. 54-55). O'Brien adds that Camus would never have accepted this analogy as just.

Alastair Horne notes that "even great-hearted Camus, who was among the first to expose the dreadful economic plight of the Algerians, both shortly before and after the Second World War, occasionally reveals a curious blindness, almost amounting to indifference, towards them as human beings." Thus Oran in The Plague seems almost to lack any Arabs at all and the shoe-shine boys ("the only men still in love with their profession") appear to be part of the tourist backdrop; Camus does not question the poverty that accompanies this beloved profession" (Horne, p. 55).

The British journalist Geoffrey Bocca points out that in Algiers the European community of 200,000 was more numerous than the 165,000 Moslems, but the communities overlapped. In Oran, the Moslems clustered in shantytowns at the outer rim of the city, which created a kind of apartheid. This explains in part why Camus does not find any need for Moslem characters in his novel (Bocca, p. 36).

The final lines of The Plague, warning of the danger of a recurrence of the plague, were unfortunately prophetic in Algeria itself. On April 8, 1962 the French voted in a referendum in favor of Algerian independence, and the violence of the abandoned Europeans now reached a crescendo. Geoffrey Bocca notes that at that point the pieds noirs (Europeans) could "hate with a good conscience...Any Moslem was fair game. The ratonade (rat hunt) became the vogue. The fashionable new attitude was 'there are nine million Moslems in Algeria and one million Europeans; if we each kill nine the problem is solved'" (Bocca, p. 198).

As regards Algiers, Bocca writes: "The plague had come to the land of Camus, even as he had described it in his novel. It was not only the hideous death in the streets, the blood in the gutters and the smell of gunpowder and plastic in the dry spring air; it was also the moral massacre, the decay of civilized principle on both sides, the total indifference to horror, brutality and pain" (Bocca, pp. 199-200).

Oran had not experienced the war before 1960. But an incident there in which Moslems attacked the family of a baker named Quiricos in his car and incinerated them all unleased the plague in Oran too. Numerous Moslems were then victimized as they returned home to their quarters (Bocca, p. 36). The ultimate lunacy of the French colons (settlers) was the so-called Secret Army (OAS), the underground organization that was determined to maintain French Algeria by attacks and outrages not only against the Moslems but also the French army and government which had approved Algerian independence. When they confronted French soldiers in the Bad el Oued section of Algiers, the army replied with a bombardment which put an end once and for all to all visions of French Algeria (Johnson, p. 504).

Criticisms of Camus for supposed insensitivity regarding Algerian independence came from many French leftists, notably Sartre and Simone de Beauvoir; but

123

even Conor Cruise O'Brien, agreeing with Sartre, takes Camus to task. He writes: "Eight years after the publication of Le Peste the rats came up to die in the cities of Algeria...And this eruption came precisely from the quarter in which then narrator had refused to look: from the houses which Dr. Rieux never visited and from the conditions about which the reporter Rambert never carried out his inquiry...The source of the plague is what we pretend is not there, and the preacher himself is already, without knowing it, inflected by the plague." (58-59). Yet, despite its flaws, the Plague is for O'Brien "a great allegorical sermon" (O'Brien, pp. 54-59).

Differences regarding Algeria caused a break between Camus on one side and his former friends Jean-Paul Sartre and Simone de Beauvoir. Camus condemned terrorism even-handedly, refusing to endorse the FLN, the Algerian "liberation" movement, because it practiced terrorism, whereas Sartre and Simone de Beauvoir openly endorsed it. Sartre, speaking at a 1956 protest meeting, attacked the "neocolonialist mystification" of a supposedly tamer French Algeria. "There are no good colonists and bad colonists. A colonist is a colonist," he maintained, denouncing the concentration of land ownership in Eurpean hands (Cohen-Solal, pp. 368-369). Speaking of Sartre's efforts to promote Algerian independence, Roland Dumas notes: "The Algerian war was his war...He missed all the important political events of his time except the Algerian war, which was, in a way, the meeting of a great cause and a great personality" (Cohen-Solal, pp. 440-441). For Simone de Beauvoir, by early 1958 the sight of French uniforms in the streets had "the same effect on me that swastikas once did...I was living in an occupied city, and I loathed the occupiers even more fiercely than I had those others in the forties." Camus, however, attacked "a section of opinion" that "thinks obscurely that the Arabs have acquired the right somehow to slit throats and to mutilate" (Horne, p. 235).

Camus was not insensitive to the moral issues raised by the Algerian war, as brought out in numerous interviews and articles. When he wrote The Plague in 1947, the wave of Algerian Arab unrest was only two years old, having started at Sétif in 1945 with the massacre of about 100 Europeans--to which the French replied with massive reprisals. Camus could not have foreseen the dimensions that the movement would assume by the late fifties.

In an interview published in _Demain_ October 24, 1957, Camus states: "My role in Algeria never was and never will be to divide...I share the fate of all those, French or Arab, who suffer...But I can't all by myself rebuild what so many men are trying to destroy. I did what I could. I shall try once more when there will once again be a chance to aid in the reconstruction of an Algeria delivered of all the hatreds and all the racism" (Lottman, p. 609). On December 12, 1957, at an informal question and answer session at Stockholm University, after Camus was awarded the Nobel Prize for Literature, he was confronted by an Algerian Moslem militant who demanded to know why Camus intervened so readily in eastern Europe, but not Algeria. Camus replied that he had been the only French journalist forced to leave Algeria for having defended the Moslems, that he favored a fully democratic regime and that some of the Algerian militants were alive because of actions of which his interlocutor was not aware. But he added: "I must also denounce a terrorism which is exercised blindly, in the streets of Algiers, for example, and which so me day could strike my mother or my family. I believe in justice, but I shall defend my mother above justice" (Lottman, pp. 617-618). In a letter to _Le Monde_ later, Camus denied that he had said that French government had committed only minor faults in Algeria.

Camus's biographer, Herbert Lottman, comments: "Most of Camus's friends realized that the fear of blind terrorism, the bomb in a public place which could kill his mother, was the very real motivation for his opposition to the FLN" (Lottman, p. 624).

By the beginning of 1958 Camus came out in support of the plan proposed by Marc Lauriol of the University of Algiers under which a federation would be established in the French Commonwealth similar to the Swiss cantonal system. A reconstituted French parliament would consist of two sections; in the second there would be about one hundred Moslems and fifteen European Algerians, and this section would have complete control over strictly Moslem affairs. Both sections together, with a majority of metropolitan French, would legislate on matters affecting France and Algeria jointly. If that solution were not adopted, said Camus, "Algeria will be lost and the consequences terrible, for the Arabs as for the French." Nothing came of this plan, however (Horne, p. 235).

Far from being indifferent or insensitive to the Algerian dilemma, Camus wrote extensively about it, gathering his main articles together in his Chroniques algériennes (Algerian Reports). In the preface of his Chroniques he notes: "...I have long been alert to Algerian realities and cannot approve, either, a policy of surrender that would abandon the Arab people to an even greater misery, tear the French in Algeria from their century-old roots, and favor, to no one's advantage, the new imperialism how threatening the liberty of France and of the West." He strongly condemns the repression and torture used by French forces in Algeria; but he condemns equally the terror practiced by the FLN against French and also Arab civilians (Camus, Resistance, pp. 111, 114-115). He objects to condemnation of the French in Algeria by some metropolitan Frenchmen. The men in his own family "being poor and free of hatred, never exploited or oppressed anyone. But three quarters of the French in Algeria resemble them and, if only they are provided reasons rather than insults, will be ready to admit the necessity of a freer and juster order" (Camus, Resistance, p. 119). "I believe in a policy of reparation in Algeria rather than a policy of expiation...And there will be no future that does not do justice at one and the same time to the two communities of Algeria" (Camus, Resistance, p. 120). "An Algeria made up of federated settlements and linked to France seems to me preferable (without any possible comparison on the plane of simple justice) to an Algeria linked to an empire of Islam which would bring the Arab peoples only increased poverty and suffering and which would tear the Algerian-born French from their natural home" (Camus, Resistance, pp. 124-125).

Camus saw the Algerian Arabs and French as "condemned to live together." He could not conceive tearing up the roots linking the French to Algeria; but the French had 'no right...to destroy the roots of Arab culture and life.'" His hope was that "Arabs and French, reconciled in freedom and justice, will make an effort to forget the bloodshed that divides them today" (Camus, Resistance, p. 130).

Camus's Algerian Reports represent a voice of moderation and conciliation, not at all the voice of a bearer of the plague. His program for equal justice for the French of Algeria and for the Arabs fell, unfortunately, on deaf ears, and extremism won the day, though Camus did not live long enough to experience the French abandonment of Algeria and the hasty departure of more than 1,380,000 persons, including some Moslems.

Conor Cruise O'Brien says that "politically Camus and his tribe, the Europeans of Algeria were casualties of the post-war period" and that Camus "flinched from the realities of his position as a Frenchman of Algeria" (O'Brien, p. 105). Such statements as well as O'Brien's reference to the preacher himself being infected with the plague, do not appear very appropriate to me. After all, in the former British colony of Rhodesia, now Zimbabwe, which faced a situation similar to that of Algeria, a final settlement recognizing an independent Zimbabwe still left a role for British settlers who wished to remain and who made a vital contribution to the economy of the country.

Perhaps the European settlers, by their support of the ultimate lunacy represented by the Secret Army, the terrorist underground of the settlers, forfeited any claim to representing justice. But the FLN, for which Sartre worked with so much enthusiasm, is not universally accepted either as representing justice.

Paul Johnson in his <u>Modern Times</u> notes that the end of the revolt came in March 1962 "in an orgy of slaughter and intolerance." The Great Synagogue was sacked and marked with Nazi slogans. Of the 250,000 Moslem officials who had served France faithfully, only 15,000 managed to get to France; the rest were "shot without trial, used as human mine-detectors..., tortured, made to dig their own tombs and swallow their military decorations before being killed; some were burned alive, castrated, dragged behind trucks, fed to the dogs; there were cases where entire families including tiny children were murdered together."

"...The new nation owed its existence to the exercise of cruelty without restraint and on the largest possible scale. Its régime, composed mainly of successful gangsters, quickly ousted those of its members who had been brought up in the Western tradition...The new Algeria had not kept its crimes to itself, it became and for many years remained the chief resort of international terrorists of all kinds...It set a pattern of public crime and disorder which was to be imitated throughout the vast and tragic continent..." (Johnson, pp. 504-505). Was

Camus wrong to refuse to endorse the ganster-like, terrorist "liberation" movement? Was he wrong to stress that the European population, many of whom were simple working men whose families had lived for several generations in Algeria, also had rights and that a Swiss type solution should have been attempted?

The theme of the plague, the supreme symbol of evil and injustice, again becomes the subject of another work by Camus, the play State of Siege (Etat de siège). The scene is Cádiz in Spain and the plague appears as a general wearing a field-gray uniform and rimless glasses, suggestive of Hitler's Gestapo chief, Himmler (Cruickshank, p. 212). The play, like the novel, is a generalized attack on totalitarianism. Gabriel Marcel objected to the Spanish setting; he would have preferred an east European country. Camus in his reply denounced both the Soviet and Nazi concentration camps, but especially the Franco regime in Spain. "You have forgotten that in 1936 a rebel general in the name of Christ gathered an army of Moors to hurl them against the legal government of the Spanish Republic, brought about the triumph of an unjust cause after inexpiable masacres and from then on started an atrocious repression which has lasted ten years and is not yet finished" (Camus, Essais, pp. 392-393).

Camus's play Caligula, first presented in 1945 and based primarily on Roman historical sources, obviously brought out striking similarities between the megalomania of Caligula and that of Hitler, between Caligula's attitude and that of Nazi intellectuals, and between Caligula's suicide and that of Hitler (Cruickshank, pp. 198-199). The death of his sister and mistress, Druisilla, reveals the absurd to Caligula, who exclaims: "Men die and are not happy." "Things as they are do not seem satisfactory to me" (Camus, Caligula, pp. 26-27). Having discovered the absurd, Caligula feels free to act according to his whims, to try to change the order of the world, to assert his freedom as "the only free man in this empire." He decrees a famine and makes himself the agent of death, killing on the most trivial pretexts; but in the end he recognizes that his freedom has not been good. He is obsessed with a death wish and appears to allow himself to be assassinated.

Les Justes (literally, "the just ones," but translated into English as "The Just Assassins)" was first produced in 1949 and is based on the memoirs of a Russian terrorist of the early twentieth century, Savinkov. The terrorist group plans to assassinate Grand Duke Sergei in order to advance the day of the revolution that will liberate Russia. But at the last moment, the would-be assassin, Kaliayev, sees children in the Grand Duke's carriage and will not hurl the bomb. Stepan, who believes that the end justifies the means, scolds his comrade for his supposed lack of courage; Dora, who is in love with Kaliayev, says the organization would lose all influence if it consented to murder children. Killing children, Kaliayev says, is contrary to honor. He tries again and succeeds; this time there are no children in the Grand Duke's carriage. In prison he refuses the consolations of religion and accepts death stoically. Dora will hurl the next bomb with the full expectation of a similar fate for herself. In his Actuelles, Camus writes: "They had chosen action and terror to serve justice, but at the same time they had chosen to die, to pay for a life with a life, so that justice might remain alive" (Camus, De l'Envers, p. 152). Let us recall that in The Plague Rieux had already said: "Until my dying day I shall refuse to love a scheme of things in which children are put to torture" (Camus, Plague, pp. 196-197).

Death came to Albert Camus on January 4, 1960 at the age of forty-six, two years after he was awarded the Nobel Prize. André Malraux as Minister of Culture issued this statement: "For over twenty years the work of Albert Camus was inseparable from the obsession with justice. We salute one of those through whom France remains present in the hearts of man" (Lottman, p. 669).

In his final summation of Camus's influence on his time, Conor Cruise O'Brien comments: "Probably no European writer of his time left so deep a mark on the imagination and, at the same time, on the moral and political consciousness of his own generation and of the next...No other writer, not even Conrad, is more representative of the Western consciousness and conscience in relation to the non-Western world." Camus was "above all an artist, and his primary and most enduring concern was not with justice, but with artistic truth. Yet the artistic truth of the novelist, dramatist, and essayist has social and political implications and is a form of justice" (O'Brien, p. 102).

Both of Camus's novels are a passionate cry for justice and a condemnation of the bigotry and oppression of the modern world. The Plague, in particular, seves as an everlasting warning that the fight for justice is never completely won, but must be constantly fought anew wherever tyranny and opression arise. More than twenty-five years after his death Camus has retained his image as the "just man," and this well deserved reputation is likely to endure.

BIBLIOGRAPHY

Bocca, Geoffrey. The Secret Army. Englewood Cliffs,
N.J.: Prentice-Hall, 1968

Brée, Gemaine and Margaret Guiton. An Age of Fiction:
The French Novel from Gide to Camus. New
Brunswick, N.J.: Rutgers Univesity Press, 1957.

Brée, Germaine. Camus. New Brunswick, N.J.: Rutgers
University Press, 1961.

Brée, Germaine. Camus: A Collection of Critical
Essays. Englewood Cliffs, N.J.: Prentice Hall,
1961.

Camus, Albert. Caligula, suivi de Le Malentendu.
Paris: Gallimard, 1958.

Camus, Albert. De l'Envers et l'Endroit à l'Exil et
le Royaume, Laurel Language Library, edited by
Germaine Brée. New York: Dell, 1963.

Camus, Albert. Essais. Bibliothèque de la Pléiade.
Paris: Gallimard et Calmann-Lévy, 1965.

Camus, Albert. L'Étranger. Edited by Germaine Brée
and Carlos Lynes. New York: Appleton-Century-
Crofts, 1955.

Camus, Albert. The Myth of Sisyphus and Other Essays.
Translated by Justin O'Brien. New York: Vintage
Books, Random House, 1955.

Camus, Albert, The Plague. Translated by Stuart
Gilbert. New York: Modern Library, Random House,
1948.

Camus, Albert. The Rebel: An Essay on Man in Revolt.
Translated by Anthony Bower. New York: Vintage
Books, 1957.

Camus, Albert. Resistance, Rebellion, and Death.
Translated by Justin O'Brien. New York: Vintage
Books, Random House, 1960.

Camus, Albert. The Stranger. Translated by Stuart
Gilbert. New York: Vintage Books, Random House,
1942.

Camus, Albert. Théâtre, Récits, Nouvelles.
Bibliotheque de la Pléiade. Paris: Gallimard, 1962.

Cohen-Solal, Annie. Sartre: A Life. Translated by
Anna Cancogni. New York: Pantheon Books, 1987.

Cruickshank, John. Albert Camus and the Literature of
Revolt. Westport, CT: Greenwood Press, 1978.

Gaillard, Pol. La Peste, Camus. Profil d'une oeuvre.
Paris: Hatier, 1972.

Hanna, Thomas. The Thought and Art of Albert Camus.
Chicago: Henry Regnery Co., 1958.

Horne, Alastair. A Savage War of Peace: Algeria 1954-
1962. New York: Viking Press, 1978.

Johnson, Paul. Modern Times: The World from the
Twenties to the Eighties. New York: Harper and
Row, 1983.

Kellman, Steven G. (editor): Approaches to Teaching
Camus's 'The Plague'. New York: Modern Language
Association, 1985. (Pages 102-109: Martha O'Nan,
"Biographical Context and Its Importance to
Classroom Study")

Lévi-Valensi, Jacqueline. Les critiques de notre
temps et Camus. Paris: Garnier, 1970.

Lottman, Herbert R. Albert Camus: A Biography.
Garden City, N.Y.: Doubleday, 1979.

O'Brien, Conor Cruise. Albert Camus of Europe and
Africa. New York: Viking Press, 1970.

Peyre, Henri. The Contemporary French Novel. New
York: Oxford University Press, 1955.

Rey, Pierre-Louis. L'Étranger, Camus. Profil d'une
oeuvre. Paris: Hatier, 1970.

7.

FILM PERSPECTIVES OF JUSTICE:
LITERARY SOURCES

Leonard Bloom
Modern Languages
University of Bridgeport

Ineluctably, one's concept of justice in relation to man, of his position and function in a global perspective, is unattainable without awareness and comprehension of how the forces of law and order operate in a given society. Like the proverbial 'man of a thousand faces,' we have come to address issues pertaining to justice from different levels of meaning in a broad sociopolitical framework irrespective of time, place, or events in history. Sometimes justice functions under well-fashioned laws designed to protect human rights as designated in the American Constitution and the Charter of the United Nations. In other instances, however, in non-democratic systems of government, those very rights which we all too often take for granted, are not the realities of everyday existence. Examples abound down through the ages of totalitarian-run governments, of police states, and zealots usurping territories for their own gain and destroying anything or anyone who might come in their way. Consequently, the violation of human rights has echoed worldwide from Biblical times to the present. As sources of information concerning justice, much can be found on pages of literature in all languages, representative of different writers across the centuries. Its theme is universal as it often conveys the problems and preoccupations, mores, morals, and concerns of a particular individual, institution or moment in a particular environment. Much of what has focused on justice from a literary perspective has also been transposed onto film, a technological medium that has radically changed the way we live, the way we perceive, and the way we comprehend world events, current or past.

While literature may seem to some people merely the accumulation of an author's thoughts through the use of words on paper, film, whether historical or contemporary, document or fiction, is implicitly an interpreted version of the human scene as well as an extension of reality into an imaginative dimension.

How fictional narrative treats the subject of justice in works of cinema is a fascinating study not only in the crossover, but in its adaptation.

Since motion pictures were first projected onto a screen in front of an audience back in 1894, film as a medium of art, has long struck a balance between its selective literary sources and subsequent cinematic adaptations. Yet, from its pristine manifestations down to the present time, there has existed a persistent paradox: on the one hand, writers argue that no record could be more literally exact than a film, while on the other, movies are essentially recognized as creations of illusion. This kind of duality affects not only the judgment, for instance, of the film maker, but of the discriminating public as well.

Moreover, in the twentieth century, replete with its spate of worldwide crises, including major and minor wars, the collapse of empires and political upheavals, Nazi Germany, the atomic holocaust, the debacle of the Vietnam War, and so forth, authors of popular literature and screenwriters have assumed increasing significance as repositories of factual, eyewitness reports on the political, social, and economic scene, ostensibly capturing the viewer's imagination for purposes of sociological and psychological analysis or dialogue.

In all these troubled times, certain writers and film makers (particularly those working in the area of documentary reportage) have used their collective talents in search of some guiding principle that could be translated into a mechanism for human understanding of world situations, and solutions to grave problems affecting people of different ages and socioeconomic status. Serious basic universal questions have frequently emerged from a better awareness of cross-cultural societies throughout the world such as the philosophical quest for the funadmental meaning of life and for truth, and primarily designed toward a fuller comprehension of human values, embracing justice and the right to free speech and movement.

Some interesting authors, ranging, for instance, from Herman Melville to Truman Capote, representing different genres and spirits of intellectual creative style, have sought to portray and examine issues surrounding justice or injustice in such diverse works as <u>Billy Budd</u> and <u>In Cold Blood</u>, respectively. Likewise, film makers have chosen to approach both stories through a physical and visual language, rendering statements about personal points of view underlying a social and philosophical nature germane to the theme of justice in one or another fashion.

In terms of film adaptations, since the beginning of world cinema, artists representing diversified segments of the movie industry have generally extrapolated a writer's story on specific issues reflecting the concerns of his or her age group preoccupied with often emotionally charged topics such as judicial polarities, conflicts between social classes, racial, societal and ideological tensions, psychological repercussions of war and the unending pursuit of peace, man's inhumanity to man, corruption in political office regardless of state or country, mob violence, police action, denial of gay rights, anti-abortion demonstrations, demagoguery, and so forth. These and sundry other related issues fill pages of literary works, to say little about their impact on the printed media or through other channels of daily communication such as the silver screen, television, radio, or even via word of mouth from neighbor to neighbor, and the like.

All these concerns project a vital, often violent reflection of our age and, indeed, even past events are occasionally reexamined, reinvestigated in some cases, raising new questions that beg for answers to specific problematic political and social issues, including drug abuse, the violation of human rights, and so on. Consequently, we may view a bond of marriage that has frequently co-existed between literature and cinema; in fact, the former has notably provided the latter with a rich source of fictional and sometimes non-fictional background information for movie studios to produce films exploring multifaceted concepts and ideas dealing with, for example, the obstruction of justice, the denial of civil rights, capital punishment, and other topical issues pertaining to the broad thesis of justice. It is not too rare that a film version may present a story more dramatic and provocative than the original piece of fiction or non-fiction on which it was based.

The number of fictional sources dealing with the theme of justice and their adaptations to the screen is rather extensive and varied, if one were to follow the development of cinema from decade to decade, and from nation to nation. While this writer believes that the present study in no way attempts to exhaust the subject of justice and its impact on or application to film, it must be pointed out that cinematic realism can only be judged from the perspective of the film maker and interpretations of his or her work must be left up to the observer for more complete scrutiny. On the subsequent pages, therefore, this writer aims to introduce certain perceptions of justice as they shape our understanding of the rights and wrongs of any politico-social order confronted with issues relative to the administration of justice.

The majority of books and their film versions for examination below are primarily American in origin, although some foreign cinematic works of interest to the theme of justice, or conversely, the miscarriage of its tenets during specific times in history, will be briefly mentioned. It is important to observe that film adaptations of literary texts generally attempt to reflect the writer's message of what justice is or is not, with the understanding that the film maker always injects into his work a personal vision or attitude on the subject he is treating.

Moreover, it should be noted that literature that records a mature, perceptive, and evocative understanding of the role justice assumes in any given society, can aid in the production of a film. Similarly, while numerous screenwriters through the years have based their scripts on often widely known literary sources, the raw material for their films emanates, in certain instances, from what they know best--their personal lives and intense recollections of growing up in a town, a region, or country under some kind of political siege.

For example, in 1971, the celebrated Italian director and actor, Vittorio de Sica, in his film "The Garden of the Finzi-Continis," depicts a hauntingly beautiful and deeply disturbing narrative about the gradual disintegration of Jewish freedom and dignity in Fascist Italy of the 1940's, treating human fear with personal touches of compassion and respect. More recently, in 1987, the English film maker, John Boorman, produced "Hope and Glory," and in the subsequent year, Louis Malle, the French director, came out with "Au Revoir les Enfants," two films brought to the screen with vivid realism about memories surrounding their childhood years during

World War II, with images of death, destruction, and the violation of human rights.

No matter how one, therefore, perceives or interprets the reality of life vis-à-vis justice, objective and/or subjective insights into man's quest for the proper administration of the law generally produce polarities of diverse opinion and frequent self-serving judgments. In short, irrespective of how one might attempt to unravel the seemingly complex nuances of justice, its identity or meaning, ironically, and sometimes tragically, can be obfuscated under changing masks of deception and intrigue.

Prior to an open discussion of particular novels, short stories, or plays on which specific films have been based, it must be noted, for our purposes, that fictional sources can be likened to an artist's conception of world events along various levels of personal exegesis or rationality. Curiously, in 1933, as a keen observer of the so-called human condition of world politics, the French writer, André Malraux, in his novel La Condition Humaine (transl. "Man's Fate") observed that man's eternal, passionate wish is to find a meaning for existence and that human individuals do not count in cases where the ends justify the means. Moreover, according to Malraux, as men strive against the forces of destruction, which is their ultimate destiny, they are dedicated to action and are passionately introspective.

While Malraux, in his perception of life, complains of the elusive and often indistinguishable ubiquity of justice to the mind and eye, other observers of the human condition maintain that no clear-cut guidelines can uniformly prevail in all situations, even where law enforcement and justice as mandated by constitutional governments and their public officials for the common good of their society, do exist. In general, we are given to believe that the law exists in such a manner as to defend and protect human rights and that impartiality and fair practices must be applied, through basic due process and other self-protective avenues of justice, for the benefit of every citizen. Nonetheless, justice is never that well-exercised or dispensed for any two similar cases in every American courtroom and certainly not in comparable foreign settings, whose laws will unalterably be administered differently

137

according to the rulings handed down by the   presiding
judge.

Those literary works and their film versions
that, in the writer's opinion, reflect carefully the
theme   of   justice will be presented   below   in
chronological order of appearance. In each case, a
brief synopsis of their narratives will be offered as
they focus on the topic of justice. Among those
works/films selected for discussion, their titles and
dates are as follows: Potemkin (1926), M (1933), Les
Misérables (1935), The Informer (1935), Mutiny on the
Bounty (1935), Fury (1936), Winterset (1936), The Ox-
Bow Incident (1942), Open City (1945), Ivan the
Terrible, part one (1947), and part two (1959), The
Winslow Boy (1950), Cry the Beloved Country (1951),
The Caine Mutiny (1954), Anatomy of a Murder (1959),
Witness for the Prosecution (1958), Inherit the Wind
(1960), Judgment at Nuremberg (1961), Billy Budd
(1962), The Trial (1963), The Fixer (1968), and Z
(1968). Some shorter commentaries will be made on
other films--among this writer's favorites--that
depict as well certain aspects of justice and its
treatment of human beings. Those specific titles
include the following: I Am a Fugitive From a Chain
Gang (1932), Odd Man Out (1947), Call Northside 777
(1947), High Noon (1952), Bad Day at Black Rock
(1954), Compulsion (1959), Birdman of Alcatraz (1962),
The Battle of Algiers (1967), Catch-22 (1970), In the
Heat of the Night (1967), and Midnight Express (1978).

To begin, in 1926 the legendary film director,
Sergei Eisenstein produced an exciting piece of
recreated   cinema   reportage based on an actual
occurrence during the abortive Russian Revolution of
1905. That event was the mutiny of the sailors aboard
the Czarist battleship Potemkin, assigned to naval
duties in the Black Sea. The film highlights, in
part, the massacre of the people who sympathized with
the sailors, and in particular, the leader who died
during the mutiny. In depicting the merciless
slaughter of dock workers who came to mourn the heroic
sailors of the Potemkin, Eisenstein's early silent
film clearly underlines the injustice of the Czarist
regime in committing acts of inhumanity toward its
countrymen and demonstrating callousness for failing
to understand the motives behind the revolt of the
officers of the vessel. After the film appeared,
policies in the Soviet Union changed: mutiny could no
longer be sanctioned, nor could experimental film
techniques thereafter be permitted; also, under

Stalin, Eisenstein was purged, later partially reinstated, and then repurged.

In 1933, the brilliant Viennese-born film director, Fritz Lang, produced his first sound film--a work based on a story of Thea von Harbou concerning the fiendish killings which spread terror among the inhabitants of Düsseldorf in 1929, and which captured the imagination of her readers and subsequently of movie audiences. The original book and its film adaptation concentrate on the psychological problems of a child-murderer as he is pursued by the police and others in pre-Nazi Germany. Thus, Lang's film, like that of some of his later works--for example, Fury (1936)--renders a powerful dramatic treatment of social problems involving victimization of the individual by society, as it relentlessly hounds a demented slayer until his final capture by crooks eager to collect their reward. Some of the most interesting scenes in the book as well as the film are devoted to the murderer's trial in which he bleats that he is a killer against his will, whereas those before him committed crimes because they so desired. A thief is allowed to preside at the trial, and while the murderer's lawyer claims that his client needs a doctor more than punishment, the court shows him no mercy but sentences him to death.

Two years later, in 1935, three important films were released that focused, in some measure, on the subject of justice. The first, Les Misérables, is an adaptation of Victor Hugo's celebrated 19th-century tale based on the themes of the hunted and the hunter--of Valjean, the tragic and eternally defeated man whose lifetime purgatory began when he stole a loaf of bread to feed his sister's starving family in the France of 1800, and Javert, the policeman, who had to pursue his quarry night and day, even down the labyrinthine ways of his own mind, because the law was his religion, his blood, and his life.

Similarly, in 1935, the exciting sea adventure known as Mutiny on the Bounty was turned into a film, based on the novels of Charles Nordhoff and James Norman Hall. This work recounts the infamous naval case surrounding a mutiny in 1787 aboard the HMS Bounty, commanded by the able, but intolerably savage Captain Bligh, who exacted justice with the aid of a flogging whip--a man whose mania for discipline increased in fury on a daily basis as his ship left England bound for Tahiti. Bligh, in a way, became a

139

kind of archetype for later naval officers drawn from the pages of literature--observe, for a second, the likes of Claggart in Billy Budd and Queeg in The Caine Mutiny--two men who abide by and rigidly enforce naval rules and regulations on their respective wartime ships. Bligh's commands and penalties for minor infractions are the judgments of a maniac, deriving as he does a lewd joy as the lash strikes a sailor across his nude back. Curiously, despite Bligh's reign of terror on the Bounty, at his subsequent court-martial, the film punishes Bligh by subjecting him to the contempt of his fellow-officers. History, nonetheless, with its occasional twists of fate, reveals that the Captain eventually was rewarded by being named an admiral in the King's navy.

One of the most penetrating novels written about Ireland in the troubling 1920's was Liam O'Flaherty's "The Informer." The story dramatizes the themes of treachery of retribution in strife-torn Dublin in 1921. The somber action of the narrative centers on Gypo Nolan, the Irish outcast who betrays his best friend, a fugitive rebel named Franki McPhillip, to the Black and Tans for a 20-pound reward, and then cracks beneath the pressure of the avengers and the mounting comprehension of his guilt. Both the novel and the film adaptation attempt to portray a drama of dishonor--a revelation of one man's weaknesses driving him to deceive not only his closest friend but, more significantly, himself. Here, also, the organization operating outside the law is that of the Irish Rebellion, viewed by many observers at the time as a romantic and patriotic cause, endowed dramatically with an aura of valor and heroic self-sacrifice.

In 1936, two estimable films were released in this country which focused on the theme of justice. The first was called Fury, which was completed by the aforementioned director, Fritz Lang, and was based on a story penned by Norman Krasna. The text centers on the subject of mob violence against an innocent man, and the narrative's approach is coldly judicial in its treatment of social injustice in a small-town American southern setting back in the 1930's. The second notable film appearing in 1936 was Winterset, based on the acclaimed play of Maxwell Anderson. Primarily, it is a story concerning the question for truth, the determination of the son of a fearless liberal to prove his father innocent of the murder charge that sent him to his death years before. This absorbing and perceptive account raises so many questions about the approaches taken by our judicial system in with disposing of its charges with seemingly unbiased decisions, oftentimes without foundation, in the sentencing of a just man to death.

Using the camera almost as if it were a poetic instrument to record the tragedy of mob rule some years later, was the 1943 film titled "The Ox-Bow Incident." Adapted from Walter van Tilburg Clark's novel of the same name, both the book and film provide an uncompromising examination and condemnation of mob justice and lynch law. On the surface, the film, in particular, tells a concise story of the tragic punishment of innocent people--in this case, a rancher, accompanied by a Mexican and a senile old man camped by the Ox-Box in Nevada, 1885. But the larger theme--that ordinary, moral persons can be induced en masse to commit grievous acts of cruelty and injustice, is meticulously worked out with the blunt style of a psychological treatise. The tale further catalogues a wide range of human foibles--bloodthirsty revenge, brutality, cowardice, moral weaknesses or ambivalence, demagoguery, and irrationality. The forces on the side of goodness, justice, and reason in the story are, as is often the case in the real life, relatively powerless and ineffectual. Examples of this kind of mob injustice without counsel or due process have occurred all too often in past eras of our history right down to the twentieth century. It is said that audiences who viewed the film upon its release in 1943 could not have missed an obvious implication; the same base human traits that Americans found so appalling in Nazi Germany existed here at home, embodied in the cherished frontier ethic of the American West. In brief, the settings were, of course, different as were the circumstances, but the miscarriage of justice was in plain sight in both instances, regardless of fact or fiction.

If we turn our attention momentarily to Europe, it was toward the end of the Second World War that many prestigious Italian film directors got caught up in a new genre of filmmaking which they styled "neo-realism." One such master was Roberto Rossellini, whose classic film Open City (1946), based on a screenplay by Sergio Amidei and Federico Fellini, reflects a devastating chronicle of the Nazi occupation of Rome--that dismal period between the collapse of the Fascist government of Mussolini in 1943 and the liberation of the Nazi-held city in June 1944. The story documents a violent, impassioned

141

drama of human atrocities and the tough, realistic
resistance of the workers' organized underground to
combat the cruelty and depravity of their foes.
Moreover, the film presents a candid, overpowering
spectacle of human fortitude in the grips of what
appear to be unconquerable odds, as justice, human
rights, and free speech are trampled upon by the
insidious German patrols guarding the city. The
sentiment that flows most vividly through watching the
film is one of supreme admiration for the people who
struggle for freedom's cause. Rossellini, and his
compatriots, Fellini and De Sica, in particular,
produced films based on screenplays that mirrored the
blackest days during and after the war in Italy.

Earlier we referred to the Russian film director
Eisenstein and his work based on actual events
surrounding the mutiny on board the ill-fated
battleship Potemkin. By 1945, the same director chose
to retreat once more into his nation's history and
surfaced with the idea of producing a film on the life
and times of the 16th-century despotic ruler, Ivan the
Terrible. In Part One of the film, for which
Eisenstein also wrote the screenplay, what we see is a
historical drama focusing on the subject of absolute
power and reflecting similtaneously on the ageless
axiom that the man who must be a tyrant must
inevitably lose his own soul. Eisenstein's conception
of Ivan as a fierce and tempestuous man, given to
behead his mistresses without provocation, while at
the same time bent on bringing all Russians into the
nationality at the expense of anyone who stands in his
way, is conspicuously totalitarian. A second part to
the tale of the crazed Russian Ivan was released
twelve years after the original in 1959, with a
screenplay by the same director. In this next
installment of the tale, we follow the Czar's career
that embraced his return to Moscow from foreign
adventures and his immediate suppression of
malcontents in his country. Interestingly, it is
rumored that the reason the 1959 version was supressed
for so long was because it made Ivan look maniacal--
this may have had some truth in its portrayal.

One of the most glaring and disturbing injustices
of the 20th century has been the racist policy of
apartheid, or the cruel and blatantly enforced
separation of whites and blacks in South Africa. The
distinguished writer, Alan Paton in 1951, completed a
screenplay called "Cry the Beloved Country," which was
adapted for the screen and received, generally

speaking, approval from both critics and audiences across America and abroad. The narrative stresses the damages that apartheid causes to all societies and not simply the struggle of blacks alone. In addition, Paton attempts to show the importance of the efforts of men like Arthur, a white man, and the son of a wealthy farmer, in mending wounds caused by the police-state's restrictions on the rights of the majority in that land. The lyrics of a song heard in the film titled "Train to Jonannesburg" contain the theme of the story in its most essential terms: "White man go to Johannesburg. He come back. Black man go to Johannesburg. Never come back." It is this dichotomy of spirit and reality, indicative of human inequality and injustice, which represents the core of the film. Today, more than thirty-five years after the release of this film, another statement on the subject of white supremacy in South Africa was filmed, namely "Cry Freedom," an account of the life and death of Stephen Biko, the martyred black activist, who showed the world the Afrikaaner régime as the repressive, fascist state that it is.

The theme of justice, directly or indirectly related to naval warfare, was again the content of a very interesting book called "The Caine Mutiny," written by Herman Wouk and adapted to the screen in 1954. Although there has never been a mutiny in the annals of U.S. naval history, or even a trial for a mutiny, this story deals with the way in which men respond to certain crises under duress. At issue is the relief of the captain of the U.S.S. Caine by his executive officer Maryk during a typhoon, aided by a fellow officer named Willie, a young, clean-cut Princeton graduate, previously involved in numerous conflicts of authority. Captain Queeg is depicted by Wouk as a disciplinarian who runs things "by the book." At his subsequent court-martial, he is portrayed as a mentally disturbed man who should never have been assigned to command a destroyer during the Second World. War. We learn that it is really Keefer, a writer and pseudo-intellectual who is the veritable antagonist of Queeg with his fanatical aversion to military authority. In the end, Wouk leaves both his readers and film viewers with a complex question regarding the legitimate responsibilities of both the Captain and his officers as the court-martial draws to a conclusion.

Courtroom dramas, as a kind of film genre, have often attracted considerable attention from a viewing audience. There are five works of topical interest in terms of each one's references to justice, or lack of it, in specific situations that this writer would like to introduce at this point. First, in 1957, the American playwright, Reginald Rose, completed a teleplay called "Twelve Angry Men," which later was adapted for the screen. Although the action of the narrative occurs almost entirely in one room with twelve sequestered jurors, Rose selects a cross-section of human types, whose charge is to determine the fate of an accused murderer. The defendant, a product of the slums who never had a chance--he is a member of an unspecified minority and his father did not love him--is never seen by the film audience. However, as the melodrama unfolds one hot summer evening, we come to learn the attributes, sensibilities, passions, and strong prejudices of certain jurors who must render their decision in the case. The jury process is carefully examined as all the evidence is skillfully examined by one particular juror, a liberal, fair-minded architect who voices his uncertainty about some details brought up during the trial. On the other hand, from the outset, the remaining eleven jurors claim the young man to be guilty, stating in the process that the information proves, without a shadow of a doubt, that the defendant is culpable. Ultimately, all twelve jurors see "the light of day," and they concur that the alleged murderer had to be innocent of the crime for which he was prosecuted.

Second, in 1957, the film "Witness for the Prosecution" appeared on the screen, which was adapted from Agatha Christie's mystery play. The story concerns a man held for trial for murder, and the play's popularity, like that of the film version, was based primarily on its multifaceted trick ending. The cinematic adaptation has greater touches of masquerade, verbal wit, and intimations of a corrupt environment that lend an intelligent balance of courtroom drama, suspense, and multilevel humor to the narrative. When Christine, wife of the accused killer, is called as the surprise witness for the prosecution, she sets herself up for a perjury conviction and a prison term to ensure her husband's freedom. The dénouement provides a twist revealing the husband as the real murderer, who is then stabbed by his wife. Sir Wilfred, the killer's counsel addresses the chain of events by sighing these thoughts: "The wheels of justice grind slowly, but they grind finely." In short, justice comes unexpectedly through the hand of a spurned woman.

Third, in 1959, a film called "Compulsion," derived from Meyer Levin's engrossing book on he infamous Leopold-Loeb kidnapping-murder case was released. The film adhered closely to Levin's text by presenting as clearly as possible the causes and effects of the trial of two alleged killers in the 1930's and their impact on public opinion in America. Together Levin and the screenplay focus attention on jurors sitting in solemn judgment of two people indicted for a capital crime. In the end, the work becomes a study of the natures and reaction of jury members whose verdict is based on a straight interpretation of the law and morality.

Fourth, in the same year, 1959, a compelling film reached the screen titled "Anatomy of a Murderer," based on Robert Traver's novel of the same name. The storytelling concerns a small-town lawyer, portrayed by actor James Stewart in one of his very best performances, who prepares and makes his defense of a moody young Army lieutenant accused of killing the rapist of his attractive spouse. Incidentally, the name Traver is a pseudonym, for the novel was penned by John Voelker, once Justice of the Michigan Supreme Court. Whereas the film version is a refreshingly honest and realistic courtroom melodrama which hews to a line of dramatic but reasonable behavior in and out of court, the book is primarily autobiographical, centering on a lawyer's memoir of a sensational murder trial in the Midwest in which justice, in the end, was served.

Fifth, the popular Broadway stage play "Inherit the Wind," was adapted into a forceful social drama for the screen in 1960. The two playwrights, Jerome Lawrence and Robert Lee, followed closely in time on the heels of the McCarthy era, and the work's implications were very much an allegory of its day. In essence, both the play and the film adaptation are really thinly disguised dramatizations of the scandalous "monkey" trial of 1925, wherein Clarence Darrow, for the defense, and William Jennings Bryan, for the prosecution, clashed over the right of John T. Scopes, a twenty four year old biology instructor to propound Darwin's theory of evolution to the high school students of Dayton, Tennessee. Actually, Scopes volunteered to be the test case challenging a state statute which deemed it unlawful for anyone to teach any theory that denies the story of the divine creation of man as given in the Bible. The whole question of the legitimacy of school board members and teachers to choose appropriate reading materials in classrooms, often a knotty subject on its own terms, is secondary to the point that the defense attorney makes concerning the student's right to think for himself in a secular educational environment.

Censorship still exists today in some schools throughout America where parents have demanded, and in certain cases, won their arguments to have specific books removed from reading lists they consider anathema to their children's education. It is ironic, in our age of exposure to blatant acts of sex, crime, drug addiction and the like, which are openly visible in the media, in magazines, films and television, to see restrictions placed on someone's reading a work like Salinger's A Catcher in the Rye and many others-- amid the glaring examples of social and political ills at the present time. Such restrictions seem ludicrous and unforgivable.

Another very interesting courtroom drama as it was depicted in a film in 1961 is "Judgment at Nuremberg," based on a teleplay by the talented writer, Abby Mann. After the hideous Nazi regime, which represented the great machinery for human annihilation during the Second World War, ceased to exist, accountability on the part of those German jurists who presided over their own courts had to be settled. The story is based primarily on information about the Nuremberg trials of Nazi war criminals, which were conducted by the Allies in the immediate postwar years. By placing the war trials in the context of political pressure from the occupation forces, Mann sets up a parallel between those Allied trials and the Nazi cases which are "on trial" throughout the teleplay and film. The same kind of constraints which led Nazi judges to situate "national interest" over justice are present at the Nuremberg proceedings.

As scenarist, Mann tries to show that justice can justice can be made expedient in any society, particularly in the guise of nationalism, which views justice as anything that is good for the country. "Judgment at Nuremberg," however, is a double-edged title which applies to the judgment of both the Nazis and Americans, for each can be judged by different codes of justice and morality. The chief Nazi on trial, Ernst Janning (played by Burt Lancaster in the film) is not a caricature of the evil Nazi machine. Rather, he is an extremely respected and learned man of the law, who agreed in the years just prior to the war to a temporary suspension of justice. He permitted his courtroom to be a forum for the erosion of human rights under inhumane Nazi laws.

Why a judge of of obvious integrity would concur to uphold immoral laws is a question which each character in the drama attempts to answer. At one point in the film, Janning says that those who say "the law is the law" and that violators of unjust laws must be punished are those people no court can afford to condone. Further, in one of Janning's most eloquent speeches, he traces the subversion of justice in his own court and the patriotism which motivated it, a patriotism which hindsight shows him is indefensible. Despite mounting pressures from the military and the sympathy created by Janning's stirring oratory, the presiding judge, named Haywood, and played by actor Spencer Tracy, decides to conclude all the hearings by sentencing Janning to a maximum term of incarceration. When a departing Haywood queries Janning as to his motives for obeying completely all the insideous Nazi laws to their fullest extent, Janning replies: "I did not know it would come to that. You must believe it." Dazed by the judge's response, Haywood responds: "I came to that the first time you sentenced to death a man you knew to be innocent." In the end, Judgment at Nuremberg shifts the balance of the trial away from the subject of Nazi atrocities to the corruption that can arise from nationalism at its worst.

Returning again to the sea for an examination of the theme of justice, or perhaps its misapplication in the truer sense, the British film "Billy Budd," released in 1962, based on Herman Melville's trenchant novel of the same name, is an interesting case in point. The story begins in 1797 when a handsome young merchant seaman, Billy Budd, is impressed into service by the English Navy, then at war with France. His innate goodness blinds him to the evil in other men, particularly the sadistic and despised master-at-arms, Claggart, who remains always aloof, unable to comprehend Budd's simple and honest nature.

Claggart attempts to cause the foretopman's downfall by falsely accusing him of instigating a mutiny. Captain Vere, however, recognizes that Claggart is lying and asks Billy to deny the charge;

147

but he is so stunned by the accusation that a speech impediment renders him incapable of uttering a word in his defense. Instead, he strikes Claggart in the presence of the captain in his quarters, causing him to fall, fracture his skull, and die.

At the subsequent court-martial aboard ship, all the officers agree that Billy's act was accidental and he should, therefore, be acquitted. Nonetheless, Vere indicates that they should concern themselves solely with the rules governing naval law, not justice, and that Billy must pay with the death penalty for fatally taking a superior officer's life.

Finally the board decides Billy's fate--he must hang from the yard-arm "on the morrow." That next morning, as the rope is placed around his neck, Billy prevents a possible mutiny among the crew when he stoically cries out---"God bless Captain Vere."

The tale of Billy Budd is an excellent example of the classic conflict of good versus evil and is filled with sundry negative ironies. Apart from Melville's preoccupation with the major issue of crime and punishment, we observe that Vere, a stickler for naval conduct of the highest order and strict adherence to ship regulations, is ultimately torn by the demands of his authority. Perhaps what gives the author's sea drama its fascination and greatness is the suggestion that Claggart, with his rather one dimensional character embodying with wickedness and scorn, is merely the underling doing the crafty Captain's bidding in disposing of young Budd.

Leaving the sea behind us, we can now turn our attention to a comic horror story that attempts to examine, in a bizarre way, the often puzzling question of justice--Franz Kafka's "The Trial." In the book and later, in 1963, when Orson Wells adapted the tale to the screen, the underlying point centers around Kafka's efforts to say something about the tyranny of modern social systems. Consequently, both the novel and film version stress the brutal, relentless way in which the law as a social institution reaches out and traps men in its complex vortex until they eventually are crushed to death by the system. Replete with all forms of symbolistic references, it is virtually an eerie account of the serialistic experiences of a baffled, yet rebellious bank clerk who one morning is mysteriously arrested by secret agents who come to his boarding room. Later, some kind of formal trial is prepared for which he has no inclination for self-defense because he was never informed of the charges brought against him.

Parenthetically, one of the best scenes in the narrative is when Joseph K, the central figure, having dismissed his ineffectual advocate on the grounds that the latter always delayed in hastening the case for trial, encounters a priest who recounts to him an allegorical tale of a man waiting all his life at the door of the LAW, but who died without ever gaining admittance. Briefly, Kafka's nightmarish story is about the inscrutable, brutal, and unrelenting fashion in which the law as a corruptible social institution can sentence men to death without any viable justification. From a critical point of view, however, both the book and film adaptation remain unclear and confusing, never arriving at an intellectual conclusion that is readily understood.

Another interesting film of the 1960's that was based on an important literary work was Bernard Malamud's "The Fixer," for which the author won both the Pulitzer Prize and the National Book award. It is the account of an ordinary man, Yakov Bok (in German, bock means "goat"), a real Jew living in Czarist Russia, who is accused of "ritual murder" and persecuted by agents of a remote and all-powerful state. The work's vitality is demonstrated in Bok's determination to survive as the odds mount against him and threaten to destroy his human will through brutality and degredation.

In one of the best lines in the film, Bibikov, the Investigating Magistrate tells Yakov: "It is not madness that turns the world upside down. It is conscience." Later, Malamud asks two pertinent questions regarding Bok's fate, which he also answers with the contemptuousness of his oppressors: "Where's reason? Where's justice?...But the Russian State denies Yakov Bok the most elemental justice, and to show its fear and contempt of humankind, has chained him to the wall like an animal." In short, Bok was an innocent victim, a scapegoat of the Czarist régime and its anti-Jewish decrees that spewed calumny and prejudice against his people. Curiously, it seems that Bok draws his courage primarily from the injustices perpetrated against him--he has no family or beliefs to justify his life--for he never yields to his persecutors despite the oppression, suffering, and harrassment he experiences in prison. In short, Yakov

149

Bok survives his agonizing ordeals; hence he becomes a kind of hero in the spirit of one's unending struggle for self-identity and freedom.

The endearing story written by Harper Lee called "To Kill a Mockingbird" was given a screen rendition in 1963. Lee's prize-winning novel is based loosely on her own childhood experiences in the South as she traces the lives of two children and their widowed lawyer-father in a small town back in the 1920's. Consequently, the action occurs in the Depression era before the term "desegregation" even existed in the common vernacular. Both the novel and the film adaptation strike the heart and mind in unfolding a social crisis wherein a Negro farm hand named Tom Robinson is brought to trial for allegedly raping a poor white girl. In the film, the doomed victim is admirably defended by Gregory Peck, who plays the role of Atticus Finch. It is really through the two children's eyes that the question of justice is challenged, for they do not understand how an innocent man like Tom could be indicted for a crime which he most assuredly did not commit from their viewpoint, Obviously, in her storytelling, Harper Lee is attempting to decry the issue of bigotry as it pertained to the jury's biased pre-judgment of a black defendant, as the court failed to consider all the documented evidence presented in the case that should have otherwise overturned the final ruling.

From another perspective relative to the theme of justice, the matter of capital punishment in America is chillingly detailed in Truman Capote's non-fiction novel "In Cold Blood." The book graphically describes the Clutter murders that took place on the night of November 15, 1959 in Holcomb, Kansas and then chronicles the investigation of the killings by Alvin A. Dewey, chief investigator of the case involving two convicted killers, Perry Smith and Richard Hickock. The true impact of the novel as well as Richard Brooks's 1967 film version lies in its approach to the serious and controversial issues regarding the death penalty in our society. In this writer's viewpoint, Brooks not only recreates Capote's exhaustively researched and thoughtful docudrama of the brutal slaying of the Clutter family, but he picks up the search for truth where Capote effectively stopped in his narrative. The description of the capture, trial and execution of the two young murderers five years after the heinous crime was committed is rendered with unswerving clarity and honesty. In particular, the hanging of Smith and Hickock is filmed in a realistic, blood-curdling ritual. Perhaps no better statement against capital punishment has been written or filmed before than the final frame of the executed Smith, with the sound of a heart beating slowly. Finally, only blank film is left. From an objective point of view, "In Cold Blood" demonstrates how witless murders and acts or other forms of random violence have become symbols of the forces of evil that pervasively are allowed to roam unsuspectingly, and all too frequently, nowadays in our nation.

Another topical melodrama that manipulates our emotional responses and appeals to our best prejudices is the popular 1969 French film designated simply "Z." The work is a highly fictionalized account of the actual 1963 assassination in Salonika of Gregarios Lambarakis, a professor of medicine at the University of Athens and a leading activist opposing the placement of Polaris missiles at that time in Greece. In the course of the scandal, the Greek government toppled and the persons morally and directly responsible for the murder were summarily brought to trial. The film was based on the novel by Vassili Vassilikos, which, in turn, is a narrative also detailing the official investigation of a political murder that was approached with some government reluctance, and which eventually uncovered a plot involving highly positioned officials as well as a secret right-wing organization of patriotic strong-armed men. Four years after the existing government fell, a military _coup d'état_ took place, and almost everyone connected with the assassination was conveniently "rehabilitated" and exonerated. Overall, the investigation of Lambrakis was an effort to demonstrate how the mechanics of Fascist corruption might be hidden under the mask of law and order.

Some miscellaneous film adaptations of books depicting in one way or another the theme of justice are the following titles for brief discussion below: Odd Man Out (1947); Call Northside 777 (1947); The Winslow Boy (1950); High Noon (1952); Bad Day at Black Rock (1958); Birdman of Alcatraz (1962); The Battle of Algiers (1967); In the Heat of the Night (1967); Cool Hand Luke (1967); Catch-22 (1970); and Midnight Express (1978). There are any number of other references to justice either adapted from novels or taken from original screenplays such as the popular "The Verdict," with Paul Newman, completed in 1986,

but the aforesaid list contains some of this writer's
favorite films dealing with justice.

First, the 1947 release "Old Man Out" is an
interesting film based on F.L. Green's novel of the
same name. The story concerns the desperate endeavor
of a wounded man to escape the police in the night-
shrouded alleys of an Irish city after committing
murder for a political cause. The theme of the
fugitive from justice is well laid out in the
dramatization of James Mason, the actor whose
performance in the role of the quarry is a penetrating
examination that mirrors how injustice stems from
prejudice and mass hysteria based on unfounded
evidence discharged against an innocent victim of
society's wrath.

In the same year, James Stewart appeared in a
film titled "Call Northside 777," which was based on
actual newspaper articles about a journalist who
succeeded in helping to gain the release of a man
wrongly imprisoned for the murder of a Chicago police
officer in 1932. The story, in effect, is an
indictment against the courts for failing to
investigate thoroughly all the essential documents and
even minor details pertaining to the case. The
judge's ruling was also deemed judgmental and biased
according to many observers at the time.

The British film "The Winslow Boy" reached the
screen in 1950 and was a striking, even inspiring
drama adapted from Terence Rattigan's play centering
on a 12-year-old naval cadet unjustly accused of
theft. His case was carried to intransigent Crown
authorities, and the barrister who defended the young
man carried out his responsibilities with consummate
skill and admiration, proving in the end the
youngster's innocence of a crime.

From the vast lore of Western films, the
estimable Stanley Kramer produced an inspiring work of
art in this genre in the 1952 film called "High Noon,"
based on a screen play by Carl Forman. The story
imparts ideas on the fundamental issues and morals
surrounding the decision of a courageous, but stubborn
sheriff in a town full of do-nothings and cowards, who
must face the impending ordeal on the scheduled day of
his retirement of placing his life on the line against
a vengeful killer arriving on the noon train. Two
major questions arise as the sheriff awaits the
desperado in town: first, Should he leave town

quickly with his new bride or should he come to grips head-on with the situation from which he cannot escape as the noon hour slowly approaches? Like a beating clock, the lawman accepts his duty as each minute ticks by feverishly until the killer and his three companion outlaws face off against each other with guns blazing under the hot, mid-day sun. Naturally, in the end, the hero successfully carries out the perilous, righteous task of protecting the decent and law-abiding citizens who have entrusted him with their care against the marauders.

A similar theme is treated in another Western film called "Bad Day at Black Rock," adapted from a story by Howard Breslin and released in 1955. In this story, a lone man again must pit himself against those who threaten his own life. Briefly, the plot deals with a stranger who arrives at a sun-baked desert whistle-stop to deliver a posthumous war medal for the son of a Japanese farmer who has "disappeared." No one seems to know the whereabouts of the farmer, and as the stranger probes into the matter, there are those in the tiny town who want to murder him. Ultimately, justice wins out, and the truth is determined as to the reason for the disappearance of the victim.

In 1962, a striking prison drama based on the true story of Robert E. Stroud, who used his long confinement behind bars to become a scholar and scientific authority on ornithology, came out called "Birdman of Alcatraz." Taken from a book by Thomas E. Gaddis, the scenario tends to leave the viewer asking two significant questions--first, why was such a man never paroled and second, why do we know very little about his background or of the two murders for which he was given a life-long sentence of imprisonment? From the author's perspective, many questions arose at that time, and for that matter many people are of the same opinion today. Such question remain unanswered concerning the dispensation of justice within our penal system, as it concerned Robert Stroud's case.

In the year 1967, three significant films were released touching individually on the subject of justice. The first, "The Battle of Algiers," is a remarkably stark and realistic re-enactment of events as they substantially occurred between 1954-57 in the rebellion of the Algerian people against French occupation of their capital. The basic theme is one of valor--the valor of people who fight for liberation

from economic and political oppression. The second
work, "In the Heat of the Night," based on a novel by
John Ball, is a scorching drama centering on the
confrontation between an arrogant small-town white
policeman and a visiting Black detective from
Philadelphia, who determinedly solves a murder case.
Racial prejudice permeates the southern town as
evidenced, in particular, by the bigotry of the local
sheriff.

The third film of interest appearing in the same
year is "Cool Hand Luke," based on a screenplay by
Donn Pearce. Atypical of prison films, this story of
a chain-gang prisoner is truly memorable in its
depiction of the brutal display of "justice" that
prison guards and other members of the "law" dispense
to convicts under their supervision. The story is
reminiscent of a much earlier satire on our prison
system, namely the 1932 classic "I Am a Fugitive from
a Chain Gang," starring the renowned actor, Paul Muni,
in the title role. The story centers on Robert Eliot
Burns, who unwittingly becomes an accomplice in an
armed robbery, is apprehended, and is sentenced to six
to ten years of hard labor. Under the watchful eyes
of a sadistic warden, Burns eventually escapes, but
later is turned over to the police by his scheming
wife. As powerful today as when it was made, this
film is a mesmerizing indictment against injustice
everywhere.

As an epic human comedy, about the insanity of
war Joseph Heller's book "Catch-22" represents a
series of brilliant mirror images where the system of
rewards and punishments as seen by the author in World
War II is perfectly disordered, and human panic is
both a positive and fruitful trait of character. The
work is also construed as a black comedy of sorts in
that exaggeration, fantasy, and reverse logic seem to
guide the lives of Air Force officers who are stranded
on a remote Mediterranean island, while its hero,
Yassarian, lives in a state of perpetual, irrational
dismay, which he believes is justifiably normal. In
short, this interesting book and film adaptation point
to the human condition as it thwarts attempts at
engaging in war, ever mindful of its tragic impact on
humanity.

The final work for discussion here is "Midnight
Express" (1978), which is a film based on a book co-
authored by Billy Hayes and William Hoffer.
Basically, the tale recounts actual events in the life

of an American student, Hayes himself, who in 1970, possessed hashish while attempting to board a plane at the Istanbul airport. The story chronicles the student's arrest, imprisonment, and final escape back to the United States. The narrative offers a stern lesson against disregard for another country's laws; yet from a critical perspective, it is a manipulative film, depicting a one-sided account--Hayes's version-- from beginning to end. Nevertheless, both the book and film adaptation are riveting and powerful accounts photographing a horror tale about the nightmare of painful existence in a foreign prison, and how justice seemingly is "thrown to the wind" insofar as it may be compared in its administration and interpretation with our American judicial and penal systems.

In sum, whatever the intention or purpose films accomplish for a viewing audience--entertainment, drama, document--they are inevitably reflections of the time and place of their origin and, as such, delineate firsthand evidence of both past and current events. In practicality, one should never underestimate the social and cultural impact of the movies and their pervasive and inescapable influence, for instance, on our notions of 20th century man and his world. Hence, to produce works of cinematic realism with any artistic significance, many screenwriters have adapted literary or non-literary sources to recount incidents that actually occurred and then robed them in the texture of the times, or have reinvented the past in pursuit of comprehending such a major facet of our culture as--JUSTICE.

Moreover, visual experience seems incontrovertible when the viewer, who may have previously read an account on which a particular film is based, finds himself or herself engaged as it were in all the physical and psychological conditions and dimensions that appear on the screen as the narrative unfolds. In a case where the film's subject is justice, it would seem that an audience would be rigorous in its demand for the explicit form of pictorial documentation which is supposedly objective and authentic. Any excellent piece of cinema, like those discussed above, will help to guide the discriminating and informed film goer appreciative of critical analysis, challenging discourse, and debate, especially on as broad theme as justice. In trying to explicate the law and its relationship to justice, writers, in cultivating their sense of topicality and history, must also concern themselves with lasting esthetic qualities, so that fairness and impartiality in their judgments do not subvert the truth of events or weaken, in fact, the credibility of their arguments.

From any literary sojourn into the realm of provoking opinion on sundry aspects of justice, there are consistently two inherent and characteristic pathways: dissent and controversy. Such human criticism abounds in the aforementioned works that have been strikingly adapted to the screen predicated on the artistic interests of the film maker's integrity for his or her métier. In brief, on these foregoing pages, therefore, only a small fraction of an enormous range of literary sources focusing on the theme of justice and their adaptation to film have been included for examination. The models given then have been culled with a view not so much for their individual merit or commercial value, but instead for their objective of depicting insightful concepts of justice and their implications in the continuous flow of world happenings.

8.
ECONOMIC JUSTICE

Charles J. Stokes
Charles Anderson Dana
Professor of Economics
University of Bridgeport

Definition

Economic justice is a concept that assumes we can measure in terms of fairness or rightness the performance of an economic system. In that sense, it involves a conmparison between what did happpen and what "ought" to have happened. The "ought" in the argument arises from standards and measures that do not necessarily come from actual performance.

An example will help. Suppose that we agree - from evidence about nutrition, clothing, housing conditions among other sources - that a family "needs" some minimum amount of money to pay for "necessities." But suppose that the economic system in Country X simply cannot perform, cannot produce enough to permit more than a few Xian families receive incomes that leave them "poor." As a result, a large number of Xian families receive incomes that leave them "poor." It could certainly be said that such a society is unjust.

Some, however, would argue that economic justice would be achieved if every Xian family received the same income, even if no Xian family got enough to meet its "needs."

On the one hand, deciding whether the Xian economic system is just turns on questions of overall performance. On the other hand, the measure of justice is that of equality of distribution of the results of economic performance, even if enough is never produced.

Notice that neither measure of fairness or justice asks how the system works. Each such measure takes what the economic system does or what it produces and asks whether it is enough as against some measure. Or such a measure asks how the results were spread out and shared among Xians.

Such measures have the inherent difficulty of being "irrelevant." What they do not suggest is what can be done to improve performance. In short, complicated as it may seem, we have to begin our analysis of economic justice with an assessment of performance, an understanding of how any given economic system actually works. In the light of what we can learn about the economic mechanisms, we can begin to hew out a relevant theory of economic justice.

Note, further, that one inference to be drawn from what we have said thus far is this. One cannot determine a priori whether a particular economic system is just. Put differently, any system may be just if it meets the two criteria inferred above -

- that "enough" is produced

- that this "enough" or more is distributed "fairly"

Poverty

Probably only poverty is as indicative of the lack of economic justice. Poverty is the lack of essentials - food, clothing, shelter. Poverty is absolute when a whole class in society suffers from this lack. Poverty is relative when the position of the poor is compared with that of the privileged, those who have as against those who have not.

Just how to measure poverty depends on whether one approaches the matter absolutely or relatively. In advanced countries, a "poverty line" is determined by setting basic standards for food and nutrition, for clothing and for shelter. All those households having less than the minimum amounts in the poverty line are poor. By the same token, those nations where the average household does not meet these basic standards of necessity are said to be poor.

Relative poverty is in many ways a more meaningful concept. Whatever the average standard for the typical household in the United States, the Soviet Union, the United Kingdom, France or Sweden, those households having only a fraction of the goods and services in that average standard are poor. This is true even if a good share of these households in

158

advanced countries may have goods and services in amounts well above some minimum poverty line.

Thus it is possible to be poor in America and yet be substantially better off than the poor in India or Haiti. It is by measures of relative poverty that economic justice can probably more appropriately be measured. Relative poverty in advanced nations can probably be substantially reduced and even eliminated by distributing incomes more equitably. The closer to the average standard each and every household is, the less likely it is for the number of the poor to be large or significant.

No matter which of these approaches is used, economic systems can hardly be said to be just if there is poverty. If whole nations are poor, then it is the international economic system that must be examined to determine the cause of this poverty. If large numbers of households in any nation are poor, then the question is one of how fairly the income of the nation is distributed.

Yet the discussion of poverty cannot stop here. For one thing, poverty in many nations is a condition of long and persistent standing. Indeed, one can argue that the poor were here first. After all, the achievement of pure survival, a condition that must have marked the early period of human existence, meant simply that the household got to the stage of having just enough to live. The question in this context is not so much why is there poverty as why development above the level of poverty took place. What activities create the surplus that makes it possible for households and nations to move well above the survival level? Thus expressed, the challenge is not so much to eliminate poverty as to create development. Only with development can the possibility of eliminating poverty be entertained.

A society that cannot produce a surplus will not escape poverty. Thus poverty arises as an index of fairness and of justice in developing societies, for what the extent of poverty says is what surplus is being produced is not being used to cut the level of human misery.

There is a cruel paradox in all this. Malthus pointed out that a society that ate up its surplus as its population grew could not escape poverty. The seed corn must be preserved even if this means that

159

some have less than they should. Some of the surplus must be used to buy tools, to enlarge the barns, to transport and mill the grain. Some must be traded for other goods. In short, poverty cannot be escaped unless even some necessities are gone without to gain a surplus from which to get a leg up on economic progress.

Thus, there is a balance between "saving" or accumulating the surplus to a sufficient level and "oversaving" that produces inordinate wealth for the few and misery for the many. Some argue that the misery is lessened if the state by careful planning does the saving and the investment. The evidence of the last two centuries does not permit a clear decision in favor of the market place as against government planning. One thing though is apparent. The market because it is anonymous does the job of distribution with less turmoil than does the state.

Surplus

Whatever the basic requirements in food, clothing, and shelter, human society in most cases has been so organized to achieve a total produce well in excess of those requirements. Whether in Egypt, in the Euphrates Valley, the Altiplano in Peru, or the valley of Mexico, among other favored places, human society was so organized that the combination of labor, land, technique and management yielded results well beyond what was needed. This surplus, to whatever cause it is assigned, permitted these societies to live well indeed.

Significantly, what remains of such societies - temples, monuments, tombs, fortresses and walled cities - indicates that much of the surplus went into glorification of the present and the past, into religious and national ceremonial monuments. We have little evidence about the living standards of the ordinary family during these times of plenty, but more than enough evidence that the rulers lived in luxury.

Marx assigned the surplus to labor. The 18th century French "économistes" assigned the surplus to land. In the 19th century, Austrian and English economists assigned the surplus to all factors of production, arguing that the factor relatively most scarce was the most productive. The point is not what causes surplus so much as what happens to the surplus.

From the late 18th century on, it became increasingly accepted that all members of a society were entitled to share in this surplus. There was less and less willingness to accept a distribution of the surplus that favored the nobility, lay or ecclesiatic. And given the nouveau riche status of the merchants and the capitalists, there was even less willingness to let them keep an inordinate share of the surplus.

Increasingly, there arose the concept of income as an incentive to produce more rather than income as a reward for having worked. The theory of fair distribution came to have two key elements. One was that those whose work was productive of more surplus were entitled to a larger share of the surplus. The other was that in any case, there ought not to be any group, class or individual without some share of the surplus. Poverty, especially in Western countries, seemed for the first time in human history, to be within the possibility of elimination.

What one needed in such a context was a rule for distribution that took these two elements into plan. Classical economists developed the rule of marginal productivity, a rule that no matter how it was manipulated or polished seemed to say that wages and benefits from the economic system "ought" to go to those who produced surplus. Indeed, the more productive of surplus, the more one was entitled to. One heard in all this an echo of Jean Calvin's dicta in Geneva. But this left the unproductive without a share. What is worse, marginal productivity was consistent with a pyramidal income structure that could never be called fair. Not in modern terms.

The Marxist rule, from each according to his ability, to each according to need, seemed to provide for a melding of the two key elements. In practice, socialist societies have not found out how to achieve this melding. To assure full employment to all ran the risk of low producitvity. To reward the more productive with perquisities produced the same class distinctions that presumably made capitalist society so unattractive.

Clearly, if an economic society produces a surplus above necessity, above poverty, the key issue in the obtaining of economic justice, is how best to distribute this surplus. But there is an issue that is not obvious. It is this. If an increase in the surplus can be attained by "saving," that is to say by not consuming, and by using this saving as "investment," then part of the distributive justice question revolves around who should "save." Equally important is the question of in what to invest these savings.

As you ponder these issues, it may become clear that the real issue is who should control the saving and investment functions. For in these two functions rests the future destiny of economic society. A society that fails to save its "seed corn," ultimately dies. A society that uses its seed corn only to provide for its immediate consumption needs, for food, clothing and shelter will have an ultimate accounting to face. How much of the seed corn, the saving, should be used for temples, mausoleums, and how much for highways, warehouses, and harbors? How much for the goods of war, to defend or to conquer?

Those who control the saving and investment function stand at the center of the economy. One answer is to turn all this over to a market system. Another is to apply the best knowledge of the wise to a planned phasing of growth. Many observers are suspicious that if a few have this power to set the pace of the future development of the society, they have the ability to favor their own interest at the expense of the whole society.

The market is a social invention that compromises the diverse interests of two groups in the economic society. One group, the sellers of that which they produce, wish to obtain the highest gain above cost possible, and thus to increase their share of the social surplus. The opposed group, the buyers, the consumers, the wage earners, wish to pay the lowest price possible, and thus to increase their share of the social surplus.

In the market place, a price is arrived at, a price that at once makes what is bought equal to what is sold. But that price does more than clear the market. It also distributes the gain in social surplus. It was Alfred Marshall, a Cambridge don, who among others pointed out that buyers are generally willing and able to pay more than they did for what they buy. The difference between what they could have been induced to pay rather than go without is a consumer surplus.

In the same manner, the sellers are generally willing and able to receive less than they did for what they brought to the market place. The difference between the minimum price they could have received to cover their production and other costs and what they do receive in the market is a producer surplus. The sum of these two - consumer and producer surplus - is the social surplus.

This social surplus arises from the operation of the market. Society has more as a result of the buying and the selling than it would have had had there been no market. This is the gain from trade, from selling and buying, from the operation of the market, that economists from Adam Smith through Marx to Samuelson have noted. But it is also a concept hard for many to see.

Goals and the Achievement of Economic Justice

One approach to the achievement of economic justice, an approach that reaches far back into ancient times, is that of setting goals and limits to the operation of an economy. The Mosaic Law provided, for example, that there was to be no permanent alienation of landed property. It futher provided that there were to be limits to interest charged on loans and, indeed, loans to the poor were to be considered largely as gifts. In the reaping of fields, gleaning by the poor was permitted so that the deprived could with permission of the owner obtain food and sustenance by following the harvesters and picking up what was left over. Widows had levirate privileges to assure that their children retained the family property. And so it went.

The goal of Hebrew Law was equality of wealth. And where by the operation of the market place, inequality of distribution occurred, there was a Sabbatical year, the 50th Jubilee Year, when all property was to return by right to the family "owning" it. Economic justice was retention of patrimony by the family, provision for the widows and other deprived individuals, and the avoidance of burdensome loans that could drive the honest and hardworking into poverty.

On more careful examination of this concept of economic justice, it must be observed that the purpose of all these rules, laws and practices was to

163

preserve a given and even ordained social order. No
matter what the effect of market forces, of buying and
selling, the social order was to be restored and
preserved.

Aquinian Justice

Thomas Aquinas in his Summa Theologica describes
economic justice as being under attack from
mercantilism and incipient capitalism. A society in
which the King was the executor on earth of God's
purposes for His people, in which the Church and its
prelates and priests were to instruct and guide His
people, and in which the whole panoply of teachers,
lawyers, writers, scholars, philosophers and even
artists served to enlighten and better human life, was
in danger from the wealth enhancing activities of
butchers, bakers, candlestick makers and merchants,
not to leave out bankers. Since in the good Saint's
view, money was "barren," it could not give birth to
interest except by extortion. By the same token, to
gain profit, "lucrum," from the ordinary and necessary
tasks of making a living was unjust. Even more unjust
was a system that elevated these common and necessary
folk to positions of great wealth and power, while
God's priests and His Church were poor and abandoned.

Once again, a given social order is defined as
superior and worthy of being preserved. And the
workings of the market place are seen as deleterious,
if as a result what is good and just is changed into
that which is unjust and indefensible.

Marxian Justice

Rather different from these concepts of economic
justice, concepts that are traditional and defensive
of ideal states of society, is the Marxist view.
While Karl Marx begins his analysis of the workings of
an emergent capitalist system with a theory of value
widely held by economists in the late 18th and early
19th century, he takes that theory to limits Adam
Smith, David Ricardo or Thomas Robert Malthus were not
apparently willing to go.

In essence, what Marx says is that the standard
of economic justice is the contribution of the
laborer. All value, whether it be value in use or
value in exchange, arises from the human effort

expended to produce a bushel of wheat, a bolt of cloth, a book, a steam engine or what have you. At the very least, that human labor must be paid for at wages that permit the laborer and his family to survive. On this all economists tended to agree.

Yet, to pay the laborer a subsistence wage, and to sell the products of his labor at a price well above that wage, was to incur a surplus value - the difference between the exchange value or price of the commodity in the market place and the wage paid.

If the laborer and his family remained poor while the transactions in the market place made the employer, the merchant and the banker rich beyond measure, this was unjust. Without the laborer's input, there would be no goods to sell, no profit to be made, no wealth to store up.

A whole social class was supported by this surplus value, a class of capitalists who added no value but extracted from the market an inordinate return on a minimum of investment. To be sure, Marxian economics is not as naive or simple as this exposition suggests. Marx lived, after all, in that period in which technological progress was especially rapid, a period in which the West was being transformed from an essentially agrarian society beholden, some insisted, to urban mercantilism, to a society of machines, of vast factories, urban rookeries, and capitalist "robber barons." The trans- forming agent was innovation, not simply the piling up of money as investment. And Marx masterfully outlined the unique transformation of money and old wealth into new machines and progress.

The result, however, was the same. The transforming power of invention and innovation, the unique place in the social scheme of entrepreneur did not mask the fact that at base, the laborer was not sharing fairly in the vast new wealth being created. The surplus grew but the distribution of the social surplus benefitted the working proletariat but little.

This, at least, is the essence of the socialist critique. Yet that critique must not be taken to be a call to return to simpler pre-capitalist economic systems. While the romanticism of the Moasaic Law or Aquinian theology is a call for a return to former ways of doing things, because they are superior in moral value to the social order of today, the

165

socialist critique argues that it ought to be possible to redistribute wealth, income and, most important, power or control over one's destiny in these complex times. It is precisely there that the socialist critique fails.

National socialism, especially in the Third World, argues that the poor countries at the Periphery have sold their goods, largely food, metals and oil, at prices set in the Metropolis, while the Periphery has been forced to pay prices for its machinery, energy, and necessary productive inputs that are set to provide high wages for Western laborers and substantial profits for Western merchants and capitalists. The multi-national monopoly firms buy, sell and produce the goods that the Periphery buys and sells. The MNCs become the agents of the new imperialism.

The simplistic answer is to nationalize the farms, the factories, the warehouses, docks, railways, telecommunications and energy companies and allow new entry into the Third World only under very stringently controlled conditions.

Capitalist Justice

Capitalist economics as developed in Vienna and in England in the 19th century stresses the principle of marginal productivity. The marginal product for each individual and each factor of production is the increment of total production that is the result of the "last" unit of human effort or other factor input. In the market place, the factor that is relatively scarce receives the higher marginal product.

Since capitalist economics is essentially descriptive rather than normative, capitalist economists are not in a position to judge the fairness of the distributive pattern of income. Yet, the marginal productivity doctrine holds that each individual is entitled to the fruits of his/her labors. What this doctrine does not do is give a rule for equality of distribution. Indeed, there is the risk that more quality can only be obtained at the cost of economic efficiency.

It is true that if people are basically alike, then the total utility of society will be greatest when income is distributed equally, assuming, of

166

course, that there is diminishing marginal utility. The citicism is that there is little evidence that people are in, fact, alike. What is worse, any utility as between individuals is probably impossible.

In the United States, evidence appears to suggest either that income distribution changes little over the years, or that as it changes, the direction is that of more equality. As contrasted with other capitalist nations at all levels of development, the United States has a fairer income distribution than most. However, as compared with major socialist countries, indices of equality of distribution are lower in the U.S. than in those countries.

Summary

Economic justice, then, is defined in terms of two basic factors -

- how well the national economy performs, and

- how equally the income of a nation or a world of nations is distributed.

Performance is a question of how much is produced as against what is possible to produce. It is also a question of how well and fully the resources of the nation were used in attaining a given level of production. Especially important, to some observers, is how well employed the labor force of the nation was in this productive process.

Equality is much more more complex. One measure of whether equality has been achieved is the extent of poverty in a nation and in the world. Obviously, if a nation is poor, then equality of income distribution makes little effective difference. Thus, performance is critical to the achievement of economic justice and the elimination of poverty.

Yet if the world is composed of rich and poor nations, then economic justice would seem to require a determination of how better to distribute all income so that no nation would remain poor. Perhaps, too, it is necessary to assist all nations to achieve levels of economic performance so that poverty at the national level can be reduced.

PART III.   JUSTICE IN SELECTED PARTS OF THE WORLD

9.

SOCIAL JUSTICE IN THE USSR[1]

Albert J. Schmidt
Arnold Bernhard Professor
of History
Professor of Law
University of Bridgeport

I. The Promise of Revolution: A Social Contract

Nearly three-quarters of a century have passed since the Bolshevik Revolution. The architects of that upheaval had set forth goals of egalitarianism and utopianism, both of which were to have been achieved under communism. Circumstances have shown that in this flight from capitalism, the Soviet populace has received something less than the social contract it had been promised.

Stalin's planned economy, although it proved a stimulus to a backward country in the 1920s and 1930s, has in recent years become burdensome, actually retarding economic growth.[2] Coupled with the harsh totalitarian methods employed by Stalin to implement it, this lessening productivity suggests that the injustices of one system have simply replaced those of another. The failure of the Stalinist system both to produce goods and to diminish social injustice reached crisis proportions in the late Brezhnev era when the many Soviet institutions appeared unworkable and corruption and privilege appeared pervasive.[3]

Secretary Mikhail Gorbachev's program, enunciated at the 27th Party Congress,[4] is really a four-fold program of Restructuring, Openness, Democratization, and Social Justice. 1) Restructuring (perestroika) aims at rebuilding the economy in a fundmental way -- by shifting power from monopolistic ministries (i.e. centralized planning) to relatively autonomous enterprises, allowing some individual enterprise, and introducing a limited market economy -- all in order to increase production. Perestroika necessarily depends on greater worker discipline, which has, among other things, activated an anti-alcohol campaign. 2) Glasnost' is "openness" whether dealing in statistics, natural, or human disasters, or Soviet history.[5] The thinking here is that the Soviet people should be

171

mature enough to handle the truth, especially if they
are expected to be more responsible in the workplace.
3) Demokratizatsiia, democratization, in current
Soviet parlance means involving people in a more real
way in the system, specifically the electoral process
and in the workplace.[6] Here, too, the intent is to
grant certain political rights in return for a more
responsible attitude toward work. 4) Social justice
(sotsial'naia spravedlivost'), called by Soviet
sociologist Tatania Zaslavskaia the "human factor" in
perestroika, is perceived as crucial to the success of
the latter. Her definition, while somewhat unusual,
speaks to improving the lot of the Soviet populace
through increased productivity.

Although the Brezhnev regime's corruption and
social malaise contradicted the whole idea of justice,
it did provide a model statement which is embedded
both in chapters three and seven of the 1977
Constitution.[7] Chapter 3, entitled "Social
Development and Culture," states in article 19 that
"the state helps enhance the social homogeneity of
society, namely the elimination of class differences
and of the essential distinctions between town
and country and between mental and physical labor and
the all-round development and drawing together of all
the nations and nationalities of the USSR." Although
this chapter further discusses work conditions,
compensation, health, social security, sport, and
education, chapter seven is more explicit in these
matters.

Designated "The Basic Rights, Freedoms, and
Duties of Citizens of the USSR" this chapter is
introduced by article 39, which states:

> Citizens of the USSR enjoy in full the
> social, economic, political and personal
> rights and freedoms proclaimed and
> guaranteed by the constitution of the
> USSR and by Soviet laws. The social system
> ensures enlargement of the rights and
> freedoms of citizens and continuous
> improvement of their living standards
> as social, economic, and cultural
> development programs are fulfilled.

Successive articles touch specifically on rights
related to social justice: (40) the right to work,
(41) rest and leisure, (42) health protection, (43)
maintenance in old age and sickness, (44) housing,

(45) education, (46) enjoyment of cultural benefits, and (47) the freedom of scientific, technical, and artistic work.

The next several -- those generally coinciding with our notions of human rights, include: (48) participation in the management and administration of state and public affairs, (49) submission of proposals to state bodies and the right to criticize shortcomings in their work; (50) freedom of speech, press, and assembly; (52) "freedom of conscience, that is, the right to profess or not to profess any religion and to conduct religious worship or atheistic propaganda"; (54) inviolability of the person, (55) the home, (56) privacy of citizens, and (57) respect for the individual and protection of the rights and the right to such protection by the courts.

The Brezhnev Constitution, therefore, is quite explicit in both what we term economic rights (social justice) and political (human) rights. Because Soviet leaders are reluctant to distinguish between these two, terming both "human," they respond to Western criticism of their violations of individuals' rights of privacy, speech, and assembly as being wide of the mark. "Genuine" human rights, they contend, are those having to do with housing, education, work, health, etc. -- rights frequently not fulfilled in the West.

Human rights defined as economic rights is rather more complicated than the simple phrase suggests. Recently, in the context of perestroika, the Soviets appear to have modified the Constitutional usage. General Secretary Gorbachev's appears to conform to that devised by Tatania Zaslavskaia, who has noted that "For the human factor to function effectively in production, the most important thing is the social and economic aspect of social justice, which basically means consistent implementation of the principle 'From each according to his abilities, to each according to his labor'."[8]

What then does this mean? According to one commentator "social justice" presently has quite as strong an ideological as socio-economic connotation. "In essence, 'social justice' is a code word for the application of an incentive system that the new leadership seems to believe is prerequisite to an improvement of the economy. The Soviet leadership is not as concerned with 'income differentiation' or inequality as with modes of labor

173

organization that stifle individual initiative and hamper economic productivity."[9]

The Soviet leadership since Lenin has resisted the temptation to embrace social equality (ravenstvo). Although Zaslavskaia suggests that social justice and equality may converge in the future, her concern, too, is for the present. Worrying about speculation and non-labor income from the "shadow economy", she has also challenged practices grounded in Soviet life such as subsidized bread, meat and dairy products, and housing by noting that they, too, constitute non-labor income.[10] She has criticized the "right to work" concept by suggesting that Soviet workers may have to join the ranks of the unemployed if their enterprise fails or if they become redundant. Further, she has attacked the sacred cow of privilege, critical of those who receive non-labor income in the form of preferential health care, better food, comfortable dachas, foreign travel, and many other luxuries denied the Soviet populace.

The ideas of Zaslavskaia and her fellow intellectuals appear to exercise considerable influence on Secretary Gorbachev. Their kind of social justice is both unprecedented and daring and carries potential risks for those who espouse it.[11] Is such drastic reform necessary? To answer we are forced to look at Soviet society in 1988 to determine whether the social justice as spelled out in the Constitution of 1977 is working or whether Gorbachev's inheritance from Stalin and Brezhnev is inherently flawed and in critical need of Zaslavskaia's brand of social justice.

II. Problem Areas for Improving the Quality of Life

Discussing social justice in the USSR really has to do with the old adage of "throwing stones at glass houses." While it is easy to discover lapses of social justice in the USSR, Americans in 1988 are troubled by their own homeless and hungry in an apparently affluent society. Bearing this in mind, we undertake a critique of the Soviet social system with considerable humility. That there are nagging problems in Soviet society -- those pertaining to the "quality of life" or social justice, as we use the term -- is no longer denied by either the Soviet leadership or media.[12]

A survey of some of the issues which appear most grievous follows in this order: 1) poverty, 2) privilege, 3) nationalities, 4) urban/rural dichotomy, 5) housing, 6) consumerism, 7) work conditions, and 8) health care. Space limitations do not permit discussion of many others.[13]

Even the candor spawned by glasnost' has not as yet resulted in an extensive discussion of poverty in the USSR.[14] While dwelling on poverty under capitalism, the Soviet leadership has evaded an admission of its existence at home. Until recently Western scholars rather gullibly bought this proposition. Mervyn Matthews, utilizing the meager statistical information at hand, has concluded that poverty is widespread in the USSR with 40% of the population subsisting on less than what has been designated the poverty wage. Despite this condition the Soviet Union does not have the grinding poverty of some Third World countries: "There is no significant amount of absolute poverty....there are no real slums or poverty districts in the Soviet Union."[15]

The low salaries of unskilled manual workers and service personnel account for the nearly 40 million whose wages are near the poverty level. Service people include not only clerks and secretaries but also professionals like agricultural experts and school administrators. The wage differential between agricultural workers, very poorly paid, and those in industry is perhaps 11%. Although the USSR takes pride in its social services, the aid rendered to needy large families, single parent families, and pensioners has been inadequate. Basic foodstuffs and housing have been subsidized; but unsubsidized food, housing repairs and maintenance, and clothing consume much of the income. The hopelessness created by this situation has fuelled the Second Economy and further indicates the risks of tampering with job security and the present pricing system.[16]

A concomitant to poverty and presumably as demoralizing to a socialist population is privilege. The events of 1917 were thought to have eradicated it, but it never really disappeared and even flourished blatantly during the Brezhnev era.[17] Privilege has taken many forms in the USSR. It must be remembered that even the highest officials receive relatively modest salaries; their reward comes in the perquisites of the position they hold--for instance special clinics, food and liquor commissaries, automobiles (perhaps with chauffeur), splendid dachas, superior housing, access to prestigeous educational institutions and subsequently employment for their offspring, special closed restaurants, foreign film showings, and permission to travel abroad. As Matthews has concluded: "Although elitism in the Soviet Union may have been for some periods reduced, it has never been removed. This is surely one of the strangest ironies produced by the Soviet attempt at social revolution."[18] Although Secretary Gorbachev has stated repeatedly his opposition to privilege, it is questionable whether the forces of social justice have the clout to dislodge it, perestroika notwithstanding.

Soviet propaganda speaks eloquently of the comradely relations among the diverse nationalities of the USSR. This viewpoint, which contrasts sharply with Western colonialism in Africa, Asia, and Latin America and even Tsarist Russia's aggrandizement, has become a centerpiece of Soviet ideology. The question remains just how successful has the leadership been in integrating the non-Russian peoples into the Soviet domain.[19]

While there has undoubtedly been an improvement in the lot of many non-Russian nationals, harmony is by no means pervasive. Kazakh nationalism, which had exploded in Stalin's day, reared its head again at the end of 1986 in the disturbances in Alma-Ata.[20] The Crimean Tatars' urge to return to their homelands has been for some years a rallying cry of human rights activists in the USSR.[21]

Baltic restiveness, evident in demonstrations in Vilnius, Riga, and Tallinn in August, 1987, were linked to wartime Nazi collaborators and provocative Western "radio voices".[22] The most recent, and by all odds the most serious, nationalties' problem is that concerning the republics of Armenia and Azerbaijan over the Nagorno-Karabakh region, predominantly Armenian but within the Azerbaijan Republic.[23] One hears of Soviet anxiety for the effects of Iranian religious fundamentalism on the Central Asian borderlands, fears deepened by the prevalence of Shiite Islam in Azerbaijan.[24]

Ukrainian and Lithuanian nationalism, sometimes identified with persistent Roman Catholicism, is always worrisome.[25] Jewish agitation to emigrate,

while not characteristic of all Soviet Jewry, is also
troublesome, perceived as setting a poor example
for other nationalities and impinging on Soviet policy
in the Arab world and with the US.[26] Not only are
there separatist sentiments among Soviet peoples,
there appear to be ethnic prejudices among Russians,
especially with a resurgence of Great Russian
nationalism.[27] It, too, is disturbing to a Soviet
regime which consistently has tilted toward the Great
Russians.

Finally, the Soviets have borne a heavy burden
subsidizing less economically developed nationalities,
particularly highly prolific ones such as the Uzbeks
in Central Asia. Muslim and Caucasus peoples have,
moreover, resisted Soviet efforts to eliminate
customary bride-price, polygamy, and feuding --
matters which were of little concern to the Tsarist
regime.[28] The Soviet policy of allowing for cultural
differences but enforcing political unity has not been
to the liking of many of the nationalities in the
USSR. Social justice in this instance is in the eye
of the beholder. It is perceived as potentially an
explosive issue in the USSR, especially as it combines
with matters of demography as in Central Asia.[29] How
the regime deals with it is one of the great questions
looming in the Soviet future.

The Soviet rural/urban dichotomy is less apparent
to a Westerner as an issue in social justice than are
some of the others.[30] It is, nonetheless, critical.
The casual tourist who visits Moscow and Leningrad has
no idea of the gulf separating those cities from the
dismal life in the countryside. The bezdorozhnost',
or roadlessness, caused by rain and mud or even the
absence of roads, is by no means a thing of the past
or a figment of literature. Villages buried deep
inside Russia -- in the Russian North, in Siberia --
bear only too many likenesses to their nineteenth
century counterpart.[31] What of the quality of
existence of Kirghiz or Kazakh herdsmen or the
peasants of Moldavia and the Russian North? The
Soviet Union clearly has a diverse rural character.

A peasantry uprooted from its own land and placed
on collective farms has become, we are told, unmindful
of traditional values, destructive of nature, and
often brutalized by the local bureaucracy. Children
and old people, in particular, have been victims of
this callousness. Medical services are often
wanting.[32] Stores are poorly stocked;[33] wages

177

are low; life is drab and monotonous. Small wonder that productivity suffers under such conditions. Current efforts to weed out privilege speak eloquently to the inequalities in the rural areas.

Increasing production requires improving the quality of leisure of the countryman, notably diminishing his consumption of alcohol. Making radio and television ever more available, establishing libraries, organizing clubs and cinemas, promoting hobbies and sports -- these are some of the antidotes applied to the troubles affecting rural Russia. Arguably, the present regime has ascribed a priority to the realization of greater social justice where slightly less than half its population resides, but the task is such as to obscure the effort.

The housing problem in the USSR has been widely publicized and impinges on many aspects of Soviet life.[34] The dismal legacy in housing from Imperial Russia was made worse by Stalin's emphasis on heavy industry. Only after Stalin's death did the authorities attempt to right the problem. Although spectacular building accomplishments have been proclaimed, the shortage remains: a large deficit is evident when one matches households with housing. The building, moreover, has not kept up with migration into the cities, the needs of the newly married, and the rising expectations of those unwilling to stay with the low-standard dwellings of the early Khrushchev era. That the housing shortage has had a demoralizing effect on Soviet society is evident by the time consumed trying to engineer housing exchanges, engaging in sub-leasing, the second home market in dachas, undertaking marriages and divorces of convenience, and offering bribes to officials.[35] Inadequate housing contributes both to escalating divorce and declining birth rates, consequently having a negative effect on productivity. Despite the Constitution's guarantee of housing and the absence of an army of homeless in the USSR, the present stock with its shortcomings represents a notable breach of social justice and one that threatens the success of perestroika itself.

Just as the Soviet housing shortage is well known in the West so are other problems confronting the consumer.[36] Among these are food shortages resulting from either poor harvests or distribution. Antiquated retailing practices often result in queues for each kind of item, curt salespeople, shoddy merchandise,

178

outdated fashions, and laboriously slow computing of costs on an abacus. When this process combines with favoritism (bribes) and dishonesty, which have both infected the retail trade, the burden on the consumer (usually the housewife after a full day of work) is horrendous. That such "double-duty" has often left Soviet wives exhausted and their marriages shattered is hardly surprising.

Despite the considerable poverty in the USSR, the extant "shortage economy" allows for a relative abundance in potential purchasing power. Small wonder that there has been great demand for such durable household goods as appliances, telephones, and cameras.[37] Privately owned automobiles continue to be a rarity in Soviet households although there is notable regional variation. Estonia with its 61 cars per thousand households in 1982 was highest.[38]

Low wages in the service sector may contribute to the poor service one encounters in retail shops, from waiters in restaurants, or from those engaged in repair work. Repairmen are especially hindered by the low priority assigned to the production of spare parts.

After Stalin's death Khrushchev put a high premium on satisfying consumer needs; generally, this trend has continued. Soviet citizens in the cities, at least, enjoy greater creature comfort and dress more stylishly than they did several decades ago; yet the prospects for significantly improved consumerism are not altogether promising despite recent rhetoric. There will be little change in either the allocation patterns or the minimal investment in services; for if the market mechanism is employed in food staples, housing, and transportation -- costs will rise appreciably with no assurance that quality will follow.[39] Under these circumstances it is not surprising that the Soviet consumer is apprehensive about a kind of social justice which threatens to strip him of his security blanket.

The Soviet consumer is most often the Soviet worker in whose name the day was won in 1917. Work conditions have not always improved to match expectations.[40] Vera Dunham has noted that Bolshevik romanticizing of the worker, "marching en masse toward a radiant future," is a thing of the past as today's worker looks to his private wellbeing with an acquisitivess far removed from the ideal of the New

Soviet Person, the true builder of socialism.[41] The same worker, often perceived as slothful in his work habits, has been exposed to anything but an exhilarating workplace. What Marx said of the worker alienation in the capitalist system has indeed become a problem in the Soviet Union today.[42] The recent outburst of labor dissatisfaction at the Iaroslavl' motor works (December, 1987) vividly indicated the problems confronting the perestroika reformers.[43]

Worker morale, greatly weakened by Stalin's draconian labor legislation, has not really improved as had been hoped with automation. Skilled and better educated workers, having retreated to the realm of private concerns, have reacted to a work environment of material shortages and mechanical failures by absenteeism. Their alienation is increased when intrashift down-time caused by centralized planning mismanagement causes a reduction in their wages. Women, caught in the trap of "double duty", worry more about day care and shopping than work productivity.[44] Labor shortage, not labor unions, provide Soviet workers with their best bargaining chip.[45] This leverage and sense of security now appear at risk with perestroika. Spokesmen for the latter, determined to increase production, reiterate the themes of "labor discipline," enterprise "accountability," work "according to his abilities," wage, price, and rent reforms, and relocation and retraining needs.[46] The appeal of equal access to consumer benefits may not exceed the discomfort caused by abandoning old and familiar ways.

In the capitalist world of spiraling medical costs, the Soviet system of health care appears to approximate the essence of social justice.[47] Even though like food and housing subsidies and free education such care is paid by hidden taxes, it seems worth it. Whether Stalin's introduction of socialized medicine was motivated more by the societal than individual considerations seems less consequential than that it has been preserved by his successors. Perceptions of a profession are, however, fostered to an extent by its reward system: in the USSR medical personnel are paid low salaries. When a point is glowingly made that large numbers of women are physicians, it should be remembered that they are really poorly paid functionaries of the state, thus confirming gender discrimination.

180

The state of Soviet health has had a poor press. We hear of the general unhealthiness caused by diet, alcohol abuse, excessive tobacco, and unsatisfactory health care. Infant mortality, which appears to have improved recently, has come under particular scrutiny of Western scholars.[48] Field notes that it increased by more than 25% in the last ten years.[49] The hospital in the USSR, which like other institutions has its officious fuctionaries and shortages of technology and supplies, is often crowded, drab, and even antiquated. Several eighteenth or early nineteenth century structures, admittedly architectural monuments, still function as hospitals in Moscow today.

Access to medical services has never been regarded as an egalitarian right in the USSR. While place of residence determines access for the general populace, the elite have special clinics and superior personnel at their disposal. For those living in remote regions of the USSR, health care is probably precarious. Besides this stratification the system suffers from a bureaucracy characteristic of other Soviet institutions in which meaningless rules impinge on quality of service. An obsession for fulfilling quotas for such services, accompanied by inevitable falsification of figures, also detracts from the central purpose of health care. While there are undoubtedly many caring health professionals in the USSR, a common perception is that the Soviet system fosters insensitivity by physicians and nurses toward patients. Finally, notable deficiencies in medical equipment and shortages in pharmaceutical products are additional impairments. To a considerable extent these shortcomings indicate that the Soviet health care system requires an infusion of funds. Field estimates that the expenditures are only a third of that in the United States, although seepage from the "hidden economy," i.e. patient payment of illegal fees, improves this percentage.[50]

The quality of life in the USSR is lessened by the unsatisfactory conditions affecting women,[51] the young, and the elderly,[52] by an increase in social deviance often aggravated by excessive alcohol consumption, drug abuse, and prostitution.[53] Crime, punishment, and shortcomings in the legal system have also come under increasing scrutiny recently.[54]

The state's apparent willingness recently to tolerate, at least on occasion, some ethnic, religious, and political non-conformity has improved the quality of life for a small segment of the population.[55] Talk and even demonstrations have occurred recently about a cultural and spiritual crisis which embraces education and its perceived failures,[56] environmental destruction,[57] a similar destruction of historic and cultural monuments,[58] and the persistence of traditional religion.[59] It is not surprising that some Soviet intellectuals have lamented a genuine cultural and spiritual crisis, while, in turn, conservatives appear to question the wisdom of excessive glasnost'.[60]

III. Social Justice in the USSR: the Prospects

The present leadership in the USSR, in assessing the obstacles to social justice, has concluded that they are inseparably linked to low productivity. Under these circumstances economic restructuring will take precedence, as it always has, over social justice. Whether the two will join hands in the future depends on Secretary Gorbachev's success in implementing his program.

For that reason social justice, as defined by Tatania Zaslavskaia, is crucial: if worker productivity is to increase, fairness no less than worker discipline will have to prevail. The privileged, those who have vested interest in the status quo, must either give way or perestroika, glasnost', Democratization, and Social Justice will be but empty slogans soon forgotten.[61] Reducing this resistance is a tall order, for it is both considerable and powerful.[62]

Secretary Gorbachev spoke about the matter to a group of editors on January 8, 1988 when he soberly discussed the necessity for change but offered assurances that the primacy of the Communist Party would not be altered. With respect to glasnost' he stated, as if to mollify his critics on this point: "We are for openness without reservations, without limitations, but for openness in the interests of socialism." He added, significantly: "The Soviet press is not a private shop. Let us recall again Lenin's premise that literature is part of the common cause of the party. This is a fundamental provision and we continue to be guided by it."[63]

Secretary Gorbachev's dilemma is clear: he must resolve his domestic problems without unleashing forces on his left or affronting those on his right. He is, moreover, at a crossroads in his foreign relations, particularly those with the US whom he has appeared to accommodate in order to improve his prospects at home.[64] The alternative to better relations with the US is still another round in the armaments race which will be for the Soviet Union and well as for the US both costly and risky. Social justice would be the loser in both places.

NOTES

1. This paper is directed to the general reader or undergraduate who has an interest in social justice in contemporary Soviet society and who may wish to pursue it through additional reading or writing. For that reason citations are to works in English. The bibliography contained herein is by no means inclusive. A useful bibliography, which complements the present one, may be found in Donald D. Barry and Carol Barner-Barry, Contemporary Soviet Politics, 3rd ed., (Englewood Cliffs, N.J., 1987).

2. See Ed A. Hewett, "Soviet Central Planning: Probing the Limits of the Traditional Model," Occasional Paper #194, Kennan Institute for Advanced Russian Studies (Washington, 1984), 1-59; Ed A. Hewett, Reforming the Soviet Economy: Equality versus Efficiency (Washington, D.C., 1988); Boris Rumer, "Realities of Gorbachev's Economic Program," Problems of Communism (May-June, 1986), 20-31; Victor Kontorovich, "Discipline and Growth in the Soviet Economy," Ibid. (Nov.-Dec. 1985), 18-31; and Marshall I. Goldman, Gorbachev's Challenge: Economic Reform in the Age of High Technology (N.Y., 1987).

3. See George Feifer, "Russian Disorders: the Sick Man of Europe," Harper's (Feb. 1981), pp. 41-55; John Bushnell, "The New Soviet Man Turns Pessimist," Survey, 24/2 (Spring, 1979), 1-18; and Hedrick Smith, The Russians (New York, 1976), pp. 25-52, 81-101. James R. Millar, in Politics, Work, and Daily Life in the USSR (Cambridge, 1987) uses data from the Soviet Interview Project (recent emigrants) to analyze the late Brezhnev era. Aaron Trehub, "Suicide in the Soviet Union," Radio Liberty Research (Oct. 26, 1987) focuses on causes of suicide in he USSR as discussed in a Kirghiz literary journal and concludes that the article "explicitly refutes the old propaganda lie that the capitalist West has a monopoly on despair." (p. 4).

The corruption of the Brezhnev regime has been broadly criticized in the Soviet press in early 1988.

4. See "The Documentary Record of the 27th Congress of the Communist Party of the Soviet Union," Current Soviet Policies IX (Columbus, O.: Current Digest of the Soviet Press, 1986. The 27th Congress of the Communist Party of the Soviet Union: A Report from the Airlie House Conference (Santa Monica , Calif.: RAND/UCLA Center for the Study of Soviet International Behavior and N.Y.: W. Averell Harriman Institute for Advanced Study of the Soviet Union, 1986) and Keith Bush, "Gorbachev's Speech to the Twenty-Seventh Party Congress: the Economy," Radio Liberty Research (Feb. 25, 1986). See also Current Digest of the Soviet Press, passim. Hereafter cited as CDSP.

Numerous works have appeared on the Gorbachev reform program. The reader may wish to refer to Mikhail Gorbachev, Perestroika: New Thinking for Our Country and the World (New York, 1987); Timothy J. Colton, The Dilemma of Reform in the Soviet Union, Rev. ed. (New York, 1986); Marshall Goldman, Gorbachev's Challenge (mentioned above). Recent Soviet economic decline is discussed in the context of the "social contract" between the state and society in Peter Hauslohner, "Gorbachev's Social Contract," Soviet Economy, III, i (1987), 54-89.

See also Alexander Yanov, The Russian Challenge: the USSR and the Year 2000. Iden J. Rosenthal transl. (London, 1987); Maurice Friedberg and Heyward Isham, Soviet Society under Gorbachev (Armonk, N.Y,, 1987), and Moshe Lewin, The Gorbachev Phenomenon (Berkeley, Calif., due Mar., 1988).

Several papers, some as yet unpublished, show the continuity of reform from the late Brezhnev period to the present: Darrell Slider, "Experimentation as a Reform Strategy in the Soviet Union," presented at the national convention of the American Association for the Advancement of Slavic Studies, Boston, November, 1987. See also his "The Brigade System in Soviet Industry: An Effort to Restructure the Labour Force," Soviet Studies XXXIX, 3, (July, 1987), 388-405; Joel C. Moses, "Worker Self-Management and the Reformist Alternative in Soviet Labour Policy, 1979-85" Soviet Studies, XXXIX, 2 (April, 1987), 205-228; see also his "The Political Implications of Reform -- the View from IGPAN, 1978-86," presented at the annual meeting of the American Political Science Association, Sept., 1987 and his "Gorbachev and the Democratization Issue", presented at the 1987 meeting of the American

Association for the Advancement of Slavic Studies in Boston. Finally, see Linda J. Cook, "Gorbachev's Reforms, Workers, and Welfare: The Threat to Employment Security and Its Political Implication", also presented at the AAASS meeting in Boston. While these papers relate to the worker, they deal with broader aspects of reform as well.

5. Vera Tolz, "Gorbachev's Speech to the Twenty-Seventh Party Congress: Reaffirmation of 'Glasnost'" Radio Liberty Research (Feb. 26, 1986), 1-4. Julia Wishnevsky, "Socialist Legality and the Falsification of History," Radio Liberty Research (Aug. 20, 1987), 1-5. "A Call for a Better-Informed Public," CDSP, XXXVII, 49 (Jan. 1, 1986), 6-7. "Pros and Cons of Printing the Hard Facts," CDSP, XXXVIII, 7 (Mar. 19, 1986), 21; "Does 'Glasnost' Encourage Nationalism?" CDSP, XXXIX, 27 (Aug. 5, 1987).

6. See Joel C. Moses, "Gorbachev and the Democratization Issue," a paper delivered at the national convention of the American Association for the Advancement of Slavic Studies, November, 1987.

7. See Robert Sharlet, The New Soviet Constitution of 1977: Analysis and Text (Brunswick, O., 1978) and the appendix of Barry, Contemporary Soviet Politics.

8. "Zaslavskaya Prescribes for Social Justice," CDSP, XXXVIII, 41 (Nov. 12, 1986), 10.

Other recent references to Zaslavskaia and "social justice" readily available in English are as follows: the entire August, 1987 issue of Survey, 29, no. 4 (127), devoted to "Social and Economic Rights in the Soviet Bloc," includes some of her writings. "How Close is the USSR to Social Justice?" CDSP, XXXVIII, 5 (Mar. 5, 1986), 1-5. "Benefits Distribution vs. Social Justice," CDSP, XXXVIII, 52 (Jan. 28, 1987), 6-7. "Sociology's Role in Restructuring Society," CDSP, XXXIX, 6 (Mar. 11, 1987), 1-4. "Zaslavskaia Talks about her Life, Theories," CDSP, XXXIX, 16 (May 20, 1987), 6-9. "A Soviet Voice of Innovation Comes to Fore," [Zaslavskaia] New York Times, Aug. 28, 1987. "Interview with Tat'yana Zaslavskaya," Radio Liberty Research (Sept. 15, 1987), 1-20. Aaron Trehub, "'Social Justice' and Economic Progress," Radio Liberty Research (October 7, 1986), 1-9. "Current Reformist Thinkers in the USSR," Summary of paper delivered by Rolf Theen (Sept. 10, 1986), Kennan Institute for Advanced Russian Studies, hereafter cited as KIARS.

It is instructive to compare Zaslavskaia's "social justice" with that discussed in the press before perestroika. See "What Does Social Justice Mean Today?" CDSP, XXXV, 45 (Dec. 7, 1983), 10, 17-18.

9. See Valdimir Shlapentokh, "Social Values and Daily Life in the Soviet Union," Contemporary Soviet Society: Values and Lifestyles (Washington, D.C.: Kennan Institute for Advanced Russian Studies, Woodrow Wilson International Center for Scholars, 1986). This is not a direct quote from Shlapentokh but rather a summary of his presentation.

10. A decree on "non-labor" or "unearned" income was promulgated jointly by the Central Committee and the Presidium of the Supreme Soviet in July 1986. See summary of presentation of Oct. 1, 1986 by W. Patrick Murphy, "The Soviet Campaign Against Unearned Income," KIARS Meeting Report. See also "Clamping Down on Unearned Income," CDSP, XXXVIII, 21 (June 25, 1986).

11. Aaron Trehub, "Gorbachev and the Soviet Social Contract," Radio Liberty Research (Sept. 7, 1987) suggests that what the West perceives as a Soviet social contract based on egalitarianism, stability, and security appears threatened by perestroika. Sergei Voronitsy, "Where Will the Restructuring of Soviet Society Lead?" Radio Liberty Research (Nov. 13, 1986) also discusses the possible consequences of changes in wages and bonuses, pensions and social security, and the pricing structure.

See also Peter Hauslohner, "Gorbachev's Social Contract," Soviet Economy, III, 1 (Jan.-Mar. 1987).

12. See Aaron Trehub, "Gorbachev's Speech to the Twenty-Seventh Party Congress," Radio Liberty Research (Feb. 27, 1986).

See also Walter D. Connor, "Social Policy under Gorbachev," Problems of Communism (July-Aug. 1986), 31-46 and Aaron Trehub, "The Twenty-Seventh Congress of the CPSU: Lip Service Paid to the Same Old Social Problems," Radio Liberty Research (Mar. 11, 1986).

13. For recent general works see Horst Herlemann, ed., Quality of Life in the USSR; Murray Yanowitch, The Social Structure of the USSR (Armonk, N.Y., 1987) consists of essays by Soviet scholars; Aaron Trehub,

"Social and Economic Rights in the Soviet Union: Work, Health Care, Social Security, and Housing," Radio Liberty Research Bulletin (Dec. 29, 1986), 1-51; the August, 1987 issue (vol. 29, no. 4) issue of Survey, which is devoted to "Social and Economic Rights in the Soviet Bloc."

14. On the other hand, "Profiling the Soviet Vagrant," CDSP, XXXIX, 14 (May 6, 1987) suggests the prospects of open discussion of this subject.

See Mervyn Matthews, Poverty in the Soviet Union: the Life-styles of the Underprivileged in Recent Years (Cambridge, 1986), which is more current than A. McAuley, Economic Welfare in the Soviet Union (London, 1979). Matthews has an excellent bibliography. See also his shorter articles: "Poverty in the Soviet Union," The Wilson Quarterly (Autumn, 1985); "Aspects of Poverty in the Soviet Union," in Horst Herlemann, ed., Quality of Life in the Soviet Union (Boulder, 1987), 43-63; "Poverty in the Soviet Union" in Contemporary Soviet Society: Values and Lifestyles (KIARS, 1986).

Cf. Gertrude E. Schroeder, "Soviet Living Standards in Comparative Perspective," Quality of Life in the Soviet Union, ed. Herlemann, pp. 13-30.

15. As quoted from Matthews, "Poverty in the Soviet Union," Contemporary Soviet Society: Values and Lifestyles, p. 5. This source is a summation of Matthew's address.

16. See Sergei Voronitsyn, "Decree Issued on Benefits for the Underprivileged," Radio Liberty Research (June 18, 1985) and "The Less Well-off Sector and the Pending Price Reform," Ibid. (Sept. 24, 1987); Aaron Trehub, "Politburo on Job Placement and Unemployment Benefits," Radio Liberty Research (Nov. 20, 1987); Allan Kroncher, "Restructuring and Prices," Radio Liberty Research (Nov. 23, 1987); "Inflation, Price-Hike Fears Addressed," CDSP, XXXIX, 43 (Nov. 25, 1987).

17. See Mervyn Matthews, Privilege in the Soviet Union: A Study of Elite Life-Styles under Communism (London, 1978); David Lane, The End of Social Inequality? (London, 1982).

See also Hedrick Smith, The Russians; Elizabeth Teague, "Lifestyle of the Elite Called into Question,"

Radio Liberty Research (Feb. 14, 1986); "Special Schools Cater to Elite's Children," CDSP XXXIX, 8 (Mar. 25, 1987), 1-5, 14.

18. Matthews, Privilege in the Soviet Union, p. 185.

19. The myth that Soviet nationalities are one happy family is explored in Lowell Tillett, The Great Friendship: Soviet Historians on the Non-Russian Nationalities (Chapel Hill, N.C.: U of North Carolina Press, 1969).

See also Michael Rywkin, Moscow's Muslim Challenge (Armonk, N.Y., 1982) and Rasma Karklins, Ethnic Relations in the USSR: the Perspective from Below (Winchester, Mass., 1986). The newsletter Soviet Nationality Survey (London) is intended to provide current news and analysis of the subject.

Soviet anxieties are evident in "Does 'Glasnost' Encourage Nationalism?," CDSP, XXXIX, 27 (Aug. 5, 1987); "Charting Worrisome Ethnic Patterns," Ibid., XXXIX, 7 (Mar. 18, 1987); "'Legitimate' Ethnic Pride is Called Good," Ibid., XXXVII, 51 (Jan. 15, 1986); and "Combatting Ideas of Bourgeois Nationalism," Ibid., XXXVII, 34 (Sept. 18, 1985).

Recent disturbances (early 1988) in Armenia and Azerbaijan have focused Western attention on the Soviet nationalities' problem. See "Rumbles Round Russia's Rim," The Economist (Jan. 30, 1988), pp. 35-36 and "The Soviet Disunion," Ibid. (Mar. 5, 1988), pp. 11-12.

20. "The Riots in Alma-Ata: What Caused Them?" CDSP, XXXIX, 1 (Feb. 4, 1987).

21. See, for example, Petro Grigorenko, Memoirs transl. Thomas P. Whitney (New York, 1982), 347-66, passim; "Crimean Tatars Voice Demands Openly," CDSP, XXXIX, 30 (Aug. 26, 1987); "Tatars Keep Heat on in Uzbekistan, Crimea," CDSP, XXXIX, 42 (Nov. 18, 1987); Ann Sheehy, "Crimean Tatar Commission Works Against Background of Continuing Protests," Radio Liberty Research (Oct. 13, 1987); Ann Sheehy, "Commission Makes Cultural Concessions to Crimean Tatars," Radio Liberty Research (Oct. 23, 1987).

22. See "Baltic-Republic Demonstrations Reported," CDSP, XXXIX, 34 (Sept. 23, 1987).

23. See Elizabeth Fuller, "More Demonstrations in Armenia," _Radio Liberty Research_ (Feb. 22, 1988); "Demonstrations over Nagorno-Karabakh in Armenia," _Ibid._, RL 90/88 and "Armenians Demonstate for Return of Territories from Azerbaijan," _Ibid._ RL 441/87, (Oct. 20, 1987). A massacre of Armenians in Sumgait, Azerbaijan has only complicated matters.

24. Cf. Ann Sheehy, "Iranian Religious Propaganda in Turkmenistan," _Radio Liberty Research_ (Sept. 22, 1987) and John Soper, "Seminar Reveals Dispute over Role of Islam in USSR," _Radio Liberty Research_ (Dec. 11, 1987).

25. The vitality of Roman Catholicism in Lithuania is hardly surprising. What is more intriguing is the survival and persistence of Eastern Rite Catholicism, or the Uniate Church, in the Ukraine. See Roberto Suro, "For Vatican, Gorbachev's 'Openness' is a Solid Wall," _New York Times_ "Week in Review" (Jan. 3, 1988), which focuses on both. Cf. also Roman Solchanyk, "Ukrainian Catholic Activist Iosyp Terelya in the West," _Radio Liberty Research_ (Sept. 20, 1987).

26. The literature on Soviet Jewry is voluminous, although not in _CDSP_, for the authorities have no wish to make so much of the issue. Nonetheless, see "Refusenik Demonstration Prompts Reiteration of Legal Grounds for Denying Exit to Some," _CDSP_, XXXIX, 48 (Dec. 30, 1987). See also Julia Wishnevsky, "Liberalism in the USSR and the Situation of Russian Jews," _Radio Liberty Research_ (June 5, 1987) for the implications of _glasnost'_ for anti-Semitism.

27. "Russian National Sentiments Surface," _CDSP_, XXXIX, 13 (Apr. 29, 1987); "Ultranationalist Russian Group Denounced," _CDSP_, XXXIX, 21 (June 24, 1987); "'Pamyat' Nationalists: The Debate Continues," _CDSP_, XXXIX, 30 (Aug. 26, 1987). For the relationship of Russian nationalism and monuments preservation, see Albert J. Schmidt, "Soviet Legislation for Protection of Architectural Monuments: Background," to be published in _Law and Perestroika_, a volume in the _Law and Eastern Europe_ series, U. of Leiden, The Netherlands. This represents the proceedings of "Law and Perestroika," a symposium held at the University of Bridgeport, November 12-15, 1987.

See especially John B. Dunlop, _The Faces of Contemporary Russian Nationalism_ (Princeton, 1983) and various articles which he has written. David K. Shipler, _Russia: Broken Idols, Solemn Dreams_ (New

York, 1983), pp. 323-46 touches on the subject.

28. See F.J. M. Feldbrugge, "Criminal Law and Traditional Society: The Role of Soviet law in the Integration of Non-Slavic Peoples," Review of Socialist Law, III (1977), 3-51.

29. See Ann Sheehy, "Kazakh Demographer Forecasts Twelve Million Kazakhs by the Year 2010," Radio Liberty Research (July 1, 1985).

30. See Horst Herlemann, "Aspects of the Quality of Rural Life in the Soviet Union," Quality of Life in the Soviet Union, pp. 163-73; Alfred Evans, Jr., "Equalization of Urban and Rural Living Levels in Soviet Society," Soviet Union/Union Sovietique, VIII, 1 (1981), 38-61; Carol Nechemias, "Regional Differentiation of Living Standards in the RSFSR: The Issue of Inequality," Soviet Studies, XXXII, 3 (1980), 366-78; Elizabeth Teague, "Inhumanity of Rural Life Blamed on Party Bureaucrats," Radio Liberty Research (Dec. 10, 1986), 1-3.

In his new work The Fire the novelist Valentin Rasputin depicts the moral degeneration of a logging town in Siberia. See "Rasputin Novella Probes Social Problems," CDSP XXXVII, 49 (Jan. 1, 1986), 8-9.

31. One finds little to romanticize about the old Russian village where life was often brutal. See Cathy Frierson, "Crime and Punishment in the Russian Village: Rural Concepts of Criminality at the End of the Nineteenth Century," Slavic Review (1987), 55-69.

32. See "Rural Medical Services Needs to be Improved" CDSP, XXXV, 36 (Oct. 5, 1983) and "Medicine/Public Health" Ibid. XXXVI, 42 (Nov. 14, 1984).

33. See Elizabeth Teague, "Villagers Protest About Shortage of Sugar," Radio Liberty Research (Aug. 27, 1987).

34. Henry Morton has written most extensively on housing in the USSR. Particularly useful are his "Housing Quality and Housing Classes in the Soviet Union," Quality of Life in the Soviet Union ed. Horst Herlemann, pp. 95-115; "Who Gets What, When and How? Housing in the Soviet Union," Soviet Studies, XXXII, 2 (1980), 235-59; "Local Soviets and the Attempt to Rationalize the Delivery of Urban Services: the Case of Housing," Soviet Local Politics

191

and Government ed. Everett M. Jacobs (London, 1983), 187-203.

See also articles by Aaron Trehub: "Some Home Truths About Soviet Housing," Radio Liberty Research (Aug. 22, 1985); "Young People's Residential Complexes," Ibid. (Oct. 22, 1985); "The Outlook for Cooperative Housing," Ibid. (Nov. 9, 1985); "Housing: More Power to the City Soviets?" Ibid. (Nov. 19, 1985); "Social and Economic Rights in the Soviet Union: Work, Health Care, Social Security, and Housing," Radio Liberty Research Bulletin (Dec. 29, 1986); "Down and Out in Moscow: Homelessness in the Soviet Union" (Mar. 14, 1988).

See also Donald D. Barry, "Soviet Housing Law: the Norms and their Application," Soviet Law After Stalin 3 vols., I. eds. Barry, George Ginsburgs, and Peter Maggs (Leyden, 1977); Henry W. Morton and Robert C. Stuart, The Contemporary Soviet City (Armonk, N.Y, 1984) and Gregory D. Andrusz, Housing and Urban Development in the USSR (Albany, N.Y., 1985).

35. Henry Morton, "Who Gets What..." Soviet Studies, passim.

36. See "Wolfgang Teckenberg, "Consumer Goods and Services: Contemporary Problems and Their Impact on the Quality of Life in the Soviet Union," Quality of Life in the Soviet Union ed. Horst Herlemann, pp. 31-41. Numerous articles in the CDSP deal with consumer goods. A few of these are as follows: "Gorbachev Restates Food Program's Aims," CDSP, XXXVII, 37 (Oct. 9, 1985); "Party Hits Consumer Goods, Food Dearth," Ibid. XXXIX, 21 (June 24, 1987); "Explaining the Meat Shortage in the USSR," Ibid. XXXVII, 10 (Apr. 3, 1985). Consumer goods and/or services: "Consumer Goods and Services Program I, II, and III" Ibid. XXXVII, 41, 42, 43 (Nov. 6, 13, 20, 1985); "Inequities in Consumption Draw Resentment," Ibid., XXXVI, 44 (Nov. 28, 1984); "The Service Sector: Some Ideas for Change," Ibid., XXXVII, 33 (Sept. 11, 1985).

See also Andreas Tenson, "New Measures to Fulfill the Food Program," Radio Liberty Research (Jan. 3, 1986); Dina Kaminskaia, "Another Campaign in the Struggle Against Production of Inferior-Quality Goods and Padding of Results," Ibid. (Aug. 9, 1985); and "Nothing to Lose but Your Queues," The Economist (Dec. 19, 1987) 46.

37. "Russian Telecoms: Talking with Comrade Bell," The Economist (Dec. 19, 1987), 60, 62.

38. Theckenberg, "Consumer Goods," p. 33.

39. The prospects of inflation have been discussed above. Cf. note #16.

40. See generally Leonard Schapiro and Joseph Godson, eds., The Soviet Worker from Lenin to Andropov (New York, 1984); Robert Conquest, ed., Industrial Workers in the USSR (London, 1967); Anna-Jutta Pietsch, "Self-Fulfillment Through Work: Working Conditions in Soviet Factories," Quality of Life in the Soviet Union, pp. 117-31; Hedrick Smith, The Russians, pp. 199-240; Vera Dunham, "The Image of the Worker in Contemporary Soviet Literature," Contemporary Soviet Society: Values and Lifestyles, pp. 10-13; Gail W. Lapidus, ed., Women, Work, and Family in the Soviet Union (Armonk, 1982).

See also Aaron Trehub, "Social and Economic Rights in the Soviet Union: Work, Health Care, Social Security, and Housing," Radio Liberty Research Bulletin (Dec. 29, 1986); "Elizabeth Teague, "Izvestia Advocates Legalization of Private Enterprise in the Service Sector," Radio Liberty (Aug. 23, 1985); Elizabeth Teague, "Soviet Citizens Told to Get Down to Work," Radio Liberty (Mar. 18, 1985). Additional articles on the subject have appeared in Radio Liberty in recent years.

Aspects of perestroika and work are discussed in the following: "Restructuring and the Working Class," CDSP, XXXVIII, 43 (Nov. 26, 1986) 7, 14; "New Law Sanctions Individual Enterprise," CDSP, XXXVIII, 46 (Dec. 17, 1986), 1-8; "Individual Enterprise Makes Slow Gains," CDSP, XXXIX, 36 (Oct. 7, 1987), 1-4; "The Law on the State Enterprise" CDSP, XXXIX, 30, 31 (1987); "Zaslavskaya on Motivating Soviet Workers," CDSP, XXXVII, 22 (June 26, 1985; "Tying Pay More Closely to Performance," CDSP, XXXVIII, 39 (Oct. 29, 1986); "Gorbachev Spurs Drive to Update Economy," CDSP, XXXVII, 15 (May 8, 1985); "Drive for Labor Discipline Resurfaces," CDSP, XXXVII, 5 (Feb. 27, 1985); "Will the Need for Workers Stay High?" CDSP, XXXVII, 3 (Feb. 13, 1985); "Rethinking Employment as Economy Shifts," CDSP, XXXVIII, 3 (Feb. 19, 1986); "A Survey of Soviet People's Work Attitudes," CDSP, XXXVII, 18 (May 29, 1985). These are a mere sampling of the articles on the subject in CDSP over the past several years.

41. "The Image of the Worker in Contemporary Soviet Literature," p. 13. It is Dunham's view that Stalin killed the spirit of comradery among workers "by destroying all lateral connections in Soviet society, by sowing distrust, and making all associations perilous." Ibid., p. 12.

42. Anna-Jutta Pietsch observes that "The elimination of private ownership of the means of production did not lead to the elimination of the alienation of labor, even though this postulate still holds a firm place in Soviet ideology." ("Self-Fulfillment through Work: Working Conditions in Soviet Factories," p. 118).

43. See Sergei Voronitsyn, "The Lessons of the Dispute at the Yaroslavl Motor Works," Radio Liberty Research RL 77/88 (Feb. 22, 1988).

44. See Carola Hansson and Karin Liden, eds., Moscow Women (New York, 1983), passim.

45. See Murray Feshbach, "Population and Labor Force," in Abram Bergson & Herbert S. Levine, eds., The Soviet Economy: Toward the Year 2000 (London, 1983) 79-111.

46. See Linda J. Cook, "Gorbachev's Reforms, Workers, and Welfare: The Threat to Employment Security and Its Political Implications," paper delivered at the national convention of the American Association for the Advancement of Slavic Studies, November, 1987; "Glasnost' and Unemployment: the Labour Pains of Perestroika," The Economist (Dec. 26, 1987), 15-18.

Cf. also Bill Keller, "Nervous Soviet Awaits Local Factory Control," New York Times, Dec. 31, 1987 which describes open labor unrest in the Iaroslavl Engine Factory -- a worker refusal to work Saturdays just as plant managers are pressed to increase enterprise profits.

Articles in CDSP on the new state enterprise and individual enterprise legislation are relevant here. See "Individual Enterprise Makes Slow Gains," CDSP, XXXIX, 36 (Oct. 7, 1987).

47. See Mark Field, "Medical Care in the Soviet Union: Promises and Realities," Quality of Life in the Soviet Union, pp. 65-82; Field's Soviet Socialized Medicine (New York, 1967) is now somewhat dated, but

he has written many articles since then; William
A. Knaus, Inside Russian Medicine (New York, 1981);
John C. Dutton, "Causes of Soviet Adult Mortality
Increases," Soviet Studies, XXXIII, 4 (Oct. 1981),
548-59; Christopher Davis and Murray Feshbach, "Rising
Infant Mortality in the USSR in the 1970s,"
U.S. Department of Commerce, Bureau of the Census
(Washington, D.C., 1980). Feshbach's ingenious use of
the Soviet census for diverse information, especially
that pertaining to health matters, is evident in
Murray Feshbach, "Between the Lines of the 1979 Soviet
Census," Problems of Communism (Jan.-Feb.1982).

See also summary of Murray Feshbach's paper of
Oct. 5, 1987 in "Glasnost and Health Issues in the
USSR," KIARS Meeting Report; summary of Mark Field's
paper of Nov. 9 in "Soviet Infant Mortality," KIARS
Meeting Report; Aaron Trehub, "Social and Economic
Rights in the Soviet Union: Work, Health Care, Social
Security, and Housing," Radio Liberty Research
Bulletin (Dec. 29, 1986) pp. 13-24; Trehub, "More
Glasnost' on Soviet Health Issues," Radio Liberty
Research (Oct. 12, 1987); Trehub, "First
Fee-For-Service Hospital in USSR to Open in Moscow,"
Radio Liberty Research (Sept. 14, 1987); Vladimir
Voinovich, "Free Medical Care," Radio Liberty Research
(Jan. 23, 1985); Elizabeth Fuller, "USSR Minister of
Health Cites Data on Infant Mortality and Infectious
Diseases in Two Transcaucasian Republics," Radio
Liberty Research (Oct. 16, 1987).

The CDSP has had innumerable articles on Soviet
health care of which the following are
examples: "Georgia's Health Care in Sorry State,"
CDSP, XXXV, 49 (Jan. 4, 1984); "Major Reforms in
Soviet Medicine Planned," CDSP, XXXIX, 19 (June 10,
1987); "Pediatrician Asks Better Neonatal Care," CDSP,
XXXVI, 12 (Apr. 18, 1984); "Combatting Mother and
Infant Mortality," CDSP, XXXVI, 29 (Aug. 15, 1984).
Medical education has been discussed in "How Can
Medical Schools Teach Better?" and "Setting Up Annual
Medical Exams for All," CDSP, XXXVI, 6 (Mar. 7, 1984);
"Why are Physicians Often Incompetent?" CDSP, XXXV,
47 (Dec. 21, 1983).

Much of the very considerable body of literature
on alcoholism in the USSR relates to health. See
Valdimir Treml, "Alcohol Abuse and the Quality of Life
in the Soviet Union," Quality of Life in the Soviet
Union, pp. 151-62 and innumerable articles in Radio
Liberty Research and CDSP.

48. See Bill Keller, "Mother Russia Makes a Comeback on Births," New York Times (Dec. 26, 1987).

49. "Medical Care in the Soviet Union," p. 68.

50. For this paragraph the author has drawn extensively on Mark Field, "Medical Care in the Soviet Union," pp. 70-80.

Although space limitations prevent discussion of other aspects of health care, the reader may wish to refer to "Why Has Soviet Dentistry Deteriorated?" CDSP, XXXVII, 1 (Jan. 30, 1985). The Russian and East European Studies Program (directed by William McCagg) at Michagan State University sponsored April 11-13, 1985 a program on "The Handicapped in the USSR and Eastern Europe," which this author believes is the most determined effort to date to study this important theme. See also "Education of the Handicapped in the USSR: Exploration of the Statistical Picture," Soviet Studies, XXXIX, 3 (July 1987), 468-88.

In contrast to the handicapped, no Soviet medical theme has likely been probed more in the West than psychiatry. Usually such study has focused on psychiatric abuse of political dissidents. From the voluminous literature on the subject, the reader may wish to consult Harvey Fireside, Soviet Pyschoprisons (New York, 1979) and Sidney Bloch and Peter Reddaway, Soviet Psychiatric Abuse (Boulder, Col., 1985). The Soviet account of their psychiatrists' withdrawal from the World Psychiatric Association may be read in "Soviet Psychiatrists Leave World Body," CDSP, XXXV, 13 (Apr. 27, 1983). One of the notable features of glasnost' has been the extensive self-criticism of psychiatric practices in the USSR. Cf. "How Psychiatry is Abused in the USSR," CDSP, XXXIX, 29 (Aug. 19, 1987); "Does Soviet Psychiatry Need a Tighter Rein?" CDSP, XXXIX, 46; Julia Wishnevsky, "Revelations of Corruption Among Soviet Psychiatrists" Radio Liberty Research (Feb. 12, 1987) and Peter Reddaway, "Does Moscow's Purge of Corrupt Psychiatrists Threaten the Psychiatric Gulag?" Radio Liberty Research (July 23, 1987). Also note Bill Keller, "Mental Patients in Soviet to Get New Legal Rights," New York Times (Jan. 5, 1988).

51. Works on women in Soviet society have not been lacking in the West. Those by Hansson and Liden and Lapidus have been cited above. Another is Gail W. Lapidus, Women in Soviet Society: Equality,

Development, and Social Change (Berkeley, Calif., 1979). CDSP has much to say on the subject. Recent articles in Radio Liberty Research by Julie Moffett include "Contraception in the Soviet Union," (July 15, 1985); "Sex Education and Attitudes Towards Sex in the USSR," (July 23, 1985); "The High Abortion Rate in the USSR" (Aug. 23, 1985.

For a recent account of the family see Peter H. Juviler, The Family in the Soviet System, published as #306 in The Carl Beck Papers by the University of Pittsburgh Center for Russian and East European Studies.

52. See Murray Feshbach, "The Age Structure of Soviet Population: Preliminary Analysis of Unpublished Data," Soviet Economy, I, 2 (1985). The young and elderly are frequent topics in Radio Liberty Research and CDSP since 1983. Cf. "Neglected Children: Making Amends" CDSP, XXXIX, 32 (Sept. 9, 1987); Aaron Trehub, "Children in the Soviet Union," Radio Liberty Research (Dec. 15, 1987).

Juvenile behavior, in particular, has been broadly covered, i.e. "Press Studies Moscow's Suburban Toughs," CDSP, XXXIX, 10 (Aprf. 8, 1987); and Valerii Konovalov, "Educational-Labor Colonies and the Problems of Reeducating Juvenile Deliquents," Radio Liberty Research (Nov. 17, 1987). Informal youth groups independent of Komsomol are discussed in Sergei Voronitsyn, "'Informal' Youth Groups in an Authoritarian Society," Radio Liberty Research (Nov. 20, 1987).

The elderly have often been discussed for their usefulness to society, i.e. "Employing Retirees, Caring for the Elderly," CDSP, XXXVI, 46 (Dec. 12, 1984); "Pensions: A Closer Link to Performance," CDSP, XXXVII, 31 (Aug. 28, 1985). Similarly, Stephen Sternheimer explores "The Vanishing Babushka: a Roleless Role for Older Soviet Women?" in Quality of Life in the Soviet Union, pp. 133-49. Proper housing for the elderly is a common theme for discussion in CDSP.

53. Treml's writings on alcohol have already been cited. The reader is also referred to Walter D. Connon, Deviance in Soviet Society (New York, 1972). CDSP has had broad coverage of alcohol, drugs, and prostitution since 1985. Cf. such recent accounts as "Soviet Drug Scene Get Heavy Coverage," CDSP, XXXIX, 2 (Feb. 11, 1987); "A Hard Look at Prostitution

in the USSR," <u>CDSP</u>, XXXIX, 11 (Apr. 15, 1987).

54. On law and order generally, see Peter H. Juviler, <u>Revolutionary</u> <u>Law</u> <u>and</u> <u>Order</u> (New York, 1976). <u>CDSP</u> has over the past several years carried diverse articles on abuses and the need for reform in the judicial system. Cf. "Courts Ordered to Stop Abusing the Law," <u>CDSP</u>, XXXVIII, 50 (Jan. 14, 1987) in which the supreme court took action against wrong convictions and inadequate investigations. The need to alter the roles of prosecutor and defense counsel has also been discussed.

55. The literature of dissent in the USSR is so vast as to require no listing here. A widely read account is Joshua Rubenstein, <u>Soviet</u> <u>Dissidents</u>: <u>Their</u> <u>Struggle</u> <u>for</u> <u>Human</u> <u>Rights</u> (Boston, 1980).

The reader might wish to consult Peter Reddaway, "Soviet Policies on Dissent and Emigration: The Radical Change of Course since 1979," KIRS Occasional Paper #192 (Washington, D.C., Aug. 28, 1984). The emergence of "informal groups" in the wake of glasnost' are particularly interesting. See Vera Tolz, "'Informal Groups' in the USSR" <u>Radio</u> <u>Liberty</u> <u>Research</u> (June 11, 1987); Vera Tolz, "'Informal Groups' Hold First Officially Sanctioned Conference," <u>Radio</u> <u>Liberty</u> <u>Research</u> (Sept. 23, 1987); and Julia Wishnevsky, "The Emergence of 'Pamyat' and 'Otechestvo'" <u>Radio</u> <u>Liberty</u> <u>Research</u> (Aug. 26, 1987). The <u>CDSP</u>, in the second half of 1987, <u>passim</u> carried numerous articles on informal groups and the demonstrations (i.e. Latvians and Crimean Tatars) they waged. See Lyudmila Alekseeva, "Public Unrest in the USSR," <u>Radio</u> <u>Liberty</u> <u>Research</u> (Sept. 9, 1985) for unrest before <u>glasnost'</u>.

Note also as a change of the times Felicity Barringer, "90 Meet in Moscow at Rights Seminar," <u>New</u> <u>York</u> <u>Times</u> (Dec. 12, 1987); Bill Keller, "Pravda Warns of Offenses by New Political Clubs," <u>New</u> <u>York</u> <u>Times</u> (Dec. 28, 1987); and Bill Keller, "For Soviet Alternative Press, Used Computer is New Tool," <u>New</u> <u>York</u> <u>Times</u> (Jan. 12, 1988). The latter, indeed, is indicative of some changes from the days of primitive <u>samizdat</u> carbons. But there are limits: see Julia Wishnevsky, "Western Radio Stations and Soviet Law," <u>Radio</u> <u>Liberty</u> <u>Research</u> (Jan. 16, 1985).

56. A standard work on contemporary Soviet education is Mervyn Matthews, Education in the Soviet Union: Policies and Institutions since Stalin (London, 1982). The notable educational reforms since this book's publication can be traced in CDSP, Radio Liberty Research, and releases of KIARS. Cf. in particular Sergei Voronitsyn, "Educational Reform on the Eve of the Central Committee Plenum," Radio Liberty Research (Dec. 23, 1987) and a summary in a KIARS Meeting Report of a presentation by Harley Balzer at the Kennan Institute Oct. 29, 1986 on the 1984 reform of general education and the 1986 reform of higher and specialized secondary education.

57. The classic account is Boris Komarov, The Destruction of Nature in the Soviet Union (White Plaines, N.Y., 1980), a broad indictment of Soviet environmental practices. Although there is still a mighty conflict between Soviet developers and environmentalists, the cause of the latter has received much publicity as evidenced by the numerous articles in CDSP over the past few years. Cf. Elizabeth Fuller, "Mass Demonstration in Armenia Against Environmental Pollution," Radio Liberty Research (Oct. 18, 1987).

Recent legislation and the prospects of more have also buttressed the environmentalists' cause.

58. The monuments theme has been embraced by Great Russian nationalists, as noted by Dunlop and Schmidt (see above), and as evidenced by the group called Pamiat, mentioned frequently in CDSP and Radio Liberty Research during 1987. Beyond that, there appears a genuine concern for deteriorating monuments and regrets for the destruction that occurred in the 1930s, during World War II, and in the Khrushchev years, especially to ancient churches. Recent legislation is intended to protect this heritage.

59. Despite an official policy of religous freedom, the state remains hostile to established religion as a competitor to the Party and ideology. CDSP has had many articles on the subject -- Islam, Orthodoxy, Protestant sects -- since 1983; moreover, Radio Liberty Research has had an extraordinary number of commentaries. That the forces of religion have persisted is evident in Oxana Antic, "What changes in Religious Legislation are Being Proposed by Soviet Citizens?" Radio Liberty Research (Nov. 11, 1987).

One of the most intensely debated subjects of the moment that of "God-seeking," especially among writers, in Soviet society. See, for example, "Yevtushenko Assesses Religion, Morality," CDSP, XXXVIII, 52 (Jan. 28, 1987); "'Gullible' Intellectuals Dabble in the Occult," CDSP, XXXVI, 33 (Sept. 12, 1984); and Oxana Antic, "Soviet Writers and the Search for God," Radio Liberty Research (May 26, 1987). These writings suggest that a religous revival may be occurring. Is it aided by glasnost'?

60. See, for example, "Bondarev: Russian Culture, Land in Peril," CDSP, XXXVIII, 32 (1986) and Vera Tolz, "The Morality Crisis in Soviet Society: Its Treatment in Samizdat and in the Official Press," Radio Liberty Research (Sept. 12, 1986). A greater tolerance for diversity in the arts appears a consequence of glasnost'. Cf. "Kommunist Sets Out New Cultural Policy," CDSP, XXXIX, 47 (Dec. 23, 1987).

Closely related to Bondarev's concern for Russia's inheritance is the crisis engendered by pervasive corruption. Once again, it is important to note that corruption is endemic in most societies; however, the builders of socialism in the USSR had hoped to spare its citizens that fate. Such has not been the case. Cf. Konstantin Simis, USSR: The Corrupt Society. The Secret World of Soviet Capitalism (New York, 1982) and Nicholas Lampert, Wistleblowing in the Soviet Union: Complaints and Abuses under State Socialism (New York, 1985). The literature is plentiful about corruption, the Second Economy, and theft of socialist property, particularly for the past few years in CDSP and Radio Liberty Research. The suggestion has been made that the "gulag" penchant for trimming and stealing has had a corrosive effect on society at large as a result of the substantial former inmate population unloosed upon it.

Cf., too, "Ligachev to Media: Don't Go Too Far," CDSP, XXXIX, 37 (Oct. 14, 1987); "Unofficial Groups Mushroom: What Limits?" CDSP, XXXIX, 39 (Oct. 28, 1987).

61. Gavril K. Popov, Professor of Economics at Moscow State University and an advocate of change, has recently called innovations in Soviet industry on January 1, 1988 a "fiction." Bill Keller, "A Gorbachev Ally Calls Latest Changes 'Fiction'" New York Times (Jan. 6, 1988).

62. See "Can Vested Interests Stall Restructuring?" <u>CDSP</u>, XXXIX, 3 (Feb. 18, 1987); "Stalinism Linked to Restructuring's Foes," <u>CDSP</u>, XXXIX, 18 (June 3, 1987).

The ouster of El'tsin is generally interpreted as a victory for those opposing broad changes under <u>perestroika</u>. See Elizabeth Teague, "Signs of a Conservative Backlash," <u>Radio Liberty Research</u> (Nov. 18, 1987); "Yeltsin ousted, His Faults Assailed, I and II, <u>CDSP</u>, XXXIX, 45, 46 (Dec. 9, 16, 1987); "El'tsin Sacked as Moscow Party Boss," <u>Radio Liberty Research</u> (Nov. 11, 1987). Hugo Young laments El'tsin's ouster in "The Triumph of Trumpery," <u>Manchester Guardian Weekly</u> (Jan. 3, 1988), 9.

63. Philip Taubman, "Gorbachev Sees Crucial Period for His Changes," <u>New York Times</u> (Jan. 13, 1987), and his follow-up, "Gorbachev: Middle Path," (Jan. 14, 1988). See also Taubman, "A Power Struggle Is Seen in Moscow," <u>ibid</u>. (Apr. 14, 1988).

64. See Flora Lewis, "Moscow at a Crossroads," <u>New York Times</u> Op. Ed. page (Dec. 12, 1987) and "A Different East-West Rivalry?" <u>Ibid</u>. (Jan. 15, 1988).

JUSTICE AND THE PALESTINIANS

Alfred G. Gerteiny
Professor of History
University of Bridgeport

With Art. 22 & 23 of the Covenant of the League, the Universal Declaration of Human Rights, the 1948 Convention on the Prevention and Punishment of the Crime of Genocide, the four basic Geneva Conventions of 1949 and the 1977 Geneva Protocols on victims of Armed conflicts, we have come a long way since customary international law was only minimally and indirectly concerned with human rights. Yet violations of human rights continue unabated in large segments of the political world. In the Middle East, one of the by-products of the conflict over Palestine is a situation where the human rights of the autochthonous are being violated, with little outcry heard here in the United States; indeed, despite legislation prohibiting aid to states violating human rights, Israel remains the largest recipient of U.S. foreign assistance. Does this constitute moral myopia or guilt by association?

There are, of course, special problems associated with conflicts involving at their core the issue of national liberation. Here, too often, governments ordinarily designate partisans as "terrorists" and therefore criminals and claim that different laws apply to them, that indeed the relevance of the laws of war are inappropriate in their case. We must vehemently disagree with this interpretation for it is precisely in these conflicts, where civilians, civilian sanctuaries and cultural centers become the targets of institutional violence, that the laws of war are most needed. It is with this in mind that the following article has been written; it is a plea for better justice not only to the Palestinians but to all destitute and subject peoples around the world. The article deals with violence ordinarily meted out by the Israeli military government in the occupied territories; indeed, no effort was made to capitalize on the even more heinous violation of international law during the Palestinian uprising of 1987-88.

The Palestine problem is multiphased, multidimensional and multifaceted. It is anchored in a bedrock of competing claims of sovereignty over the same territory by two main groups of people, one Palestinian Arab, the other Israeli Jewish. The first category is represented by a native population that has inhabited the land from time immemorial, often and periodically changing its religion to meet requirements imposed by successive invading masters. The claim of this population to the land of Palestine is no different from that of any autochthonous population to the territory they inhabit under International Law. Furthermore, this claim has been legitimized by international recognition, extended by an overwhelming majority of nation states, and confirmed by numerous actions by the United Nations. The second category is represented by a settlers' population with complex cultural-religious-emotional roots in and attachment to that same land. Their sovereignty over part of the land has been recognized by an ample number of nation states and is concretized by effective control over the territory.

In their struggle for exclusive or shared, partial or total title over Palestine the first group is aided and abetted by all Arabic-speaking countries and, to a somewhat lesser degree of militancy, by the Islamic and other Third World states. Generally, the capitalist and socialist worlds support "the legitimate rights of the Palestinian people" as well. The second group is aided and abetted by an overwhelming majority of Jews throughout the world; and it finds varying degrees of support and assistance from those nations where Jews, by virtue of their citizenship and militancy, exercise political power and influence. Among these the United States government is singularly important. To a lesser extent, Israel receives support from large segments of Christian fundamentalist groups in largely Protestant countries.

Successive military campaigns waged by the immediate protagonists in a war that began effectively in May 1948, have extended Israeli control over an area well beyond the original confines of the Zionist state as defined by the United Nations' Partition of Palestine Resolution of November 29, 1947, and in fact even beyond the totality of the territory considered by that resolution--including territories of adjacent states. Consequently, Israel today finds itself exercising control not only over the territory allocated to it by that resolution, but well beyond and over an alien population roughly equivalent to more than half the size of its own population. Given this situation, a relationship has developed between occupier and occupied that deserves consideration in light of existing international law and custom, taking into account both Israel's need for security and Arab civil and human rights. In Israel, particularly since the advent of the Likud coalition, extremism has prevailed in this context, resulting in a genocidal treatment of the subject population, which will be discussed in this paper. The Palestinian reaction to their subjugation or dispersion is too well publicized and will, therefore, not be submitted to either description or treatment in this paper. Suffice it to say that it consists of two methods; among the subjugated it is expressed by a generally ineffective, mostly subdued resistance, and among the dispersed by sporadic if not self-damaging terrorism. Let us then turn to the Israeli treatment of its subject people, which, by all accepted standards, is genocidal.

Indeed, the word that characterized the sanguinary rule of Ottoman Sultans, Russian Czars and Germany's Nazis continues unabated and undisturbed in many parts of the world today, with new, innocent targets being subjected to genocide. Sadly, some of the oppressors are members of formerly oppressed groups. Given the prevalence of this criminal situation in the world, Richard Rubenstein, the author of *After Auschwitz*, declared at the March 1975, New York City Conference on the Holocaust: "Perhaps we are at the beginning, not he end of the age of Genocide."[1]

One such nation evidently targeted for dissolution is the Palestinians, a people who are as old as History itself, pre-dating Judaism, Christianity and Islam, and who, at one time or another, espoused one or the other of these Abrahamic traditions.

Zionism, as practiced today by the Israeli hierarchy in the occupied territories, is to these Palestinians, and more recently, to a lesser extent, to Lebanese and Syrians, what Nazism was to the Jews of Europe--an ideology whose aim is to "purify" a state of undesirable Semites; its methods, however, are less obvious in that they involve not the immediate physical death of the gas chambers, but the slower, more pernicious method of mental death.[2]

The original, worthy dream of Zionism to spare the Jews from the intolerance, bigotry and pogroms of Eastern Europe has turned into a nightmare: a nightmare for Jews and Gentiles of good will; a nightmare according to which Zionism has, unwittingly perhaps, adopted Hitler's way of looking at things, Hitler's way of solving the problem of a troublesome and unwanted people--by destroying them.

So that there may be no misunderstanding, let us cite the essential elements of the Genocide Convention, approved by Resolution 260A (III) of the United Nations General Assembly on December 9, 1948, as well as its interpretation by its outstanding progenitor--Raphael Lemkin. The Genocide Convention is now incontestably an integral part of the customary phase of the Law of Nations. [3] It declares, _inter alia_: "Genocide, whether committed in time of peace or in time of war, is a crime under International Law which [adherent member States] undertake to prevent and punish." [4]

It defines genocide as "any of the following acts committed with intent to destroy, in whole or in part, a national, ethnical, racial or religious group as such." [5] (Now, it is exceedingly clear that Israel has been attempting to destroy the Palestinians as a people, as a nation, through a variety of means, some of which we shall describe later. In fact General Sharon's call for "purification," along with the assertion that Israel will pursue and destroy the "terrorists" to the far corners of the world, is a familiar call for genocide. The word "terrorists," let me remind you, is an Israeli euphemism for Palestinians. It seeks their dehumanization. It also seeks the conditioning of the world to thinking of the Palestinians only as criminals.)

The Convention goes on to list the acts that fall under the term Genocide. The intent, of course, has to be the destruction of a human group as such:

a. Killing members of the group.
b. Causing serious bodily or mental harm to members of the group.
c. Deliberately inflicting on the group conditions of life calculated to bring about its physical destruction [as such] in whole or in part.
d. Imposing measures intended to prevent births within the group.

206

        e. Forcibly transferring children of the
        group. [6]

Furthermore,   the   Convention   renders   punishable
"Genocide; conspiracy to commit genocide; direct and
public incitement to commit genocide; attempts to
commit genocide; complicity in Genocide." [7]

        Of course, as is customary, a Convention, in this
case the Genocide Convention, should be read with the
interpretation of its progenitor. With this in mind
we shall now consider the interpretation of Raphael
Lemkin:

        Generally   speaking,   Genocide   does   not
        necessarily mean the immediate destruction
        of a nation....It is intended, rather, to
        signify a coordinated plan of different
        actions aiming at the   destruction   of
        essential   foundations   of   the life of
        national groups, with the aim of annihilat-
        ing the groups themselves...Genocide has two
        phases: one, destruction of the national
        pattern of the oppressed group; the other,
        the imposition of the national pattern of
        the oppressor. This imposition, in turn,
        may be made upon the oppressed population
        which is allowed to remain, or upon the
        territory alone, after removal of   the
        population and the colonization of the area
        by the oppressor's own nationals. [8]

        This point of view is supported by Professor
Richard   Arens,   past   President   of   Survival
International USA,   an organization whose primary
concern is discovering, unmasking and exposing
genocide, who has published extensively on the
subject. Thus genocide "can take the form of what
anthropologists have called deculturation, and it can
involve the disintegration of some or all of the
following: political and social institutions, culture,
language, national feelings, religion, economic
stability, personal [and group security], liberty,
health [mental and physical], and dignity." [9]

        It certainly does not take arduous research and
reflection to recognize the manifestations of most of
these elements in the lands occupied or claimed by
Israel. And while the aim of the Israeli leadership
is not death per se, it is at least Palestinian
depopulation through constant official hounding and

its consequent generalized despair. Another scholar
of genocide, Chaim Shatan, notes that "there is
suggestive evidence that pervasive and persistent
despair kills through a complex psychic and hormonal
process which exhausts the cortex of the adrenal
glands and...destroys the ability to adapt to
stress....This 'psychic death,'" he continues, "is
real, not mysterious; it [despair] kills more surely
than malnutrition." [10] Indeed, recent evidence has
established a strong causal relationship between
psychological stress and serious psychological dis-
orientation, including psychosomatic symptomatology.[11]

Stephen Goroye, writing in the Washington
University Law Quarterly on "Mental Harm in the
Genocide Convention," has demonstrated unequivocally
that mental harm is not restricted to the imposition
of stupefying and mind-altering drugs, but extends to
deculturation as well.[12] The dislocation suffered by
the Palestinians in refugee camps, those who have been
evicted from their dwellings because of security
considerations and those whose houses have been
demolished under suspicion of having been used as
havens for people sought by Israeli authorities; the
constant and lengthy curfews, the separation of family
members, the night searches, the constant checking of
identity cards; and the general helpless situation of
a disarmed population subjected to incessant bullying
and shooting by armed alien settlers: all these nerve-
racking harassments are at least as devastating in
psychological terms as bodily harm and physical
torture, which the Israelis inflict on the
Palestinians as well.

According to Arens and Shatan, the term "broken
heart," a prevalent condition among the Palestinians,
"ceases to be a deeply felt metaphor and becomes the
product of a compelling and predictable interaction
between a [once] familiar [and harmonious] environment
that has become hostile and the cortical responses of
people within the victimized group." [13] The extreme and
dehumanizing conditions imposed upon the natives of
the occupied territories--where agglomerations,
including refugee camps, have been turned into
suffocating ghettos and reservations--produce a life-
threatening despair, which is a crime under
International Law and specifically constitutes
genocide according to the Convention. More
accurately, such systematic harassment, with a view to
discouraging the Palestinians from remaining on their
native land, with a view to depopulating the occupied

territories, constitutes genocide par excellence. If we used Dr. Lemkin's interpretation of the Genocide Convention, however, the lives the Palestinians of the occupied territories are forced to live are characterized by the disintegration and destruction that genocide produces.

Let us now discuss in greater detail selected practices constituting genocide according to Dr. Lemkin's interpretation. We have, of course, become conditioned, mentally numbed and emotionally desensitized so that most of us have come to accept these practices because they are justified in the name of security and because they are directed by what is purported to be a "civilized, democratic" society against the "subhuman, two-legged animals and terrorists"--the Palestinians. Let us also remember that the Nazis used similar terms to justify their dehumanizing of their Jews.

Eretz Israel, under the Begin and Shamir rule, includes, beyond the pre-June 1967 Israel, Cisjordan (the West Bank), the Gaza Strip and the Golan Heights. These have, for all practical purposes, been annexed, or to use the official terminology, "liberated." Indeed, the "liberated territories" need not be annexed, according to Israeli ruling circles, since they have always been deemed an integral part of Eretz Israel. A few more years of occupation in Southern Lebanon, which is the geographic extension of Galilee, and that territory, too, will have become "liberated." As a matter of fact, the irrigational network of Israel, as it stands now, has been designed to use the waters of Lebanon's Litani River.[14]

Eretz Israel, then, includes some 3.5 million souls, among them .5 million second-class Israeli non-Jews.[15] These constitute Israel's citizens. To them must be added approximately 1.5 million undesirable Palestinians, latent, potential or actual terrorists according to Israel and generally referred to as Arabs. Democracy is the privilege of Jewish citizens throughout Eretz Israel. The others do not enjoy this privilege; they are subject people in much the same way as the non-Greeks in ancient Sparta. Worse, they are, and are made to feel, undesirable.[16]

There is some explicit evidence that the undesirability of the Palestinians in Eretz Israel is not developmental--that is, resulting from the negative interaction between settlers and natives--but planned, in that it has always been considered indispensable to the erection a Jewish State. Here lies another genocidal factor. Witness the suggestion of Theodor Herzl, in his Diaries, to "spirit the Arabs across the border after denying them work in the Jewish State." Witness also the statement of Chaim Weizmann, his successor and first President of Israel, in Trial and Error, his fascinating diaries: "Palestine must become as Jewish as England is English." Let me also invoke the words of another great early Zionist, Joseph Weitz, the former Head of the Jewish Agency's Colonizing Department. He wrote in his Diaries, in 1940, "Between ourselves, it must be clear that there is no room for both people together in this country....the only solution is Palestine...without Arabs....And there is no way but to transfer the Arabs from here to neighboring countries; to transfer all of them; not one village, not one tribe should be left."

More recently, we have seen evidence of this policy of depopulation and dispersion in statements attributed to Ben-Gurion by Itshac Rabin (whose book was subsequently censored) during the 1948 year. Rabin reported that Ben-Gurion called on him to rid Galilee of the Palestinians. And, of course, we have the constant lament of Moshe Dayan about the undesirability of the Palestinians in the Occupied Territories. We also know about the Israeli sociological studies warning against the threat of "Levantinization of Israel," the inevitable consequence of the presence of Arabs there.

Better still are the demographic studies that describe the threat of an Arab majority in Israeli in the not-too-distant future if the Occupied Territories are annexed with their population. And how about General Sharon's "final solution of the terrorist problem" by means of a forcible dispersion of the Palestianians as far away as possible from Israel? Has he not called the operation ordered by him and carried out by his Phalangist henchmen in Sabra and Shatila "purification"? We also know, of course, that what Mr. Begin calls "full autonomy" for Judea and Samaria and the Gaza Strip is a process by which the land is actually separated from its native Palestinian population, the land being Israeli, the natives not.

These would be allowed to manage their civil affairs (and there lies his concept of autonomy--just

210

civil affairs). They would be allowed to remain in their ghettos, in their quasi Bantustan, under the constant watch of Israeli agents, so long as they desist from any political or cultural activity that may be construed as nationalistic. They would provide menial labor at rates well below Israeli wages. Should they fail to exhibit docility and submission to the Zionist masters, they would be subject to immediate deportation. Thus Begin's concept of autonomy for the Occupied Territories, based as it is on the separation of land from people, seeks de-Palestinization by depopulation and despair, and Judaization of the territories, an act of genocide under the Convention.

We are in the habit of condemning, as we must, the Soviet Union for the restrictions it imposes on those among its citizens who defy the totalitarian system. Should we not also condemn the Israeli government for similar treatment of its subject Palestinians and non-Jewish citizens?

Let us look more closely at Israel's treatment of its subject people. Habeas corpus does not apply to them. The territories are under a military government whose inhumane decrees apply to the native populations, not to the Jewish settlers. The former are subject to arrest and long incarceration if found with any sort of weapon; they are kept incommunicado and without benefit of counsel; they may have the house in which they dwell razed with only a few minutes' notice.

Conversely, the Jewish settlers are issued submachine guns which they carry at all times and use liberally on youngsters, boys and girls suspected of being disrespectful or of throwing stones in defiant gestures. These settlers are never punished for shooting and killing Palestinians.[17] Should any one of the settlers, however, be hit by a stone, the army of occupation joins in the posse, shooting and ultimately arresting and physically abusing large numbers of suspects. The more primitive forms of torture during the subsequent interrogations include beatings on the back, feet and sexual organs. Detainees are forced to stand naked for long periods exposed to heat or cold, sometimes under a cold dripping shower. Their sleep is often disrupted by bright lights. They are held in minuscule cells, living with the stench of their own excrement.

211

Often the army barges, at any time of the night, into Palestinian dwellings of youngsters suspected of throwing stones at Israelis or of exhibiting nationalistic feelings with Palestinian flags or literature. The suspects are then carried away under the horrified and helpless eyes of their families and held incommunicado, sometimes for weeks. [18]

Article 78 of the Fourth Geneva Convention[19] permits an occupying power to use internment or house arrest "for imperative reasons of security," provided that each such case is reviewed every six months. For persons detained under authority of Israel's Emergency Defense Regulations a review proceeding is an exercise in futility, as neither the detainee nor his counsel is permitted to know the grounds upon which suspicion rests.

Town regulation orders are liberally decreed. These forbid people to leave their villages and homes for indefinite periods of time, even if their livelihood requires such travel. People are forced to report to distant police stations every day at specific times. These dictatorial practices are undertaken allegedly "for the security of the State of Israel," despite the fact that most of those placed under restriction are never charged with committing an illegal act. Town restriction orders serve as tools to create despair. More palpably, they are used to deny freedom of expression. They are directed toward newspaper editors, mayors and national Palestinian figures. Denials of free expression are most acute in the educational field, especially with respect to the three universities on the West Bank--Bir Zeit, An Najah, and Bethlehem. These are often subjected to forcible closure. The faculty and students are subjected to constant and varying degrees of harassment. Indeed, those members of the faculty who refuse to sign "commitments" which place unacceptable limits on their right of expression are deported. Foreign faculty invited to teach at these universities must sign a pledge not to engage in any activity, including academic activity, that may suggest sympathy for the Palestinian national cause. Failure to sign such a document results in denial of association with the college. [20]

Furthermore, these institutions have lost their tax-exempt status, and Israeli taxes now take a large percentage of their budget. Intense censorship places many intolerable restrictions on academic freedom.

Faculty and student research papers and books, including imported books, are censored and some 1500 of these have been totally banned. Foreigners of Palestinian origin interested in teaching in the Occupied Territories are denied the necessary work and residence permits. Student are very often arrested, interrogated, detained and mistreated, usually without being charged with a specific crime. Their books and notes are scrutinized and sometimes destroyed.

The press is also subjected to censorship. Arabic papers are severely censored, closed down completely or simply seized. Editors and correspondents are subjected to town restriction orders, which adversely affects the quality and effectiveness of the profession.

The right to political expression is also denied. There have been no local elections in the Occupied Territories since 1976. Most mayors and members of municipal councils have been dismissed and replaced by Israeli appointees and village leagues. Political parties and meetings are banned and any political expression, even symbolic, is prohibited. In short, the Israeli authorities are using thought-control tactics, civil and intellectual restrictions, beating, torture and the like to terrorize the inhabitants into submission or emigration.

Furthermore, terrorization is obtained by the imposition of collective punishment, in contravention to Article 33 of the Fourth Geneva Convention. In fact, the Convention adopted Article 33 as a direct reaction to similar practices under Hitler's Third Reich.

The Israeli military government in the occupied territories uses three forms of collective punishment:

1. Curfews: Whole towns, villages and refugee camps are often placed under curfew as a reprisal for demonstrations or other "security incidents." These curfews often last as long as 24 hours per day for several days. Some agglomerations have been placed on curfew for weeks at a time, with occasional brief intervals for minimal shopping.

2. Demolition of houses: Homes are indiscriminately blown up on suspicion that one of the inhabitants is connected with "anti-Israeli

activities." Since 1967 over 20,000 demolitions have taken place.

3. **Mass arrests and round-ups**: Hundreds of people are routinely arrested and detained, or forced to perform corvees. Such incidents occur following demonstrations, which are forbidden. Often the demonstrators are fired at, resulting in casualties including death. We are all appalled when the Polish authorities break up Solidarity demonstrations by using water cannon (they used gunfire only once or twice); yet we take it for granted when Israeli authorities kill demonstrating children. On the other hand, when Jewish settlers demonstrate or even shoot and kill Palestinians, they are seldom arrested. If they are apprehended they are usually exonerated.[21]

In an article published in the New York Times of September 12, 1982, reference is made to a study conducted by Jerusalem's former Deputy Mayor, Meron Benvinisti and eight other specialists and financed principally by the City University of New York's Institute for Middle East Peace and Development.[22] The study details the massive Israeli seizure of Palestinian land in the West Bank and explains the various methods used for that purpose. The New York Times article, headlined "Israel Dramatically Changing Face of West Bank," makes it plain that Israel has already Judaized the West Bank in contravention to the Camp David Agreement and International Law, the aim being to squeeze the Palestinians out of their native land, a genocidal practice under the relevant Convention. By September 1982, the Benvinisti study disclosed, 65 per cent, or 942,000 of the 1.4 million acres, of the West Bank had been seized and converted to Israeli ownership. Mr. Benvinisti remarks that this is "just the beginning...because the Israeli Government has adopted, since 1979, a new approach toward land ownership, which has enabled it to seize practically any land needed for unlimited Jewish settlement in the West Bank."[23] We should realize that this policy has continued, has even been accelerated, after the Camp David Agreement on "total autonomy" for the West Bank and Gaza, raising serious doubt as to Israel's good faith in the negotiations.

The Data Base Project reports that since Israel captured the West Bank in 1967, seizure, or Judaization, of most of the land was effected by seven different methods, to satisfy Israeli legal requirements. It must be recalled, however, that such

214

arbitrary deprivation of land runs counter to Article 17 of the Universal Declaration of Human Rights; it also runs counter to the Fourth Geneva Convention. Successive Israeli governments seized "absentee property" and leased it to settlers. They seized land registered as state domain, in other words in the name of the Treasury of Jordan or of the King, and leased it to settlers. They requisitioned land for military purposes and likewise leased it for settlement. Perhaps the most extreme among the militant Jewish settlers have created, near Hebron, the town of Qiryat Arba on such land requisitioned "temporarily" for security reasons. Other areas were expropriated for "vital and military requirements." In two per cent of the cases the Israeli government reintegrated land that had been owned by Jews before Israeli's creation.

When in 1979 Israel's Supreme Court ruled that the creation of civilian settlements on land requisitioned for military and security considerations was illegitimate, the Begin government invoked Article 103 of the Land Code of the defunct Ottoman Empire, claiming that Israel, as a successor state, had a right to do so.

While the seizure of land in Cisjordan has accelerated since 1979, the practice was begun under the Labor Party's leadership in 1967 by the issuance of decrees such as Military Government Order #291 of 1968, which also curtailed the natural right of the native Palestinians to purchase land or expand their property. Today only Jews can lease or buy land seized by the State of Israel. Furthermore, Military Government Orders put severe limits on what the Palestinians can do on their own property; witness, for instance, Order 1039, which prohibits Arabs from planting eggplant and tomatoes, among other vegetables, on their own land without prior military government authorization.[24] This order has been issued by the authority of a State which prides itself on having otherwise "turned a desert into a garden."

Mr. Benvinisti's study indicated that by 1982 most of the West Bank was in the process of becoming State of Israel's Domain by the following simple procedure. Israeli authorities post public notices that a certain number of plots are in the process of being declared State property. The notice further states that the local inhabitants have 21 days to file their objections. But when they do so, their appeal, instead of being heard by a civil court, is considered by an administrative appeals commission whose chairman is a legal advisor to the Land Authority. This procedure, curiously, was upheld by Israel's Supreme Court, thus legitimizing the Government's claim that all Jewish settlements in the West Bank are legal, since they are built on State land.

The situation on land-use planning is equally hopeless for the Palestinians. Even before the Begin coalition's access to power, the Labor Government prohibited Arab buildings beyond the confines of clearly defined Arab agglomerations and municipalities. The Likud Government went even further by declaring all "unclaimed land," that is, most of the West Bank, off-limits to Arabs whether for residence or business. Any infraction of this law carries heavy fines and demolition of structures. Meanwhile, Jewish home and business building is proceeding posthaste to create _faits accomplis_ and forestall any possible restitutions. Such behavior surpasses the ukases under the worst of the anti-Semitic East European governments of old.

Maps and master plans clearly show those areas of the West Bank purified of Arabs--the Nazis would have used the term "_Araberrein_." These maps show vast regions, including most of Jerusalem, designated as "exclusively for Jews." In their midst, Arab agglomerations and neighborhoods seem as though they are being squeezed out. Indeed, this policy reminds one of South Africa's Bantustan practices under the apartheid system.

The Data Base Project found that despite general Israeli fear that the annexation of the occupied territories will surely lead to an Arab majority in a Greater Israel, the actual demographic trends indicate a gradual Jewish gain on the Arabs, as the Arabs have been moving out of the territory. Here again we see the effectiveness of Israel's genocidal policy of depopulation by sowing fear, despair, deculturation and political and economic strangulation. In the West Bank, the average annual growth rate for Palestinians stands at 1.4 per cent, against 2.5 per cent for Jews in Greater Israel. For a people who rate among the most prolific in the world, this rate of growth is anomalous and, again, indicative of the efficacy of Israel's genocide in the West Bank. The study also shows that in the period between 1968 and 1980, over 100,000 Palestinians left the territory. Further scrutiny indicates that the flight of Palestinians is dramatically increasing. In 1980 alone, the natural increase of 20,000 in the Palestinian population was offset by over 17,000 departures. Israeli settlements in the West Bank numbered 120 at the close of 1982. This, the expropriation of land and prohibitions imposed on the natives to use living space, renders the West Bank virtually closed to Palestinians. Most of it has, in fact, become Araberrein.

A brief legal summation on the question of Israeli expropriation of Palestianian land and of settlements on the West Bank is imperative. Article 49 of the Geneva Civilians Convention, to which Israel became a state party on July 6, 1951, prohibits the transfer of an occupant's own population into occupied territory. The Israeli government's argument that the Convention does not apply because Jordan is not the reversioner is supporter by neither the text nor the negotiating history of the Convention. Begin's contention that Israel's claims to the West Bank are at least as good as those of Jordan is irrelevant. W.T. Mallison, Professor and Director of International Law Programs at George Washington University, argues in this context that "as long ago as the Civil War, the U.S. Government claimed to be the legitimate sovereign of the entire country but applied the humanitarian law of occupation to territory it recovered from the Confederate States....In addition, application of this law has never depended on the aggressive or defensive character of an armed conflict, although the Nazis did and now the Israelis claim the contrary." Furthermore:

> customary law, as set forth as early as 1833 by Chief Justice Marshall in United States vs. Perchemen and as codified in Article 46 of the regulations annexed to The Hague Conventions of 1899 and 1907, forbids the taking of private property by an occupying power. Article 55 states that the occupying power is only the administrator and usufructuary of public property and has only limited and temporary rights, and Article 56 includes the property of municipalities as private property.

Thus, Professor Mallison comments: "Even at the time of The Hague Conventions there was no property in occupied territory that could be taken by an occupying power under the established and customary law." Indeed, he points out that Israel's Supreme Court has stated "in the Elon Moreh case that the Hague Law is now binding on Israel as universal customary law." [25]

Basically, therefore, the conclusion from this quick summary of the relevant law is that Israeli settlements and seizure of land in the Occupied Territories not only constitute genocide but also are violative of conventional International law, and that Israel is legally bound by the Geneva Convention on Civilians. Indeed, Dr. Nathan Feinberg, professor emeritus of international law at Hebrew University, has decisively rejected the legal arguments of the Israeli authorities on the subject.

The Israeli government claims that the abridgment of civil and human rights in the Occupied Territories is necessitated by security requirements. Further, it rejects the contention by specialists and human rights bodies that such severe restrictions represent contraventions to International Law. The situation is additionally complicated by that government's affirmation that the West Bank has been "liberated," that it is not occupied and that it forms an intrinsic part of Eretz Israel; its non-Jewish population remain aliens. An equivalent situation involves the Syrians of the annexed Golan Heights. It may soon apply to an indefinitely occupied Southern Lebanon.

Obviously, Israel may not, with impunity, acquire territory through conquest; it may not differentiate arbitrarily between land and people on religious and cultural grounds without incurring charges and accusations of discrimination and violation of human rights and without expecting both passive and active resistance from the local populations. It cannot systematically decree rules through its military government destined to discourage populations from remaining on their native land without having its inhumane policy termed genocidal.

Israel may not pick and choose among the various United Nations resolutions concerned with the Palestinian problems; indeed, it may not arbitrarily choose parts of resolutions only and reject the remainder while claiming the United Nations to be anti-Semitic and therefore unfit to deal with the Arab-Israeli problem. It will either have to respect General Assembly Resolution 181 in its entirety or desist from invoking that part of the partition resolution calling for the establishment of a Jewish state as legitimizing its existence, as it does in its

218

Declaration of Independence. 26 Furthermore, if Israel's policy seeks acceptance within the Middle East, it should not exclude itself from it; as a transplanted organ in the Middle East body Israel must be compatible with that body or expect rejection.

Indubitably, the Palestinian leadership and its Arab supporters, by originally rejecting Resolution 181 and vowing to put an end to the State of Israel, have contributed to Israel's paranoia; indubitably such negativism, no matter how understandable and legitimate, has fueled the maximalist designs in Israel. The same is true of the ensuing frustration-and-despair-caused terrorism carried out by Palestianian maximalists against Israel.

What then is the solution to that cycle of blunders and counter-blunders, to that seemingly intractable dilemma? Do freedom and identity for either Israeli or Palestinian necessitate danger and expulsion for the other? The answer is a qualified no. For one thing, all Israelis and all Palestinians are not maximalists in their attitude, needs and requirements, even though they seem to be dominated by such leaders. On the other hand, the answer hinges on a certain number of premises, including attitudinal change, which may prove difficult to obtain.

Above all, the Arab-Israeli dispute must be removed from U.S. internal politics. It is obvious that only a highly emotional minority in the United States takes this dispute to heart. This vocal minority, by virtue of this monopoly, imposes its views on the politicians. These politicians should be equally concerned about the wishes of the silent majority, which is fairer in its assessment of the needs and requirements of the situation in the Middle East and more widely representative of the views of the people of the United States.

United States policies should be more concerned with the issue of justice in the matter than with the pressures of the lopsided situation described in the previous paragraph. The lessons of Iran and Lebanon should teach us that obstinacy in supporting a regime against the majority wishes of an allied nation leads to disaster. Such a lesson must be translated at the regional level. For, indeed, our support of Israel's whims, right or wrong, for internal political gains, against the requirements of justice as perceived by liberal elements in Israel and the majority of the

Arab peoples, is likely to perpetuate the dispute, increasingly radicalizing the regions against American interests and providing opportunity for the Soviet Union to prevail in an area where she is not otherwise welcomed. Rationally, therefore, our concern in global politics dictates a change in attitudes and policies.

Second, we must officially open channels of communication with the PLO because it represents the only Palestinian accepted leadership available, and the basis of the problem at hand is the question of Palestine-Israel. Recognition of and dealings with the PLO would humanize that organization, providing it with an alternative to the terror which is, after all, the only language available to the dispossessed, vilified and ignored people. Terror is, above all, a cry seeking recognition by affirmation.

Third, Syria cannot be ignored either, and its views and wishes must be aired and taken into account by all parties to the ultimate settlement. Indeed, Syria, by virtue of history, culture and geography, is a party to the dispute. Fourth, the Soviet Union, with a border only 250 miles from the contested territory, must be a party to the agreement if we do not want it to act as a spoiler. An agreement settling the dispute as envisaged below is likely to be acceptable to the Soviet Union and is even more likely to help the U.S. in its Middle Eastern concerns.

Fifth, the spirit of General Assembly Resolution 181 must be reaffirmed; its relevance concerning the legitimacy of Israel and of Palestine must be reconfirmed and accepted by the protagonists. The shifts from acceptance to rejection by Israel and from rejection to acceptance by the Palestinians must be reconsidered in the interest of peace. Indeed, early in 1949 a conference of the United Nations Conciliation Commission was held at Lausanne, attended by representatives of the United States, France and Turkey; it resulted in an agreement, reached May 12 of that year, to negotiate borders on the basis of Resolution 181. Unfortunately, Israel, which had extended its control over a territory fifty per cent larger than that assigned to it by that resolution, rejected that agreement. [27]

Sixth, the question of Jerusalem must be resolved in the context of the spirit of the recommendation of the special commission established by Resolution 181 to consider that question. That resolution called for the election by the General Assembly of a five-member commission with exclusive representation from states not directly involved in the conflict to produce a detailed proposal for a permanent international régime for the Jerusalem area. According to the recommendations, Jerusalem was to be divided into two sections, one to be administered by an international body under the United Nations. Such a solution, or one inspired by it and accepted by the parties, is indispensable to peace and security and these, in turn, are sine qua non to mutual acceptance and respect.

Seventh, until peace comes to the area and a Palestinian state is allowed to coexist side by side with Israel, it is incumbent upon the community of nations to see that Israel replaces its genocidal rules in the Occupied Territories by new ones insuring the protection of the alien civilian populations in accordance with recognized International law and custom. In this context, a balance between respect for human rights and the requirements of security must be struck, [29] as conceived by the two main international instruments concerned with this issue, The Hague Regulations of 1907[30] and the Geneva Convention of 1949.[31] The necessity for the occupier to preserve a decent vie publique is indispensable to future harmonious relations between the protagonists.

Eighth, Israel must immediately freeze the erection of Jewish settlements in the occupied areas, in accordance with the unanimous wishes of the community of nations and the requirements of International Law and customs. The establishment of Jewish settlements exacerbates the relations between occupiers and occupied; it indicates an unwillingness to recognize the existence of rights for the Palestinian people; it confirms the perception that Israel is expansionist; it negates the contention that Israel seeks peace through accommodation; it dehumanizes both Israelis and Palestinians by subordinating the human element to ideological imperatives.

Ninth, Israel must, prior to negotiations leading to a final settlement, humanize its occupation in the territories acquired by force. Such a measure could be obtained by ceasing to discriminate in law among the inhabitants according to their religions and

221

national identities. A single legal system--except perhaps in personal matters--applying to natives and settlers would leave a definite mellowing effect on the severity of laws and a general salutary effect on inter-community relations--a sine qua non to Israel's ultimate acceptance in the Middle East and, therefore, to inter-community, regional and international peace. A single law in the Occupied Territories would also frustrate the expansion of the settlements.

The Israeli government has made much hay of the contention that the West Bank has been liberated, that as it has "always been part of Eretz Israel" it need not be annexed formally. International Law, however, makes it very clear that occupation of an alien country is characterized by the establishment of some kind of administration there that is separate from the legitimate government of the occupier. It further states that such administration neither displaces nor transfers sovereignty. Such transfer may only occur by official treaty, official annexation without treaty, an illegal procedure, or extension of the occupier's laws, including that of nationality over the territory and its inhabitants.[32]

Tenth, the Palestine Liberation Organization must openly and firmly stand against all forms of terrorism in this transitional stage. It must opt for a diplomatic solution. Its position must be strengthened by a league of Arab states that for once would have an interest in a just and practical solution to the Palestine-Israel problem rather than in furthering particular national interests in the cause of an illusive Arab unity. Ultimately, of course, peace and security in this hub of the world would work in the interests of all parties. It would, if nothing else will, minimize if not altogether eliminate terrorism for any side. Indeed, the force of arms will neither insure peace among the regional protagonists nor bring about an end to terrorism. In fact, violence only begets violence. If there is to be a genuine and permanent peace between Israel and her neighbors, the minimal needs and requirements of all the protagonists must be satisfied. In this context the following principles are most important:

a. An Israel within secure, well defined and recognized boundaries.

A cornerstone of Security Council resolutions 242 and 338 is an Israel that is geographically defined

222

once and for all. Such agreed-upon definition is indispensable because it will abort the natural tendency of a geographically undefined state to expand, seeking new and ostensibly more favorable boundaries. It will also establish beyond contest the reciprocal areas of sovereignty, eliminating border disputes. It will allay the fears of Israel's neighbors regarding maximalist Zionist designs, such as an eventual Israel "from the Nile to the Euphrates," and allow them to sell peace to their own populations.

A well defined Israel at peace and in cooperative relations with its neighbors will minimize the need for military expenditure, allowing that state to recover some semblance of solvency and therefore dignity.

The frontiers before the 1967 war, with minor and reciprocal adjustments, are at this point in history the most realistic for Israel and her neighbors. Thus for Israel they represent an approximately fifty per cent accretion over the area originally recommended by the 1947 UN Partition Resolution and specifically accepted by the nascent state as evident in Israel's independence proclamation:

> This recognition by the United Nations of the right of the Jewish people to establish their State is irrevocable....Accordingly...by virtue of our natural and historic right and on the strength of the United Nations General Assembly, [we] hereby declare the establishment of a Jewish state in Eretz-Israel, to be known as the State of Israel. [33]

In order to insure the economic viability of that state, allay fears of expansionism beyond the borders and regularize the situation of Jews abroad whose loyalties have come under severe questioning, the laws of return and of citizenship should be amended to apply only to Jewish victims of persecution abroad.

On the other hand, Israel must provide for compensation to or repatriation of Palestinian refugees, in accordance with UN General Assembly Resolution 194 (III) of November 19, 1948.[34] This provision should be subject to a statute of limitations.

b.   A Sovereign Palestine within secure, well defined
      and recognized boundaries.

      It   must be clear that no solution to the
Palestine problem could be reached without a sovereign
Palestinian state, in accordance not only   with
Resolution 181, but also with previous partition
proposals (Peel in 1937 and Woodhead in 1938).
Furthermore,   if,   as   Israel's   declaration   of
independence deems, Resolution 181 is "irrevocable" as
it applies to one part of Palestine, the Jewish State,
does it not ipso facto make sense to deem   it
irrevocable for the other part?   That the Palestinian
people should have for a time refused to accept the
amputation of part of their territory does in no way
diminish their rights over the remaining part.

      The whole community of nations, and now a growing
number of people in Israel and the United States,
recognizes the need for and accepts the legitimacy of
a sovereign independent Palestinian   state.   The
Palestine Liberation Organization, furthermore, has
indicated willingness to negotiate with Israel a
mutual recognition based on that principle.

      A sovereign independent Palestine would include
East Jerusalem, the West Bank and the Gaza Strip;
contact between the two main territories would be
insured along agreed-upon highways patrolled by joint
motorized police.   Highway maintenance would   be
jointly borne.

      The state would have its own security and defense
establishment.   The quality and quantity of the armed
forces would be defined by a regional agreement.
Besides insuring the security of the state, this
establishment would also prevent illegal incursions
and excursions across the borders by terrorists, in
cooperation with neighboring security forces.

      The Palestinian citizens should be allowed to
elect their own leaders and set up a governmental
system compatible with their wishes and inclinations.
Such government would function under a constitution
that would replace the temporary and now obsolete
National Charter.

      The   Jewish   settlers would be given   the
opportunity to become Palestinian citizens or be
repatriated.   All Palestinians in the diaspora would

224

be granted a right of return subject to a statute of limitations.

The economy of Palestine would be based on tourism, off-season agriculture, light and assembly industry, foreign (mostly Arab) investments and contributions from diaspora relatives. A common market with Jordan, Israel, and Lebanon is indispensable. Perhaps Syria, Egypt and the Arab Oil states may be included in the future.

c. Restitution of Syrian, Egyptian and Lebanese territory and demilitarization of Sinai and the Golan Heights.

No lasting peace between Israel and its neighbors is possible so long as territories continue to be held in contravention to International Law and so long as Israel continues to feel threatened by her two mightiest neighbors. Territorial restitution is embodied in all United Nations resolutions concerned with Arab-Israeli conciliation. The third paragraph of the preamble of Security Council Resolution 1242 stresses "that all member states in their acceptance of the Charter of the United Nations have undertaken a commitment to act in accordance with Art. 2 of the Charter which outlaws war and the use of force in the settlement of international dispute," thus restating the obligations of the parties to the Kellogg-Briand Pact of 1928, itself enforced by the Nuremberg and other war crimes tribunals following World War II. The preamble of Security Council Resolution 242, furthermore, refers to the Charter of the United Nations, which was accepted "unreservedly" by Israel upon that state's admittance to membership in the United Nations,[35] and emphasizes "the inadmissibility of the acquisition of territory by war."

Restitution of the territories occupied by Israel since 1967, at least, is an indispensable legal, psychological and political condition for peace, security and normalization in the area. Demilitarization of strategic areas and reduction of armaments represents another important cornerstone to security and peace. The demilitarization of Sinai has already been obtained through the Camp David Accords. Indubitably, it has contributed to the peace process; a similar situation involving a restituted Golan Heights is a sine qua non to establishing feelings of security in northern Israel.

d.   Neutralization of Palestine, Israel, and Jordan.

In addition and as a complement to demilitarization of Sinai and the Golan Heights, a neutralization treaty patterned after the Austrian model should insure the inviolability of Palestine, Israel, Jordan and Lebanon. These four relatively equivalent states need not be burdened by debilitating military budgets. Furthermore, their neutralization will contribute to defusing the reciprocal paranoia that poisons international relations in the area. The neutralization of what may be called the Greater Holy Land should be guaranteed unconditionally, irrevocably and perpetually by the United Nations generally and the great powers particularly. As in the case of Switzerland, perpetual neutrality should allow the Greater Holy Land member states to erect mutually-agreed-upon defensive establishments in the context of a defensive alliance.

e.   Association of the Greater Holy Land.

An ultimate confederation on the Helvetian model would be a welcome complement to perpetual neutralization among the three states of the Greater Holy Land. Such a confederation would be enhanced by a defensive alliance, an economic union, a common market and a single currency; it may also constitute itself as a duty-free zone within the Middle East.

There would be many advantages to a confederation. Above all it would give a sense of depth to small, virtually indefensible states; it would preserve local laws, culture and customs within each member state while creating freedom of movement everywhere, thus respecting the Zionist concept of a Jewish state at the infra level while creating a unitary system at the supra level. It would bring back together the original mandate area by including Jordan and give a sense of security to the Christians of Lebanon through the political weight of the Jews and other Christians in Jordan and Palestine.

But such an ideal solution is most certainly utopian at this point; instead, an intermediate Benelux-type association, provided that good will exists, is probably feasible and desirable. Its objective would be to bring about a total circulation of persons, goods, capital and services. A coordinated policy in the economic, financial and social fields and a common policy with regard to foreign trade would equally be instituted, and the day-to-day operations of the association would be conducted by a permanent General Secretariat. The executive authority of the organization would rest with a Committee of Ministers meeting quarterly.

A confederal labor-sharing convention would regularize the labor market, creating a richer, more diversified pool of workers.

A human and civil rights convention would establish commissions to regulate, safeguard and supervise the treatment of all member states' citizens wherever they may reside or work.

f. <u>The</u> <u>status</u> <u>of</u> <u>Lebanon.</u>

The Lebanese problem seems as intractable as the Palestine-Israel conundrum. Its solution, nevertheless, is equally possible, given good will and reasonableness. Furthermore, peace and normality in Lebanon are indispensible to security and harmony in the whole Levant. In the search for peace in that tormented country, the wishes and interests of its various communities as well as those of Syria must be taken into account. Those of the great powers should be subordinated to them. In our opinion, a solution on the Helvetian model, including neutralization, would be most appropriate. The achievement such a settlement could be enhanced by some of kind of economic union with either Syria or the Greater Holy Land.

CONCLUSION

The cycles of unrest and violence, ushered in in the Near East following the dismemberment of the Ottoman Empire at the end of World War I and the ensuing Balkanization of this part of the world by Great Britain and France through the League of Nations, an organization they for all practical purposes controlled, cannot be solved by force of arms. Furthermore, the superpower involvement in it threatens a wider cataclysmic Armageddon spelling the end of the human species. A solution is imperative. It lies in the recognition of the danger at hand, of the mutual interests and rights of all concerned, and of mutual recognition, the whole leading to positive negotiations among all the protagonists without any exclusion whatever, under the auspices of the United Nations, which, in this case at least, is the successor to the League of Nations in whose womb the Middle East problem was conceived.

Peace is indeed conceivable. But only good will, mutual respect and cooperation would make it possible. The road to a solution based on the prescribed formula could be long and tortuous; but in the end the rewards would be redeeming to humanity as a whole. In the area where the present prevailing civilization and conscience find their roots, however, hatred would give way to love; intolerance, genocide and terrorism to ethnic and religious tolerance and mutual respect, security and tranquility; suspicion to trust; disharmony, division and greed to unity in diversity and to sharing and cooperation. Basically and ultimately the three Abrahamic faiths would finally fulfill, in the Greater Holy Land, their destiny to create a "city of God."

Without peace, however, without the acceptance of its need and possibility, without the tangible preliminary steps of mutual recognition and acceptance, the prevailing cycle of mutual denial, violence and hatred will continue to exacerbate the elements that would eventuallly lead to an ultimate apocalyptic world conflageration.

NOTES

1

Report in <u>The New York Times</u>, March 7, 1975.

2

Israel has been repeatedly condemned by international human rights organizations for its treatment of Palestinians; most recently, the United Nations Human Rights Commission, meeting in Geneva, adopted two condemnatory resolutions: one for Israeli settlement policy in the West Bank and Gaza, the other for "inhuman treatment" of the population of Syria's occupied Golan Heights. Report in N.Y. <u>Daily News</u>, February 24, 1984.

3

"Law making treaties create general norms for future conduct of the parties in terms of legal propositions....The Genocide Convention of 1948...[is an example] of this type....Such treaties are in principle binding only on parties, but the number of parties, the explicit acceptance of rules of law, and in some cases, the declaratory nature of the provisions produce a strong law-creating effect at least as great as the general practice considered sufficient to support a customary rule." (I. Brownley, <u>Principles of Public International Law</u> [Oxford: Clarendon Press, 1973], p. 12.) See also Sohn and Buergenthal, <u>International Protection of Human Rights</u>, pp. 1284 and 1300-22.

4

United Nations General Assembly, 78 UNTS 277 (1951).

5

Ibid.

6

Ibid.

7

Ibid.

8

Raphael Lemkin, <u>Axis Rule in Occupied Europe</u> (New York: Carnegie Endowment for International Peace, 1944), p. 79.

9

Richard Arens, ed., <u>Genocide in Paraguay</u> (Philadelphia: Temple University Press, 1976), p. 137.

10

Chaim Shatan, "Genocide and Bereavement," in ibid., p. 116.

11

See D. Davies, <u>The Last of the Tasmanians</u> (London: Trinity Press, 1972); B. Bettleheim, "Individual and Mass Behavior in Extreme Situations," <u>Journal of Abnormal and Social Psychology</u>, 38 (1943), 417; and C. Bendy, "Problems of Internment Camps," in ibid., 453.

12

See S. Gorove, "Mental Harm in the Genocide Convention," <u>Washington University Law Quarterly</u>, 1951, p. 17.

13

See Richard Arens, op. cit., p. 138, and, for further cooroboration, A.H. Crisp and R.R. Priest of the Department of Psychiatry at St. George's Hospital Medical School, London, in "Psychoneurotic Status During the Year Following Bereavement," <u>Journal of Psychosomatic Research</u>, 16 (1973), 351.

14

See Thomas R. Stauffer, "Price of Peace, Spoils of War," in <u>American Arab Affairs</u>, 1 (Summer, 1982), pp. 43-54.

15

See David K. Shipler, "Jews and Arabs of Israel: Worlds that Don't Mingle," and "Melting Pot is not Goal," <u>The New York Times</u>, December 27, 1983; also, in same issue, "In Textbooks, Stereotypes of Arabs." See also Shipler, "Arabs and Jews of Israel: The Bigotry Runs Deep," <u>The New York Times</u>, December 28, 1983, and "Israeli Arabs: Scorned, Ashamed and 20th Class," <u>The New York Times</u>, December 29, 1983.

16
Ibid.

17
David K. Shipler, "Israel Admits Laxity on Offenses by Settlers," The New York Times, February 8, 1984.

18
For a sampling of reports on dehumanizing the illegal treatment of Palestinians under Israeli rule, see Shipler, "Boys in West Bank Arrested at Night for Weeks of Questioning by Israelis," The New York Times, February 27, 1982; "Gulf of Bitterness Divides West Bank Jews and Arabs," ibid., September 13, 1982; The Sunday Times (London), June 18, 1977; Felicia Langer, With My Own Eyes (London: Ithica Press, 1974); Swiss League of Human Rights, Violations of Human Rights in the West Bank (1977), reprinted in The Link (Fall, 1977).

19
Fourth Geneva Convention, of August 12, 1949, 6 U.S.T. 3516, T.I.A.S. 3365, 75 U.N.T.S. 287.

20
See, inter alia, "Teachers Reject Israeli Demand," The New York Times, September 13, 1982.

21
See, inter alia, David K. Shipler, "Israelis Drive Bedouins of Negev into Closed Zones," The New York Times, December 26, 1981; "Israelis Survive Storm Over Bedouin Baby's Death," ibid., March 18, 1982; "A Mayor Is Ousted in the West Bank," ibid.; Anthony Lewis, "A West Bank Incident," ibid.; "Two More Shot in West Bank Amid Growing Fears on Both Sides," ibid., March 21, 1982; "West Bank Boy Dies as Israelis Fire on Protesters," ibid.; "Violence Continues to Spread on West Bank," ibid., March 23, 1982; Anthony Lewis, "Destroying the Dream," ibid., April 1 and 5, 1982:

"One of the ugliest realities in the West Bank is the vigilante activity of some Israeli settlers. The extremists among them are frankly intent on driving the Arab

inhabitants out; they use violence and
to intimidation that end."

See also David K. Shipler, "West Bank Occupaton
Leaves Scars on Israel Too," ibid., May 2, 1983;
and the documents of the Committee for Defense of
Political Prisoners in Israel, P.O. Box 157, Um
El-Fahm, Israel, and those of the American-Arab
Anti-Discrimination Committee, Washington, D.C.,
particularly The Bitter Year: Arabs Under
Israeli Occupation, 1982.

22

See Meron Benvinisti, et al, West Bank and Gaza
Data Base Project, Interim Report (Jerusalem:
The West Bank Data Base Project, 1982).

23

See David K. Shipler, "Israel Dramatically
Changing Face of the West Bank," The New York
Times, September 12, 1982.

24

See David K. Shipler, §In West Bank, Even Crop
Joins Conflict," ibid., February 11, 1982:

"...a tomato is not just a tomato, nor a
mere eggplant a mere eggplant. Its destiny
is determined by whether it was grown by
Arab or Jewish hands....Under the rules, the
Israelis may sell produce on the occupied
West Bank but West Bank Arabs are severely
limited in what they may sell in
Israel....Europe is not open to Arab farmers
from the West Bank and Gaza."

25

See W. T. Mallison, "Status of the West Bank
Under Customary International Law," The New York
Times, October 9, 1983.

26

See text of the Proclamation of Independence of
Israel, in Walter Z. Laqueur, ed., The Israeli-
Arab Reader (New York: Bantam, 1970), pp. 125-28.

27

See Quincy Wright (assisted by M. Khadduri), "The
Palestine Conflict in International Law," in

Major Middle East Problems in International Law, ed. Majid Khadduri (Washington, D.C.: American Enterprise Institute for Policy Research, 1972).

28

General Assembly Resolution 194 (111) December 11, 1948; text in *U.N. Yearbook, 1948-49*, pp. 174-76.

29

See Myers S. McDougal and Florentino Feliciano, *Law and Minimum Public Order: The Legal Regulation of International Coercion* (New Haven: Yale University Press, 1960), p. 75.

30

James Brown Scott, ed., *The Hague Conventions and Declarations of 1899 and 1907, Section III: Military Authority Over the Territory of the Hostile State* (New York: Oxford University Press, 1915), pp. 122-27.

31

The Geneva Convention Relative to the Protection of Civilian Persons in Time of War, August 12, 1949 (Washington, D.C.: Department of State Publications 3938, August, 1950), pp. 164-216.

32

Lord McNair and A.D. Watts, *The Legal Effect of War* (Cambridge University Press, 1966), pp. 367-69.

33

"Declaration of the Establishment of the State of Israel," reprinted from Israel's Official Gazette No. 1 of the 5th Iyar, 5708 (14 May, 1948), in *Israel's Struggle for Peace* (New York: Israel Office of Information, 1960), pp. 161-64.

34

See Ralph H. Magnus, ed., *Documents on the Middle East* (Washington, D.C.: American Enterprise Institute for Public Policy Research, 1969), p. 161. Paragraph II reads as follows:

"Resolved that the refugees wishing to return to their homes and live at peace with their neighbors should be permitted to do so at the earliest practicable date, and that compensation should be paid for the

property of those choosing not to return   or
for loss and damage to property which, under
the principles   of International Law or   in
equity,   should   be   made   good   by   the
Government or authorities responsible."

35

See   General Assembly Resolution 273 (111) of May
11, 1949,   on   the   admission of Israel   to   the
United Nations.

11.

IS THERE GENOCIDE IN THE MIDDLE EAST?

Jesse Levitt
Prof. of Modern Languages
University of Bridgeport

May 14, 1948 was the date of the proclamation of the independence of the state of Israel; the following day armed forces from Transjordan, Egypt, Syria and other Arab countries entered Palestine in order to put an end to the new state of Israel. They failed; forty years later, with the exception of the separate Egyptian-Israeli peace treaty of 1979, the confrontation continues, without any peace settlement in sight. In 1967, following the intervention of Jordan in the Egyptian-Israeli hostilities, Israel occupied the west bank of the Jordan, thereby completing the occupation of what had been the Palestine mandate. This occupation has now lasted more than twenty years and has inevitably produced frustration and resentment among the Palestinian Arabs subject to the Israeli occupation. These resentments flared into a widespread campaign of civil disorder in December 1987, and it is still in progress as of April 1988.

The West Bank, known to Israeli "hard-liners" as Judea and Samaria, has never been formally annexed to Israel and still remains occupied territory; East Jerusalem, however, has been annexed. Undoubtedly there have been serious cases of human rights violations as the Israelis seek to control a hostile population. The increasing number of Israeli settlements in the area is also a source of strong resentment. The status of the West Bank population, however, is vastly different from that of Arab residents in "old Israel," i.e., the area that constituted Israel between 1948 and 1967, where Arab residents are Israeli citizens, although (with the exception of Druse volunteers) they do not serve in the army and therefore lack some of the privileges available to those who have completed their military service. Some Israeli Arabs have even been elected to the Knesset, the Israeli Parliament. The frequent comparison of Israel with South Africa is therefore out of place; there is no apartheid in Israel.

The very real violations of human rights in the occupied West Bank and Gaza areas have led Arab propagandists and even some scholars to talk or write about an alleged "genocide" perpetrated by the Israelis against the Palestinian Arabs. Such allegations should be received with considerable skepticism.

The term "genocide" is in no way synonymous with mere violation of human rights. In Chile, for example, there have been flagrant violations of human rights since 1973, when General Pinochet assumed power after the death of President Salvador Allende. But there is no genocide. Even in wartorn Lebanon and racist South Africa there is no genocide.

Genocide represents the most heinous violation of human rights involving the deliberate murder of thousands or even millions of human beings. It is extremely doubtful that the term can be properly used to denote notions such as "cultural genocide" or mental anguish, which do not involve the physical extermination of large numbers of human beings. The Soviets often confine political dissidents in psychiatric hospitals, which is an outrageous violation of human rights, but not genocide.

In Spain the Franco regime (1939-1978) prohibited the Basques from using their language (at least in public), writing in it, teaching it or broadcasting in it. Printing of Basque books was forbidden; there were no Basque newspapers or magazines. Obviously, this was a flagrant violation of human rights. But under the present democratic régime in Spain, the Basques have local autonomy and are free to teach the language, broadcast in it and publish Basque books and periodicals. The victims of "cultural genocide" are thus very much alive and able to enjoy their current cultural freedom.

Officially, genocide is defined in the United Nations Convention of December 9, 1948 as "any of the following acts intended to destroy, in whole or in part, a national, ethnical, racial or religious group, as such: (a) killing members of the group; (b) causing serious bodily or mental harm to members of the group; (c) deliberately inflicting on members of the group conditions of life calculated to bring about its physical destruction in whole or in part; (d) imposing measures intended to prevent births within

236

the group; (e) forcibly transferring children of the group to another group" (Kuper, Genocide, p. 19).

Dr. Leo Kuper, professor emeritus of the University of California, in his book Genocide: Its Political Use in the Twentieth Century (1981) broadens the scope of the term to include "cases where the victims of massacre were political groups (or economic classes)." He also includes "conflicts marked by genocidal massacres, expressed characteristically in the annihilation of a section of a group--men, women and children, as for example in the wiping out of whole villages" (Kuper Genocide, pp. 9-10). Nowhere, in his book does Dr. Kuper make any mention of an alleged Israeli genocide against Palestinian Arabs.

In a more recent book, The Prevention of Genocide (1983) Dr. Kuper notes that the U.N. Commission on Human Rights on February 15, 1983 condemned "in the strongest terms the large scale massacre of Palestinian civilians in the Sabra and Shatila refugee camps near Beirut for which the responsibility of the Israeli government has been established"; the Commission described the massacre as "an act of genocide." The massacre had in fact occurred in September 1982 in the Beirut area during the Lebanese campaign of the Israeli army, after the assassination of the Christian Phalangist leader and newly elected President of Lebanon, Bashir Gemayel. The Israeli army had arranged with the Lebanese Christian militia to disarm Palestinians in the camps; but the Christian militia massacred an estimated 300 to 800 Palestinians. An Israeli government commission of inquiry stated that the Israeli forces did have direct responsibility. The Israeli forces should have anticipated some kind of revenge on the part of the Christian militia and should have intervened sooner.

Former President Jimmy Carter in his book The Blood of Abraham puts the final toll at more than 1400 dead and missing. No evidence was presented about PLO troops being in the camps. "Nowhere," says Carter, "was the reaction more angry or anguished than in Israel's democratic society...." Opposition leader Shimon Peres referred to "this abominable act which the rabbis said is the absolute antithesis of the traditions of Judaism." When Begin's government refused to start an investigation, 400,000 citizens took to the streets, i.e., more than ten percent of Israeli's total population (Carter, pp. 2-3).

237

Dr. Kuper notes that the U.N. resolution carefully avoided any reference to the role of the Christian militia; an effort to incorporate such a reference was rejected. Dr. Kuper adds: "Against the background of the United Nations protective stance in many past genocides with tens of thousands, indeed hundreds of thousands of victims, it is clear that there is a special animosity at work in the resolution on Israel." He adds that the grievance against Israel could have been submitted to the International Court of Justice, under the terms of the Genocide Convention, to which Israel is a signatory, and "this at least would have been a judicial process" (Kuper, Prevention, pp. 169-170). Again there is no reference whatever to any other supposed Israeli genocide.

The "special animosity" of the United Nations toward Israel had already been amply documented by the resolution of the General Assembly on November 19, 1975 that called Zionism "a form of racism." The resolution, strongly supported by the Communist and Arab blocs, was passed on the anniversary of Kristalnacht, November 10, 1938, when the Nazis broke windows in Jewish stores and homes, thus announcing their ultimate intention to annihilate the Jews.

The notion of Zionism as racism is utterly absurd. Judaism has adherents of all races; in recent years Israel has absorbed hundreds of thousands of immigrants from Africa and Asia, including the black Falasha Ethiopians. It is not correct to describe Israel as a "settler society" analogous to French Algeria or British Rhodesia before the sixties, or to make specious comparisons with the Union of South Africa. Far from being a society predominantly of white Europeans, Israel, as Barry Rubin notes in The Arab States and the Palestine Conflict, now has a majority of Jews emigrating from Arab countries and their descendants. "The driving out of these people by Arab governments made a tremendous contribution to the success of their enemy; cases of mistreatment destroyed Arab credibility of possible coexistence. With or without the existence of Zionism, rising Arab nationalism would probably have led to the same end" (Rubin, p. 11).

Nor is Israel a society in which a ruling élite suppresses a majority of different ethnic origins. Even counting the occupied West Bank, Israel still has a majority of Jews and a minority of Arabs in its

238

population. Besides, Judaism, while not a
proselytzing religion, does accept converts. Zionism
is a form of Jewish ethnic nationalism with which one
may or may not agree; but it is not racism in any
sense of the term. Palestinian Arabs, both Moslem and
Christian hold citizenship in "old Israel," the area
it held between 1948 and 1967, and there is no
apartheid.

The U.N. resolution, as Jeane Kirkpatrick former
U.S. ambassador to the U.N. points out "symbolized the
death of the dream of the U.N. as an institution
dedicated to reason, democracy, and peace." In U.N.
language, she adds, "'racism' is the ultimate
political crime, the ultimate violation of political
rights" and a state based on racism is supposedly
"unworthy" of membership in the "family of nations."
The Palestine Liberation Organization has been endowed
with the rights of a member state, while Israel,
according to a growing number of U.N. resolutions, is
declared to be "the moral equivalent of Nazi Germany--
a state guilty of 'war crimes' and 'genocide' whose
very existence is a violation of international law"
(Kirkpatrick).

This resolution, which has never been disavowed or
repudiated, clearly establishes the unfitness of the
United Nations General Assembly to play any
constructive role in the effort to secure a just and
lasting peace in the Arab-Israeli conflict. Dr. Kuper
notes that the United Nations "provides no protection
against genocide, and that the Commission on Human
Rights...actually condones the crime by delay, evasion
and subterfuge" (Kuper, Genocide, p. 183).

Potentially, the U.N. resolution on Zionism, so
warmly supported by the Communist and Arab worlds,
lays the groundwork for possible new genocides against
Jews.

David K. Shipler of the New York Times, who says
he is neither Jew nor Arab, notes in his book Arab and
Jew: Wounded Spirits in a Promised Land that the
Palestinian Arabs "have suffered powerlessness and
deprivation of liberty, but never genocide" (Shipler,
p. 9). The United States did not ratify the U.N.
Genocide Convention of 1948 until 1986 precisely
because some Senators feared that hostile propaganda
would use the convention to attack the United States
for imaginary genocides (e.g. the "genocide" of black

people, of Puerto Ricans, of Vietnamese, of Hiroshima).

The massacre of some 250 inhabitants of Arab village of Deir Yassin near Jerusalem in April 1948 is sometimes cited as an example of genocide. Conor Cruise O'Brien in his book The Siege, which is generally pro-Israel, cites this massacre as "the most frightful atrocity of the entire Arab-Jewish conflict" in 1948. Responsibility rests with the Irgun zvai Leumi, an extremist right-wing underground movement led by Menachem Begin. The Jewish Agency condemned the Irgun action. An Arab reprisal raid killed 77 doctors, nurses, university teachers and students bound for Hadassah Hospital and Hebrew University on Mount Scopus (O'Brien, p. 282). Massacres and atrocities were practiced on both sides of the conflict; but the number of victims in such cases was not large enough for one to be able to refer plausibly to a "genocide."

On the Arab side, threats against Israel at various times seem to suggest genocidal intentions-- which could not be implemented due to Arab military defeats. On May 15, 1948 Azzam Pasha, Secretary of the Arab League, said at a press conference: "This will be a war of extermination, a momentous massacre which will be spoken of like the Mongolian massacres and the Crusades" (Rubin, p. 203). In May 1948, just before the entry of Transjordanian armed forces into Palestine, King Abdallah told the British representative in Amman that his forces would invade Palestine on May 14. Asked about the Jewish forces, he replied: "It does not matter how many there are. We will sweep them into the sea" (Rubin, p. 202). In June 1967, according to the London Daily Telegraph, Ahmad Shukairy, head of the Arab Liberation Organization, said at a press conference in Amman that hardly any Jews would survive in Israel after the invasion of the Arab armies (Laqueur, Road, p. 20).

General Yehoshafat Harkabi, former chief of the Israeli military intelligence, in his book Arab Attitudes Toward Israel, considers that the formula frequently used in the Arab world, "to throw the Jews into the sea" "has an undoubted genocidal significane." He also sees genocidal motifs in a typical caricature depicting the killing of a scorpion to symbolize the liquidation of Israel. A manifesto published in 1964 in the Egyptian newspaper Al-Ahram

240

for distribution to Jews abroad warns them not to migrate to Israel, since such a move would be a "free one-way road to death" (Harkabi, p. 38).

General Harkabi says that from the Arab point of view the establishment of Israel was an "international crime" and that "her extinction must be carried out as a punitive operation and a massacre." Any dream of making an Arab country of Palestine "inevitably includes a genocidal element" (Harkabi, pp. 38-39).

Obviously, no such genocide has occurred because of Arab military defeats in every war with Israel. But the confrontation is by no means over. Kuper notes that genocide is preceded by a process of dehumanization. He cites an article by Herbert C. Kelman who notes that "victims must be deprived of their human status if systematic killing is to proceed in a smooth and orderly fashion." Denial of a common humanity, categorization of the target group in pejorative terms and demonization are often preludes to genocide (Kuper, Genocide, pp. 87-88). We know that centuries-old European anti-Semitism reached its ultimate expression in Hitler's gas chambers and crematories. Since the Second World War, anti-Semitism has greatly receded in the Western world, but has taken on a vigorous new existence in the Arab world, where the discredited myths and lies of European anti-Semitism are continually propagated. The motivation is of course anti-Zionism, the determination to destroy the state of Israel. It is true, however, that some politicians and writers distinguish between anti-Semitism and anti-Zionism, repudiating the former, while espousing the latter.

Yasir Arafat, leader of the PLO, in his speech to the U.N. General Assembly on November 13, 1974, claimed that the PLO did distinguish between Judaism and Zionism, stating: "While we maintain our opposition to the colonial Zionist movement, we respect the Jewish faith." He claimed that if the Jews had been willing to settle peaceably alongside Palestinian Arabs, like the Armenians and Circassians, "we would have opened our doors to them as far as our homeland's capacity for absorption permitted...." But he could not accept the goal of an immigration "to usurp our homeland, disperse our people and turn us into second-class citizens..." (Lilienthal, pp. 202-203).

241

Dr. Edward Said of Columbia University, who is often a spokesman for the Palestinians has written: "Anti-Semitism and racial theory of that sort is our natural enemy as much as it is the enemy of the Jews: that almost goes without saying. I am happy to say parenthetically, that the leading Arab organization to which I belong, the AAUG, has gone on record publicly to condemn the proposed march through Skokie, Illinois--a predominantly Jewish Chicago suburb--of the American Nazi Party" (Said, The Palestine Question and the American Context, p. 24).

In the troubled area of Arab-Jewish relations, there are all the same a few brighter spots. In Morocco, during the Second World War, King Mohammed II stopped the Vichy government and the Nazis from deporting Moroccan Jews to the death camps. At present King Hassan II appears to maintain a cordial relationship with the local Jewish community, and American Jewish tour groups often visit Morocco. The King has also sought to discuss possible peace terms with a number of Israeli journalists and politicians who have been invited from time to time to Morocco. The Tunisian government under President Bourguiba has also sought to protect Jewish rights. Before the civil war, Jews in Lebanon appear to have enjoyed full civil rights. During the Lebanese civil war, the Jews of Beirut actually received assistance from th PLO when they were caught between warring factions (Lilienthal, p. 753).

The United States was also able to persuade the Sudanese government, for a time, to permit the entry of Black Falasha Jews from Ethiopia fleeing famine conditions, and their transfer by air to Israel. But such flights have now ended, since the overthrow of the Nimeiry government.

Most Arab propagandists and spokesmen, however, prefer to combine anti-Zionism with anti-Semitism, reviving the forgeries of the czarist government of Russia and repeating the myths of medieval European superstitition.

The present Syrian Minister of Defense, Mustafa Tlas, is the author of an anti-Semitic book, the Matzah of Zion, which revives the spurious medieval blood libels against the Jews. "...Every mother was warning her child: do not stray far from home. The Jew may come by and put you in his sack to kill you and suck your blood for the Matzah of Zion" (Response, August 1986, p. 1).

Even in Egypt, which has been at peace with Israel since 1979, anti-Semitic statements abound, although they are clear violations of article 3, clause 5 of the Camp David accords, which specify that both sides will "strive to cultivate mutual trust and understanding and refrain from hostile propaganda...." A study by the Simon Wiesenthal Center for 1986-1987 finds anti-semitic accusations in more than twenty-two newspapers. Thus El-Jumhuriya, a semi-official government daily wrote on January 9, 1987: "Israeli terrorism is of special characteristics, since terror and betrayal is the nature of Jews. Jews are traitors" (Response, February 1988, p. 1).

The attitudes of Arab writers and spokesmen toward Hitler and Nazi Germany have been ambivalent. Nasser and other leaders in the past stressed opposition to Fascism and Nazism. Logically, since Nazi persecution and genocide against the Jews were probably the major reason for the successful creation of Israel, the Palestinian Arabs could be considered as the ultimate victims of Nazism (Laqueur, Road, p. 20).

Mohammed T. Mehdi, an Iraqi who is the founder of the American-Arab Relations Committee, has said: "The real father of Israel is Hitler even more than Herzl, and Israel is the by-product of anti-Semitism even more than of Zionism." Mehdi considers the very existence of Israel "an act of terrorism against the Palestinians." He proposes that the Jews leave Israel and that the United States open its doors to them. But he declares that he hates anti-Semitism because it drove the Jews to realize their national identity (Goot, p. 123).

Nevertheless, the powerful wave of anti-Semitism (not just anti-Zionism) that was unleashed in the Arab world by the creation of Israel has often led to the portrayal of Hitler's Germany in very sympathetic terms. British historian Paul Johnson (as well as many others) has described Hitler's extermination of the European Jews as "the greatest single crime in history" (Johnson, p. 413). Expressions of approval for the greatest practitioner of genocide in world history and attempts to minimize or deny the Holocaust can only be interpreted as a possible preparation for a repeat performance when the time is considered ripe.

In 1943 Haj Amin el Husseini, Mufti of Jerusalem, wrote to Nazi Foreign Minister von Ribbentrop asking for German intervention in the Balkans to prevent Jewish migration to Palestine (Shipler, pp. 334-335). British historian Paul Johnson describes Haj Amin as "a dedicated killer who devoted his entire adult life to race murder. There is a photograph of him taken with Himmler: the two men smile sweetly at one another; beneath, a charming inscription by the SS chief to 'His Eminence the Grossmufti': the date was 1943 when the 'Final Solution' was moving into top gear" (Johnson, p. 481).

The Mufti, says Johnson "outrivalled Hitler in his hatred for Jews." He organized the systematic destruction of Arab moderates, of whom there were many in Palestine in the 1920s. "Arabs and Jews might have lived together as two prosperous communities," Johnson notes. But the Mufti used terrorist leader Emile Ghori "whose assassination squads systematically murdered the leading Arab moderates--and silenced the rest. By the end of the 1930s Arab moderate opinion had ceased to exist, at least in public..." (Johnson, p. 481).

There is also strong circumstantial evidence linking the Mufti to the assassination of King Abdallah of Jordan at the Al-Aqsa mosque in Jerusalem in 1951; the actual assassin was Mustafa Shuqri Asha, a nineteen-year old veteran of the Mufti's shock troops, who was himself immediately gunned down (Rubin, pp. 214-215). Abdallah had been the only Arab leader willing to negotiate openly with Israel over a possible division of territory in Palestine, and his assassination served as a warning to other Arab leaders who might have the temerity to negotiate with Israel.

"One of the best kept secrets in the Arab world," says David K. Shipler, "is the extent to which prominent Arabs--including some from Saudi Arabia--journey to Jerusalem to be treated at Hadassah Hospital by Jewish doctors they are sworn to hate and are raised to respect. Relatives of PLO officials receive treatment there as well." King Hussein of Jordan was born in the original Hadassah Hospital in Jerusalem. "The Israelis would love to boast about all this, but they insist on keeping medical confidences. Their pride comes in having built an institution where the two peoples can merge and care together. Hadassah has a good name in the Arab world, and some Jordanians kept their Hadassah cards from 1948 to 1967, returning to use the hospital after the end of the Six-Day War." The Israeli government pays the bills of poor West Bank residents who cannot afford hospital care; in the fiscal year ending March 30, 1984 it amounted to 1.5 million dollars (Shipler, pp. 552-554).

Obviously such medical assistance does not point the way to any stable political solution, but it is a far cry from notions of genocide.

On May 1, 1964 Egyptian President Nasser said that in the Second World War "our sympathies were with Germany" and that the "lie of the murdered six million Jews is not believed by anybody." Nasser also stressed on another occasion the relevance of the anti-Semitic Protocols of the Elders of Zion for understanding the key issues of our time (Laqueur, Road, p. 22).

The Jordanian officer Abdallah al-Tall who defected to Egypt wrote approvingly of the extermination of the Jews by the Nazis, declaring: "The blame applies first and foremost to the Jews themselves, and their characteristics of treachery, deceitfulness, crime and treason, and in the second place to European civilization, which apparently could not long suffer the vile Jewish character, and in the course of time hatred of the Jews and loathing for their vices led to a movement of collective killing" (Shipler, pp. 334-335).

The Egyptian fundamentalist monthly El Mukhtar El-Islami wrote in April 1986: "The Jews were responsible for World War II. They initiated this war in order to crush Nazi Germany which was the last obstacle before Jewish domination of the world. Europe was indeed destroyed and Zionist strategy had its victory. The Jews were also behind the murder of President Abraham Lincoln."

El-Ahram, the leading Egyptian semi-official daily newspaper, on March 3, 1987 carried a book review of "The First Terrorists," in which critic Adb El-Muneim Qandil stated: "I lower my pen in respect to the author who presents proof from Israeli books to the malice of the Jews who wish to kill all male newborns and pregnant women in order to uproot the

245

Palestinians...The author speaks about turning   facts
upside   down...such   as   their   claim   that   the   gas
chambers used by Hitler to get rid of people   infected
by   the   plague   were especially built   to   burn   Jews
alive."

    El   Masa,   another semi-official organ,   wrote   on
April   21,   1987:   "...Jews distributed a   'ridiculous
lie'   after   the   Second   World   War   concerning   the
Holocaust.   They started with the claim that   100,000
Jews were exterminated but later reached the figure of
eight   million.   Jews are inflating these numbers   in
order   to   achieve   bigger   help   from   the   U.S.A."
(Response, February 1988, pp. 1, 2).

    Evidently,   the   Egyptian-Israeli peace treaty has
had   only   limited   effect   stemming   the   race   hate
propaganda   in   Egypt.   If   dehumanization   and
demonization   are preludes to possible genocide,   one
cannot help wondering whether genocide is the ultimate
Arab objective for Israel.   Of course, this may all be
super-heated   rhetoric   stirred   up   by   rejection   of
Israel   and   sympathy   for   the   Palestinian   Arabs.
Perhaps.   But   then,   no one took Hitler at his   word
when he first came to power.

    There   have   been numerous propaganda attempts   to
portray Israel as assuming the role of Nazi Germany in
its   relations with   the Palestinian Arabs.   The   New
Republic   cites,   as   "the   most   stunningly   stupid
example"   of this,   an editorial from the Boston Globe
on   February   18,   1988 comparing the "horrors" in   the
occupied   territories with "the czarist pogroms,   the
centuries   of homelessness and persecution,   the   mass
graves   at Babi Yar,   the piled bodies found   at   Nazi
death camps in 1945" (New Republic, March 14, 1988, p.
18).

    A   Saudi Arabian paper Al Gumhuriya   editorialized
in   1983:   "Now   one can ask the leaders   of   Israel:
'Did   not   the   Nazis   torture   you   or   in   previous
generations did you not represent the Nazis before the
world as wild,   cowardly beasts?   And is what you are
doing   less than what the Nazis   did?"   (Shipler,   pp.
334-5).

    Shipler   reports   visiting the Ansar prison   camp,
where   Palestinian Arab prisoners started chanting   in
heavily accented English: "Ansar is Auschwitz!   You
are   Nazis" (Shipler,   p.   333).   The   comparison   of

246

course, is invalid; however bad conditions were at Ansar, it was not an extermination camp, like Auschwitz. Shipler comments: "The Holocaust has become a vehicle of hurt and outrage between Arabs and Jews, a symbol of immense grievance on both sides, an event without analogy, yet one used often as analogy to inflate the scope of each side's transgressions. Arab propagandists frequently liken Israel to Nazi Germany and the Palestinians to the Jews of Europe. Menachem Begin, for his part, routinely accused the PLO of conspiring to commit genocide against the Jews. The respectability of the forum has been no deterrent to this sort of nonsense" (Shipler, p. 334).

Shipler makes this overall comment on the Palestinian Arabs and the Jews: "The hardships of the Palestinian Arabs in modern history bear no resemblance in scope or depth to those of the Jews. Subjected to Turkish brutality under the Ottoman Empire, British rule under the Mandate created by the League of Nations, political arrest by the Jordanian monarchy, and rough controls under Israel, the Arabs from this crucial slice of Palestine have suffered powerlessness and deprivation of liberty but never genocide. Their sense of distinctiveness as a Palestinian people has come not from an ancient source but largely in reaction to the creation and growth of Israel on part of the land where they lived" (Shipler, p. 9. Underlining added.).

According to the New Republic, Professor Edward Said, the leading American spokesman for the Palestinian Arabs, said in his latest book: "We have had no Holocaust to protect us with the world's compassion," and he rejected the comparison with the Nazis on television in early March 1988 (New Republic, March 18, 1988, p. 18).

In fact there is no valid comparison between the crimes of Nazi Germany, which meant mass extermination, and the violations of human rights that have been committed by Israel. The flight of the Palestinian Arabs in 1948 was ultimately caused by the refusal of the Arab states to recognize Israel and the terror and confusion resulting from war conditions. The refusal of the Arab states to negotiate a peace with Israel has left these refugees in limbo, since Israel cannot be expected to readmit them in the absence of a firm peace. It would have been possible to resettle the refugees elsewhere. When twelve

247

million Germans were expelled from Poland and Czechoslovakia after the Second World War, the German Federal Republic successfully resettled them and integrated them into the West German economy.

The Arab states, on the contrary, have preferred to leave the refugees in virtually unlivable camps; with the exception of Jordan, they have withheld citizenship from the Palestinians, keeping most of them confined to their camps in an effort to maintain animosity against Israel and stimulate a desire for vengeance. It must also be noted that 600,000 Jews were either forced to leave Arab lands or else left because living conditions had become intolerable. All were resettled in Israel and integrated into Israel society. A comprehensive peace agreeement, if it is ever achieved, must take into account the justified claims of Palestinian Arab refugees outside their homeland; but it must also provide for Jews forced to leave Arab lands.

While David K. Shipler describes genocide threats as nonsense, such threats are not taken lightly in Israel, which, as Seth P. Tillman notes, is dominated by a "politics of fear." Arie Lova Eliav, a former Knesset member, wrote of the "continual trauma" produced by Arab threats against Israel's existence, "the constant fear and misgivings that gnaw at our hearts and sometimes craze us." This fear "dictates our psychological reactions, which appear so incomprehensible and sometimes irrational to our enemies and friends." Terrorism by the PLO has perpetuated the trauma, especially when the victims have also been victimized by the Nazis (Tillman, pp. 123-4).

Marie Syrkin, a long-time Labor Zionist leader who favors an Israeli withdrawal from occupied territories, warns about distortions in the press comparing Israel with Nazi Germany; the "unbearable conditions" in Arab rhetoric, she says, "do not represent a physical reality but a political demand. Evenhanded journalists who blandly echo the PLO vocabulary should be more wary of Orwellian doublespeak, in which words have contrary meanings when applied to Arabs or Jews. For Jews, 'camps' meant barbed-wire enclosures from which death was the only escape; for Arabs it is a willed concentration determined by Arab strategy. For Jews, 'genocide' meant the numerical extermination of a people; for

Arabs a population explosion." She ridicules the "obscene comparison" of the PLO ship "filled with well-heeled Arab agitators, terrorists and assorted journalists," that was supposed to imitate the journey of the refugee ship Exodus (Congress Monthly, March-April 1988, p. 11).

On the other hand, Dr. Edward Said, who is of Palestinian origin and who is a member of the Palestine National Council, sees the Israeli fear of a recurring genocide as victimizing the Palestinian Arabs. He writes in his Question of Palestine: "I do sympathize with, I understand as profoundly as I can, the fear felt by most Jews that Israeli's security is a genuine protection against future genocidal attempts on the Jewish people. But it is necessary to remark that there can be no way of satisfactorily conducting a life whose main concern is to prevent the past from recurring. For Zionism, the Palestinians have now become the equivalent of a past experience reincarnated in the form of a present threat. The result is that the Palestinians'° future as a people is mortgaged to that fear, which is a disaster for them and for the Jews." He feels that there can be reconciliation "if both peoples make the attempt to see each other within a common historical perspective. Better fully acknowledged conflict than hidden and unstated fears, rigidly theologized fantasies about the Other" (Said, The Question of Palestine, pp. 231-232).

Is there genocide in the Middle East, or is there an imminent danger of it? If genocide is understood in its basic meaning of systematic, organized mass murder of thousands of human beings, there has been no genocide. The Israelis, as Shipler confirms, have not practiced any genocide against the Palestinian Arabs. As for the Arab nations, in their forty year struggle with Israel there have been frequent statements suggesting the planning of a genocide; but none has been carried out because of the failure of Arab military force to overcome Israel. There has of course been considerable repression and there have been atrocities on both sides, but genocide has not occurred, unless the meaning of the term is deliberately distorted to cover offenses of a lesser order against human rights.

This tentative conclusion is not meant to gloss over the numerous atrocities that have taken place in the Middle Eastern area, some of which have already been mentioned. But it should also be noted that some of the worst atrocities have been carried or by Arab factions against each other--the PLO against Lebanese Christians and vice versa, Amal Shihites in Lebanon against Palestinians, Druse and Maronites against each other, and the crushing of a Moslem Brotherhood revolt in Homs by the Syrian army.

While there has not been any real genocide in the Arab-Israeli conflict, the danger still persists as long as the conflict remains unsettled. There is also the larger problem of a new Arab-Israeli conflict spreading to the superpowers and provoking a worldwide holocaust vastly exceeding the proportions of even a sizable genocide. A solution thus becomes ever more urgent.

What hope is there now, in 1988, for a reasonable settlement? Such a settlement must of necessity be one of compromise, avoiding maximum demands by extremists on both sides and showing a willingness by both sides to be flexible. Public attention is focused in the spring of 1988 on the Palestinian disturbances on the West Bank, brought on by twenty years of Israeli military occupation. The New Republic, normally pro-Israel, in an editorial on February 15, 1988, sharply attacks Israeli Defense Minister Rabin. "Rabin has sanctioned brutalities that should burden the conscience of Israel and the whole Jewish people. Supporters of Israel--the U.S. government and the American people, for example--are entitled to expect that this official thuggery cease" (New Republic, February 15, 1988, p. 10).

It is often proposed that a true settlement of the Israeli-Palestinian impasse lies in mutual recognition by the PLO and Israel. Any such mutual recognition, however, would call for each side to moderate extremist demands, and there seems little indication that this will occur in the foreseeable future. The Palestinian National Charter states in article 21: "The Arab Palestinian people, expressing themselves by the armed revolution, reject all solutions which are substitutes for the total liberation of Palestine and reject all proposals aiming at the liquidation of the Palestinian problem or its internationalization." Other resolutions adopted in Cairo in 1974 refuse regotiations on the basis of Security Council Resolution 242 which "treats our national cause as a

250

refugee problem." Another resolution states: "The PLO will struggle against any proposal to set up a Palestine entity at the price of recognition, peace and secure boundaries, giving up the historic right and depriving our people of its right to return and to self-determination on its original soil" (Laqueur-Rubin, pp. 369-71).

Yasir Arafat said very recently in an interview with Anthony Lewis of the New York Times that he was prepared to make peace with Israel and that he accepted all United Nations resolutions. As for mutual respect for Israeli-Palestinian borders, he declared that international guarantees would be implemented; "we are in need of the guarantees more than they." "I say from the beginning, peace needs courageous men. Peace for both of us." In the opinion of Anthony Lewis, these comments represent Arafat's "most unambiguous commitments yet to a negotiated peace with Israel." But Lewis also notes Arafat's opposition to the Shultz peace mission. Secretary Shultz had gone to Jerusalem inviting fifteen Palestinians to confer with him; none had accepted his invitation. According to Arafat, Shultz did not have the right to choose the Palestinian delegation.

While this declaration by Arafat is encouraging, it does not necessarily mean a clear-cut shift in the PLO position. It has been noted that Arafat made similar statements in the past to the foreign press, while saying something quite different in Arabic. Besides, the PLO does not operate by a majority vote of its council, but by the principle of consensus, which always gives radical fringe groups the opportunity to upset any agreements reached. In a PLO conference in Lisbon in 1983, Sartawi, a close friend of Arafat, spoke of the need for peace with Israel, and was promptly shot to death at the meeting.

The peace mission undertaken by U.S. Secretary of State George Shultz in February 1988 has now been rejected on both sides. "Hard-line" Israeli Premier Shamir (who in 1978 had voted against the Egyptian peace treaty) refuses to consider trading any territory at all for the sake of peace. Secretary Shultz's invitation to fifteen Palestinian leaders was boycotted by all of them on Yasir Arafat's instructions.

Where does justice lie in this seemingly endless controversy? Neither the destruction of Israel nor the permanent annexation of the West Bank could be considered just. If Israel is here to stay, so are the Palestinian Arabs and some accommodation is urgent. The problem transcends the interests of the immediate parties to the dispute. World peace itself is threatened by the continuing unresolved conflict. "It was the ordering of the American armed forces in the Eastern Mediterranean into battle dress and full battle preparedness to prevent Russia from direct intervention in the Arab-Israeli war that stopped the spread of the fighting into World War III in June of 1967, not any U.N. action or prestige" (Polin, pp. 223-224). Again in 1973, during the next Israeli-Egyptian war, President Nixon proclaimed a worldwide alert of all American armed forces, including nuclear units.

The need to preserve world peace and avoid a worldwide nuclear holocaust requires that an equitable solution be found for the Arab-Israeli dispute. After all, it was the assassination of an Austrian archduke in 1914 and the commitments of the great powers to smaller client states that eventually plunged all Europe, and eventually the world into the First World War.

The United States must use its influence with Israel persuasively, but firmly to secure the necessary flexibility on Israel's part which might make a just solution possible. Despite the stubbornness of Shamir, there are many in Israel who do support the Shultz initiative.

Former Foreign Minister Abba Eban, now Chairman of the Committee on Foreign Relations and Defense of the Israeli Knesset, in a recent article in the New York Times (February 24, 1988), stresses the futility of any Israeli attempt to retain the West Bank permanently. All the weaponry of the United Staes, he says "would not save it from disintegration and collapse if it were to try to incorporate 90 million Russians--a proportion equal to the 1.5 million Palestinian Arabs in a Greater Israel--and rule them against their will." The spotlight, he adds should be fixed on the Palestinians. "If they refuse to consult with Mr. Shultz, they will be true to their worst tradition never having lost a chance to miss an opportunity. The most urgent task is to promote the

252

election or agreed nomination of a Palestinian leadership..." (<u>NY</u> <u>Times</u>, February 24, 1988).

In fact, up to now, the Palestinian Arabs have indeed refused to consult with Secretary of State Shultz, on instructions from Yasir Arafat.

Israeli General Harkabi says: "Israel cannot defend itself if half its population is the enemy...If an individual claims that he can live only provided that he sits on the shoulders of another individual, and further, that he has the right to drive his finger nails into the other's body (that is, in this instance by establishing settlements), people will begin to question whether it might be better if such an individual did not exist. Never before has Israel prejudiced its claim to legitimacy as by the argument that it cannot exist without the West Bank" (<u>Time</u>, April 4, 1988, p. 50).

He adds that the Arab dream of the disappearance of Israel may continue, but that Jordan and the PLO have adapted to the realistic need of accommodation. "What is important to su is that the goal of eliminating Israel ceases to be 'policy' as distinguished from 'grand design.' There is no way of extinguishing a people's vicious dreams which are liable to persist even after political accommodation. A political settlement eventually uproots the vicious dreams and cancels them out, while lack of political accommodation establishes and reinforces them" (Anthony Lewis in the <u>New</u> <u>York</u> <u>Times</u>, March 27, 1988, p. A29).

General Harkabi recently wrote in the newspaper <u>Ha'aretz</u>: "Israel is a candidate for inclusion in Barbara Tuchman's <u>March</u> <u>of</u> <u>Folly</u> as a country working against its own best interests, a looking-glass world in which political positions that subvert the country's continued survival are called patriotic." The Arabs have ceased considering Israel "a wise country." It can still achieve peace, "but the longer such a settlement is put off, the worse our situation will grow, until we find ourselves facing an absolutely hopeless tangle" (F. Lewis, <u>New</u> <u>York</u> <u>Times</u>, April 10, 1988).

Statements like those of Abba Eban and General Harkabi are a far cry from the self-defeating intransigence of Premier Shamir and his associates in the Likud party. If Likud cannot be dislodged from power in the coming Israeli elections, there may eventually be a sharp confrontation between Israel and the United States. Professor Tony Smith of Tufts University in a New York Times article notes that if Shamir's views become the majority view, the United States will have to "review critically the many ways our ability to act in world affairs is hampered by an inflexible ally..." (New York Times, March 26, 1988, p. 31). It would be well for the Israeli voters to take heed of such warnings.

It is sometimes claimed that the "Jewish lobby" hampers U.S. foreign policy and that Israel should amend the "law of return" by limiting it to Jewish refugees only, rather than to all Jews. But many American Jews have voiced strong objections to Shamir's policies. Thus, Theodore R. Mann, President of the American Jewish Congress, stresses that "a continuation of the status quo (on the West Bank) is a prescription for disaster" (Congress Monthly, March-April 1988, p. 6).

As for amending the "law of return," it is really an imaginary problem. The great majority of the Jews living in the disapora in the Western world have no intention of migrating to Israel. When Algerian independence became a reality in 1962, the vast majority of the Algerian Jews went to France. Even Soviet Jews permitted to leave for Vienna by the Soviet government tend to prefer resettlement in the United States rather than migration to Israel. The "law of return" does not realistically threaten neighboring Arab states with possible Israeli expansion. As for the alleged "double loyalties" of American Jews, the closeness of American Jew to Israel is entirely analogous to the feelings of Irish-Americans for Ireland or of Greek-Americans for Greece and Cyprus.

In any case, the search for peace in the Arab-Israeli dispute has become an urgent necessity, and in this task Soviet cooperation can be of considerable, perhaps decisive, importance. The two superpowers can and should bring their influence to bear on their respective client states to moderate their maximum demands and arrive at a stable peace. If this is not accomplished in a not too distant future, we face the prospect of a situation resembling that of the summer of 1914. Future Arab-Israeli confrontations might

254

even involve the possibility of the use of nuclear weaponry. It appears to be a certainty that Israel has nuclear capabilities, and the possibility of Arab nuclear capabilities is not out of the question either. Any nuclear confrontation would easily escalate and the resulting Holocaust might well exceed any genocide perpetrated up to now. It is thus a matter of increasing urgency that a just solution be actively sought in the forty-year old Arab-Israeli confrontation.

BIBLIOGRAPHY

Carter, Jimmy. The Blood of Abraham. Boston: Houghton-Mifflin, 1985.

Eban, Abba. "Israeli's Main Goal and Mr. Shultz's," New York Times, February 24, 1988, op. ed. page.

Goot, Amy Kaufman and Steven J. Rosen. The Campaign to Discredit Israel. Washington, D.C., American Israel Public Affairs Committee, 1983.

Harkabi, Yehoshafat. Arab Attitudes Toward Israel. New York: Hart Publishing Co., 1972.

Johnson, Paul. Modern Times: The World from the Twenties to the Eighties. New York: Harper and Row, 1983.

Kirkpatrick, Jeane. "An Anniversary of Open Season on Israel," Stamford Advocate, November 11, 1985.

Kuper, Leo. Genocide: Its Political Use in the Twentieth Century. New Haven: Yale University Press, 1981.

Kuper, Leo. The Prevention of Genocide. New Haven: Yale University Press, 1985.

Laqueur, Walter. The Road to Jerusalem: The Origins of the Arab-Israeli Conflict 1967. New York: Macmillan, 1968.

Laqueur, Walter and Barry Rubin, editors. The Israel-Arab Reader: A Documentary History of the Middle East Conflict. New York: Viking-Penguin, 1984.

Lewis, Anthony, "Arafat on Peace, New York Times, March 13, 1988, p. 29.

Lewis, Anthony, "Passing in the Night," New York Times, March 27, 1988, p. 29.

Lewis, Flora, "The Lessons of Hate," New York Times, April 10, 1988, part 4, p. 31.

Lilienthal, Alfred M. The Zionist Connection: What Price Peace? New York: Dodd, Mead and Co., 1978.

Mann, Thomas R., "Mission to the Middle East," Congress Monthly, March-April 1988, pp. 3-6. (Published in New York by the American Jewish Congress).

Morrow, Lance, "Israel at Forty, the Dream Confronts Palestinian Fury and a Crisis of Identity." Time, April 4, 1988, pp. 36-50.

O'Brien, Conor Cruise. The Siege: The Saga of Israel and Zionism. New York: Simon and Schuster, 1986.

Peretz, Martin, "Occupational Hazards," New Republic, March 14, 1988, pp. 14-20.

Polin, Raymond. Modern Government and Constitutionalism. Chicago: Nelson-Hall, 1979.

Response, August 1986 and February 1988. Los Angeles: Simon Wiesenthal Center.

Rubin, Barry, The Arab States and the Palestine Conflict. Syracuse: Syracuse University Press, 1981.

Said, Edward W. The Palestine Question and the American Context. Beirut: Institute for Palestine Studies, 1979.

Said, Edward W. The Question of Palestine. New York: Times Books, 1979.

Shipler, David K. Arab and Jew: Wounded Spirits in a Promised Land. New York: Times Books, 1986.

Smith, Tony, "No Blank Check for Israel," New York Times, March 26, 1988, p. 31.

"Soul of the Jewish State," New Republic, February 15, 1988.

Syrkin, Marie, "Doublespeak about Israel," Congress Monthly, March-April 1988, pp. 9-12.

Tillman, Seth P. The United States in the Middle East: Interests and Obstacles. Bloomington: Indiana University Press. 1982.

PART IV. SOME ISSUES OF JUSTICE

12.

GENDER EQUALITY: STILL A CHALLENGE TO JUSTICE

Kim M. Blankenship
Department of Sociology
Yale University

It is increasingly difficult to deny the existence of gender inequality in our society. In the United States this inequality manifests itself in, among other things, a sizeable sex-based earnings gap, tremendous occupational segregation, huge sex differences in the amount of time spent on household chores and childrearing duties, disproportionately high rates of poverty among women, and a large and growing incidence of violence against women.

This paper considers both the meaning of gender inequality for women's lives and the possibilities for challenging this inequality. It begins with an examination of some of the evidence regarding the persistence of inequities between men and women. It then considers why gender equality is viewed as such a radical idea. The third section of the paper examines the various ways in which feminist scholars have sought to understand women's oppression and the implications of their analyses for promoting gender equality. In the final section, the ways in which gender equality have been defined in the law and public policy are considered. The paper concludes with a reassessment of gender equality.

EVIDENCE OF GENDER INEQUALITY

The past century has witnessed a dramatic change in the extent of women's paid employment; yet this has not been accompanied by much significant change in their economic and social status. In 1890 only 19 percent of all women over the age of sixteen worked in the paid labor force (Golding, 1984:Table 1). By 1984, the comparable figure was 53.5 percent: more than half of all women worked for wages (Sidel, 1986:60). More dramatic still has been the increase in the proportion of employed married women, from 4.6 percent in 1890 (Goldin, 1984:Table 1) to 52 percent in 1980 (U.S. Bureau of the Census, 1983:Figure 5). Prior to 1960 older women returning to work accounted for most of this growth. After 1960, younger married women first with school-aged children and most recently with preschoolers have entered the labor force in larger numbers. During the same period, men's labor force participation rates have fallen. It might seem that women's increased participation in the labor force would be accompanied by a trend towards greater equality between men and women. Such has not been the case, however.

Working women earn much less than working men. In 1955 the median earnings of full-time year-round working women was 64 percent of their male counterparts' earnings. This meant that women earned 64 cents for every dollar that a man earned (Blau, 1984:308). The figure declined to 59 percent in 1981 and then returned to its 1955 level of 64 percent in 1984 (Sidel, 1986:61). Does this earnings difference between men and women reflect sex differences in educational attainment? According to United States Census Bureau figures, the answer is a resounding "no." In 1980, women aged 25 or over with a college degree earned 62 percent of what a male college graduate earned. Indeed, men who had not graduated from high school earned more than women with a college degree (U.S. Bureau of the Census, 1983:21). Studies based on more disaggregated data replicate these findings. For example, an examination of the careers of 1972 graduates of Harvard's schools of law, dentistry, design, divinity, education, public health, and arts and sciences reveals that seven years after having received their degrees, and regardless of their family or marital status, women graduates in every field had lower salaries than their male counterparts (cited in Marxhall and Paulin, 1984:201).

If the sex-based earnings gap does not reflect sex differences in education, it also does not reflect broad occupational differences between the sexes. In each broad occupational category, full-time year-round working women earn less than their male counterparts. Women do best in professional and technical occupations and craft and related jobs where they earn 64 percent of similarly located men. They fare worst in sales jobs where they earn only half of what men sales workers earn (Blau, 1984:308). Furthermore, the wage gap persists even when occupations are defined more narrowly. A comparison of average weekly earnings for men and women in 1981 for example, showed that in the 91 occupations in which both men and women

worked, there was not a single job in which women made
as much or more than men (Rytina, 1982).

In addition to educational and occupational
differences between the sexes, it might seem that such
factors as ability, experience, quality of education,
and labor force commitment would explain these large
sex-based earnings disparities. Yet, in a
comprehensive review of twenty-five years of social
science research on the causes of the pay gap, a
National Academy of Sciences study found that no
single study could account for more than half of the
gap in such individualistic terms. And most could
account for only one-quarter to one-third of the
difference (Treiman and Hartmann, 1981).

That women do not earn as much as men, even when
they do the same work, is but one of the ways in which
gender inequality manifests itself in our society. As
important, most men and women do not do the same
work: occupational segregation by sex is pervasive
and pronounced. Thus, the majority of women are
concentrated in only 25 of the 420 occupations
identified by the Census Bureau (Marks, 1984:1666).
Much attention is given to the fact that women have
made significant inroads into the professions.
Between 1962 and 1982 the proportion of women
engineers grew from 1 to 6 percent; of women doctors
rose from 6 to 15 percent; and of women college
professors from 19 to 25 percent (Sidel, 1986:61).
These gains however have been offset by women's
continued tendency to enter clerical jobs and their
lack of success in entering traditionally male blue-
collar jobs (Beller, 1984:26-28). Thus, in both 1970
and 1980, 75 percent of all women worked in female-
intensive occupations (defined as 80 percent or more
female), while 16 percent worked in neutral
occupations, and 9 percent in male-intensive jobs
(more than 80 percent male). And, in 1983 almost half
of all women employed worked in technical, sales, and
administrative support occupations.

As significant as the fact that women are
concentrated in only a limited number of occupations
is the fact that these are among the lowest-paying
jobs. Empirical evidence suggests that earnings are
30 to 50 percent higher in traditionally male
occupations than in traditionally female jobs (Beller,
1984:23). Moreover, according to the National Academy
of Sciences, one of the most important reasons these
jobs pay so little is the sex of the job incumbent.

263

Indeed, the study found that even when differences in both the characteristics of individuals and the requirements of the job were accounted for, every percentage point increase in the proportion female in the job lowered the average wage by $28 (Treiman and Hartmann, 1981).

Paid work is not the only work that women do. Housework, which includes such tasks as preparing and cleaning up after meals, doing laundry, shopping, keeping up the house and family members and managing finances, also is women's work. Indeed, numerous studies indicate that women are disproportionately responsible for these tasks (Hartmann, 1981a; Berch, 1982:Chapter 6; Berheide, 1984; Berk and Berk, 1979; Yancey and Eriksen, 1979). Women who do not work in the paid labor force spend an average of over fifty hours per week on household chores. In contrast, their husbands' contribution averages ten hours per week. Moreover, the average amount of time spent on housework by husbands does not change when their wives work. Thus, while employed women spend fewer hours on housework a week than do non-working women, their total work weeks are longer. Full-time working women spend slightly more than thirty hours a week on household duties. Their total work week averages seventy-six hours long. In contrast, their husbands spend a total of fifty-five hours working, which is about ten hours less than the work week of husbands with non-working wives (Hartmann, 1981a:Figure 1).

In another smaller study, Berheide (1984) found that wives performed between 74 and 92 percent of household tasks including cooking, cleaning the kitchen, doing laundry, straightening, ironing, running errands, caring for children, and completing miscellaneous chores. With the exception of errand running, their husbands performed only 12 to 24 percent of these tasks. These and similar studies indicate that women's increased participation in the paid labor force has not relieved them of responsibility for housework. Moreover, not only are they paid poorly for their work outside the home, but they are not paid at all for the many hours they spend on housework. Yet estimates suggest that, in 1980, women's work in the home was worth at least $15,000. In other words, if families had been forced to hire someone to do this work, it would have cost them at least this much (Berch, 1982:95-96).

Another symptom of gender inequality in our society is the disproportionately high rate of poverty among women. In 1983, 35.2 million Americans, or 15.3 percent of the population lived in poverty. This represents the highest rate of poverty since 1966. Although the rate decreased by nearly one percentage point between 1983 and 1984, most of this decline resulted from changes in men's economic status. About three-fourths of those families who escaped from poverty during this period were headed by white men (Sidel, 1986:10-11). Thus, any discussion of poverty in our country must focus on women and children, and particularly women and children of color (eg. see Sidel, 1986; Pearce, 1986; Shortridge, 1984; Ehrenreich and Piven, 1984; Coalition on Women and the Budget, 1986). Indeed, 75 percent of the nation's poor in 1984 were women and children (Coalition on Women and the Budget, 1986). Indeed, 75 percent of the nation's poor in 1984 were women and children (Coalition on Women and the Budget, 1986:6). Although the majority of these poor people were white, a much higher proportion of people of color were poor in 1984 than were whites. While 11.5 percent of whites were poor, 28.4 percent of Hispanics and 33.8 percent, or one-third of Blacks fell in this category (Sidel, 1986:12).

One of the most significant social changes to take place in the last two decades has been the rapid increase in the number of female-headed families. Between 1976 and 1984 the number of such families grew by 80 percent, from 5.5 to 9.9 million (Sidel, 1986:16). As a result, 29 percent of all children were living in families where their father was absent, unemployed or out of work. This was especailly true for black and Hispanic children, more than half of whom lived in families maintained by women (Goldsmith, 1985:8). As the proportion of these households has increased their relative status has declined. In 1983 the poverty rate among female-headed households was 36 percent as compared to a poverty rate of 7.6 percent among married couple families (U.S. Bureau of the Census, 1984:Table B). Again, the situation was worse for black and Hispanic families maintained by women, with poverty rates of 54 and 53 percent respectively (Goldsmith, 1985-8). To put it another way, three-fourths of all black children under the age of six living in female-headed households lived below the poverty level (Sidel, 1986:18). Women and their children comprise 93 percent of all AFDC recipients, 84 percent of all food stamp recipients, two thirds of all public housing residents, and two-thirds of all legal services clients (Coalition on Women and the Budget, 1986:15-27).

If women escape poverty in their younger years, they are at risk again after reaching the age of 65. Indeed, half of all older women have personal incomes below or within $1000 of the poverty level. As a consequence, 71 percent of the elderly poor are women. As with their younger counterparts, elderly women are extremely dependent on federal government welfare programs. They comprise 75 percent of aged Supplemental Security Income (SSI) recipients and three-fourths of Medicaid recipients over the age of 65 (Coalition on Women and the Budget, 1986:45-49).

Domestic violence is yet another way in which gender inequality manifests itself in families. For many years wife-beating remained a matter of private shame. Wives, their relatives, and their neighbors, not to mention public officials seemed to assume that some amount of violence was a part of normal female/male relationships. In the last decade however, it has become a matter of public concern and debate (for discussion of the development of the battered women's movement and public response to it see e.g. Wexler, 1982; Tierney, 1982; Gelb, 1983). Still, families hesitate to admit that battering occurs, making it difficult to know precisely how many women are affected. A 1976 national survey estimates that at least 1.8 million women are beaten in their homes every year (cited in Sidel, 1986:44). According to others however, these figures seriously underestimate the extent of the problem. For example, one-third of all homicide victims were killed by husbands or lovers. A 1979 Louis Harris poll found that 10 percent of all women interviewed experienced domestic violence during the year (cited in Gelb, 1983:250). And other estimates indicate that 10 to 20 percent of the male population engages in regular beating of their wives.

Battering is a problem that cuts across socioeconomic groups, geographical regions, age, race and ethnicity. Across all of these categories, battered wives tell similar stories of fear, love and self-blame. Consider the story of this woman told in Ruth Sidel's excellent book about women and poverty.

At twenty I met my first husband, lived with him and decided to get married. I never

should have married him. He used to beat me
up, he drank a lot, but I stayed with him.
I thought a baby would make the marriage
better. So our first child was born on our
second anniversary.

He spent a lot of money drinking and
wouldn't support us, so I had to. He became
violent when he was drinking, but I saw good
in him when he was not. He would smash
things; he almost choked me a few times.
The only time he would leave me alone is
when I pretended I was dead, or when I was
pregnant (1986:41).

A wife's hesitation to report crimes of battering
is mirrored in society's behavior. Police in
particular and the criminal justice system in general
respond slowly, if at all, to reports of domestic
violence. According to one study conducted in the
Cleveland, Ohio area, during a nine month period in
1979 police received 15,000 complaints which resulted
in only 700 reports filed and 460 arrests (cited in
Sidel, 1986:45).

Wife-battering is not the only institutionalized
form of violence against women. Rape, date rape,
sexual harassment and incest also stand as constant
reminders of gender inequality in our society. One in
three women will be raped in her lifetime (Grossholtz,
1983:59). Furthermore, while violence generally is
associated with rape, this need not be the case.
Recent studies reveal that date rape and other forms
of acquaintance rape have reached epidemic proportions
on college campuses (cited in Herman, 1984:26). For
example, according to a 1980 Cosmopolitan magazine
survey, of the 106,000 women responding, one-fourth
said they had been raped at least once. More than
half of those had been raped by friends, 37 percent by
strangers, 18 percent by relatives and 3 percent by
husbands.

Sexual harassment is another form of abuse faced
solely by women. In a recent review of survey
findings regarding the extent of sexual harassment,
Martin (1984) observes that the problem "is pandemic--
an everyday, everywhere occurence" (p. 56). Sexual
harassment ranges from serious intrusions on women's
lives like unwanted letters, phone calls, materials of
a sexual nature, pressure for sexual favors, or
physical contact (such as touching or pinching) to

267

less severe intrusions such as unwanted pressure for dates, suggestive looks or gestures, or teasing. According to recent surveys somewhere between one-third and one-half of women have experienced at least one of these forms of harassment.

Like sexual harassment and family violence, incestuous abuse crosses socioeconomic, geographic and race and ethnic boundaries. As with other forms of violence, the vast majority of offenders are men and the vast majority of victims females (Begus and Armstrong, 1983). As Begus and Armstrong point out, incestuous abuse ranges from indecent exposure and fondling to masturbation, cunnilingus, fellatio and intercourse (1983:237). Moreover, it is rarely an isolated act. Instead, it occurs over a long period of time.

Evidence from other countries indicates that gender inequality, which, as we have seen manifests itself in a wide variety of ways, knows no national boundaries. In the words of the United Nations: "Women constitute one half of the world's population, perform nearly two-thirds of its work hours, receive one-tenth of the world's income, and own less than one-hundredth of the world's property" (cited in Phillips, 1987:5). Although the sex-based wage gap in the United States is second only to Japan (with a male/female wage ratio of 52.7 percent) among the 16 OECD nations, in no country have women achieved economic parity with men. For example, in 1982 the sex-based wage ratio in the United Kingdom was 69 percent, in Greece 74 percent, in Denmark 84 percent, in Australia 85.2 percent and in Sweden 90 percent (International Labor Organization, 1985).

Occupational segregation in other industrialized countries is pronounced as well. In Britain for example, over half of all women work in the two occupational categories of clerical and service work. As in the United States, women in Britain have made significant inroads into the professions over the past decade. Yet within this category they dominate the lowest ranks: More than a third are nurses and almost another third are primary and secondry school teachers (Ruggie, 1984:65-67). A similar pattern holds in Sweden. Secretarial work is the most common occupational affiliation of women in this country. While nearly 40 percent of women workers in Sweden are professionals (technical and medical workers), here too they remain in the lower ranks of nursing and pre-

268

school and primary school teachers (Ruggie, 1984:67).
Although somewhat more evenly distributed across the
occupational spectrum than their European
counterparts, women in the Soviet Union also are
concentrated more heavily in the lower-paying sectors
such as education, trade, public health and welfare
and cultural work (Berch, 1982:Table 11-3).

It seems that women in other industrialized
countries also are responsible for a disproportionate
share of housework. In Britain and Sweden this
manifests itself in the tendency for women with small
children to work part-time (Ruggie, 1984:72-74). In
Britain, nearly 40 percent of all employed women
worked part-time and in Sweden the comparable figure
was 46 percent. In contrast only about 10 percent of
all employed men in these countries worked part-time.
In the Soviet Union, where women spend as much time as
men on their jobs they also spend more than twice as
much time on housework. As a consequence, they report
having less than two-thirds the amount of free time as
men (Berch, 1982:Table 11-4). In the words of one
Soviet woman:

> Although women are now legally equal to
> men, male psychology has not changed. For
> many women, marriage means a working day
> equal to a man's plus another working day at
> home. Men seldom view marriage as a joint
> venture. A man I know is a good example.
> When he married, he couldn't boil water and
> he felt imposed upon if his wife asked him to
> go to the bakery. After his divorce, he lived
> alone and became a wonderful cook and
> housekeeper. But when he remarried he
> reverted completely to type(cited in Berch,
> 1982:188).

As in the United States, most industrialized
countries have witnessed a rapid increase in the
number of female-headed households and have noticed a
disproportionately high risk of poverty among such
families (Kamerman, 1986). A 1981 report of the
Commission of European Communities, for example, finds
that the incidence of poverty among such families in
the European Economic Community is "above or far above
average" (cited in Kamerman, 1986:41). Other
countries such as Canada, Australia and Sweden have
launched similar investigations and arrived at similar
conclusions.

Violence against women also appears to know no national boundries. Indeed, the problem of wife-battering first received contemporary public attention in England in 1971, with the establishment of the first battered women's shelter (Gelb, 1983; Tierney, 1982). Maria Mies (1983) tells of the pervasiveness of the problem in Germany as she recounts efforts to establish a shelter in Cologne in the face of skeptical municipal authorities. In the less industrialized world, the forms of violence against women most publicized in the West include female infanticide, the Indian rite of suttee or widow-burning, and genital mutilation.

Such compelling figures have led concerned scholars backwards asking whether gender equality has ever existed and forwards wondering whether it shall ever be known. Although there is a vast amount of literature, particularly in anthropology, addressing the former concern (eg. Leacock, 1978; Sacks, 1979: Draper, 1975; Gough, 1975; Blumberg, 1978), this paper is concerned primarily with the latter. Can we ever hope to achieve gender equality? If so, what form will it take? And how will we get there? To begin to answer these questions it is important to consider why efforts to promote gender equality meet with such tremendous resistance.

Gender Equality: A Radical Idea

Given the worldwide prevalence of gender inequality, it may seem hard to imagine that so many have refused to act against it. Yet history demonstrates time and time again not only disagreements over what should be done, but disagreements over whether a problem exists in the first place. The development of efforts to eliminate employment discrimination in the U.S. serve as but one example of this.

In 1964, Congress began debating Title VII of the Civil Rights Act. The bill was intended to prohibit employers from discriminating on the basis of race, religion, and national origin in hiring, firing, and setting any other term, condition or privilege of employment. In what appears to have been a joke, Congressman Smith of Virginia proposed that title VII be amended to include prohibitions against employment discrimination based on sex. In so doing, the conservative Congressman hoped to kill the entire

270

bill; he assumed that his colleagues would find the idea of "sex discrimination" so ridiculous that they would vote against the Act altogether. It seems that the Congressman knew at least some of colleagues quite well. His proposal met with considerable laughter. When the laughter died down and members turned their attention to debating the amendment, it became clear that many did find it difficult to accept the existence of discrimination against women or to imagine what might happen if women were granted equal rights. Consider for example, the response of Congressman Celler, a liberal Democrat and supporter of Title VII:

> You know, the French have a phrase for it when they speak of women and men. When they speak of the difference, they say 'vive la difference.'
>
> I think the French are right.
>
> Imagine the upheaval that would result from adoption of blanket language requiring total equality. Would male citizens be justified in insisting that women share with them the burdens of military service? What would become of traditional family relationships? What about alimony? Who would have the obligation of supporting whom? Would fathers rank equally with mothers in the right of custody to children? What would become of the crimes of rape and statutory rape? ...Would the many state and local provisions regulating working conditions and hours of employment for women be struck down? (Congressional Record, Vol. 110, 1964:2577).

Congressman Celler and many of his colleagues were convinced that the problem of sex discrimination and the resulting gender inequality simply were not as pervasive as the problems of race discrimination and racial inequality. This was articulated quite well by Congresswoman Green in the same debates:

> May I submit to my women colleagues, while I join with you in objecting to the discrimination against women, may I say that in all fairness the discrimination against the female of the species is not really a 'way of life,' and , I repeat, it is a way of life against Negroes in many parts of the

271

country and has been for far too many years. And I must admit to my male colleagues that sometimes, in some ways, maybe women do get some advantages (Congressional Record, Vol. 110, 1964:2581).

Eventually Title VII was passed with the "sex" prohibition intact. But not until Congress added another section to the bill specifying that under certain conditions, it was legal to discriminate against women. Specifically, Section 703 (e)(1) provides that when sex is a "bona fide occupational qualification reasonably necessary to the normal operation of [a] particular business of industry" it is appropriate to make an employment decision based on sex.

Slightly less than twenty years later, the Equal Rights Amendment fared less well in Congress. Indeed, in June 1982 the deadline for ratifying the amendment passed, three states shy of the thirty-eight necessary to secure it in the U.S. Constitution. The amendment simply demanded that: "Equality of rights under the law shall not be denied or abridged by the United States or by any State on account of sex." Yet it met with tremendous resistance (Mansbridge, 1986; Marshall, 1984; Boneparth, 1982) with critics charging that it would, among other things, force women onto the battlefields and into the bathrooms with men.

Why have these apparently simple efforts to promote gender equality met with such resistance? Why is gender equality viewed as such a radical idea? In part at least, the answer lies in the tendency to assume that the demand for gender equality denies sexual difference; to assume it is a demand for women to be just like men. Yet, since women clearly differ from men in their reproductive capabilities, how can they ever be like men? Sexual difference appears then to be inescapable and gender equality to be not only unachievable but undesirable. Undoubtedly it was this concern that lay behind Congressman Celler's invocation of the famous French phrase, "vive la différence." Moreover, given that by the early 1960s it was increasingly more difficult to justify race inequality in the name of biological difference, it is not surprising that Congress was more wiling to address race inequality than it was to address gender inequality. Unlike women's reproductive structure a person's skin color was no longer so likely to be seen as a symbol of insurmountable difference.

That gender equality is counterposed so quickly to sexual difference is itself a reflection of the liberal context within which such debates frequently take place. For a central dilemma of liberal social and political theory is the relationship between individuality and equality. Liberal theory distinguishes between freedom or liberty on the one hand, and equality on the other (Mill, 1969; see also Tawney, 1964 on the liberal view of equality). From this perspective society is viewed as an aggregate of individuals not any one of whom is exactly the same. The just society is the society that allows for individual freedom: freedom of consciousness or opinion; freedom to pursue those opinions so long as others are not harmed; and freedom to unite for any purpose not involving harm to others. According to Mill, "to give any fair play to the nature of each, it is essential that different persons should be allowed to lead different lives" (1969:18). Freedom or liberty so described is contrasted with equality: "the wearing down into uniformity all that is individual in [persons]" (1969:77). In this view equality comes to mean collective mediocrity. It is precisely this fear that underlies popular wisdom, which holds that a society emphasizing equality is a society that would have all of its peoples thinking the same thoughts, wearing the same clothes, living in the same kind of houses, and eating the same kinds of foods. And oh how drab such a society would be! Instead, the best that can be hoped for, this wisdom tells us, is a society in which each is allowed to express her/himself and s/he wishes. In such a society, individual difference would thrive and oh how exciting life would be!

To be sure there is strength in liberal theory, especially when it is considered in the context of the seventeeth and eighteenth century thought in which it first emerged. By introducing the notion of free and equal beings, liberal theory rejected the feudal belief in the "natural order" of things whereby monarchs ruled through "divine right" and peasants submitted through obligation. Liberal theory announced that people had rights not just duties, and in so doing challenged tyranny and arbitrary power (Phillips, 1987:6). With respect to gender equality, this has meant that even though liberals fear it is impossible to overcome the biological differences between the sexes, it is possible to promote the freedom of individual women. Women may be different from men, liberal theory tells us, women may be able to bear children while men cannot, but society should not force them to have children when they do not want them. On the other hand, if women want to lead different lives, if they want to stay at home and raise children they also should be allowed to do so. It may never be possible to promote total equality between the sexes, just as it will never be possible to promote total equality in a society comprised of unique individuals. But it is possible to provide for the freedom of each individual to live the life s/he chooses.

If liberal theory has emphasized individuality which it contrasts with equality, it also has tended to focus on political and legal rights which it disassociates from social and economic status. From the liberal perspective we are all citizens regardless of our socio-economic status (see for example, Phillips, 1987:7). Yet this argument implies that status differences do not matter, and here the liberal argument runs into trouble. For status differences do matter. If persons are illiterate, as many poor people are, they cannot read campaign literature and are unlikely to vote. If persons have no money they are unlikely to bring cases to court. By separating politcal-legal rights from questions of socio-economic condition, liberal theory separates the issue of equality from the context in which it occurs. It abstracts equality from the reality of social inequality. Allowing for individual difference to thrive only promotes equality in a society that attaches no value to those differences, in a society in which no one is disadvantaged systematically for his or her differences. Demanding that all be free to live the life they choose only promotes equality in a society which does not systematically reward some lifestyles over others. Liberal theory requires that we all are equal before it can guarantee our equality.

There is an analogy to be drawn here with the contrast between sexual difference and gender equality. Those who view the demand for gender equality as a denial of biological difference tend to assume that biological differences between the sexes do not, or at least should not matter anyway--that they do not play a part in determining social and economic status or legal and political rights. If women's biology makes them more suited to raising children than to digging ditches, this perspective tells us, they should be allowed to do so. Indeed, differences in reproductive capacities are viewed as one of the many differences that make individuals have blue eyes and some have brown, that make some individuals good at painting pictures and others good at building bridges. Absent from this perspective is an understanding of the way in which society gives meaning to biological difference, just as there is absent from liberal theory an understanding of how social and economic status structure political and legal rights. Nowhere is it recognized that in our society as presently structured, those who raise children are disadvantaged relative to those who dig ditches. In this way, liberal theory fails to acknowledge the extent to which society devalues women; and to the extent that women are defined biologically, devalues women's biology. It fails to recognize that socially, women and men are not equal; that the society that gives meaning to gender differences is a society in which women are subordinate. In short, the social context which gives biology its meaning has constructed women's biology as inferior to men's. Thus, biology does not simply signify individual diversity in our society as popular wisdom would seem to have it. It signifies inequality.

Gender equality then is viewed as a radical idea by many, at least in part because it is viewed as a denial of biological difference between the sexes. From this perspective, to demand gender equality is to call for a radical state of androgyny, which, from the point of view of liberal theory, is highly undesirable. Under closer scrutiny however, it becomes clear that to address the question of gender equality in these terms is to justify inequality in the name of biology, much as occurred in the eighteenth and nineteenth centuries when it came to race-based inequality. Today it is no longer socially acceptable to argue (at least openly) that biological differences between the races make it impossible to promote racial equality. Rarely is the argument made any more, as once it was made by white plantation owners and Nazis, that skin color or race/ethnic background makes some inferior to others. Moreover, history has shown that this perspective actually served to justify race inequality--an inequality from which certain groups drew concrete benefits. So too does it seem that the argument against gender equality which draws on biological difference and invokes the spectre of radical androgyny serves to hide the fact that certain groups benefit from the existence and perpetuation of gender inequality. Indeed, when we look at why such seemingly simple efforts to promote gender equality as Title VII of the Civil Rights Act of 1964 and the more recent proposed Equal Rights Amendment met with such resistance, we see that it was not just because the idea of gender equality offended people's sensibilities. Certain groups actively opposed these measures because they stood to lose from their implementation. By way of elaborating this, it is useful to turn to an examination of the ways in which feminists have discussed gender equality.

GENDER INEQUALITY: SOURCES OF WOMEN'S OPPRESSION

Feminism is a tradition rich in debate. Yet feminists have at least two things in common. They agree that inequality between the sexes exists and they are committed to gender equality. They do not, however, agree either on the sources of this inequality or on the form that equality should take (for detailed discussions see Jaggar and Rothenber, 1984; Walby, 1986:esp. Chapter 2; Phillips, 1987: Barrett, 1980; Hooks, 1984; Buechler, 1984).

In very concrete terms this means that feminists will interpret the same evidence of gender inequality differently. Take the sex-based wage gap discussed earlier as an example. According to some feminists the wage gap only symbolizes gender inequality under certain circumstances. These feminists agree that there are some valid reasons to expect individual earnings differences because they agree that earnings reflect individual qualities. Those with more education, with greater ability, with more skills will earn more than others. If, however, a comparison of men and women who are equal in all of these terms reveals that women still receive lower pay than men, these feminists will conclude that the difference is based solely on sex and is therefore illegitimate. Thus, when seemingly unequal outcomes reflect relevant individual differences they are considered legitimate. When, on the other hand, they reflect irrelevant, arbitrary group distinctions such as sex, they truly signify inequality

In contrast, other feminists focus on the context in which difference is constructed. With regard to the earnings gap they ask us to question the criteria by which work is valued. Who decides what these criteria should be? according to what logic? and who

276

benefits from these decisions?   Is there any inherent
reason to expect education to be related to   earnings
or is this relationship socially created? Who decides
what skills are and what makes some individuals less
skilled than others?   Who says that it takes more
skill to operate a fork lift than it does to type a
letter?   And how do we decide which tasks are more
important? Is there something inherent in a task that
makes it so or does it derive its meaning from
society?   In all of these ways they assert that it
makes no sense to talk of individual differences
independent of the context which gives these
differences their meaning; and they direct our
attention to the nature of that context. According to
these feminists, ours is a society characterized by
inequality. It is a society where some have power and
others do not; a society where some get where they are
by oppressing others.   The sex-based wage gap then
signifies a difference in power, not in individual
abiliies, skills, etc. Given this context, it is hard
to justify any wage differences.

    This difference among feminists over how to
interpret the sex-based wage gap reflects a more
general and longstanding debate among theorists and
activists alike over the relationship between feminism
and liberalism.   As is clear from the way that each
interprets the sex-based wage gap, liberal feminists
advocate reform of existing structures as a means of
accomplishing gender equality. They demand that sex
not be a factor in wage-setting.   In contrast, more
revolutionary feminists call for fundamental changes
in social relations as a means to equality.   They
challenge the system of wage-setting itself, not just
the way in which the system has treated women.

    Intersecting this "reform vs. revolution" debate
is a second one regarding the significance of
biological differences between the sexes and the
relationship between these differences and gender
inequality. With regard to wages, liberal feminists
assert that biological differences between the sexes
are not, or should not be a relevant basis for denying
women a fair wage.   More revolutionary-minded
feminists accept the possibility of gender difference
but focus on challenging the standard in relation to
which the differecne is defined. They questin whether
there is such a thing as a fair wage or a relevant
difference.

Liberal feminism then, bears much in common with the liberal perspective discussed earlier. It agrees with the distinction made in liberal theory between freedom and equality and demands that women have the same freedom as men. While it acepts that at some level women can never be totally equal with men due to their biology, it agrees that such a definition of equality is undesirable anyway. Instead, it demands that biological differences not be allowed to restrict women's freedom to be what they want to be and to live as they want to live. As the early liberal feminist Mary Wollstonecraft argued, if women appear to be inferior to men it is not their biology that makes them so. Rather, it is the barriers that have kept them from realizing their full potential that are to blame. Hence, liberal feminism has focused its attention on removing barriers to equal opportunity as a means of promoting gender equality. This it has done at the expense of providing an explanation for why these barriers exist in the first place.

Liberal feminism also accepts the distinction between political-legal rights and socio-economic condition that lies behind the liberal view that we are all citizens no matter what our status. Indeed, liberal feminists have devoted considerable energy to securing political and legal rights for women, equal to those of men. Thus it was that early feminists fought for women's right to property (see Salmon, 1986 for an excellent discussion of women and property laws) and to the vote.

Most significant of all, liberal feminism, like liberal theory in general, requires that men and women be equal before it can guarantee their equality. For, liberal feminism reflects the liberal tradition in the way it abstracts discussions of gender equality from the reality of social inequality between the sexes. It demands that men and women be treated the same when they are the same without adequately addressing the fact that they are not the same. They are unequal. To the extent that they address this inequality, liberal feminists assert that it takes the form of barriers which prevent women from becoming like men. Yet they question neither the source of these barriers nor the one-sidedness of the demand that equality means women should be allowed to become the same as men and not that men should be allowed to become like women.

In contrast, more revolutionary-oriented feminists focus directly on the sources of the barriers to women's equality and challenge the standards against which women's difference derives. Unlike liberal feminists who would have it that biological differences can be made irrelevant simply by ignoring them, this group of thinkers argues that biological differences are significant in our society and will continue to be so until society itself changes. For the most part however, the significance of these differences does not rest in biology per se. Rather, it derives from the social conditions that give meaning to those differences. The nature of this society, how it oppresses women, and who serves as the standard against which women's differences are judged however, is the subject of debate among these feminists. In short, revolutionary-oriented feminists disagree among themselves over what are the fundamental structures and who are the primary agents of power. Radical feminists view patriarchy, the system of male dominance, as the fundamental structure of power and men as the primary agents of power. Men oppress women and men provide the standard against which women's differences are judged. Marxist-feminists assert that capitalism is the fundamental structure of power and classes the agents of power. Gender inequality then derives from capitalist social relations and women's differences are judged according to class-based standards. Socialist-feminists maintain that both capitalism and patriarchy structure the social world and both men and classes are the agents of power. In this view, women are evaluated according to class- and gender-based standards. Finally, race-conscious feminists focus on the interconnectedness of three power structures: capitalism, patriarchy, and racism (colonialism); and assert that women's differences are evaluated according to a race-, class- and gender-based standard.

Before looking at these perspectives in greater detail, it is useful to consider how they affect the interpretation of the specific aspects of gender inequality discussed earlier. Consider for example, the issue of violence against women. From the perspective of radical feminism, violence against women signifies men's power in our society. Indeed, men's violence against women is viewed as an important basis of their control over women. It is something that all women, as women, fear. As Susan Griffin writes, "rape and the fear of rape are a daily part of

279

all women's consciousness (Griffin, 1983:159). A Marxist-feminist, in contrast, would focus on the association between class and men's violence against women. From this perspective, ours is a capitalist society, and in this context men are oppressed as workers. Lacking power at the workplace and few opportunities to express or assert their power, they take their anger and feelings of powerlessness out on women. But they are not acting as men when they do so. They are acting as frustrated and alienated workers. In a non-capitalist, classless society this perspective would argue, where men have more power and control over work and their lives in general, there would be no violence against women. Socialist-feminist thinkers would attribute such violence to both class and gender. This perspective recognizes that violence against women transcends class boundaries. It involves a class component insofar as it tends to occur more frequently among certain class groups and it tends to take different forms among different class groups. But it also cannot be denied that it is men who are the abusers and women who are the victims. Thus, according to socialist-feminists, violence involves a gender component as well. There is no reason to believe that a classless society would be a society free of domestic violence, or any other form of violence against women. Finally, according to race-conscious feminists, domestic violence contains a race component and also as involves class and gender divisions. From this perspective, men's violence against women reflects the powerlessness associated with race-oppression as well as class oppression and the power of men as men in our society.

As the above discussion indicates, from the radical feminist perspective gender is the most salient division in our society, from which all others derive. Many who fall within this category however, leave the precise origins of women's subordination unexplained, emphasizing instead, the persistence and pervasiveness of gender inequality across time and place (Jaggar and Rothenberg, 1984:86-87). For this reason radical feminists often are criticized for treating patriarchy--the structure of male domination--as a universal, and to some extent a historical category. Although some have paid attention to the different forms that patriarchy has taken in different historical moments (Lerner, 1986) and others have demonstrated the way in which patriarchal relations appear in all aspects of social life (eg. Millet, 1977), patriarchy remains a relatively undertheorized concept. Thus, the basis of women's subordination, and the dynamic of patriarchy remain unclear. Shulamith Firestone (1970) stands as an exception in this regard, for she does offer a more complete theory of patriarchy. Firestone locates women's oppression in their biological difference from men. Because women menstruate, nurse and get pregnant, they are vulnerable relative to men. Among other things, men have controlled women by controlling reproduction. Like liberal feminists then, Firestone accepts that biological differences between the sexes relate fundamentally to the possibility of gender equality. Unlike liberal feminists however, she views these differences as neither inescapable nor irrelevant. According to Firestone, women must transcend (not ignore) their biology. And it is technology that will allow them to do so. Indeed, technology provides the key to women's emancipation from male dominance. For technological developments can make it possible to remove reproduction from women's bodies and thereby put an end to women's dependence on men. Gender equality will follow.

The focus on biological difference and the capacity of technology to overcome this difference contains two major flaws. First, it tends toward biological reductionism. Indeed, radical feminism in general falls prey to this criticism. For, by neglecting to address the basis and dynamic of patriarchy while emphasizing its historical persistence, radical feminists all imply that biology (defined broadly enough to include psychology) explains male domination. Yet biological differences appear immutable. The only way to escape the implied inevitability of gender inequality then is to hypothesize a route through which to transcend biology. Hence, Firestone's emphasis on technology. Yet herein lies the second problem with this perspective. It places us in a hopeless dilemma because technology is social. That is to say, technological development not ony takes shape within a social context but also, it reflects that context. If that context is one of gender inequality, of male domination, as Firestone suggests, then it is difficult to imagine how it would create the technology necessary for women's emancipation.

It would seem instead that women must control, or at least participate equally in the process of technological development before that technology can free women from their biology. Yet it seems also that it is only when women are once free of their biology that they can participate equally in the process of technological development. In short, the transformation of social relations is necessary for the development of emancipatory technology at the same time as the emancipatory technology is necessary for the transformation of social relations.

The tensions within Firestone's perspective and radical feminism in general appear more concretely in current debates over reproductive technology. With in-vitro fertilization, surrogacy, and embryo transfer now possible, the technologies necessary for realizing Firestone's vision seem close at hand. And yet these technologies have received an all but consistently warm welcome from feminists. On the one hand, they seem to have opened a wide range of reproductive choices. On the other hand, feminists caution us to consider the context which constructs these reproductive choices (Mies, 1985; Arditti et al., 1984; Hubbard, 1985; Stanworth, 1987). It is a context, they argue, in which those most affected by the technology have little to no control over its development. This in turn raises the very real possibility that these technologies will be used to control and oppress women rather than to free them. Some feminists conclude that inherently, the technology is neither empowering nor enslaving and that it can be used by, for, or against women (Rothman, 1984:32-33). Others conclude even more radically that:

> Technical progress is not neutral...It is always based--not just in its beginnings--on exploitation and subjection of women, exploitatin and oppression of other peoples...(emphasis in original, Mies, 1985:555)

> Exploitative and opressive relations cannot be overcome by more technologies--even if it [sic] were in the hands of women--but only by revolutionizing these relations (Mies, 1985:553).

This effort to direct our attention toward the context of social inequality characterizes the three remaining feminist traditions. Like Firestone and other radical feminists, feminists writing in this tradition recognize biological differences between the sexes. They do not, however, go as far as Firestone in attributing gender inequality to these differences. Instead, Marxist-feminists locate gender inequality in capitalist social relations. According to the most orthodox versions of this perspective, class is the most salient division from which all others, including gender divisions derive. Women's oppression is viewed as secondary to class oppression. It is important only insofar as it functions on behalf of capitalism, which it does in at least two ways. First, gender inequality serves an economic function because it preserves women as a reserve army of labor. Because of their family responsibilities women provide an especially cheap source of workers available for the worst jobs. Moreover, when unemployed they can return to the household. As a result, they are not a socially volatile group of unemployed workers. Gender inequality also serves a second, more political function for capitalism. According to these theorists gender divisions undermine class consciousness and worker organization and thereby help to reproduce capitalist control.

The more orthodox versions of Marxist-feminism border on economic reductionism in their tendency to reduce all social relations to class relations and all social inequality to class inequality. In focusing on women as workers, they ignore the importance and dynamics of family life. Families are not, as many Marxists would have it, a "haven in a heartless world" (Lasch, 1979)--the place where alientated workers can find loving and caring relations. They are a central location of women's oppression. Also, by focusing on gender divisions as they function for capitlism, the orthodox perspective understates the extent to which men benefit as men from gender inequality (for more extensive critiques of the orthodox perspective see e.g. Eisenstien, 1979; Hartmann, 1981b; Walby, 1986; Barrett, 1980). In attempting to address these problems, others have sought to formulate Marxist theory in a way that more directly acknowledges women's situations. Steve Buechler nicely summarizes the contribution of this perspective in these terms:

> Among the most important of these contributions is the attempt to grasp the larger economic significance of seemingly privatized labor [domestic or household work], its explicit theorization of women's unique dual labor role as it relates to the contradictory needs of capitalist economies, and its broader attempts to approach the

283

institution of work and the family as part
of a wholistic totality (1984:26).

Still, the focus of this perspective is the relevance
of women's work and of family for capitalism. Gender
inequality is not viewed as independent from class
inequality and so no independent structure of gender
inequality is the subject of theorizing.

   In contrast, socialist feminists stress the
importance of inequality between men and women in and
of itself. From this viewpoint an understanding of
social organization requires an analysis of the
interconnectedness of capitalism and patriarchy, of
class and gender relations. In this way, social-
feminists accept important insights from both radical
feminism and Marxist feminism. Society, they argue,
is organized around both productive and reproductive
activity.   Social feminists disagree among themselves
however, over how precisely to characterize the
relationship between the structures of these two
activities. Most of this debate revolves around two
issues. First, these feminists disagree on the amount
of relative independence they accord each system. For
some, capitalism and patriarchy are so interconnected
that we must talk of a capitalist patriarchy. Each
can be defined only by recognizing the other. Others
discuss capitalism and patriarchy as analytically
independent. Closely related to this first debate is
a second which revolves around the question of the
relationship between the two system: are they
mutually reinforcing or do they conflict with one
another?

   A final group of feminists focus on race ethnic
differences in their analyses of gender relations
(Hooks, 1984; Glenn, 1985; Combahee River Collective,
1979; Joseph, 1981). As these writers correctly point
out, there is a race ethnic component to nearly every
indicator of gender inequality we might imagine. This
means, on the one hand, that not all women are the
same. Though women as a whole fare worse than men,
women of color fare worse than white women. As
compared to white women they earn less, work in the
worst jobs, experience higher rates of poverty, and so
forth. On the other hand, the significance of race
ethnic inequality manifests itself in the fact that
not all men are the same either. If men are better
off than women it also is true that some men are
better off relative to women than are others.

284

Specifically, among men, men of color remain at the bottom of the hierarchy. Hence, race conscious feminists dirct our attention to variation in the experience of gender inequality and demand that we transform our categories to include this variety. Strategically, this means that a challenge to gender inequality must include a challenge to racist as well as patriarchal and capitalist structures.

From this discussion then, it should be clear that feminists are united in their efforts to understand and explain inequality between men and women and to promote gender equality. They disagree among themselves in some important ways as well. While liberal feminists tend to disassociate the matter of equality from the sources and relations of power, more revolutionary feminists tend to focus precisely on the issue of power. While liberal feminists and to some extent radical feminists tend to concentrate on the relationship between biological difference and gender equality, other feminists focus more on the context from which difference derives its meaning and the way in which difference becomes translated into inequality. With the exception of liberals, who do not theorize about the barriers to women's equality, feminists agree that groups actively benefit from gender divisions. Thus, there are groups as well as structural forces that act to maintain those divisions even as women may strugle to overcome them. It is appropriate then to examine what has been done to challenge gender inequality in the realm of law and public policy.

GENDER EQUALITY, THE LAW AND PUBLIC POLICY

Laws and public policy aimed at addressing gender inequality in the United States have tended to fluctuate back and forth between a focus on equal treatment and a focus on gender difference. At issue is the question of whether, on the one hand, equality should be provided for by guaranteeing that women are treated the same as men; or, on the other hand, by recognizing and accomodating women's difference from men. Or as Ruth Milkman puts the question: "Are women's interests best served by public policies that treat women and men identically, ignoring the social and cultural differences between them? Or should we view those differences positively and seek greater recognition and status for traditionally female values

285

and forms of behavior?" (1986:375). Each approach has its limitations.

The equal treatment approach reflects the liberal tradition in its assertion that equality requires men and women to be treated equally. Rarely does it go quite this far however. Instead, it reflects the modified demand that men and women be treated alike when they are situated similarly: when women are like men they should be treated like men. The limitations of this perspective have been alluded to already.

On the one hand, it is difficult to achieve such a goal in a context in which men and women are situated unequally. Hence, the equal treatment approach must confront a major dilemma: can it provide for equality in situations in which men and women cannot be compared or at times in which the differences between them are noncomparable? Biological differences form the outermost boundaries of this dilemma. And it seems that the equal treatment approach would allow biological difference to justify differential treatment. Nowhere is this more clear than in the bona fide occupational qualification (bfoq) exception to Title VII referred to earlier. The bfoq establishes that biological differences between the sexes can be relevant grounds for employment decisions and therefore, that under certain circumstances employers _can_ treat men and women on the basis of their sex. The classic examples given here are wet nurses and sperm donors.

Essentially the law protects employers who would hire only men as sperm donors (assuming such positions were ever subject to hiring and firing) from charges of sex discrimination! But as Catharine MacKinnon points out (1979:137), the exception also has been interpreted to mean that sex differences, for cultural/social reasons, may give rise to the need to discriminate on the basis of sex. Thus, guidelines of the U.S. Equal Employment Opportunity Commission (the agency responsible for enforcing Title VII) state that sex differences may give rise to a legitimate need for "authenticity or genuineness" in certain jobs, such as acting, which only one sex can provide.

Although this may seem a reasonable stipulation as regards acting, it is not hard to imagine its being abused. Indeed, for many years the airlines industry used precisely this logic in justifying its practice of hiring only women flight attendants. Presumably

286

customers preferred women attendants to men because of women's qualities "as women." Might a similar argument be made to restrict women's access to better jobs? Although the law has not upheld such an argument, it is clear that it leaves considerable room for inequality in the name of social and cultural tastes.

A second limitation of the equal treatment approach is its implication that gender equality requires women to become like men. The standard of comparison then is not neutral, it is a male standard. Women are different because they are not like men, this perspective tells us. It does not question why it is that women's ability to have a baby should make them deviate from the norm. It doesn't ask why, for example, work is structured in such a way as to make it difficult for people to bear, nurse and raise children and at the same time, maintain a good, high-paying job. It doesn't wonder about the standards according to which work presently is organized. In a differently organized society, men might be considered deviant for not being able to have a child and life might be arranged accordingly. The equal treatment approach then demands that the same standards be applied equally to men and women but does not recognize that the standard is a male one. And in a society in which men and women are unequal, women either will be far less likely to meet such a standard or will be required to become like a man in order to do so.

In contrast to the equal treatment approach, the approach to gender equality that focuses on differences, or on special treatment, takes differences as its starting point. Men and women are different, it argues, and laws and public policies ought to recognize those differences. While seemingly an alternative view of equality however, this second approach runs up against essentially the same barriers. As with the equal treatment approach, it has tended to decontextualize the demand for equality. Thus, it fails to recognize that women's differences are created in a context of social inequality between the sexes. In such a context, recognizing and accomodating women's difference runs the risk of perpetuating or reproducing that inequality.

Second, the differences or special treatment approach has tended not to confront the issue of

287

standards. This is revealed most clearly in the language of "special treatment." To contrast special and equal treatment is still to imply that women deviate from the norm. It is to accept standards that are not broad enough to include both sexes, standards by which neither group is considered special nor by which either is requred to act like the other. The problem for law and public policy then would seem to be one of constructing an approach that recognizes the differences between men and women but penalizes no one for those differences. It would be one of constructing an approach that recognizes the systematic damage done to women as women (as well as, perhaps, members of social class and race ethnic groups) and guarantees equality to all on the basis of their equal personhood. In order to illustrate the tensions within laws and public policy aimed at promoting gender equality, it is best to consider a few examples.

Protective legislation serves as one of the best examples of the special treatment or differences approach (for detailed discussions of these laws see Baer, 1978; Steinberg, 1982; Lehrer, 1987). Protective legislation placed restrictions on the number of hours women could work, the times of day during which they could work, and the amount of weight they could lift while working. It emerged as part of a struggle to improve working conditions for all workers but came to pass as protections on women's employment only. While the courts refused to uphold such restrictions on men's work, viewing them as violations of men's freedom of contract, they justified their application to women in the name of sex differences. This perspective is articulated quite well in a Supreme Court decision handed down in 1908. At issue were the protective laws in the State of Oregon, which placed a maximum on the number of hours women might work in a day. The High Court unanimously upheld the law in these terms:

> Even if all restrictions on political, personal, and contractual rights were taken away and [woman]...stood, so far as statutes are concerned, upon an absolutely equal plane with [man]...it would still be true that she will rest upon and look to him for protection; that her physical structure and proper discharge of her maternal functions-- having in view not merely her own health, but the well-being of the race--justify

legislation to protect her from the greed as well as the passion of man. The limitations which this statute places upon her contractual powers, upon her right to labor, are imposed not only for her benefit, but also largely for the benefit of all...The two sexes differ in structure, in the amount of physical strength, in the capactiy for long-continued labor, the influences of vigorous health upon the future well-being of the race, the self-reliance which enables one to assert full rights, and in the capacity to maintain the struggle for subsistence. This difference justifies a difference in legislation (cited in Blankenship, 1986:306).

Protective legislation became the increasing subject of controversy as it became clear that it operated to restrict women's access to better paying jobs. Shift differentials were paid to night work for example, yet in many states women were prohibited from holding night jobs and were therefore unable to earn these differentials. Similarly, restrictions on the number of hours women could work limited their ability to make overtime, and weight-lifting restrictions kept them out of higher paying jobs. Because these laws operated to prevent women from working in better jobs, they found tremendous support among male-dominated trade unions. But women also supported them; for protective laws offered some of the only guarantees of better working conditins available to women. Thus it was not until the 1970s that they were finally ruled to be discriminatory.

Protective laws then, were justified on the premise that women were biologically weaker than men and that such differences ought to be accommodated by public policy. To be sure, the premise itself is questionable. After all, nurses, a typically female and relatively low-paying occupation lift patients who weigh considerably more than the twenty-five pounds typically specified in weight-lifting laws. More important however, it is clear that the laws served to justify and even promote women's inequality in the name of biological difference. Given the social reality, acknowledging women's difference (even assuming it existed) did not promote but undermined gender equality. Furthermore, the standard according to which women were judged different was clearly a male one. The laws viewed the ability to lift more than twenty-five pounds or work more than eight hours in a day or work at night as the norm and women as deviating from that norm.

Tensions within the equal treatment approach manifest themselves in numerous public policies. In the area of divorce law, for example, there has been a growing movement towards no fault laws which seek to treat men and women the same by dividing property equally between husbands and wives. Yet as Lenore Weitzman (1985) convincingly demonstrates in her analysis of California divorce laws, this approach has worked to women's disadvantage. For the reality is that men and women are not situated equally, and to treat them as they are ultimately perpetuates women's inequality. For example, women typically are awarded custody of children. This means that even though husbands and wives may receive the same amount in a settlement, husbands have only to support themselves while wives must support themselves and the children. Moreover, while husbands usually have a job, wives often do not. So losing their husbands means they are left with no source of income and must search for a job, often with few skills and little experience to recommend them. Hence, Weitzman found that upon divorce husbands experience a 42% increase in their standard of living while their ex-wives and the minor children living with them experience a 73% decline in their standard of living in the first year after divorce (1985:xii).

The equal treatment approach confronts its most difficult obstacles when it must address characteristics unique to women. Pregnancy and job segregation provide but two examples in this regard. When the courts first confronted the question of whether excluding pregnancy from a disability plan constituted sex discrimination they ruled that it did not. The argument reflected the equal treatment approach in its focus on whether women who were situated equally with respect to men were treated equally. The Supreme Court ruled that to excude pregnancy was not to discriminate on the basis of sex--as if to say that pregnant men would be treated the same as pregnant women under such a plan. Instead the Court ruled that, though pregnancy is unique to women it is not universal to them (something that all women experience) and therefore, to exclude pregnancy is not to treat on the basis of sex.

Rather than accommodating women's differences, the Court allowed them to justify differential treatment. Without confronting the weakness of the equal treatment approach, Congress passed a bill in 1978 prohibiting pregnancy discrimination, and defining it as sex discrimination. The bill requires that where an employer's disability plan includes coverage for temporary disability it also must include coverage for pregnancy. In this way, Congress managed to address the issue of pregnancy within the equal treatment approach. It simply defined disability plans as the context in which to consider the treatment of men and women. In this context men and women were considered similar and therefore were required to be treated the same.

The limitations of the emphasis on equal treatment appear presently in the debate over comparable worth. Comparable worth seeks to challenge the sex-based wage gap. As mentioned in the first part of this paper, women's earnings are consistently lower than men's earnings. This is associated with occupational segregation. Indeed, one of the primary reasons women, on average, earn less than men is that they are concentrated in low-wage, predominantly female jobs. Laws relating to equality and wages take one of two forms, neither of which adequately addresses this situation. Equal pay laws require that men and women be paid the same for the same work. A clearer expression of the treatment approach there could not be. Yet because women are not situated equally (they are segregated in different jobs), it is difficult to compare them to men and to determine whether they are being treated unequally.

In contrast, equal opportunity laws (as embodied in Title VII) require the removal of barriers that restrict women's access to better-paying jobs. In this way, equal opportunity law recognizes that women are not always situated equally with men, and demands the elimination of barriers that prevent them from becoming so. The male standard remains intact however, as does the goal of equal treatment. Provisions for women's equal opportunity tell women that to get higher pay they must take a traditionally-male and therefore higher paying job. They do nothing to challenge wage-setting practices in predominantly female jobs, and for this reason seem to be telling women in those jobs that they deserve the wage they receive. Moreover, once they have gained access to better-paying jobs, women's equality rests again on

291

the equal treatment guarantee, with all of its limitations.

Comparable worth seeks to challenge the sex-based wage gap in a way that simultaneously challenges the limitations of both the treatment and the differences approach to gender equality. It attempts to formulate a way of acknowledging the differences between men and women and between traditionally female and traditionally male jobs which does not at the same time penalize women and those working in traditionally female jobs for those differences. Comparable worth does this by forcing us to confront the question of how we value work. Why is it that those characteristics typically associated with women's jobs are paid less than those associated with men's jobs? Why is it that people are considered to be working under harsher job conditions and therefore to be deserving of highesr pay when they work outside or when they lift a lot of weight (such as in traditionally male jobs) but not when they work in poorly lit offices in front of video display terminals relentlessly punching in someone else,s data day after day (such as in traditionally female jobs)?

Comparable worth requires us to answer these questions by demanding a reevaluation of work that takes into account the work that women do and in so doing, denies the male standard. On the other hand, comparable worth in practice has tended not to meet this potential. Where comparable worth plans have been implemented, they have tended to take the form of plans that pay men and women equally for comparable work. Elaborate job evaluation systems often are used to compare men's and women's jobs. Yet clearly, this form of implementation reflects the treatment approach in its assertion that only where their work is similar should men and women be treated comparably. And usually, the job evaluations used to compare jobs reflect male standards. Thus, to the extent that comparable worth plans have been implemented, they have tended to take a form quite compatible with the equal treatment approach. The larger struggle for comparable worth, however, has been a struggle to overcome the limitations of both the differences and the treatment approaches to gender inequality. As we have seen, these limitations have characterized all efforts to challenge inequality between the sexes through laws and public policy.

CONCLUSIONS

That gender inequality exists cannot be denied. It manifests itself in nearly every aspect of social life. It also seems clear that any effort to overcome this inequality will have to transcend the boundaries imposed by liberal theory and reflected in laws and public policies. It is simply too narrow to view gender equality as a choice between freedom and equality, or individuality and equality, or equal opportunity and equal outcome, or treatment and difference, or equal treatment and special treatment. Instead, we must begin to ask ourselves what type of structure it is that we live in that imposes these boundaries. Who benefits and who stands to gain from restricting gender equality to these terms? Gender equality rests in a challenge to that structure. It rests in a challenge to the power relations that constitute society. And it rests in the empowerment of oppressed groups.

At the same time, gender equality requires us to recognize difference among both women and men. We are not all "in this thing together." The experience of women and men varies depending on their class and race ethnic origins. Gender equality can be achieved only with a sensitivity to and an effort to overcome these differences as well. Only in this way is it possible to create a society in which difference can be recognized without simultaneously serving to justify inequality. Such a society requires that all people have access to the conditions necessary to live a decent, healthy, enjoyable life; and thereby all should be able to participate in the creation and continuation of social life. Only in this way can we expect to realize the liberal vision that in promoting freedom we also will promote equality.

REFERENCES

Arditti, Rita, Renate Duelli Klein, and Shelley Minden (eds.)
1984   Test-Tube Women: What Future for Motherhood? (London: Pandora Press)

Baer, Judith
1978   The Chains of Protection: The Judicial Response to Women's Labor Legislation (Westport, Connecticut: Greenwood Press)

Barrett, Michele
1980   Women's Oppression Today: Problems in Marxist Feminist Analysis (London: Verso)

Begus, Sarah and Pamela Armstrong
1983   "Daddy's Right: Incestuous Assault." pp. 236-249 in Irene Diamond (ed.) Families, Politics and Public Policy (New York: Longman)

Beller, Andrea H.
1984   "Occupational Segregation and the Earnings Gap." pp. 23-33 in U.S. Commission on Civil Rights, Comparable Worth: Issue for the 80s, A Consultation of the U.S. Commission on Civil Rights, Volume 1, June 6-7, 1984 Washington, D.C.

Berch, Bettina
1982   The Endless Day: The Political Economy of Women and Work (New York: Harcourt, Brace, Jovanovich, Inc.)

Berheide, Catharine White
1982   "Women's Work in the Home: Seems Like Old Times." In Beth B. Hess and Marvin B. Sussman (eds.) Women and the Family: Two Decades of Change (New York: Haworth Press)

Berk, Richard A. and Sarah Fenstermaker Berk
1979   Labor and Leisure at Home: Content and Organization of the Household Day (Beverly Hills, California: Sage Publications)

Blankenship, Kim M.
1986   Sex Discrimination in Employment: An Analysis of U.S. Federal Policy. PhD. Dissertation, Duke University

Blau, Francine D.
   1984 "Women in the Labor Force: An   Overview."
         Pp. 297-315 in Jo Freeman (ed.) Women: A
         Feminist Perspective, Third Edition (Palo
         Alto,   California: Mayfield Publishing
         Company)

Blumberg, Rae Lesser
   1978 Stratification: Socioeconomic and Sexual
         Inequality (Dubuque, Iowa: Wm. C. Brown)

Boneparth, Ellen (ed.)
   1982 Women,   Power and   Policy   (New   York:
         Pergamon Press)

Buechler, Steve
   1984 "Sex and Class: A Critical Overview of
         Some Recent Theoretical Work and Some
         Modest   Proposals."   The   Insurgent
         Sociologist 12(3):19-32.

Coalition on Women and the Budget
   1986 Inequality of Sacrifice: The Impact of the
         Reagan Budget on Women (Washington, D.C.)

Combahee, River Collective
   1979 "A Black Feminist Statement." Pp. 362-372
         in Zillah R. Eisenstein (ed.) Capitalist
         Patriachy and the Case for Socialist
         Feminism (New York: Monthly Review Press)

Draper, Patricia
   1975 "Kung   Women: Contrasts   in   Sexual
         Egalitarianism in Foraging and Sedentary
         Contexts." Pp. 77-109 in Rayna R. Reiter
         (ed.) Toward an Anthropology of Women (New
         York: Monthly Review Press)

Ehrenreich, Barbara and Francis Fox Piven
   1984 "The Feminization of Poverty." Dissent 31
         (Spring):162-170

Eisenstein, Zillah R. (ed.)
   1979 Capitalist Patriarchy and the Case for
         Socialist Feminism (New York: Monthly
         Review Press)

Firestone, Shulamith
   1970 The Dialectic of Sex (New York: Bantam
         Books)

Gelb, Joyce
    1983 "The Politics of Wife Abuse." Pp. 250-262
          in Irene Diamond (ed.) Families, Politics
          and Public Policy (New York: Longman)

Glenn, Evelyn Nakano
    1985 "Racial   Ethnic   Women's   Labor: The
          Intersection of Race, Gender and Class."
          Review of Radical Political Economy 17:86-
          108

Goldin, Claudia
    1984 "The   Earnings   Gap   in   Historical
          Perspective." Pp. 3-20 in U.S. Commission
          on Civil Rights, Comparable Worth: Issue
          for the 80's, A consultation of the U.S.
          Commission on Civil Rights, Volume 1, June
          6-7, 1984 (Washington, D.C.)

Goldsmith, Judy
    1985 "Testimony of the National Organization for
          Women,   Presented   by   Judy   Goldsmith,
          President." Pp. 233-249 in U.S. Congress,
          House Committee on Post Office and Civil
          Service, Options for Conducting a Pay
          Equity Study of the Federal Pay   and
          Classification Systems.   Hearings Before
          the Committee on Post Office and Civil
          Service, 99th Congress, 1st Session.
          (Washington,   D.C.:   U.S. Government
          Printing Office)

Gough, Kathleen
    1975"The   Origin of the Family."   Pp. 51-76 in
          Rayna Reiter (ed.) Toward an Anthropology of
          Women (New York: Monthly Review Press)

Griffin, Susan
    1983 "Rape: The All American Crime." Pp. 159-
          168 in Laurel Richardson and Verta Taylor
          (eds.),   Feminist Frontiers: Rethinking
          Sex,   Gender,   and Society   (Reading,
          Massachusetts: Addison-Wesley Publishing
          Co.)

Grossholtz, Jean
    1983 "Battered   Women's   Shelters   and   the
          Political Economy of Sexual Violence." Pp.
          59-69 in Irene Diamond (ed.) Families,
          Politics and Public Policy (New York:
          Longman)

Hartmann, Heidi I.
1981a "The Family as the Locus of Gender, Class, and Political Struggle: The Example of Housework." Signs 6 (Spring):366-394
1981b "The Unhappy Marriage of Marxism and Feminism: Towards a More Progressive Union." Pp. 1-42 in Lydia Sargent (ed.), Women and Revolution: The Unhappy Marriage of Marxism and Feminism (Boston: South End Press)

Herman, Dianne
1984 "The Rape Culture." Pp. 20-38 in Jo Freeman (ed.) Women: A Feminist Perspective (Palo Alto, California: Mayfield Publishing Company)

Hooks, Bell
1984 Feminist Theory: From Margin to Center (Boston: South End Press)

Hubbard, Ruth
1985 "Prenatal Diagnosis and Eugenic Ideology." Women's Studies international Forum 8(6):567-576

International Labour Organization
1985 Personal memo

Jaggar, Alison M. and Paula S.Rothenberg
1984 Feminist Frameworks: Alternative Theoretical Accounts of the Relations Between Men and Women, Second Edition (New York:McGraw-Hill Book Company)

Joseph, Gloria
1981 "The Incompatible Ménage à Trois." Pp. 91-107 in Lydia Sargent (ed.), Women and Revolution: The Unhappy Marriage of Marxism and Feminism (Boston: South End Press)

Kamerman, Sheila B.
1986 "Women, Children and Poverty: Public Policies and Female-Headed Families in Industrialized Countries." Pp. 41-63 in Gelp et al. (eds.) Women and Poverty (Chicago: University of Chicago Press)

Lasch, Christopher
  1979 Haven In a Heartless World: The Family
        Besieged (New York: Basic Books, Inc.)

Leacock, Eleanor
  1978 "Women's Status in Egalitarian Society:
        Implications for Social Evolution."
        Current Anthropology 19(2):47-275

Lehrer, Susan
  1987 Origins of Protective Labor Legislation for
        Women, 1905-1925 (Albany: State University
        of New York Press)

MacKinnon, Catharine A.
  1979 Sexual Harassment of Working Women: A Case
        of Sex Discrimination (New Haven,
        Connecticut: Yale University Press)

Mansbridge, Jane
  1986 Why We Lost the ERA (Chicago: University
        of Chicago Press)

Marshall, Susan E.
  1984 "Keep us on the Pedestal: Women Against
        Feminism in Twentieth Century America."
        Pp. 568-581 in Jo Freeman (ed.) Women: A
        Feminist Perspective, Third Edition (Palo
        Alto, California: Mayfield Publishing
        Company)

Marshall, Ray and Beth Paulin
  1984 "The Employment and Earnings of Women: The
        Comparable Worth Debate." Pp. 196-214 in
        U.S. Commission on Civil Rights, Comparable
        Worth: Issue for the 80s, A Consultation
        of the U.S. Commission on Civil Rights,
        Volume 1, June 6-7, 1984 Washington, D.C.

Martin, Susan Ehrlich
  1984 "Sexual Harassment: The Link Between
        Gender Stratification, Sexuality, and
        Women's Economic Status." Pp. 54-69 in Jo
        Freeman (ed.) Women: A Feminist
        Perspective, Third Edition (Palo Alto,
        California: Mayfield Publishing Company)

Mies, Maria
  1983 "Towards a Methodology for Feminist
        Research." Pp. 117-139 in Gloria Bowles
        and Renate Duelli Klein (eds.), Theories of

Women's Studies (London: Routledge and Kegan Paul)

1985 "Why Do We Need All This? A Call Against Genetic Engineering and Reproductive Technology." Women's Studies International Forum 8(6):553-560

Milkman, Ruth
1986 "Women's History and the Sears Case." Feminist Studies 12(2):375-400

Mill, John Stuart
1969 On Liberty, Representative Government, The Subjection of Women: Three Essays (Oxford University Press: London)

Millet, Kate
1977 Sexual Politics (London: Virago)

Pearce, Diana M.
1986 "Toil and Trouble: Women Workers and Unemployment Compensation." Pp. 141-161 in Barbara C. Gelpi, Nancy C.M. Hartsock, Clare C. Novak and Myra H. Strober (eds.), Women and Poverty (Chicago: University of Chicago Press)

Phillips, Anne
1987 "Introduction." Pp. 1-23 in Feminism and Equality (New York: New York University Press)

Rothman, Barbara Katz
1984 "The Meaning of Choice in Reproductive Technologies." Pp. 23-33 in Rita Arditti et al., Test-Tube Women: What Future for Motherhood? (London: Pandora Press)

Ruggie, Mary
1984 The State and Working Women: A Comparative Study of Britain and Sweden (Princeton, New Jersey: Princeton University Press)

Rytina, Nancy F.
1982 "Earnings of Men and Women: A Look At Specific Occupations." Monthly Labor Review April:25-31

Sacks, Karen
1979 Sisters and Wives (Westport, Connecticut: Greenwood Press)

Salmon, Marylynn
    1986 Women and the Law of Property in Early
          America (Chapel, North Carolina: University
          of North Carolina Press)

Shortridge, Kathleen
    1984 "Poverty is a Woman's Problem." Pp. 492-
          501 in Jo Freeman (ed.) Women: A Feminist
          Perspective, Third Edition (Palo Alto,
          California: Mayfield Publishing Company)

Sidel, Ruth
    1986 Women and Children Last: The Plight of
          Poor Women in America (New York: Viking)

Stanworth, Michelle (ed.)
    1987 Reproductive Technologies: Gender,
          Motherhood, and Medicine (Minneapolis,
          Minnesota: University of Minnesota Press)

Steinberg, Ronnie
    1982 Wages and Hours: Labor and Reform in
          Twentieth Century America (New Brunswick,
          New Jersey: Rutgers University Press)

Tawney, R. H.
    1964 Equality (B & N Imports)

Tierney, Kathleen J.
    1982 "The Battered Women Movement and the
          Creation of the Wife-Beating Problem."
          Social Problems 29(3):207-220

Treiman, Donald J. and Heidi I. Hartmann
    1981 Women, Work, and Wages: Equal Pay for Jobs
          of Equal Value. Final Report, Committee on
          Occupational Classification and Analysis
          (Washington, D.C.: U.S. Government
          Printing Office)

United States Bureau of the Census
    1983 American Women: Three Decades of Change
          (Washington, D.C.: U.S. Government Printing
          Office)
    1984 Characteristics of the Population Below the
          Poverty Level (Washington, D.C.: U.S.
          Government Printing Office)

Walby, Sylvia
    1986 Patriarchy at Work: Patriarchal and
          Capitalist Relations in Employment

        (Minneapolis,   Minnesota: University of
        Minnesota Press)

Weitzman, Lenore J.
    1985   The   Divorce   Revolution: The
          Unexpected Social and Economic Consequences
          for Women and Children in America (New
          York: The Free Press)

Wexler, Sandra
    1982   "Battered Women and Public Policy."   Pp.
          184-204 in Ellen Bonaparth (ed.) Women,
          Power and Policy (New York: Pergamon Press)

Yancey, W. L. and E. P. Eriksen
    1979   "The Division of Family Roles." Journal of
          Marriage and the Family 41:301-313

13.

FOOD AND HUNGER: A CHALLENGE TO JUSTICE

E. Wesley Menzel
Professor of Education
University of Bridgeport

Humankind's history and survival have been shaped by our ability to acquire a sufficient amount of food. From being food gatherers and hunters, our ancestors learned how to use simple tools, build fires for cooking, and domesticate plants and animals. Overcoming hunger and malnutrition guided the development of a worldwide food production system. However, as societies have become organized with political and economic priorities, nations have viewed resources differently. Soil and water, two essential resources, have been sometimes abused, sometimes protected. Food production is severely affected when soil is left to erode and water becomes polluted. Conservation and equitable management of these resources can provide human beings with adequate amounts and variety of food products. When land is exploited and controlled by the powerful, at the expense of the powerless, the results can be hunger and malnutrition. The thoughts that follow will describe the behavior of prehistoric food gatherers, the early beginnings of agriculture, and how the distribution of resources and technology influence hunger. Social justice requires a world agricultural system that can produce, distribute and provide enough food for those living on this fragile planet.

FOOD GATHERERS

The beginning of agriculture was the bedrock of civilization. Communities and populations flourished as food produced in the country provided city folk with basic food resources. The skill of growing food encouraged our ancestors to take up tasks other than hunting, fishing and gathering. Time became available for creative activities, thought and the art of living. Man survived as a predatory hunter during early Paleolithic times with a world population of perhaps a few thousand. Small groups of 90 to 100 prehistoric individuals, characterized as Peking Man and later Neanderthal Man, moved from place to place

303

gathering enough calories to maintain themselves.[1]
Efforts to find food and overcome hunger have been
characteristic of homo sapiens. Mankind's culture has
evolved over thousands of millenia, accumulating
behaviors that have enhanced and impoverished his
development. Homo sapiens propagated into a diverse
variety of nations with a world population numbering
nearly five billion people. Neanderthal man emerged
from being a food gatherer and hunter to becoming a
mighty landlord, farming thousands of hectares and
producing millions of tons of food.

This development required the discovery of fire,
the invention of simple tools, the planting of seeds
and the domestication of animals. The most primitive
methods of cooking food probably began between one
million and five hundred thousand B.C.[2] Early man ate
food raw until he noticed that heating meat or
roasting it in hot embers made the food tastier and
more palatable.[3] Fruits, berries and seeds could have
been mixed with heated meat creating a better taste
and providing accumulated health benefits.[4] Today we
are familiar with the benefits of different foods
prepared in a variety of ways. Cooking food adds to
the efficiency of the digestive process. Potatoes,
corn and other carbohydrates gain a better flavor, and
proteins in meat become more tender after cooking. It
seems likely that the early prehistoric chefs
recognized the improvement of cooked food and pursued
various approaches to preparing fish, meat and fruits.
It is also likely that the life span increased as the
process of cooking reduced contamination and spoilage
by some disease causing organisms.

Contaminated water continues to be a problem in
the less developed countries of the world. Unclean
water causes dysentery and diarrhea, resulting in
dehydration in infants and young children. If left
untreated, the situation is fatal. Today we are well
acquainted with the value of pasteurizing dairy
products and cooking meats, poultry and fish which are
natural hosts for pathogenic organisms.

Diversity and a sufficient quantity of food,
nutrients and calories maintained our early ancestors.
Early food gatherers searched areas as large as 30
square miles a day to satisfy their food needs. Large
amounts of energy from the food eaten was spent on
gathering food and firewood. The diets of the Kung
Bushmen in Botswana, Africa, have been studied to
determine the source of their calories. Their energy

needs of 2240 calories per day were met by eating
Mongongo nuts, meat and plant foods.[5] Unique and
creative tools for hunting and primitive pottery
containers for cooking food must have provided early
mankind with a sense of food security. Those
historical events leading to the beginning of
organized agriculture are illustrated in Figure I.[1,6,7]

EARLY AGRICULTURE

It is generally accepted that organized food
production began close to ten thousand B.C. Did these
primitive farmers notice that certain plants grew in
similar areas year after year? Perhaps those
individuals who were most observant and knew their
environment well began the domestication of plants and
animals. Southeast Asia, Africa, the Middle East and
perhaps Central America, although somewhat later, are
likely areas where food growing began. Village
communities have been uncovered where anthropologists
have found milling and pounding stones that were used
for processing wheat seeds. With food now available
close to home, our ancestors had more time and energy
available for inventing conveniences such as the wheel
and plow.[8]

Modern agriculture has continuously progressed
from these early times to the present. The majority
of the Colonial population (90%) in the mid 1700's was
engaged in food production. However, today 2.2
million farmers in the United States produce an
abundance of food. On explanation for the excellence
of American agriculture is the political, economic and
governmental support of agricultural colleges and
experimental stations. The Morrill Act of 1862
established the Department of Agriculture and a land
grant college in each state for the purpose of
conducting research in agriculture and mechanics.
These great institutions have educated students in all
the agricultural sciences and have developed programs
which help make citizens aware of the value of the
quality of food, nutrition, and health.

Hunger and poverty are the result of national and
international policies and priorities. Mankind has
demonstrated the ability to produce an abundance of
food. Power, economics, political forces, and greed
have blocked humanity from sharing an equitable
distribution of the world's resources. The air and
the oceans belong to a world community. Land, food

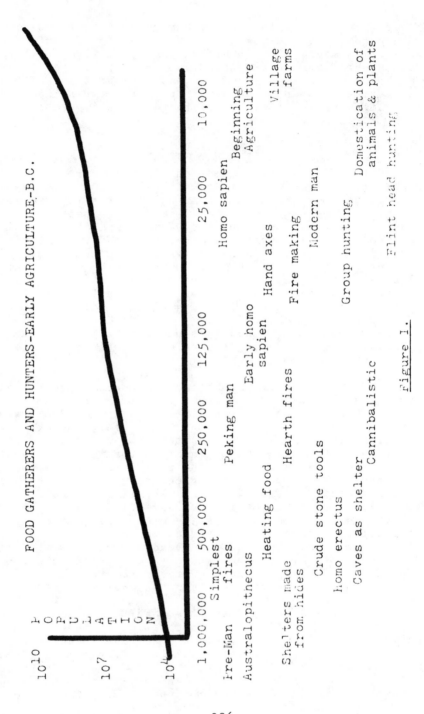

Figure 1.

production, oil and people are viewed as belonging to individual nation states. Contemporary problems of hunger in underdeveloped countries relate to lack of governmental policies, unfair land use and powerless people having nothing to say about the production and distribution of food. Indeed, these are issues related to justice. Twenty years ago in Ethiopia, forty percent of the land was covered with trees and forests. Trees have been cut down by villagers to use as fuel for cooking, and excess grazing by animals has eliminated mature plants and root systems that hold water, break the wind, and prevent erosion. Imbalance of nature occurs when more is taken from the earth than is returned. Exploitation of land and natural resources leaves an environment barren, and the possibility of producing food is diminished.[9]

Today, food production throughout the world is at record levels. Technology, efficiency and agricultural research have provided farmers with the means for producing an abundance of grain, meat, fruits and vegetables. However, hunger still exists across the continents of North and South America, Africa and Asia. "In 1985, the Physicians' Task Force calculated that hunger afflicts some 20 million Americans".[10] The estimates for world hunger are between 600 and 800 million. In a western developed culture and a land of plenty, it is more difficult to understand and explain hunger and malnutrition than perhaps in less developed sections of the earth where continuing problems of drought and limited agricultural policies exist. Explanations for hunger need to consider political, economic, social, cultural, and health priorities as well as a nation's industrial and agricultural policies.

HUNGER AND MALNUTRITION

Mankind continues to tolerate the injustice of starvation and malnutrition. In 1985, the world agriculture system produced enough food to provide each person on our planet with 3600 calories per day.[11] That is more than an adequate intake for the average individual. There is a variation of caloric requirements which relates to gender, age and physical activitiy. To prevent malnutrition and hunger there are minimum standards throughout the life cycle for calories and nutrients. Inadequate diets, especially for children and infants, when rapid growth and metabolism are taking place, have severe consequences.

A diet deficient in protein and calories (PCM--protein calorie malnutrition) results in disease. Kwashiokor is a disease caused by an inferior diet given to a child after breast feeding has been stopped. Lack of adequate protein causes apathy, poor digestion and absorption, edema, and evantually death, if the child is not treated with nutrition therapy. Children with deficient diets from birth suffer from marmasmus. As this disease progresses, muscles are wasted, temperature is subnormal and the child takes on the look of an elderly person. The brain does not develop and learning disability develops.[12]

Protein and calorie malnutrition follows hungry people living in poverty. The income of a person determines the quality, variety and caloric content of food he or she consumes. Individuals with higher incomes purchase more animal protein and less grain. Low purchasing power results in high grain diets and amounts of protein that are minimum to insufficient.

Protein, carbohydrates and fat vary somewhat in their caloric content. In comparing the same weights of protein and carbohydrates, the caloric values are similar (4 calories per gram). Fat provides 9 calories per gram. Each of these nutrients plus vitamins, minerals, water, and fiber are essential in healthy diets. In combination, these nutrients provide energy, growth, and maintenance for the human body.

It is important, when discussing food and hunger, to think of its caloric and nutritional value as well as how many calories were required to produce that food. American agriculture requires high inputs of energy. Fuel is necessary for tractors on the farm, trucks on the highway for transportation, and ocean going vessels carrying food exports. Pumping water to irrigate dry land and for "mining the Ogalal aquifer, a vast underground lake that spans eight states" in the western United States uses electrical energy.[13] Labor costs increased faster than the cost of energy during the nineteen fifties, and farmers began using larger and more powerful equipment than in the past. Treating crops such as corn with commercial pesticides, herbicides and fertilizers uses energy during planting and production harvesting. Over the last forty years, as a result of the green revolution, high yield varieties (HYV) of corn, wheat, and rice have been developed. These grains are highly productive but costly in their total energy needs.

Cost factors in deficit nations and limited governmental support could limit the use of highly productive grains.

Feeding grain to poultry and pigs produces protein more efficiently than if the same grain were fed to steers for beef protein. In the first case, the ratio of pounds of grain required to produce pounds of meat is 4:1, and in the second case, the ratio is 20:1.

The domestication of grain for humankind has had tremendous significance. Flour for bread and pasta and hundreds of other grain products have been developed. More than fifty percent of this planet's population depends on grain directly for food and energy. Grain is also basic to the four food groups, a traditional eating pattern in the United States. The basic four groups are protein, grain, dairy, and fruits and vegetables. Animal protein and dairy food are produced from grains, plus the grain group itself, leaving fruits and vegetables as the only foods not dependent on grain.

Grains and legumes and their many by-products can be consumed directly by human beings rather than by feeding them to animals and then consuming the animals for protein, fat and other nutrients. Examples of grains are wheat, corn, rye, barley, rice and millet. Legumes are a wide variety of peas and beans. Grains and legumes in combination can provide human beings with the appropriate amount of essential proteins required for health and body maintenance.

There are advocates who suggest that less grain should be fed to animals. This would provide more grain for human consumption. "Two thirds of the world's coarse grain (corn, rye, barley, sorghum, millet) are fed to livestock".[14] However, changing the eating style of the wealthy and substituting quality grain and legume protein for animal protein seems unlikely.[15]

USES OF RESOURCES

The earth's resources are unevenly distributed. Wealth, oil, soil, forests, rain, food production, and populations randomly exist around the earth. With an increasing population, will mankind ever be able to feed all the hungry? Highways, homes and projects to

satisfy the needs of cities are continuously being
constructed, and farm land is being taken out of
production. The carrying capacity of crop land and
grazing pastures are experiencing increased stress.
Carrying capacity of the land is an estimate of how
much food can be produced on existing farm land in
view of an ever increasing population. For a
humanistic answer, should world efforts be directed at
limiting population growth? It is the belief of
this writer that patterns of consumption of food,
land, oil, air, and water, indicate how political,
social, and economic forces view and use nature's
resources.

The primary function of agriculture and the use
of land is to produce food for man and animals.
Through careful planning, land can be regenerated and
maintained for centuries. Conservation of land
includes returning vital nutrients and organic
materials back to the soil; farming hillsides
susceptible to erosion differently than flat fields;
protecting top soil by building terraces and planting
trees that break the wind sweeping overland; rotating
crops that replace nutrients taken out of the soil by
certain plants and providing time for the soil to
remain fallow, rest, and rebuild itself. Land that is
overused, overgrazed, or left to erode will become
dust-like and useless.

Technology has not changed our human need for
food, soil and water. Agricultural research has
increased the productivity of land, seeds and animals.
This research has produced hybrid plants with yields
of grain and fruit far greater than more primitive
forms. Animal science using artificial insemination
based on genetic research is producing greater
qualities of milk, more young per litter, and less
carcass fat. However, more of nature's resources are
required to achieve these yields. High tech high
yield plants require more water, fertilizer and pest
controls. Large cost effective farms need long
straight fields to justify the purchase of big
tractors and machinery for planting, cultivating and
harvesting crops. This type of agriculture is capital
intense, not labor intense. Where poverty exists,
capital intense agriculture cannot always be pursued.
World markets are open to nations whose agricultural
products can be grown competitively. Food reaches a
particular market because it is produced more
efficiently and at less cost than a competitive food.

FOOD FOR PEOPLE

Foods such as soybeans from Brazil, peanuts from Africa and cassava from Thailand are sold as cash crops to wealthy developed countries, where they are used to feed cattle.[18] This capital is needed by countries like Brazil to pay interest on large debts owed to Western banks. Monies lent by the World Bank for development are expected to return 10% interest and often the bank will suggest which crops a country should plant for export.[19] Cash crops do produce assets for payment of debts in underveloped countries. However, high payments hinder a country from becoming more self-sufficient and from producing food for its own population. Much like colonialism, consumer needs in the industrialized world guide food production in less developed nations. Governmental policies designed to export large quantities of agricultural products in countries where malnourished people cannot obtain adequate food encourage continual hunger.

Temporary solutions to hunger have been demonstrated to some extent in recent years. Nations with food surpluses have provided hundreds of tons of food, medical supplies, support personnel and vehicles for transporting grain to the hungry. Churches and charities, foundations and universities have sent workers and consultants to help countries solve their hunger problems. Long term solutions and historical experience may provide different answers.

The work and thoughts of Norman E. Borlaug could provide a direction. Poverty and hunger in underdeveloped countries are problems that have multiple causes and require multiple solutions. Nations with traditional agricultural methods and political unrest have been able to meet the food needs of their growing populations. Subsidized food for urban dwellers in undeveloped countries keeps food prices below a peasant farmer's cost and prevents small land owners from maintaining their small farms. These small farmers cannot compete with the subsidized food. Third world deficit nations with large debts have difficulty purchasing food from nations with surplus grains.

Third World nations, with the aid of the industrial nations, need to make long term commitments, perhaps twenty years towards a sustainable regenerative agricultural system. Trained

311

scientists in all fields of agriculture need to be
willing to operate at a grass roots level in
conducting research within local environments. The
time for this work may take eight or ten years.
Individuals from various disciplines such as
economics, politics, medicine, and all agricultural
sciences, need to work as an integrated team towards
helping each nation achieve greater productivity.
Each government must work with this team and support
long term plans which may change existing social ,
economic, cultural and political patterns. The human
rights of individuals born into this world and
production and distribution of food for people, must
be examined together; otherwise, our social and
political systems will collapse.[20]

Nations have made great progress designing
agriculture programs that minimize hunger. Kerala,
one of the twenty-two states in India, through a
coalition government, has established a food
distribution system through land reform and Fair Price
Shops. Farmers provide food to the open market and
government storage facilities. High yield varieties
of rice and wheat were modified to meet environmental
conditions that provided the people of Kerala with a
dependable food policy. Limited and rationed
purchases of rice, sugar and oil are made at Fair
Price Shops, where prices are lower than at other
stores.[21] A political commitment to land reform,
education, and access to food has provided Kerala with
food stability.

People, given the opportunity to become self-
sufficient in food production, and with supportive
resources, can make great strides in overcoming their
own poverty and hunger. The basic resources are
access to land that can grow crops or graze cattle;
water for irrigation if rainfall becomes insufficient;
opportunities to purchase seeds and/or annual stock
within their economic means and long-term agricultural
consultation appropriate to their environmental and
cultural conditions. Small farms, using local labor
and regenerative methods for maintaining soil
fertility, are highly productive. Such farms require
less energy input, show reduced erosion, and can
provide for stable food needs. Indigenous and
genetically strong plants and animals for local
programs offer farmers production possibilities that
may not be available in selectively bred seeds where
the genetic variety has been reduced. Furthermore,
the latter types of seeds require mechanized

approaches and large economic commitments to the newer agricultural technologies of food production. Undeveloped countries will become independent food producers when governments establish equitable food and farming policies.

NOTES

1

Brothwell, Don and Pat, Food in Antiquity, Frederick A. Prager, New York, 1969.

2

Tannahill, Reay, Food in History, Stein and Day, New York, 1973.

3

Ibid

4

Jacob, H. E. Six Thousand Years of Bread, Doubleday, New York, 1944.

5

Pimental, David and Marcia, "Hunters, Gatherers and Early Agriculture;" Food Energy and Society, John Wiley and Sons, 1979.

6

Braidwood, R.J. "The Agriculture Revolution" Scientific American, Sept. 1960.

7

Washburn, S.L., "The Evolution of Man," Scientific American Vol. 239, Sept. 1978.

8

Braidwood, R., op cit.

9

Nova, "Will The World Starve?," PBC, New York, Dec. 23, 1987.

10

Brown, J.L., Hunger in the U.S., Scientific American, Vol. 256, Feb. 1987, p. 37.

11

Lappe, F.M. World Hunger, Grove Press, New York, 1986, p. 9.

12 Hamilton, E., Whitney, E. Sizer, F., Nutrition: Concepts and Controversies 3rd. Ed., West Publishers Co., 1985.

13
Batie, S. and Healy, R., "The Future of American Agriculture," Scientific American, Vol. 248, Feb. 1983, p. 47.

14
Ehrlich, A. and Ehrlich, P., "Why Do People Starve?" The Amicus Journal, Spring 1987, p. 45.

15
Ibid

16
Ibid

17
Borgstrom, George, "The Golden Age," The Feeding Web, Gussow, J. (Ed) Bull Publishing Co., 1978.

18
Oxfam America, In A World of Abundance, Why Hunger? Educational Publication, Boston, MA 1986.

19 The Politics of Food, Yorkshire TV, PBS, New York, Jan. 6, 1988.

20 Borlaugh, Norman E., "Accelerating Agricultural Research and Production in the Third World: A Scientist's Viewpoint," Agriculture and Human Values, Humanities and Agriculture Program, University of Florida, Gainsville, Vol. III, 1986.

21
Phone conversation with T. M. Thomas, former resident of Kerala, Jan. 6, 1988.

POLITICAL AND SOCIAL JUSTICE IN THE CONSTITUTION

William V. Dunlap
Associate Professor
and Associate Dean
School of Law
University of Bridgeport

Is it true that freedom of the press belongs to those who own one? Or that a woman has a constitutional right to an abortion -- if she can afford one? Why is it that the Constitution of the United States guarantees due process of law but not a minimum standard of living? Or assures equal protection of the laws while ignoring the obvious inequalities of wealth?

Each of these dichotomies presents examples of two very different forms of justice. The first I will call "political justice," which concerns the relationship between citizens and their government or, in John Rawls's terms, "those aspects of the social system that define and secure the equal liberties of citizenship."[1] The second I will call "social justice," which deals with the allocation among the population of goods and other advantages of social cooperation, or, in Rawls's phrase, those aspects of the social system that "specify and establish social and economic inequalities."[2] "Social justice" is often used in a broader sense that would include our concept of political justice; in this narrower context, it takes on a meaning similar to Aristotle's "distributive justice."

In this chapter, an examination of the Constitution will reveal a substantial concern with political justice both in the original document and, particularly, in the amendments, but an almost total lack of interest in social justice. Then we will look at three other constitutions and discover that some nations do include guarantees of social justice in their basic political documents. Next, an examination of some Supreme Court decisions will show that those few provisions of the United States Constitution that might have been interpreted as promoting social justice have been dealt with almost uniformly in a

manner that avoids social issues altogether.
Throughout, we will examine a basic, but seldom
articulated, premise of United States political and
legal thought -- that governmental behavior is
fundamentally different from private behavior -- and
see how this so-called public/private or social/-
political distinction helped shape the Constitution
and its role in the promotion of social justice.

The Original Constitution

To be sure, most of the Constitution concerns
itself not with justice at all, but rather with
technical matters determining the structure and
relationships of the various levels and branches of
government: rules governing Congress, the presidency
and the courts, for example, or the relationships
between the national and state governments.
Furthermore, most people, when they consider justice
and the Constitution, think not of the original
document, ratified in 1787, but of the Bill of Rights,
adopted four years later, and the subsequent
amendments.

The decision of the Framers at the Constitutional
Convention in Philadelphia not to include a Bill of
Rights in the Constitution was a deliberate one. Most
of the delegates did not believe that one was
necessary: They were creating a national government of
limited powers that would have relatively little
direct effect on the lives of the people; the state
governments would provide sufficient protection
against abuses by the national government. Not
everyone agreed, however. Thomas Jefferson, who had
been abroad as Ambassador to France when the
Constitution was drafted, and James Madison insisted
on a Bill of Rights to protect individual liberties
from an over-zealous government, and it soon became
clear that only a commitment to a Bill of Rights would
assure ratification of the Constitution by the state
conventions.

Nevertheless, even the original document
contained as many guarantees of political justice as
any fundamental political document to that time. A
brief review reveals the following:

* A limitation on the suspension of habeas
corpus, which has been called the most important human
right in the Constitution.

318

* A prohibition of bills of attainder and ex post facto laws by Congress and by the states.

* The Contract Clause, which prohibits states from "impairing the Obligation of Contracts."

* The right to trial by jury.

* Limitations on the prosecution of treason and on the punishment Congress may set for treason.

* The Privileges and Immunities Clause, which entitles the citizens of each state "to all the Privileges and Immunities of Citizens in the several States."

* A prohibition on religious tests as qualifications for public office.

In addition to these explicit provisions designed to protect individual rights and promote political justice, some provisions that to the Framers had little if any connection to matters of justice have been of great use to civil libertarians: For example, the Commerce Clause, which authorizes Congress to regulate interstate commerce, has been invoked to protect the right to travel and to affirm Congress's power to enact civil rights laws. It was the federal court system, established under Article III, that allowed such imaginative use of the Commerce Clause and that has proved, over the decades, to be an effective, if not perfectly consistent, defender of human rights and political justice in many contexts.

The Bill of Rights

It is, of course, the Bill of Rights that most people think of in connection with justice and the Constitution. These eight amendments form the basis of the legal protection of our civil rights and liberties and contain some of the most powerful and eloquent assertions of individual dignity and autonomy in all of political theory. The provisions of the Bill of Rights should be well known to every student in the United States, but they bear repeating here:

* The First Amendment protects against infringement of the rights of free expression and association -- speech, press, assembly, petition and

319

the free exercise of religion -- and prohibits the
establishment of religion.

* The Second, asserting the states' right to
maintain armed militias, protects the right to bear
arms.

* The Third restricts the quartering of soldiers
in private homes.

* The Fourth prohibits unreasonable searches and
seizures.

* The Fifth, like the first, contains a broad
variety of provisions, all of them quite well known
and frequently invoked: the right to indictment by a
grand jury before being prosecuted for a crime; the
prohibition on double jeopardy, so that no one may be
tried twice for the same crime; the right against
self-incrimination in criminal cases; the Due Process
Clause, which prohibits the government from depriving
a person of life, liberty or property without due
process of law; and the Takings Clause, which requires
the government to pay for any private property that it
takes for public use.

* The Sixth protects criminal defendants through
a variety of procedural rights: to a speedy and public
trial by an impartial and local jury, to be informed
of the charges against them, to be confronted by
witnesses against them and to subpoena witnesses for
them, and to have assistance of counsel.

* The Seventh preserves the right to a jury trial
in most common law civil cases and limits the
authority of courts in overruling facts found by a
jury.

* The Eighth prohibits excessive bail, excessive
fines, and cruel and unusual punishment.

The Ninth and Tenth Amendments are often referred
to as part of the Bill of Rights, although neither
amendment mentions any specific rights, and it has
frequently been argued that they have no effect. The
Ninth declares that the enumeration of specific rights
in the Constitution, including the Bill of Rights,
should not be used as an argument that other rights
held by the people are not protected. It has been
cited in cases protecting rights not enumerated
elsewhere in the Constitution, most notably the right

320

of privacy in such landmark cases as <u>Griswold</u> v. <u>Connecticut</u>, which struck down a law restricting the sale of contraceptives, and <u>Roe</u> v. <u>Wade</u>, which invalidated Texas's abortion statute.

The Tenth says that powers not delegated to the national government by the Constitution are reserved to the states or to the people. This has frequently been minimized as a tautology, but much of the recent political debate and constitutional litigation over the proper relationship between the national and state governments has focused on the meaning of this amendment.

One of the most important, but probably least understood, aspects of the Bill of Rights is that its provisions pertain only to the national government and not to the states. Of the eight articles of the Bill of Rights, only two -- the First and the Seventh -- refer specifically to the national government. The other amendments either identify a particular right as appertaining to an individual or express themselves in the passive voice, or both, so that the text does not make clear against whom the right may be exercised. For example, the Fourth Amendment is premised upon the "right of the people to be secure in their persons, houses, papers, and effects, against unreasonable searches and seizures." The Fifth, in the passive, says: "No person shall be ... deprived of life, liberty, or property, without due process of law," a sweepingly broad injunction with no indication of the subject.

Despite the ambiguity (or even by reading into the Bill of Rights an ambiguity that does not appear on the face of the amendments), the courts held early on in our constitutional history that the Bill of Rights restricted the powers only of the national government. In other words, the Fourth Amendment did not establish a right of security; it merely prohibited the national government from conducting unreasonable searches and seizures. Nor did one have a right not to be deprived of property without due process of law; it was just that the national government could not constitutionally do so. The states could, insofar as the Fifth Amendment was concerned, and any protection against such arbitrary action would have to be found in the constitutions of the states themselves.

The Later Amendments

The Constitution has been amended sixteen times in the 197 years since the ratification of the first ten amendments, and more or less half (the precise number depending upon how one classifies particular amendments or defines "political justice") deal with issues of political justice. The others are concerned primarily with the structure of government: restricting federal jurisdiction over lawsuits against states, changing the method of electing the vice president, authorizing the income tax, establishing direct election of United States senators, changing the dates of the president's term of office, limiting a president to two terms, granting presidential electors to the District of Columbia, and establishing a line of succession to the presidency. Some of these bear to some extent on political justice -- the national income tax, allowing the people to elect senators directly, allowing residents of the District of Columbia to have a voice in the indirect election of the president -- but we will not deal with them further. Two others cancel each other out: the Eighteenth, banning alcoholic beverages from the United States in 1919 and ushering in the Prohibition Era, and the Twenty-First, repealing it 14 years later and leaving the control of alcohol to the states. The rest are all designed to promote political justice in one way or another, and they include some of the most important developments in American political and social history.

The Thirteenth, Fourteenth and Fifteenth Amendments are known collectively as the Civil War Amendments. They were ratified between 1865 and 1870 -- in the wake of the Civil War -- to abolish slavery and the systematic discrimination against Blacks in the South. The Thirteenth abolished slavery and involuntary servitude in the United States. When it became clear that discrimination against the free Blacks would continue, the Fourteenth Amendment redefined state and national citizenship to include most former slaves, and then enacted a series of restrictions on state authority to interfere with the rights of citizens. When some southern states continued to deny Blacks the right to vote, not on the ground that they were Black but that they were former slaves, the Fifteenth guaranteed the right to vote irrespective of race, color, or previous condition of servitude.

322

The Civil War Amendments notwithstanding, systematic efforts to deny Blacks the right to vote continued well into the second half of this century, requiring extensive litigation, legislation, and, in 1964, another constitutional amendment, the Twenty-Fourth, prohibiting the use of poll taxes in national elections.

Meanwhile, women won the vote in 1920 with the ratification of the Nineteenth Amendment, and young adults won it in 1971 with the Twenty-Sixth, which prohibited age discrimination at the polls against any citizen aged 18 or older. The 18-year-old rule appears to be a political justice issue of a different sort from the Fifteenth and Nineteenth Amendments, however. Some age barrier is inevitable in voting, since one hardly wants infants and young children electing a government, and the decision to lower the barrier to 18 from 21 is a somewhat arbitrary political decision, arbitrary in the sense that 17 or 19 are arguably equally valid cutoffs. Gender and race discrimination, on the other hand, are not inevitable; they are the irrational results of biases and stereotyping, and the decision to prohibit them altogether is in no sense arbitrary.

Since 1971, a variety of constitutional amendments have been proposed that would have, among other things, provided that "the life of each human being begins at conception," effectively overruling a woman's constitutional right to choose an abortion without governmental interference; stripped federal courts of jurisdiction to hear school desegregation cases or to order busing as a remedy for school segregation; and prohibited gender discrimination. Only the last of these, known as the Equal Rights Amendment, ever had any real chance of adoption, and it was eventually defeated.

Other Constitutions

All of these rights -- whether in the original Constitution, the Bill of Rights, or the subsequent amendments -- promote political justice. In fact, they are collectively known as political rights, sometimes civil and political rights. None of them is designed to promote social justice, in the sense in which we have used the phrase. Is that because the promotion of social justice is inappropriate to a national constitution, which is, of course, a

political document? Or is it a result of a conscious
choice? A survey of other constitutions will help
answer that question.

The United States Constitution does not mention
the right to work or the right to employment, although
related rights have been found at various times to be
constitutionally protected. For example, the Supreme
Court, in 1905, held that the "right to purchase or
sell labor" was a liberty interest protected by the
Fourteenth Amendment. That particular holding was
overruled three decades later, but even when it still
accurately described the law, it was not a guarantee
of employment. It was a command to the states not to
interfere with the freedom of workers and employers to
set the terms of employment, such as wages and hours.
Similarly, Article 12 of the Constitution of the
Federal Republic of Germany provides, "All Germans
shall have the right freely to choose their trade,
occupation, or profession, their place of work
and their place of training." On its face, this, too,
is a guarantee of noninterference by the government, a
political rather than a social right.

In contrast, the Constitution of the Soviet Union
assures not only the right to choose one's trade or
profession, but the right to guaranteed employment:
"Citizens of the USSR have the right to work (that is,
to guaranteed employment and pay in accordance with
the quantity and quality of their work, and not below
the state-established minimum) ...." The French
Constitution appears to go even further: The Preamble
to the 1946 Constitution, incorporated by reference
into the 1958 Constitution, declares, "Every
individual has the duty to work and the right to
employment."

Both the Soviet and French documents also protect
the political, or freedom-of-choice, aspects of the
right to work. For example, the Soviet citizens'
right to work includes "the right to choose their
trade or profession, type of job and work in
accordance with their inclinations, abilities,
training and education, with due account to the needs
of society." It is very likely, and not a trivial
problem, that the "needs of society" outweigh
individual preference to such an extent that in some
countries this aspect of the right is effectively
null; it may even be true that, despite the promise of
guaranteed employment, many Soviet citizens have no
jobs, for economic or political reasons. It is

324

important to remember, however, that a country's
inability to fulfill its promises to its citizens, or
a particular government's choosing to break those
promises in political retaliation, does not mean that
the nation takes the guarantees lightly.

A variety of social and economic rights appear in
the French, German, and Soviet Constitutions. The
right to education, in somewhat different
permutations, appears in all three. France's 1946
Preamble provides:

> The Nation guarantees to children and
> adults equal access to education,
> professional training and culture. The
> organization of free, public and secular
> instruction at all levels is a duty
> incumbent upon the state.

The Soviet Constitution goes into more detail:

> Citizens of the USSR have the right to
> education. This right is ensured by free
> provision of all forms of education, by
> the institution of universal, compulsory
> secondary education, and broad development
> of vocational, specialized secondary, and
> higher education, in which instruction is
> oriented towards practical activity and
> production; by the development of extramu-
> ral, correspondence and evening courses; by
> the provision of state scholarships and
> grants and privileges for students; by the
> free issue of school textbooks; by the
> opportunity to attend a school where
> teaching is in the native language; and
> by the provision of facilities for
> self-education.

The United States Constitution, in contrast,
makes no mention of a right to education. In fact,
the Supreme Court declared in 1973 that a right to
education is neither explicitly nor implicitly
protected by the Constitution.

The French and Soviet Constitutions both
guarantee social security. France's 1946 Preamble
provides, in very general terms, "Every human being
who by reason of age, physical or mental condition, or
economic situation is incapable of working shall have
the right to obtain the means of subsistence from the

325

community." Again, the Soviet Constitution goes into somewhat more detail:

Citizens of the USSR have the right to maintenance in old age, in sickness, and in the event of complete or partial disability or loss of the breadwinner.

This right is guaranteed by social insurance of workers and other employees and collective farmers; by allowances for temporary disability; by the provision by the state or by collective farms of retirement pensions, disability pensions, and pensions for the loss of the breadwinner; by providing employment for the partially disabled; by care for the elderly and the disabled; and by other forms of social security.

The United States also has its Social Security System, of course, but it is not protected by the Constitution. The Congress is free radically to amend or even to abolish the system. The occasional warnings that the system is fiscally unsound and on the brink of collapse do not have the constitutional implications they would in France or the Soviet Union.

Both France and the Soviet Union provide constitutional guarantees of health care and of rest and leisure. The Soviet Union guarantees a right to housing and cultural benefits.

These are just a few examples of the social and economic rights that some countries have protected in their constitutions. How do these social rights differ from the political rights found in the United States Constitution (and also, to one degree or another, in the French, German and Soviet constitutions)? In two ways: substance and enforcement.

Political rights differ from social rights in their very nature. By and large, political rights require government to deal with individuals in one or more of three ways: fairly, equally, and at a distance. By "fairly," I mean that laws or governmental decisions should be rational, not arbitrary, and made pursuant to established procedures; the Due Process Clauses of the Fifth and Fourteenth Amendments are examples of political rights

326

requiring fair treatment. By "equally," I mean that government should not arbitrarily favor one individual or group over another; the Equal Protection Clause of the Fourteenth Amendment is an example. By "at a distance," I refer to those rights that create a zone of autonomy or privacy about the individual into which the government has no right to intrude; the First Amendment freedoms of speech and religion are examples. All these political rights govern the procedures by which government operates and restrain its authority in certain spheres, but they do not guarantee anything of substance to the individual.

Social rights, on the other hand, require that the government provide something of value to the individual: a job, an education, housing, health care, a pension. They entail a much different sort of claim by an individual against the government, and the difference is significant in a number of respects: First, social rights, by their very nature, require significant governmental expenditures of resources, which may not be available; seldom can such a claim be made of political rights. Second, social rights invariably involve a redistribution of goods within the population, sometimes by nationalization or expropriation, usually by taxation. Any such redistribution to promote one right will have to be balanced against the property rights of those whose property is taken. Unlike social rights, political rights may be exercised by one person without necessarily interfering with the rights of another.

Political rights and social rights also differ in their enforcement. The political rights of the United States Constitution are self-executing, which means that courts can enforce them directly, without any action by Congress. Thus, an individual whose right of free speech has been infringed by the government can take the government to court to vindicate the right. This is not true of the social and economic rights found in the Soviet Constitution. The fulfillment of the rights is solely within the power of the government, and failure to achieve the rights is not justiciable in the courts. While there is nothing in the nature of social and economic rights that requires this disparate treatment, the difference is understandable, and it is possible that, if the United States were to amend the Constitution to include social and economic rights, the new rights would be non-self-executing and not justiciable in the courts.

327

Having looked briefly at the political rights included in the United States Constitution and at the social rights excluded from it, we will turn to the judicial interpretation of those rights to see how the social/political distinction manifests itself there.

The Fourteenth Amendment

Of all the constitutional amendments ratified since the Bill of Rights, the most significant has been the Fourteenth. The "series of restrictions on state authority" mentioned casually above in the survey of amendments paved the way for a virtual revolution in the social and political structure of the United States.

By the time of the Civil War Amendments, the political situation had changed greatly from the early days of the Republic. The states were no longer the protectors of individual rights, providing a buffer between the national government and their citizens. Southern states continued to discriminate systematically against the newly freed slaves, and so the Constitution was amended once again. The Fourteenth Amendment not only granted United States and state citizenship to most of the former slaves; in three clauses, it wrote into the Constitution limitations on state powers to abridge their rights and to discriminate against them.

Two of the clauses were similar in form and language to earlier constitutional provisions. The Privileges and Immunities Clause of the Fourteenth Amendment ("No State shall make or enforce any law which shall abridge the privileges or immunities of citizens of the United States.") was clearly related to the Privileges and Immunities Clause of Article IV in the original text ("The Citizens of each State shall be entitled to all the Privileges and Immunities of Citizens in the several States."). Likewise, the Due Process Clause of the Fourteenth ("nor shall any State deprive any person of life, liberty or property, without due process of law") was almost identical to that of the Fifth Amendment, except for the specific reference to state authority. The third, the Equal Protection Clause, declared that no state should "deny to any person within its jurisdiction the equal protection of the laws" and had no national analogue.

How were these three provisions, which do not seem in the least extraordinary in light of the American tradition of individual rights and liberties, able to alter the political and social structure of the United States? In two ways -- by giving the federal courts jurisdiction over the states in matters of civil rights, and by granting Congress authority to legislate in the area of civil rights -- but both took time, because the courts, quickly recognizing the amendment's potential for radical change, deliberately interpreted the three clauses in ways that would minimize their impact for years, even till today. (A third technique, not directly relevant to the public/private distinction under discussion, was incorporation: selectively applying, on a case-by-case basis, virtually every provision of the Bill of Rights to the states by finding that they fell within the meaning of the Due Process Clause of the Fourteenth Amendment. As a technical matter, then, it is still true that the Bill of Rights does not apply to the states; the protections found in it, however, are applied to the states through the Fourteenth. In this way, the federal courts and Congress gained jurisdiction over virtually every aspect of the Bill of Rights.)

The first major test of the three clauses came 1873, in a constitutional challenge to a Louisiana statute that had created a private monopoly in a New Orleans slaughterhouse. Disgruntled butchers attempted to overturn the monopoly with a variety of arguments grounded in the Civil War Amendments: that the monopoly created an involuntary servitude in violation of the Thirteenth Amendment, abridged their privileges and immunities as citizens of the United States, deprived them of property without due process of law, and denied them the equal protection of the laws. The Supreme Court of the United States, in The Slaughter-House Cases, disposed quickly of all four arguments:

The Thirteenth Amendment's prohibition of involuntary servitude was inapplicable in light of the amendment's "one pervading purpose ... the freedom of the slave race." Likewise, the Equal Protection Clause: "The existence of laws in the States where the newly emancipated negroes resided, which discriminated with gross injustice and hardship against them as a class, was the evil to be remedied by this clause."

Unlike the slavery amendment and the Equal Protection Clause, the Due Process Clause had a history. It was virtually identical to the Fifth Amendment's restraint on national power, and, as the court observed, there was a similar restraint upon state power in the constitution of nearly every state. The court found no prior application that would regard the slaughterhouse monopoly as a deprivation of property.

The court devoted most of its attention to the Privileges and Immunities Clause, and it was this part of the case that put an indelible stamp on the Constitution. Asked by the displaced butchers to find that the monopoly had abridged their privileges and immunities as citizens of the United States, the court responded by distinguishing national citizenship from state citizenship and then by differentiating between the privileges and immunities of national citizenship and those that attach to state citizenship. The former are those that owe their existence to the national government or its national character, and among them are the privilege of the writ of habeas corpus, the right to assemble peaceably and petition for redress of grievances, and the right to use the navigable waters of the United States. The latter, which attach to state citizenship, are the fundamental rights that belong to the citizens of all free governments: protection by the government, the right to acquire and possess property and to pursue and obtain happiness and safety, subject to reasonable governmental regulation for the public good.

Should the butchers' next argument not have been that, if their complaint did not state a Fourteenth Amendment claim, then it should fall under Article IV's protection of the privileges and immunities of state citizenship? Unfortunately for the butchers, that issue already had been decided against them. The Article IV clause does not grant protection against the actions of one's own state. Instead, it grants to a citizen of one state who is present in another state the same rights that the host state affords its own citizens. It is an antidiscrimination rule, rather than a guarantee of substantive rights.

While the court's reasoning in The Slaughter-House Cases is appealing, the result was by no means inevitable. Two dissenters said quite plainly that the Louisiana statute violated fundamental rights and ought to be invalidated under the Privileges and

Immunities Clause of the Fourteenth Amendment. Justice Miller, however, in his opinion for the court, was quite straightforward about his reasons. He rejected outright the possibility that the intent of the Fourteenth Amendment was "to transfer the security and protection of all the civil rights which we have mentioned, from the States to the Federal government." Such an interpretation

> would constitute this court a perpetual censor upon all legislation of the States, on the civil rights of their own citizens [and would] radically change the whole theory of the relations of the State and Federal governments to each other and of both these governments to the people.

Justice Bradley, in dissent, responded that "it was the intention of the people of this country in adopting that amendment to provide National security against violation by the States of the fundamental rights of the citizen." Since The Slaughter-House Cases, the Privileges and Immunities Clause of the Fourteenth Amendment has been of little assistance to those attempting to safeguard civil rights against infringement by the states.

Eventually, the radical change that Justice Miller feared arrived, but by a different, arguably less appropriate route. By the end of the Nineteenth Century, the Supreme Court was routinely invoking the Due Process Clause to invalidate state legislation on the ground that it infringed some liberty or property interest protected by the Fourteenth Amendment. The best-known case, Lochner v. New York, struck down a New York statute that had established a maximum ten-hour day and sixty-hour week for bakers. The court found that the right to purchase or sell labor was a part of the liberty protected by the Fourteenth Amendment. It seems odd to many that the court would accomplish this through the Due Process Clause, which was originally intended to ensure proper procedural safeguards. The use of the clause to protect against the infringement of specific substantive rights, irrespective of procedural safeguards, came to be known as substantive due process, and the period of constitutional history from the 1890s to 1934 is frequently called the Substantive Due Process Era or the Lochner Era.

By 1934 and the repudiation of substantive due process, the basic issues had changed. The point of the repudiation was the deference the courts would thenceforth pay to the legislature when judging the constitutionality of economic regulation. Justice Miller's issue -- the proper role of the federal courts as "censors" of state legislation -- was long since moot. The national government was by this time quite active in the business of overseeing the states' treatment of their own citizens, and it involved a great deal more than judicial review of state laws. This brings us to the second major mechanism by which the Fourteenth Amendment ushered in the new world of federalism and a dramatic increase in national power over individual lives. As Section I of the Fourteenth Amendment placed restrictions on the authority of the states and opened the way for the federal courts to oversee states' treatment of their citizens, so Section V opened the way for Congress: "The Congress shall have power to enforce, by appropriate legislation, the provisions of this article." The scope of this authority was not immediately clear, but the Supreme Court soon acted to restrict it severely.

The State Action Doctrine

The Civil Rights Act of 1875 made it a federal crime to deny to anyone access to public accommodations -- inns, transit, theaters, and the like. In The Civil Rights Cases, an appeal from convictions under the act, the Supreme Court held in 1883 that the act could not be applied to discrimination by private parties: "Individual invasion of individual rights is not the subject matter of the amendment." Why? Because Section V authorized Congress to enforce the provisions of Section I, and Section I spoke in terms of states,' not individuals,' denying the equal protection of the laws. Only discrimination by the state, not by private actors, was prohibited by Section I, and therefore only state discrimination was subject to congressional enforcement. This was the birth of the State Action Doctrine, which for more than a century has impeded the use of the Constitution in combating racial discrimination in the private sector.

The court in the Civil Rights Cases based its opinion on the language of the amendment, but, as in the Slaughter-House treatment of the Privileges and Immunities Clause, that outcome was not inevitable.

332

The first Justice Harlan -- in one of his many stirring dissents -- maintained that Section V did grant congressional power to legislate against private discrimination. Going even further, he argued that, even if this were not so, the industries covered by the act were licensed by states and charged with duties to the public and were therefore state instrumentalities subject to congressional regulation.

The State Action Doctrine, while technically narrow in scope and application, is the legal embodiment of the social/political distinction that is the subject of this essay. The doctrine is still the subject of severe criticism, and predictions of its demise abound. It is, nevertheless, despite its faults and its many exceptions, the law.

Separate but Equal

Given the reasoning of the Civil Rights Cases, the State Action Doctrine clearly applies to judicial enforcement of Section I as well as to congressional implementation. In fact, the logic of the State Action Doctrine helped justify a new approach that allowed even the state to discriminate: the Separate but Equal Doctrine. Two cases shed light on the political philosophy underlying the two doctrines.

By the "logic of the State Action Doctrine," I mean the world view that distinguishes on an elemental level between state-sponsored discrimination and private discrimination or, in other words, between de jure (legal) and de facto (actual) discrimination. These Latin phrases represent a dichotomy about which the major school desegregation cases of the 1970s revolved but which has been heavily criticized as outdated or irrelevant. In constitutional civil-rights jurisprudence, the distinction dates as far back as the Civil Rights Cases, and by the end of the Nineteenth Century it had become fairly well defined, by two landmark cases in particular.

West Virginia, in 1880, was excluding blacks, among others, from its juries by limiting jury service to "white male persons who are twenty-one years of age and who are citizens of this state." The Supreme Court of the United States, in overturning the murder conviction of a Black man in Strauder v. West

333

<u>Virginia</u>, struck down that statute and held that, under the Fourteenth Amendment,

> the law in the States shall be the same
> for the black as for the white; that all
> persons, whether colored or white, shall
> stand equal before the laws of the States,
> and, in regard to the colored race, for
> whose protection the amendment was primarily
> designed, that no discrimination shall be
> made against them by law because of their
> color [and that blacks are guaranteed] the
> right to exemption from unfriendly
> legislation against them distinctively as
> colored, -- exemption from legal
> discriminations, implying inferiority in
> civil society, lessening the security of
> their enjoyment of the rights which others
> enjoy, and discriminations which are steps
> towards reducing them to the condition of
> a subject race.

Parenthetically, the court explicitly upheld West Virginia's authority to discriminate on the basis of citizenship, age, and gender.

The expansive language of <u>Strauder</u> led many to hope that the court would similarly dispose of state statutes forbidding the races from mingling in schools and theaters. Sixteen years later, however, the court sustained a Louisiana statute forbidding blacks and whites from riding in the same railroad car. The statute called for "equal but separate accommodations for the white and colored races," and the court took the opportunity to distinguish between enforced separation and political inequality:

> We consider the underlying fallacy of the
> plaintiff's argument to consist in the
> assumption that the enforced separation
> of the two races stamps the colored race
> with a badge of inferiority. If this be
> so, it is not by reason of anything found
> in the act, but solely because the colored
> race chooses to put that construction upon
> it. ... If the civil and political rights
> of both races be equal, one cannot be
> inferior to the other civilly or
> politically. If one race be inferior to the
> other socially, the Constitution of the

United States cannot put them upon the same plane."

In a stroke, the Supreme Court extended the logic of the State Action Doctrine, which confined national authority over discrimination to that sponsored by the state, to allow states affirmatively to separate the races, so long as the accommodations were "equal." That the court was willing to overlook what everyone knew -- the accommodations were not in fact equal -- is further evidence of the hold that this conceptual dichotomy had on the legal thinking of the day: So long as the law, on its face, treated the races equally, the demands of the Constitution had been met. Political inequality was forbidden, but social inequality was no concern of the Constitution. Thus the case of Plessy v. Ferguson established the Separate but Equal Doctrine, which helped define relations between the races for more than half a century.

Until 1954, "separate but equal" school systems through much of the South and Midwest helped perpetuate generations of systematic, pervasive discrimination that branded black children as inferior from the moment they walked through the kindergarten door, and then assured that they would remain inferior by denying them the education and training that would have allowed them, in adulthood, to succeed.

When the turning point finally arrived and the dual school systems fell, Separate but Equal survived. Brown v. Board of Education held that the segregated school systems were unconstitutional because they were unequal:

> To separate them from others of similar age and qualifications solely because of their race generates a feeling of inferiority as to their status in the community that may affect their hearts and minds in a way unlikely ever to be undone. ... We conclude that in the field of public education, the doctrine of 'separate but equal' has no place. Separate educational facilities are inherently unequal."

In other words, the court distinguished Brown from Plessy on their facts, and left the law of Plessy untouched. Brown touched off a civil rights

335

revolution -- political, social and legal -- in the United States, and since that time the constitutional law of equal protection has grown dramatically. The Equal Protection Clause now defends not only blacks and other racial minorities, but also women, noncitizens, and illegitimate children. As its scope grew, so did the complexity of its analysis. Equal protection cases speak today in terms of strict scrutiny, compelling state interest and tight fit. It is true that a Plessy-style statute would not survive modern equal protection analysis and that, for all practical purposes, Separate but Equal is an ex-doctrine, but it is probably significant that the doctrine has never been explicitly overruled.

The Public/Private Distinction

What is the relationship between State Action and Separate but Equal? Both depend upon what has come to be known as the "public/private distinction," but they depend upon it in somewhat different ways. The State Action Doctrine makes a straightforward distinction between state actions and private actions; the former are regulated by the Fourteenth Amendment, the latter are not. The problem of the State Action Doctrine is determining what is and what is not state action, in deciding when the government is closely enough associated with a private entity to justify treating the private entity's action as governmental action.

That is not the problem of Separate but Equal. The Louisiana statute requiring separate railroad cars for whites and blacks clearly constituted state action. The task of Plessy was to distinguish political inequality from social inequality, or political injustice from social injustice. For the state to create a jury system and to exclude blacks from it is to brand blacks as inferior. For a state to require separate (and ostensibly equal) accommodations for the races is a neutral statement; if one race wants to read messages of inferiority into it, there is little the state can do about that.

The public/private distinction of State Action and Separate but Equal is just an example, a special case, of the social/political distinction we drew at the outset. We have seen the distinction, in one form or another, at work in three separate contexts now: in the choice of rights protected in the Constitution, in the State Action Doctrine, and in Separate but Equal.

336

It is not just a historical curiosity, however. The distinction survives today. It can be found in the Supreme Court's refusal to find social and economic rights in the Constitution, in the modern State Action Doctrine that limits the reach of the Constitution in matters of procedural due process and equal protection, in First Amendment cases that restrict a legislature's power to promote diversity of speech, and in the United States government's stance on the international protection of human rights.

Supreme Court Decisions

Several attempts were made in the 1960s and 1970s to persuade the Supreme Court that the Constitution affords affirmative social rights and does not merely protect freedom of action. The attempts invariably failed. For example, after Roe v. Wade in 1973 found that a woman's right to privacy severely restricted the power of a state to prohibit abortions, two indigent women challenged a Connecticut welfare regulation that permitted the state to pay for expenses connected with childbirth but limited benefits for abortions to those that were medically necessary. In the 1977 case of Maher v. Roe, the court held: "The Constitution imposes no obligation on the States to pay the pregnancy-related medical expenses of indigent women, or indeed to pay any of the medical expenses of indigents." The opinion went on to say that such disparate treatment of childbirth and abortion did not offend the Equal Protection Clause.

Other instances abound: The right to travel means that a state may not, by denying welfare benefits, penalize those who exercise the right, but neither is the state required to provide bus fare to indigents who would like to travel. The freedom to choose the form and substance of one's children's education without state interference does not imply a right to be supplied an education.

The only significant exceptions to this general rule came in the well-known criminal procedure cases of the 1960s, when the court found that a state not only must allow a criminal defendant the assistance of counsel, but must provide a trial lawyer to indigent felony defendants. This landmark Sixth Amendment case of Gideon v. Wainwright was soon expanded to include many other phases of the criminal justice system, and

337

many came to hope that this right to be provided with counsel would be only the first of many social rights to be guaranteed by the Constitution. The Maher court said no, distinguishing right to counsel from other social rights: "These cases are grounded in the criminal justice system, a governmental monopoly in which participation is compelled. Our subsequent decisions have made it clear that [these principles] do not extend ... generally."

State Action Today

The public/private distinction is most evident today in the State Action Doctrine, which appears for the most part in three categories of cases: due process, defining the procedural limitations on a state's ability to make decisions adversely affecting a person's life, liberty, or property; equal protection, concerning challenges to a state's disparate treatment of groups of individuals; and First Amendment, dealing with challenges to governmental limitations on speech or religion. The State Action Doctrine comes into play when the entity making the adverse decision is not the government, per se, but is closely enough related to the government to give rise to the argument that the private entity's actions should be subject to constitutional regulation.

For example, a well-known series of cases arose in the 1970s defining what in the way of pre-termination hearings and other procedural safeguards the government must provide before depriving a person of welfare, Social Security disability, or comparable governmental benefits. As the Supreme Court was deciding those, a parallel line of cases challenged decisions made by private entities. In 1974, an aggrieved consumer whose electric service had been terminated for nonpayment by a privately owned utility attempted to persuade the Supreme Court that the utility's actions should be regarded as the government's and that the consumer should have been entitled to a pre-termination hearing. The court, in Jackson v. Metropolitan Edison Co., rejected the argument, despite the close relationship between the state and the utility, a state-sanctioned monopoly that was heavily regulated and that provided a service uniquely public in character. The court reached a similar result four years later when an evicted mother attempted to block the sale of her furniture by the storage company to which it had been consigned. The woman argued that the resolution of private conflicts was a function traditionally reserved to the state, that the state had delegated this function to the storage company through the Uniform Commercial Code, which had authorized the sale, and that as a result the threatened sale should be treated as a sale by the state, subject to the procedural requirements of the Due Process Clause. The Supreme Court, in _Flagg Brothers_ v. _Brooks_, decided that, because dispute resolution was not exclusively a state function and because the state had not participated in the threatened sale but had merely acquiesced, the Due Process Clause did not apply.

These decisions are reasonable on their face and might not seem so problematic had it not been for an earlier line of cases finding state action in the deeds of companies less closely related to government. The cases concerned racial discrimination, and the seminal decision of _Burton_ v. _Wilmington Parking Authority_ involved a privately owned and operated coffee shop in a parking garage owned by a municipal authority. Citing such other factors as the state and national flags' flying above the building and the reliance of the parking authority on the income from renting out the space, the court, in 1961, held that "by its inaction, the Authority, and through it the State, had ... made itself a party to the refusal of service [to Blacks]." Similar cases followed, but by 1972, the tendency to find state action, even in racial cases, had disappeared. In that year, the court declined to find state action in the racial discrimination of a private club, even though the club had been granted a liquor license by the state, liquor licenses were a scarce commodity because that community already had its state-mandated quota, and the terms of the liquor license required the club to adhere to its own constitution and by-laws, which restricted membership and guest privileges to whites.

One explanation for this reversal, which was actually a return to the traditional distinction between public and private action, is that the federal courts had been finding state action as a pretext, to give themselves jurisdiction and provide recourse to victims of state-tolerated private discrimination. Between 1961 and 1972, however, Congress had seen its authority over private discrimination dramatically increased. This came about in two ways: First, in

339

1964, the Supreme Court upheld the constitutionality of the Civil Rights Act of 1964, justifying Congress's reliance on the Commerce Clause as authority to forbid private discrimination, at least insofar as it affected interstate commerce; thus, Congress had bypassed the State Action Doctrine by not relying for its authority on Section 5 of the Fourteenth Amendment. Then in 1968, the court applied the Civil Rights Act of 1866 -- which guaranteed to all citizens the right to own, sell, and lease property without regard to race -- to the private sale of a house. Rather than invalidate that application of the statute under the State Action Doctrine, Jones v. Alfred H. Mayer Co. found that the statute was authorized by the Thirteenth Amendment, which empowered Congress to enforce the abolition of slavery. The court reasoned that restrictions on owning property were among the "badges and incidents of slavery," and that, because the Thirteenth Amendment had no state action requirement, the legislation had been constitutionally applied. Thus Congress had taken an active role in the fight against private racial discrimination, and the federal courts, no longer the only recourse for its victims, reverted to the old public/private distinction once again.

A similar reversal or backtracking occurred in the First Amendment shopping center cases. In 1968, the Supreme Court held that a shopping center was the "functional equivalent" of a municipal business district and that the First and Fourteenth Amendments prohibited the mall's owner, just as they prohibit city government, from interfering with freedom of speech. Four years later, the court established a major limitation on that ruling, and by 1976 had overruled it altogether. In 1980, however, the court ruled that a state constitution could protect speech rights in a shopping center, and since that time several state supreme courts have found that their state constitutions do so protect the rights of speakers.

The First Amendment

A third context in which the public/private distinction is seen today is in a new breed of First Amendment cases, challenging state or congressional authority to place restrictions on speech in the name of promoting diversity of expression. The distinction here is on a more fundamental level, however. It goes to the very heart of the philosophy that defines the role of government in society. Three Supreme Court decisions make the point. In 1974, <u>Miami Herald</u> v. <u>Tornillo</u> invalidated a Florida right-of-reply statute that required newspapers to provide space to political candidates whose personal character or official record had been assailed in the newspaper. This decision, heralded by newspaper publishers and journalists across the land, vindicated A.J. Liebling's caustic observation years earlier that "freedom of the press is guaranteed only to those who own one." Two years after <u>Tornillo</u>, the case of <u>Buckley</u> v. <u>Valeo</u> struck down key provisions of the Federal Election Campaign Act of 1971 that limited campaign expenditures by candidates for national office. Two years after that, <u>First National Bank</u> v. <u>Bellotti</u> invalidated a Massachusetts statute that prohibited banks and some corporations from making contributions or expenditures to influence any public referendum unless the question materially affected the property, business, or assets of the corporation.

What these three statutes had in common was an effort by a legislature to rectify what it saw as an imbalance in the "marketplace of ideas." This imbalance, in effect a "market failure," had come about, the legislature reasoned, because people with money or access to money had gained too much influence in the electoral process, and the legislature attempted to strike a balance between the First Amendment rights of those with money and of those whose voices were being drowned out.

The Supreme Court's refusal to permit this reflects the origins of the Constitution in eighteenth-century liberal thought, which viewed society as composed of individuals with government on the outside, doing as little as possible to interfere with the constant flow of the marketplace, the myriad of individual transactions among the citizens, each of whom possessed certain rights. These rights consisted of zones of freedom or autonomy of action without governmental interference, except when necessary to protect the rights of others. The court thus views the First Amendment: a restriction on governmental authority to take any action that would impinge upon an individual's freedom of speech. That the statutes were designed to promote free expression by increasing diversity and by protecting the integrity of the electoral campaign system, another First Amendment value, is not relevant to this approach.

341

There are, however, other ways of viewing the government's role in the social structure that would allow a court to sustain these statutes under the First Amendment. The world today is very different from that of the eighteenth century, and the role of government has changed radically, not only because of the doctrinal developments in the Fourteenth Amendment. Rather than standing by passively, ready to intervene when necessary, government today is actively involved in the marketplace. In the United States, it is by far the largest and most influential player: the largest employer, the largest borrower, the largest lender, a pervasive regulator of virtually every aspect of business and many facets of personal life as well. Because governmental decisions help shape society, and because the climate for free expression is determined in large part by government, it is not unreasonable to read the First Amendment broadly to allow, perhaps even to require, government to take affirmative action to promote the values the amendment was designed to protect. This view of society blurs the distinction between government and those it governs. The public/private distinction of the State Action Doctrine loses much of its clarity and meaning and becomes virtually worthless as a rule of decision. This is the view of the social welfare state.

There is yet a more extreme view, which is diametrically opposed to eighteenth-century liberalism. Marxist theory, in its many manifestations, obliterates the public/private distinction altogether. Hegel, a major source of Marxist thought, rejected the liberal view that freedom meant being left alone by the state; this he minimized as "negative freedom." Concrete freedom, to Hegel, required that men submit their wills to the laws of the state, which he viewed as the embodiment of the will of the people. Marx and Engels saw the state as the representative of the ruling class, protecting its interests against other elements of society, but predicted that, once class divisions had been eliminated, the state would become representative of all society and thus render itself redundant.

Under this view, the concept of state action and the notion of a state's interfering with a citizen's freedom of speech become meaningless, because the state and the individual are, in some sense, one. The rights to be guaranteed by the state are no longer the

342

political and civil rights of the United States
Constitution, but the social and economic rights of
the Soviet Constitution. It is in this fundamental
difference between the United States and the Soviet
philosophies of government, played out daily in the
international arena of human rights, that the United
States approach becomes most explicit.

International Human Rights

That the Soviet Union does not protect freedom of
speech and religion the way the United States
understands those concepts does not mean there are no
human rights in the Soviet Union, any more than the
failure of the United States to guarantee health care
and employment means there are no human rights in the
United States. What all this does mean is that the
two countries, each of which represents to some degree
one of the major political systems of the world, do
not agree on the definition of human rights or on how
they should be protected. It also means that neither
country performs adequately in protecting the rights
that the other holds fundamental.

It is on the international level that this
difference between political rights and social rights
is most evident, because it is an ongoing issue with
implications for world peace. The United States
government, without regard to which party controls the
White House, routinely criticizes the Soviet Union and
other Eastern Bloc countries for their failure to
respect the human rights of their citizens, and the
Soviet Union responds by criticizing the United States
for its health care, unemployment, and homelessness
problems. The United States acknowledges the
conflict. The assistant secretary of state for human
rights and humanitarian affairs said in 1987:

> We are frequently challenged by Soviet-bloc
> states to deal with economic and social
> issues at human rights meetings. ... But in
> our view, such matters do not belong at a
> human rights meeting. At a human rights
> meeting, we can engage in useful discussion
> of the meaning of the right to freedom of
> speech or to freedom of religion.[3]

The distinction has affected the form and
substance of the international legal protection of
human rights. Like the United States Constitution,

343

the United Nations Charter is primarily structural, dealing with the organization and with relations among nations. It contains relatively few references to individual rights, political or social, and those few are expressed in the broadest possible terms. In 1948, three years after the Charter went into effect, the United Nations General Assembly adopted the Universal Declaration of Human Rights. Most of the enumerated rights are of the political sort, but there are guarantees of rights to social security, to an adequate remuneration for work, to rest and leisure, and to an adequate standard of living, including food, clothing, housing and medical care. The Declaration, which had been heavily promoted by the United States, was approved, 48-0, but there were eight abstentions, including the entire Soviet Bloc.

Because the Declaration, too, was phrased in relatively general terms, and because it was a General Assembly resolution rather than a treaty, it was not likely to be regarded as binding international law. Therefore, the Commission on Human Rights began drafting two covenants that would catalogue the rights in greater detail and bind those states that ratified them. The covenants were presented to the General Assembly in 1954 and adopted in 1966; they entered into force, after ratification by thirty-five states, in 1976. The Soviet Union signed them in 1968 and ratified them in 1973. The United States signed them in 1977 but has never ratified them.

Not surprisingly, the two documents are called the International Covenant on Civil and Political Rights and the International Covenant on Economic, Social and Cultural Rights. The decision to draft separate documents and to divide them in that way was based on more than just the ideological differences of the Western and Eastern Blocs. The binding character of the obligations imposed by the covenants varies according to the kind of right protected. Specifically, the Civil and Political covenant obligates states parties "to respect and to ensure to all individuals" the rights protected by the covenant; to fulfill that sort of right is well within the power of any government that cares to do so. On the other hand, the Economic, Social, and Cultural covenant requires each state "to take steps ... to the maximum of its available resources, with a view to achieving progressively the full realization of the rights," most of which require economic resources that

344

may not be available to all countries, even those that want to provide them.

Conclusion

The protection of social and economic rights may not be a constitutional matter in the United States, but that is not to say that the rights are not satisfied. The standard of living in the United States is high enough that most people enjoy the basic social necessities without a constitutional guarantee. For most of those who do not, the state and national governments have instituted, as a political matter, welfare, social security, and health insurance systems. For those who still do not have the basic necessities, the lack of constitutional guarantees is a real issue, though not one they are likely to ponder extensively in those terms.

On the other hand, the fact that the Soviet Constitution guarantees such social and economic rights as housing and medical care does not mean that the people actually enjoy those benefits. As the assistant secretary of state put it: "The truly meaningful issue is not what rights the government has guaranteed, what promises have been made, but what has been delivered."4

This fundamental social/political dichotomy notwithstanding, a social and economic counterpart to the political Bill of Rights would not be totally alien to the United States political system. For that matter, it would not even be a new idea. President Franklin D. Roosevelt, in his 1944 State of the Union Address to Congress, urged just that: an "economic bill of rights" that would guarantee a decent home, adequate medical care, social security, a good education, and a job with a salary adequate to provide food and clothing. Piecemeal political attempts have been made at some of these proposals, but the fact that no serious effort has been made to write the "economic bill of rights" into basic law is no accident. The 200-year-old distinction between the political and social spheres survives today.

A paraphrase of Thomas Hobbes's famous dictum may make the distinction most clearly. The liberties of subjects, he wrote in the seventeenth century, "depend on the silence of the law."5 Of civil and political rights this is still quite true. Those who

345

give priority to the economic and social rights, however, might say: "The rights of subjects depend upon the action of the law." This difference can be dismissed as a problem in semantics -- the difference between a right and a liberty -- but it is more than that, much more. It determines the relationship between a state and its citizens, it sets standards for basic human dignity, and it is, more often than many governments in both systems care to admit, a question of life and death.

NOTES

1   John Rawls, A Theory of Justice, (Cambridge, Mass.: Harvard University Press, Belknap Press, 1971), p. 61.

2   Id., p. 7.

3   Richard Schifter, "Human Rights, the Soviet Union, and the Helsinki Process," State Department Bulletin, Vol. 87, No. 2021, April 1987, p. 48.

4   Id.

5   Thomas Hobbes, Leviathan, Section XXI (abridged edition, F.B. Randall, ed., New York: Washington Square Press, 1964), p. 154.

APPENDIX

Appendix I

DECLARATION OF INDEPENDENCE
In Congress, July 4, 1776

The unanimous Declaration of the
thirteen united States of America,

When in the Course of human events, it becomes
necessary for one people to dissolve the political
bands which have connected them with another, and to
assume among the Powers of the earth, the separate and
equal station to which the Laws of Nature and of
Nature's God entitle them, a decent respect to the
opinions of mankind requires that they should declare
the causes which impel them to the separation.

We hold these truths to be self-evident, that all
men are created equal, that they are endowed by their
Creator with certain unalienable Rights, that among
these are Life, Liberty and the pursuit of Happiness.
That to secure these rights, Governments are
instituted among Men, deriving their just powers from
the consent of the governed, That whenever any Form
of Government becomes destructive of these ends, it is
the Right of the People to alter or to abolish it, and
to institute new Government, laying its foundation on
such principles and organizing its powers in such
form, as to them shall seem most likely to effect
their Safety and Happinesss. Prudence, indeed, will
dictate that Governments long established should not
be changed for light and transient causes; and
accordingly all experience hath shown, that mankind
are more disposed to suffer, while evils are
sufferable, than to right themselves by abolishing the
forms to which they are accustomed. But when a long
train of abuses and usurpations, pursuing invariably
the same Object evinces a design to reduce them under
absolute Despotism, it is their right, it is their
duty, to throw off such Government, and to provide new
Guards for their future security.--Such has been the
patient sufferance of these Colonies; and such is now
the necessity which constrains them to alter their
former Systems of Government. The history of the
present King of Great Britain is a history of repeated
injuries and usurpations, all having in direct object
the establishment of an absolute Tyranny over these
States. To prove this, let Facts be submitted to a
candid world.

349

He has refused his Assent to Laws, the most wholesome and necessary for the public good.

He has forbidden his Governors to pass Laws of immediate and pressing importance, unless suspended in their operation till his Assent should be obtained; and when so suspended, he has utterly neglected to attend to them.

He has refused to pass other Laws for the accommodation of large districts of people, unless those people would relinquish the right of Representation in the Legislature, a right inestimable to them and formidable to tyrants only.

He has called together legislative bodies at places unusual, uncomfortable, and distant from the depository of their Public Records, for the sole purpose of fatiguing them into compliance with his measures.

He has dissolved Representative Houses repeatedly, for opposing with manly firmness his invasions on the rights of the people.

He has refused for a long time, after such dissolutions, to cause others to be elected; whereby the Legislative Powers, incapable of Annihilation, have returned to the People at large for their exercise; the State remaining in the mean time exposed to all the dangers of invasion fromwithout, and convulsions within.

He has endeavoured to prevent the population of these States; for that purpose obstructing the Laws for Naturalization of Foreigners; refusing to pass others to encourage their migrations hither, and raising the conditions of new Appropriations of Lands.

He has obstructed the Administration of Justice, by refusing his Assent to Laws for establishing Judiciary Powers.

He has made Judges dependent on his Will alone, for the tenure of their offices, and the amount and payment of their salaries.

He has erected a multitude of New Offices, and sent hither swarms of Officers to harass our people, and eat out their substance.

He has kept among us, in times of peace, Standing Armies without the Consent of our legislatures.

He has affected to render the Military independent of and superior to the Civil Power.

He has combined with others to subject us to a jurisdiction foreign to our constitution, and unacknowledged by our laws; giving his Assent to their acts of pretended Legislation:

For quartering large bodies of armed troops among us:

For protecting them, by a mock Trial, from Punishment for any Murders which they should commit on the Inhabitants of these States:

For cutting off our Trade with all parts of the world:

For imposing taxes on us without our Consent:

For depriving us in many cases, of the benefits of Trial by Jury:

For transporting us beyond Seas to be tried for pretended offences:

For abolishing the free System of English Laws in a neighbouring Province, establishing therein an Arbitray government, and enlarging its Boundaries so as to render it at once an example and fit instrument for introducing the same absolute rule into these Colonies:

For taking away our Charters, abolishing our most valuable Laws, and altering fundamentally the Forms of our Governments:

For suspending our own Legislatures, and declaring themselves invested with Power to legislate for us in all cases whatsoever.

He has abdicated Government here, by declaring us out of his Protection and waging War against us.

He has plundered our seas, ravaged our Coasts, burnt our towns, and destroyed the lives of our people.

He   is at this time transporting large armies   of
foreign   mercenaries   to compleat the works of   death,
desolation   and   tyranny,   already   begun   with
circumstances of Cruelty & perfidy scarcely paralleled
in   the most barbarous ages,   and totally unworthy the
Head of a civilized nation.

He   has   constrained our   fellow   Citizens   taken
Captive   on   the high Seas to bear Arms against   their
Country,   to become the executioners of their   friends
and Brethren, or to fall themselves by their Hands.

He has excited domestic insurrections amongst us,
and has endeavoured to bring on the inhabitants of our
frontiers,   the merciless Indian Savages,   whose known
rule of warfare,   is an undistinguished destruction of
all ages, sexes and conditions.

In   every   stage   of these   Oppressions   We   have
Petitioned for Redress in the most humble terms: Our
repeated Petitions have been answered only by repeated
injury.   A Prince,   whose character is thus marked by
every   act which may define a Tyrant,   is unfit to   be
the ruler of a free people.

Nor   have   We been wanting in attentions   to   our
Brittish   brethren.   We have warned them from time to
time   of   attempts by their legislature to   extend   an
unwarrantable jurisdiction over us.   We have reminded
them   of   the   circumstances   of   our   emigration   and
settlement   here.   We have appealed to   their   native
justice and magnanimity,   and we have conjured them by
the   ties   of   our   common kindred   to   disavow   these
usurpations   which,   would   inevitably   interrupt   our
connections   and correspondence.   They too have   been
deaf to the voice of justice and of consanguinity.   We
must,   therefore,   acquiesce in the   necessity,   which
denounces   our Separation,   and hold them,   as we hold
the rest of mankind, Enemies in War, in Peace Friends.

We,   therefore,   the Representatives of the united
States   of America,   in General   Congress,   Assembled,
appealing   to the Supreme Judge of the world   for   the
rectitude   of our intentions,   do in the Name,   and by
authority   of   the   good People   of   these   Colonies,
solemnly   publish   and   declare,   that   these   United
Colonies   are,   and   of   Right ought to   be   Free   and
Independent   States;   that they are Absolved from   all
Allegiance   to   the   British   Crown,   and   that   all
political   connection   between them and the   State   of
Great   Britain,   is and ought to be totally dissolved;

and that as Free and Independent States, they have
full power to levy War, conclude Peace, contract
Alliances, establish Commerce, and to do all other
Acts and Things which Independent States may of right
do. And for the support of this Declaration, with a
firm reliance on the Protection of Divine Providence,
we mutaully pledge to each other our Lives, our
Fortunes and our sacred Honor.

Appendix II

THE CONSTITUTION OF THE UNITED STATES

OF AMERICA

(Preamble)

We the People of the United States, in Order to form a
more perfect Union, establish Justice, insure domestic
Tranquility, provide for the common defense, promote
the general Welfare, and secure the Blessings of
Liberty to ourselves and our Posterity, do ordain and
establish this CONSTITUTION for the United States of
America.

Article I.
(The Legislative Branch)

SECTION 1. All legislative Powers herein
granted shall be vested in a Congress of the United
States, which shall consist of a Senate and House of
Representatives.

SECTION 2. The House of Representatives shall be
composed of Members chosen every second Year by the
People of the several States, and the Electors in each
State shall have the Qualifications requisite for
Electors of the most numerous Branch of the State
Legislature.

No Person shall be a Representative who shall not
have attained to the Age of twenty-five Years, and
been seven Years a Citizen of the United States, and
who shall not, when elected, be an Inhabitant of that
State in which he shall be chosen.

(Representatives and direct Taxes shall be
apportioned among the several States which may be
included within this Union, according to their
respective Numbers, which shall be determined by
adding to the whole Number of free Persons, including
those bound to Service for a Term of Years, and
excluding Indians not taxed, three fifths of all other
Persons.) The actual Enumeration shall be made within
three Years after the first Meeting of the Congress of
the United States, and within every subsequent Term of
ten Years, in such Manner as they shall by Law direct.

The Number of Representatives shall not exceed one for
every thirty Thousand, but each State shall have at
Least one Representative; and until such enumeration
shall be made, the State of New Hampshire shall be
entitled to chuse three, Massachusetts eight, Rhode-
Island and Providence Plantations one, Connecticut
five, New-York six, New Jersey four, Pennsylvania
eight, Delaware one, Maryland six, Virginia ten, North
Carolina five, South Carolina five, and Georgia three.

When vacancies happen in the Representation from
any State, the Executive Authority thereof shall issue
Writs of Election to fill such Vacancies.

The House of Representatives shall chuse their
Speaker and other Officers; and shall have the sole
Power of Impeachment.

SECTION 3. The Senate of the United States shall
be composed of two Senators from each State, chosen by
the Legislature thereof, for six Years; and each
Senator shall have one Vote.

Immediately after they shall be assembled in
Consequence of the first Election, they shall be
divided as equally as may be into three Classes. The
Seats of the Senators of the first Class shall be
vacated at the Expiration of the second Year, of the
second Class at the Expiration of the fourth Year, and
of the third Class at the Expiration of the sixth
Year, so that one-third may be chosen every second
Year; and if Vacancies happen by Resignation, or
otherwise, during the Recess of the Legislature of any
State, the Executive thereof may make temporary
Appointments until the next Meeting of the
Legislature, which shall then fill such Vacancies.

No Person shall be a Senator who shall not have
attained to the Age of thirty Years, and been nine
Years a Citizen of the United States, and who shall
not, when elected, be an Inhabitant of that State for
which he shall be chosen.

The Vice President of the United States shall be
President of the Senate, but shall have no Vote,
unless they be equally divided.

The Senate shall chuse their other Officers, and
also a President pro tempore, in the absense of the
Vice President, or when he shall exercise the Office
of President of the United States.

The Senate shall have the sole Power to try all Impeachments. When sitting for that Purpose, they shall be on Oath or Affirmation. When the President of the United States is tried, the Chief Justice shall preside: And no Person shall be convicted without the Concurrence of two thirds of the Members present.

Judgment in Cases of Impeachment shall not extend further than to removal from Office, and disqualification to hold and enjoy any Office of honor, Trust or Profit under the United States: but the Party convicted shall nevertheless be liable and subject to Indictment, Trial, Judgment and Punishment, according to Law.

SECTION 4. The Times, Places and Manner of holding Elections for Senators and Representatives, shall be prescribed in each State by the Legislature thereof; but the Congress may at any time by Law make or alter such Regulations, except as to the Place of Chusing Senators.

The Congress shall assemble at least once in every Year, and such Meeting shall be on the first Monday in December, unless they shall by Law appoint a different Day.

SECTION 5. Each House shall be the Judge of the Elections, Returns and Qualifications of its own Members, and a Majority of each shall constitute a Quorum to do Business; but a smaller number may adjourn from day to day, and may be authorized to compel the Attendance of absent Members, in such Manner, and under such Penalties as each House may provide.

Each House may determine the Rules of its Proceedings, punish its Members for disorderly Behavior, and, with the Concurrence of two thirds, expel a Member.

Each House shall keep a Journal of its Procedings, and from time to time publish the same, excepting such Parts as may in their Judgment require Secrecy; and the Yeas and Nays of the Members of either House on any question shall, at the Desire of one fifth of those Present, be entered on the Journal.

Neither House, during the Session of Congress, shall, without the Consent of the other, adjourn for more than three days, nor to any other Place than that in which the two Houses shall be sitting.

SECTION 6. The Senators and Representatives shall receive a Compensation for their Services, to be ascertained by Law, and paid out of the Treasury of the United States. They shall in all Cases, except Treason, Felony and Breach of the Peace, be privileged from Arrest during the Atendance at the Session of their respective Houses, and in going to and returning from the same; and for any Speech or Debate in either House, they shall not be questioned in any other Place.

No Senator or Representative shall, during the Time for which he was elected, be appointed to any civil Office under the Authority of the United States, which shall have been created, or the Emoluments whereof shall have been encreased during such time; and no Person holding any Office under the United States, shall be a Member of either House during his Continuance in Office.

SECTION 7. All Bills for raising Revenue shall originate in the House of Representatives; but the Senate may propose or concur with Amendments as on other Bills.

Every Bill which shall have passed the House of Representatives and the Senate, shall, before it become a Law, be presented to the President of the United States; If he approve he shall sign it, but if not he shall return it, with his Objections to that House in which it shall have originated, who shall enter the Objections at large on their Journal, and proceed to reconsider it. If after such Reconsideration two thirds of that House shall agree to pass the Bill, it shall be sent, together with the Objections, to the other House, by which it shall likewise be reconsidered, and if approved by two thirds of that House, it shall become a Law. But in all such Cases the Votes of both Houses shall be determined by Yeas and Nays, and the Names of the Persons voting for and against the Bill shall be entered on the Journal of each House respectively. If any Bill shall not be returned by the President within ten Days (Sundays excepted) after it shall have been presented to him, the Same shall be a Law, in like Manner as if he had signed it, unless the Congress by their Adjournment prevent its Return, in which Case it shall not be a Law.

Every Order, Resolution, or Vote to which the Concurrence of the Senate and House of Representatives may be necessary (except on a question of Adjournment) shall be presented to the President of the United States; and before the Same shall take Effect, shall be approved by him, or being disapproved by him, shall be repassed by two thirds of the Senate and House of Representatives, according to the Rules and Limitations prescribed in the Case of a Bill.

SECTION 8. The Congress shall have Power To lay and collect Taxes, Duties, Imposts and Excises, to pay the Debt and provide for the common Defense and general Welfare of the United States; but all Duties, Imposts and Excises shall be uniform throughout the United States;

To borrow money on the credit of the United States;

To regulate Commerce with foreign Nations, and among the several States, and with the Indian Tribes;

To establish an uniform Rule of Naturalization, and uniform Laws on the subject of Bankruptcies throughout the United States;

To coin Money, regulate the Value thereof, and of foreign Coin, and fix the Standard or Weights and Measures;

To provide for the Punishment of counterfeiting the Securities and current Coin of the United States;

To establish Post Offices and post Roads;

To promote the Progress of Science and useful Arts, by securing for limited Times to Authors and Inventors the exclusive Right to their respective Writings and Discoveries;

To constitute Tribunals inferior to the supreme Court;

To define and punish Piracies and Felonies committed on the high Seas, and Offenses against the Law of Nations;

To declare War, grant Letters of Marque and Reprisal, and make Rules concerning Captures on Land and Water;

To raise and support Armies, but no Appropriation of Money to that Use shall be for a longer Term than two Years;

To provide and maintain a Navy;

To make Rules for the Government and Regulation of the land and naval Forces;

To provide for calling forth the Militia to execute the Laws of the Union, suppress Insurrections and repel Invasions;

To provide for organizing, arming, and disciplining the Militia, and for governing such Part of them as may be employed in the Service of the United States, reserving to the States respectively, the Appointment of the Officers, and the Authority of training the Militia according to the discipline prescribed by Congress;

To exercise exclusive Legislation in all Cases whatsoever, over such District (not exceeding ten Miles square) as may, by Cession of particular States, and the acceptance of Congress, become the Seat of the Government of the United States, and to exercise like Authority over all Places purchased by the Consent of the Legislature of the State in which the Same shall be, for the Erection of Forts, Magazines, Arsenals, dock-Yards, and other needful Building;--And

To make all Laws which shall be necessary and proper for carrying into Execution the foregoing Powers, and all other Powers vested by this Constitution in the Government of the United States, or in any Department or Officer thereof.

SECTION 9. The Migration or Importation of such Persons as any of the States now existing shall think proper to admit, shall not be prohibited by the Congress prior to the Year one thousand eight hundred and eight, but a tax or duty may be imposed on such Importation, not exceeding ten dollars for each Person.

The privilege of the Writ of Habeas Corpus shall not be suspended, unless when in Cases of Rebellion or Invasion the public Safety may require it.

No Bill of Attainder or ex post facto Law shall be passed.

No capitation, or other direct, Tax shall be laid, unless in Proportion to the Census or Enumeration herein before directed to be taken.

No Tax or Duty shall be laid on Articles exported from any State.

No Preference shall be given by any Regulation of Commerce or Revenue to the Ports of one State over those of another: nor shall Vessels bound to, or from, one State, be obliged to enter, clear, or pay Duties in another.

No Money shall be drawn from the Treasury, but in Consequence of Appropriations made by Law; and a regular Statement and Account of the Receipts and Expenditures of all public Money shall be published from time to time.

No Title of Nobility shall be granted by the United States: And no Person holding any Office of Profit or Trust under them, shall, without the Consent of the Congress, accept of any present, Emolument, Office, or Title, of any kind whatever, from any King, Prince, or foreign State.

SECTION 10. No State shall enter into any Treaty, Alliance, or Confederation; grant Letters of Marque and Reprisal; coin Money; emit Bills of Credit; make any Thing but gold and silver Coin a Tender in Payment of Debts; pass any Bill of Attainder, ex post facto Law, or Law impairing the Obligation of Contracts, or grant any Title of Nobility.

No State shall, without the Consent of the Congress, lay any Imposts or Duties on Imports or Exports, except what may be absolutely necessary for executing it's inspection Laws: and the net Produce of all Duties and Imposts, laid by any State on Imports or Exports, shall be for the Use of the Treasury of the United States; and all such Laws shall be subject to the Revision and Controul of the Congress.

No State shall, without the Consent of Congress, lay any duty of Tonnage, keep Troops, or Ships of War in time of Peace, enter into any Agreement or Compact with another State, or with a foreign Power, or engage in War, unless actually invaded, or in such imminent Danger as will not admit of delay.

Article II.
(The Executive Branch)

SECTION 1. The executive Power shall be vested in a President of the United States of America. He shall hold his Office during the Term of four Years, and, together with the Vice-President, chosen for the same Term, be elected, as follows

Each State shall appoint, in such Manner as the Legislature thereof may direct, a Number of Electors, equal to the whole Number of Senators and Representatives to which the State may be entitled in the Congress: but no Senator or Representative, or Person holding an Office of Trust or Profit under the United States, shall be appointed an Elector.

[The Electors shall meet in their respective States, and vote by Ballot for two persons, of whom one at least shall not be an Inhabitant of the same State with themselves. And they shall make a List of all the Persons voted for, and of the Number of Votes for each; which List they shall sign and certify, and transmit sealed to the Seat of the Government of the United States, directed to the President of the Senate. The President of the Senate shall, in the Presence of the Senate and House of Representatives, open all the Certificates, and the Votes shall then be counted. The Person having the greatest Number of Votes shall be the President, if such Number be a Majority of the whole Number of Electors appointed; and if there be more than one who have such Majority, and have an equal Number of Votes, then the House of Representatives shall immediately chuse by Ballot one of them for President; and if no Person have a Majority, then from the five highest on the List the said House shall in like Manner chuse the President. But in chusing the President, the Votes shall be taken by States, the Representation from each State having one Vote; A quorum for this Purpose shall consist of a Member or Members from two-thirds of the States, and a Majority of all the States shall be necessary to a Choice. In every Case, after the Choice of the President, the Person having the greatest Number of Votes of the Electors shall be the Vice President. But if there should remain two or more who have equal Votes, the Senate shall chuse from them by Ballot the Vice-President.]

The Congress may determine the Time of chusing the Electors, and the Day on which they shall give their Votes; which Day shall be the same throughout the United States.

No person except a natural born Citizen, or a Citizen of the United States, at the time of the Adoption of this Constitution, shall be eligible to the Office of President; neither shall any Person be eligible to that Office who shall not have attained to the Age of thirty-five Years, and been fourteen Years a Resident within the United States.

In Case of the Removal of the President from Office, or of his Death, Resignation, or Inability to discharge the Powers and Duties of the said Office, the same shall devolve on the Vice President, and the Congress may by Law provide for the Case of Removal, Death, Resignation or Inability, both of the President and Vice President, declaring what Officer shall then act as President, and such Officer shall act accordingly, until the Disability be removed, or a President shall be elected.

The President shall, at stated Times, receive for his Services, a Compensation, which shall neither be encreased nor diminished during the Period for which he shall have been elected, and he shall not receive within that Period any other Emolument from the United States, or any of them.

Before he enter on the Execution of his Office, he shall take the following Oath or Affirmation:--"I do solemnly swear (or affirm) that I will faithfully execute the Office of President of the United States, and will to the best of my Ability, preserve, protect and defend the Constitution of the United States."

SECTION 2. The President shall be Commander in Chief of the Army and Navy of the United States, and of the Militia of the several States, when called into the actual Service of the United States; he may require the Opinion in writing, of the principal Officer in each of the executive Departments, upon any subject relating to the Duties of their respective Offices, and he shall have Power to Grant Reprives and Pardons for Offenses against the United States, except in Cases of Impeachment.

He shall have Power, by and with the Advice and Consent of the Senate, to make Treaties, provided two-

thirds of the Senators present concur; and he shall
nominate, and by and with the Advice and Consent of
the Senate, shall appoint Ambassadors, other public
1inisters and Consuls, Judges of the supreme Court,
and all other Officers of the United States, whose
Appointments are not herein otherwise provided for,
and which shall be established by Law: but the
Congress may by Law vest the Appointment of such
inferior Officers, as they think proper, in the
President alone, in the Courts of Law, or in the Heads
of Departments.

The President shall have Power to fill up all
Vacancies that may happen during the Recess of the
Senate, by granting Commissions which shall expire at
the End of their next Session.

SECTION 3. He shall from time to time give to
the Congress Information of the State of the Union,
and recommend to their Consideration such Measures as
he shall judge necessary and expedient; he may, on
extraordinary Occasions, convene both Houses, or
either of them, and in Case of Disagreement between
them, with Respect to the Time of Adjournment, he may
adjorn them to such Time as he shall think proper; he
shall receive Ambassadors and other public Ministers
he shall take Care that the Laws be faithfully
executed, and shall Commission all the Officers of the
United States.

SECTION 4. The President, Vice President and all
civil Officers of the United States, shall be removed
from Office on Impeachment for, and Conviction of,
Treason, Bribery, or other high Crimes and
Misdemeanors.

Article III.
(The Judicial Branch)

SECTION 1. The judicial Power of the United
States, shall be vested in one supreme Court, and in
such inferior Courts as the Congress may from time to
time ordain and establish. The Judges, both of the
supreme and inferior Courts, shall hold their Offices
during good Behaviour, and shall, at stated Times,
receive for their Services a Compensation which shall
not be diminished during their Continuance in Office.

SECTION 2. The Judicial Power shall extend to all
Cases, in Law and Equity, arising under this

Constitution, the Laws of the United States, and
Treaties made, or which shall be made, under their
Authority;--to all Cases affecting Ambassadors, other
public Ministers and Consuls;--to all Cases of
admiralty and maritime Jurisdiction;--to Controversies
to which the United States shall be a Party;--to
Controversies between two or more States;--between a
State and Citizens of another state;--between Citizens
of different States;--between Citizens of the same
State claiming Lands under Grants of different States,
and between a State, or the Citizens thereof, and
foreign States, Citizens or Subjects.

In all Cases affecting Ambassadors, other public
Ministers and Consuls, and those in which a State
shall be Party, the supreme Court shall have original
Jurisdiction. In all the other Cases before
mentioned, the supreme Court shall have appellate
Jurisdiction, both as to Law and Fact, with such
Exceptions, and under such Regulations as the Congress
shall make.

The trial of all Crimes, except in Cases of
Impeachment, shall be by Jury; and such Trial shall be
held in the State where the said Crimes shall have
been committed; but when not committed within any
State, the Trial shall be at such Place or Places as
the Congress may by Law have directed.

SECTION 3. Treason against the United States,
shall consist only in levying War against them, or in
adhering to their Enemies, giving them Aid and
Comfort. No Person shall be convicted of Treason
unless on the Testimony of two Witnesses to the same
overt Act, or on Confession in open Court.

The Congress shall have power to declare the
Punishment of Treason, but no Attainder of Treason
shall work Corruption of Blood, or Forfeiture except
during the Life of the Person attainted.

Article IV.
(Relation of the States to each other)

SECTION 1. Full Faith and Credit shall be given
in each State to the public Acts, Records, and
judicial Proceedings of every other State. And the
Congress may by general Laws prescribe the Manner in
which such Acts, Records and Proceedings shall be
proved, and the Effect thereof.

SECTION 2. The Citizens of each State shall be entitled to all Privileges and Immunities of Citizens in the several States.

A Person charged in any State with Treason, Felony, or other Crime, who shall flee from Justice, and be found in another State, shall on demand of the executive Authority of the State from which he fled, be delivered up, to be removed to the State having Jurisdiction of the Crime.

No Person held to Service or Labour in one State, under the Laws thereof, escaping into another, shall, in Consequence of any Law or Regulation therein, be discharged from such Service or Labour, but shall be delivered up on Claim of the Party to whom such Service or Labour may be due.

SECTION 3. New States may be admitted by the Congress into this Union; but no new State shall be formed or erected within the Jurisdiction of any other State; nor any State be formed by the Junction of two or more States, or parts of States, without the Consent of the Legislatures of the States concerned as well as of the Congress.

The Congress shall have Power to dispose of and make all needful Rules and Regulations respecting the Territory or other Property belonging to the United States; and nothing in this Constitution shall be so construed as to Prejudice any Claims of the United States, or of any particular State.

SECTION 4. The United States shall guarantee to every State in this Union a Republican Form of Government, and shall protect each of them against Invasion; and on Application of the Legislature, or of the Executive (when the Legislature cannot be convened) against domestic Violence.

Article V.
(Amending the Constitution)

The Congress, whenever two-thirds of both Houses shall deem it necessary, shall propose Amendments to this Constitution, or, on the Application of the Legislatures of two-thirds of the several States, shall call a Convention for proposing Amendments, which, in either Case, shall be valid to all Intents and Purposes, as part of this Constitution, when

366

ratified by the Legisatures of three-fourths of the
several States, or by Conventions in three-fourths
thereof, as the one or the other Mode of Ratification
may be proposed by the Congress; Provided that no
Amendment which may be made prior to the Year One
thousand eight hundred and eight shall in any Manner
affect the first and fourth Clauses in the Ninth
Section of the first Article; and that no State,
without its Consent, shall be deprived of its equal
Suffrage in the Senate.

Article VI.
(National Debts)

All Debts contracted and Engagements entered
into, before the Adoption of this Constitution, shall
be as valid against the United States under this
Constitution, as under the Confederation.

This Constitution, and the Laws of the United
States which shall be made in Persuance thereof; and
all Treaties made, or which shall be made, under the
Authority of the United States, shall be the supreme
Law of the Land; and the Judges in every State shall
be bound thereby, any Thing in the Constitution or
Laws of any State to the Contrary notwithstanding.

The Senators and Representatives before
mentioned, and the Members of the several State
Legislatures, and all executive and judicial Officers,
both of the United States and of the several States,
shall be bound by Oath or Affirmation, to support this
Constitution; but no religious Test shall ever be
required as a Qualification to any Office or public
Trust under the United States.

Article VII.
(Ratifying the Constitution)

The Ratification of the Conventions of nine
States shall be sufficient for the Establishment of
this Constitution between the States to ratifying the
Same.

DONE in Convention by the Unanimous Consent
of the States present the Seventeenth Day of
September in the Year of our Lord one thousand
seven hundred and Eighty seven and of the
Independence of the United States of America the

367

Twelth. In Witness whereof We have hereunto
subscribed our Names.

G. WASHINGTON
President and deputy from Virginia

New Hampshire   Delaware
John Langdan   George Read
Nicholas Gilman   John Dickinson
                              Jacob Broom
Massachusetts   Gunning Bedford, Jr.
Nathaniel Gorham   Richard Bassett
Rufus King
                                       Maryland
Connecticut   James McHenry
William Samuel Johnson   Daniel Carroll
Roger Sherman   Daniel of St Thomas
                                         Jenifer
New York
Alexander Hamilton   Virginia
                              John Blair--
New Jersey   James Madison, Jr.
William Livingston
David Brearley   North Carolina
William Patterson   William Blount
Jonathan Dayton   Hugh Williamson
                              Richard Dobbs Spaight
Pennsylvania
Benjamin Franklin   South Carolina
Robert Morris   John Rutledge
Thomas Fitzsimons   Charles Pinckney
James Wilson   Charles Cotesworth
Thomas Mifflin   Pinckney
George Clymer   Pierce Butler
Jared Ingersoll
Gouberneur Morris   Georgia
                              William Few
                              Abraham Baldwin

Attest:

WILLIAM JACKSON, Secretary

AMENDMENTS

Article I
(Freedom of Religion, Speech & Press)

Congress shall make no law respecting an establishment of religion, or prohibiting the free exercise thereof; or abridging the freedom of speech, or of the press; or the right of the people peaceably to assemble, and to petition the Government for a redress of grievances. (1791)

Article II.
(Right to Bear Arms)

A well regulated Militia, being necessary to the security of a free State, the right of the people to keep and bear Arms, shall not be infringed. (1791)

Article III
(Housing of Soldiers)

No soldier shall, in time of peace be quartered in any house, without the consent of the Owner, nor in time of war, but in a manner to be prescribed by law. (1791)

Article IV
(Search and Arrest Warrants)

The right of the people to be secure in their persons, houses, papers, and effects, against unreasonable searches and seizures, shall not be violated, and no Warrants shall issue, but upon probable cause, supported by Oath or affirmation, and particularly describing the place to be searched, and the persons or things to be seized. (1791)

Article V
(Rights in Criminal Cases)

No person shall be held to answer for a capital, or otherwise infamous crime, unless on a presentment or indictment of a Grand Jury, except in cases arising

369

in the land or naval forces, or in the Militia, when in actual service in time of War or public danger; nor shall any person be subject for the same offence to be twice put in jeopardy of life or limb; nor shall be compelled in any criminal case to be a witness against himself, nor be deprived of life, liberty, or property, without due process of law; nor shall private property be taken for public use, without just compensation. (1791)

Article VI
(Rights to a Fair Trial)

In all criminal prosecutions, the accused shall enjoy the right to a speedy and public trial, by an impartial jury of the State and district wherein the crime shall have been committed, which district shall have been previously ascertained by law, and to be informed of the nature and cause of the accusation; to be confronted with the witnesses against him; to have compulsory process for obtaining witnesses in his favor, and to have the Assistance of Counsel for his defence. (1791)

Article VII
(Rights in Civil Cases)

In suits at common law, where the value in controversy shall exceed twenty dollars, the right of trial by jury shall be preserved, and no fact tried by a jury, shall be otherwise reexamined in any Court of the United States, than according to the rules of the common law. (1791)

Article VIII
(Banks, Fines, and Punishments)

Excessive bail shall not be required, nor excessive fines imposed, nor cruel and unusual punishments inflicted. (1791)

Article IX
(Rights Retained by People)

The enumeration in the Constitution, of certain rights, shall not be construed to deny or disparage others retained by the people. (1791)

Article X
(Powers Retained by the States and the People)

The powers not delegated to the United States by the Constitution, nor prohibited by it to the States, are reserved to the States respectively, or to the people. (1791)

Article XI
(Law Suits Against States)

The Judicial power of the United States shall not be construed to extend to any suit in law or equity, commenced or prosecuted against one of the United States by Citizens of another State, or by Citizens or Subjects of any Foreign State. (1795)

Article XII
(Elections of the President and Vice-President)

The Electors shall meet in their respective states and vote by ballot for President and Vice-President, one of whom, at least, shall not be an inhabitant of the same state with themselves; they shall name in their ballots the person voted for as President, and in distinct ballots the person voted for as Vice-President, and they shall make distinct lists of all persons voted for as President, and of all persons voted for as Vice-President, and of the number of votes for each, which lists they shall sign and certify, and transmit sealed to the seat of the government of the United States, directed to the President of the Senate;--The President of the Senate shall, in presence of the Senate and House of Representatives, open all the certificates and the votes shall then be counted;--The person having the greatest number of votes for President, shall be the President, if such number be a majority of the whole number of Electors appointed; and if no person have such majority, then from the persons having the highest numbers not exceeding three on the list of those voted for as President, the House of Representatives shall choose immediately, by ballot, the President. But in choosing the President, the votes shall be taken by states, the representation from each state having one vote; a quorum for this purpose shall consist of a member or members from two-thirds of the states, and a majority of all the states shall be necessary to a choice. And if the House of

371

Representatives shall not choose a President whenever the right of choice shall devolve upon them, before the fourth day of March next following, then the Vice-President shall act as President, as in the case of the death or other constitutional disability of the President.--The person having the greatest number of votes as Vice-President, shall be the Vice-President, if such number be a majority of the whole number of Electors appointed, and if no person have a majority, then from the two highest numbers on the list, the Senate shall choose the Vice-President; a quorum for the purpose shall consist of two-thirds of the whole number of Senators, and a majority of the whole number shall be necessary to a choice. But no person constitutionally ineligible to the office of President shall be eligible to that of Vice-President of the United States. (1804)

Article XIII
(Abolition of Slavery)

SECTION 1. Neither slavery nor involuntary servitude, except as a punishment for crime whereof the party shall have been duly convicted, shall exist within the United States, or any place subject to their jurisdiction.

SECTION 2. Congress shall have power to enforce this article by appropriate legislation. (1865)

Article XIV
(Civil Rights)

SECTION 1. All persons born or naturalized in the United States, and subject to the jurisdiction thereof, are citizens of the United States and of the State wherein they reside. No State shall make or enforce any law which shall abridge the privileges or immunities of citizens of the United States; nor shall any State deprive any person of life, liberty, or property, without due process of law; nor deny to any person within its jurisdiction the equal protection of the laws.

SECTION 2. Representatives shall be apportioned among the several States according to their respective numbers, counting the whole number of persons in each State, excluding Indians not taxed. But when the right to vote at any election for the choice of electors for President and Vice-President of the United States, Representatives in Congress, the Executive and Judicial officers of a State, or the members of the Legislature thereof, is denied to any of the male inhabitants of such State, being twenty-one years of age, and citizens of the United States, or in any way abridged, except for participation in rebellion, or other crime, the basis of representation therein shall be reduced in the proportion which the number of such male citizens shall bear to the whole number of male citizens twenty-one years of age in such State.

SECTION 3. No person shall be a Senator or Representative in Congress, or elector of President and Vice-President, or hold any office, civil or military, under the United States, or under any State, who, having previously taken an oath, as a member of Congress, or as an officer of the United States, or as a member of any State legislature, or as an executive or judicial officer of any State, to support the Constitution of the United States, shall have engaged in insurrection or rebellion against the same, or given aid or comfort to the enemies thereof. But Congress may by a vote of two-thirds of each House, remove such disability.

SECTION 4. The validity of the public debt of the United States, authorized by law, including debts incurred for payment of pensions and bounties for services in suppressing insurrection or rebellion, shall not be questioned. But neither the United States nor any State shall assume or pay any debt or obligation incurred in aid of insurrection or rebellion against the United States, or any claim for the loss or emancipation of any slave; but all such debts, obligations and claims shall be held illegal and void.

SECTION 5. The Congress shall have power to enforce, by appropriate legislation, the provisions of this article. (1868)

Article XV
(Color and Suffrage)

SECTION 1. The right of citizens of the United States to vote shall not be denied or abridged by the United States or by any State on account of race, color, or previous condition of servitude--

373

SECTION 2. The Congress shall have power to enforce this article by appropriate legislation. (1870)

Article XVI
(Income Taxes)

The Congress shall have power to lay and collect taxes on incomes, from whatever source derived, without apportionment among the several States, and without regard to any census or enumeration. (1913)

Article XVII
(Direct Election of Senators)

The Senate of the United States shall be composed of two Senators from each State, elected by the people thereof, for six years; and each Senator shall have one vote. The electors in each State shall have the qualifications requisite for electors of the most numerous branch of the State legislatures.

When vacancies happen in the representation of any State in the Senate, the executive authority of such State shall issue writs of election to fill such vacancies: Provided, That the legislature of any State may empower the executive thereof to make temporary appointments until the people fill the vacancies by election as the legislature may direct.

This amendment shall not be so construed as to affect the election or term of any Senator chosen before it becomes valid as part of the Constitution. (1913)

Article XVIII
(Prohibition of Liquor)

SECTION 1. After one year from the ratification of this article the manufacture, sale, or transportation of intoxicating liquors within, the importation thereof into, or the exportation thereof from the United States and all territory subject to the jurisdiction thereof for beverage purposes is hereby prohibited.

SECTION 2. The Congress and the several States

374

shall have concurrent power to enforce this article by appropriate legislation.

SECTION 3. This article shall be inoperative unless it shall have been ratified as an amendment to the Constitution by the legislature of the several States, as provided in the Constitution, within seven years from the date of the submission hereof to the States by the Congress. (1919)

Article XIX
(Woman Suffrage)

The right of citizens of the United States to vote shall not be denied or abridged by the United States or by any State on account of sex.

Congress shall have power to enforce this article by appropriate legislation. (1920)

Article XX
(Terms of the President and Congress)

SECTION 1. The terms of the President and Vice President shall end at noon on the 20th day of January, and the terms of Senators and Representatives at noon on the 3d day of January, of the years in which such terms would have ended if this article had not been ratified; and the terms of their successors shall then begin.

SECTION 2. The Congress shall assemble at least once in every year, and such meeting shall begin at noon on the 3d day of January, unless they shall by law appoint a different day.

SECTION 3. If, at the time fixed for the beginning of the term of the President, the President elect shall have died, the Vice President elect shall become President. If a President shall not have been chosen before the time fixed for the beginning of his term, or if the President elect shall have failed to qualify, then the Vice President elect shall act as President until a President shall have qualified; and the Congress may by law provide for the case wherein neither a President elect nor a Vice President elect shall have qualified, declaring who shall then act as President, or the manner in which one who is to act shall be selected, and such person shall act accordingly until a President or Vice President shall have qualified.

SECTION 4. The Congress may by law provide for the case of the death of any of the persons from whom the House of Representatives may choose a President whenever the right of choice shall have devolved upon them, and for the case of the death of any of the persons from whom the Senate may choose a Vice President whenever the right of choice shall have devolved upon them.

SECTION 5. Sections 1 and 2 shall take effect on the 15th day of October following the ratification of this article.

SECTION 6. This article shall be inoperative unless it shall have been ratified as an amendment to the Constitution by the legislatures of three-fourths of the several States within seven years from the date of its submission. (1933)

Article XXI
(Repeal of Prohibition)

SECTION 1. The eighteenth article of amendment to the Constitution of the United States is hereby repealed.

SECTION 2. The transportation or importation into any State, Territory, or possession of the United States for delivery or use therein of intoxicating liquors, in violation of the laws thereof, is hereby prohibited.

SECTION 3. This article shall be inoperative unless it shall have been ratified as an amendment to the Constitution by conventions in the several States, as provided in the Constitution, within seven years from the date of the submission hereof to the States by the Congress. (1933)

Article XXII
(Limitation of President to Two Terms)

SECTION 1. No person shall be elected to the office of the President more than twice, and no person who has held the office of President, or acted as

President, for more than two years of a term to which
some other person was elected President shall be
elected to the office of the President more than once.
But this Article shall not apply to any person holding
the office of President when this Article was proposed
by the Congress, and shall not prevent any person who
may be holding the office of President, or acting as
President, during the term within which this Article
becomes operative from holding the office of President
or acting as President during the remainder of such
term.

SECTION 2. This article shall be inoperative
unless it shall have been ratified as an amendment to
the Constitution by the legislatures of three-fourths
of the several States within seven years from the date
of its submission to the States by the Congress.
(1951)

Article XXIII
(Suffrage--The District of Columbia)

SECTION 1. The District constituting the seat
of Government of the United States shall appoint in
such manner as the Congress may direct:

A number of electors of President and Vice
President equal to the whole number of Senators and
Representatives in Congress to which the District
would be entitled if it were a State, but in no event
more than the least populous State; they shall be in
addition to those appointed by the States, but they
shall be considered, for the purposes of the election
of President and Vice President, to be electors
appointed by a State; and they shall meet in the
District and perform such duties as provided by the
twelfth article of amendment.

SECTION 2. The Congress shall have power to
enforce this article by appropriate legislation.
(1961)

Article XXIV
(Poll Taxes)

SECTION 1. The right of citizens of the United
Stats to vote in any primary or other election for
President or Vice President, for electors for
President or Vice President, or for Senator or

Representative in Congress, shall not be denied or abridged by the United States or any State by reason of failure to pay any poll tax or other tax.

SECTION 2. The Congress shall have power to enforce this article by appropriate legislation. (1964)

Article XXV
(Presidential Disability and Succession)

SECTION 1. In case of the removal of the President from office or of his death or resignation, the Vice President shall become President.

SECTION 2. Whenever there is a vacancy in the office of the Vice President, the President shall nominate a Vice President who shall take office upon confirmation by a majority vote of both Houses of Congress.

SECTION 3. Whenever the President transmits to the President pro tempore of the Senate and the Speaker of the House of Representatives his written declaration that he is unable to discharge the powers and duties of his office, and until he transmits to them a written declaration to the contrary, such powers and duties shall be discharged by the Vice President as Acting President.

SECTION 4. Whenever the Vice President and a majority of either the prinicipal officers of the executive departments or of such other body as Congress may by law provide, transmit to the President pro tempore of the Senate and the Speaker of the House of Representatives their written declaration that the President is unable to discharge the power and duties of his office, the Vice President shall immediately assume the powers and duties of the office as Acting President.

Thereafter, when the President transmits to the President pro tempore of the Senate and the Speaker of the House of Representatives his written declaration that no inability exists, he shall resume the powers and duties of his office unless the Vice President and a majority of either the principal officers of the executive department or of such other body as Congress may by law provide, transmit within four days to the President pro tempore of the Senate and the Speaker of

the House of Representatives their written declaration
that the President is unable to discharge the powers
and duties of his office. Thereupon Congress shall
decide the issue, assembling within forty-eight hours
for that purpose if not in session. In the Congress,
within twenty-one days after receipt of the latter
written declaration, or, if Congress is not in
session, within twenty-one days after Congress is
required to assemble, determines by two-thirds vote of
both Houses that the President is unable to discharge
the powers and duties of his office, the Vice
President shall continue to discharge the same as
Acting President; otherwise, the President shall
resume the powers and duties of his office. (1967)

Article XXVI
(Suffrage for 18-year-olds)

SECTION 1. The right of citizens of the United
States, who are eighteen years of age or older, to
vote shall not be denied or abridged by the United
States or by any State on account of age.

SECTION 2. The Congress shall have power to
enforce this article by appropriate legislation.
(1971)

(Year ratified in parenthesis)

Appendix III

UNITED NATIONS UNIVERSAL DECLARATION OF
HUMAN RIGHTS (1948)

Whereas recognition of the inherent dignity and
of the equal and inalienable rights of all members of
the human family is the foundation of freedom, justice
and peace in the world,

Whereas disregard and contempt for human rights
have resulted in barbarous acts which have outraged
the conscience of mankind, and the advent of a world
in which human beings shall enjoy freedom of speech
and belief and freedom from fear and want has been
proclaimed as the highest aspiration of the common
people,

Whereas it is essential, if man is not to be
compelled to have recourse, as a last resort, to
rebellion against tyranny and oppression, that human
rights should be protected by the rule of law,

Whereas it is essential to promote the
development of friendly relations between nations,

Whereas the peoples of the United Nations have in
the Charter reaffirmed their faith in fundamental
human rights, in the dignity and worth of the human
person and in the equal rights of men and women and
have determined to promote social progress and better
standards of life in larger freedom,

Whereas Member States have pledged themselves to
achieve, in co-operation with the United Nations, the
promotion of universal respect for and observance of
human rights and fundamental freedoms,

Whereas a common understanding of these rights
and freedoms is of the greatest importance for the
full realization of this pledge,

Now, therefore,

The General Assembly

Proclaims this Universal Declaration of Human
Rights as a common standard of achievement for all
peoples and all nations, to the end that every

individual and every organ of society, keeping this Declaration constantly in mind, shall strive by teaching and education to promote respect for these rights and freedoms and by progressive measures, national and international, to secure their universal and effective recognition and observance, both among the peoples of Member States themselves and among the peoples of territories under their jurisdiction.

Article 1. All human beings are born free and equal in dignity and rights. They are endowed with reason and conscience and should act towards one another in a spirit of brotherhood.

Article 2. Everyone is entitled to all the rights and freedoms set forth in this Declaration, without distinction of any kind, such as race, colour, sex, language, religion, political or other opinion, national or social origin, property, birth or other status.

Furthermore, no distinction shall be made on the basis of the political, jurisdictional or international status of the country or territory to which a person belongs, whether it be independent, trust, non-self-governing or under any other limitation of sovereignty.

Article 3. Everyone has the right to life, liberty and the security of person.

Article 4. No one shall be held in slavery or servitude; slavery and the slave trade shall be prohibited in all their forms.

Article 5. No one shall be subjected to torture or to cruel, inhuman or degrading treatment or punishment.

Article 6. Everyone has the right to recognition everywhere as a person before the law.

Article 7. All are equal before the law and are entitled without any discrimination to equal protection of the law. All are entitled to equal protection against any discrimination in violation of the Declaration and against any incitement to such discrimination.

Article 8. Everyone has the right to an effective remedy by the competent national tribunals for acts violating the fundamental rights granted him by the constitution or by law.

Article 9. No one shall be subjected to arbitrary arrest, detention or exile.

Article 10. Everyone is entitled to full equality to a fair and public hearing by an independent and impartial tribunal, in the determination of his rights and obligations and of any criminal charge against him.

Article 11.--1. Everyone charged with a penal offence has the right to be presumed innocent until proved guilty according to law in a public trial at which he has had all the guarantees necessary for his defence.
2. No one shall be held guilty of any penal offence on account of any act or omission which did not constitute a penal offence, under national or international law, at the time when it was committed. Nor shall a heavier penalty be imposed than the one that was applicable at the time the penal offence was committed.

Article 12. No one shall be subjected to arbitrary interference with his privacy, family, home or correspondence, nor to attacks upon his honour and reputation. Everyone has the right to the protection of the law against such interference or attacks.

Article 13.--1. Everyone has the right to freedom of movement and residence within the borders of each state.
2. Everyone has the right to leave any country, including his own, and to return to his country.

Article 14.--1. Everyone has the right to seek and to enjoy in other countries asylum from persecution.
2. This right may not be invoked in the case of prosecutions genuinely arising from non-political crimes or from acts contrary to the purposes and principles of the United Nations.

Article 15.--1. Everyone has the right to a nationality.
2. No one shall be arbitrarily deprived of his nationality nor denied the right to change his nationality.

Article 16.--1. Men and women of full age, without any limitation due to race, nationality or religion, have the right to marry and to found a family. They are entitled to equal rights as to marriage, during marriage and at its dissolution.
2. Marriage shall be entered into only with the free and full consent of the intending spouses.
3. The family is the natural and fundamental group unit of society and is entitled to protection by society and the State.

Article 17.--1. Everyone has the right to own property alone as well as in association with others.
2. No one shall be arbitrarily deprived of his property.

Article 18. Everyone has the right to freedom of thought, conscience and religion; this right includes freedom to change his religion or belief, and freedom, either alone or in community with others and in public or private, to manifest his religion or belief in teaching, practice, worship and observance.

Article 19. Everyone has the right to freedom of opinion and expression; this right includes freedom to hold opinions without interference and to seek, receive and impart information and ideas through any media and regardless of frontiers.

Articl 20.--1. Everyone has the right to freedom of peaceful assembly and association.
2. No one may be compelled to belong to an association.

Article 21.--1. Everyone has the right to take part in the Government of his country, directly or through freely chosen representatives.
2. Everyone has the right of equal access to public service in his country.
3. The will of the people shall be the basis of the authority of government; this will shall be expressed in periodic and genuine elections which shall be by universal and equal suffrage and shall be held by secret vote or by equivalent free voting procedures.

Article 22. Everyone, as a member of society, has the right to social security and is entitled to realization, through national effort and international co-operation and in accordance with the organization and resources of each State, of the economic, social and cultural rights indispensable for his dignity and the free development of his personality.

Article 23.--1. Everyone has the right to work, to free choice of employment, to just and favourable conditions of work and to protection against unemployment.
2. Everyone, without any discrimination, has the right to equal pay for equal work.
3. Everyone who works has the right to just and favourable remuneration insuring for himself and his family an existence worthy of human dignity, and supplemented, if necessary, by other means of social protection.
4. Everyone has the right to form and to join trade unions for the protection of his interests.

Article 24. Eveyone has the right to rest and leisure, including reasonable limitation of working hours and periodic holidays with pay.

Article 25.--1. Everyone has the right to a standard of living adequate for the health and well-being of himself and of his family, including food, clothing, housing and medical care and necessary social services, and the right to security in the event of unemployment, sickness, disability, widowhood, old age or other lack of livelihood in circmstances beyond his control.
2. Motherhood and childhood are entitled to special care and assistance. All children, whether born in or out of wedlock shall enjoy the same social protection.

Article 26.--1. Everyone has the right to education. Education shall be free, at least in the elementary and fundamental stages. Elementary education shall be compulsory. Technical and professional education shall be made generally available and higher education shall be equally accessible to all on the basis of merit.
2. Education shall be directed to the full development of the human personality and to the strengthening of respect for human rights and fundamental freedoms. It shall promote understanding, tolerance and friendship among all nations, racial or religious groups, and shall further the activities of the United Nations for the maintenance of peace.
3. Parents have a prior right to choose the kind of education that shall be given to their children.

Article 27.--1. Everyone has the right freely to participate in the cultural life of the community, to enjoy the arts nd to share in scientific advancement and its benefits.
2. Everyone has the right to the protection of the moral and material interests resulting from any scientific, literary or artistic production of which he is the author.

Article 28. Everyone is entitled to a social and international order in which the rights and freedoms set forth in this Declaration can be fully realized.

Article 29.--1. Everyone has duties to the community in which alone the free and full development of his personality is possible.
2. In the exercise of his rights and freedoms, everyone shall be subject only to such limitations as are determined by law solely for the purpose of securing due recognition and respect for the rights and freedoms of others and of meeting the just requirements of morality, public order and the general welfare in a democratic society.
3. These rights and freedoms may in no case be exercised contrary to the purposes and principles of the United Nations.

Article 30. Nothing in this Declaration may be interpreted as implying for any State, group or person any right to engage in any activity or to perform any act aimed at the destruction of any of the rights and freedoms set forth herein.

UNITED NATIONS CONVENTION ON THE PREVENTION
AND PUNISHMENT OF THE CRIME OF GENOCIDE
(1951)

The Contracting Parties,
    Having considered the declaration made by the
General Assembly of the United Nations in its
resolution 96 (I) dated 11 December 1946 that genocide
is a crime under international law, contrary to the
spirit and aims of the United Nations and condemned by
the civilized world;
    Recognizing that at all periods of history
genocide has inflicted great losses on humanity; and
    Being convinced that, in order to liberate
mankind from such an odious scourge, international cooperation is required:
    Hereby agree as hereinafter provided.

    Article I. The Contracting Parties confirm that
genocide, whether committed in time of peace or in
time of war, is a crime under international law which
they undertake to prevent and to punish.

    Article II. In the present Convention, genocide
means any of the following acts committed with intent
to destroy, in whole or in part, a national, ethnical,
racial or religious group as such:
    (a) Killing members of the group;
    (b) Causing serious bodily or mental harm to
        members of the group;
    (c) Deliberately inflicting on the group
        conditions of life calculated to bring
        about its physical destruction in whole
        or in part;
    (d) Imposing measures intended to prevent
        births within the group;
    (e) Forcibly transferring children of the
        group to another group.

    Article III. The following acts shall be
punishable:
    (a) Genocide;
    (b) Conspiracy to commit genocide;
    (c) Direct and public incitement to commit
        genocide;
    (d) Attempt to commit genocide;
    (e) Complicity in genocide.

Article IV. Persons committing genocide or any of the other acts enumerated in article III shall be punished, whether they are constitutionally responsible rulers, public officials or private individuals.

Article V. The Contracting Parties undertake to enact, in accordance with their respective Constitutions, the necessary legislation to give effect to the provisions of the present Convention and, in particular, to provide effective penalties for persons guilty of genocide or any of the other acts enumerated in article III.

Article VI. Persons charged with genocide or any of the other acts enumerated in article III shall be tried by a competent tribunal of the State in the territory of which the act was committed, or by such international penal tribunal as may have jurisdiction with respect to those Contracting Parties which shall have accepted its jurisdiction.

Article VII. Genocide and the other acts enumerated in article III shall not be considered as political crimes for the purpose of extradition.
The Contracting Parties pledge themselves in such cases to grant extradition in accordance with their laws and treaties in force.

Article VIII. Any Contracting Party may call upon the competent organs of the United Nations to take such action under the Charter of the United Nations as they consider appropriate for the prevention and suppression of acts of genocide or any of the other acts enumerated in article III.

Article IX. Disputes between the Contracting Parties relating to the interpretation, application or fulfillment of the present Convention, including those relating to the responsibility of a State for genocide or any of the other acts enumerated in article III, shall be submitted to the International Court of Justice at the request of any of the parties to the dispute.

Article X. The present Convention of which the Chinese, English, French, Russian and Spanish texts are equally authentic, shall bear the date of 9 December 1948.

NOTES ON CONTRIBUTORS

KIM BLANKENSHIP is an Assistant Professor of Sociology at Yale University. Her work focuses on Women and Work, Socialist-Feminist Theory, and The American Welfare State. Her publications include "Sectoral Influences on Occupational Sex Segregation," in Ida H. Simpson & Richard L. Simpson (eds.) Research In The Sociology of Work (JAI Press, 1984) and articles in American Journal of Sociology and other journals. She is presently preparing a manuscript tracing the History of U.S. Policy Towards Sex Discrimination in Employment.

LEONARD BLOOM is a member of the Modern Language Department faculty since 1967, and has been its Chairman since 1982. His academic interests, apart from a lifelong attachment to cinema and film criticism, cover such diverse areas as medieval Spanish language and literature, Basque and Sephardic studies, classical music and travel. He has written articles extensively on topics related to the Basque people, their language and culture. Now he serves as editor of the Journal of Basque Studies in America.

DAVID R. CONRAD is a professor of education and co-director of the Center for World Education at the University of Vermont. He teaches courses in aesthetic education, global education, and philosophy of education at the University. Dr. Conrad is the author of Education for Transformation: Implications in Lewis Mumford's Ecohumanism and co-edited Global Images of Peace and Education with T. M. Thomas and Gertrude Langsam. His articles have been published in several American and Japanese journals. His recent research is in the area of peace education.

WILLIAM V. DUNLAP is the Associate Dean and an associate professor at the University of Bridgeport School of Law, where he teaches Constitutional Law, Civil and Political Rights and International Human Rights. He received a B.A. from the New School for Social Research and a J.D. from Yale University.

ALFRED G. GERTEINY is a professor of History at the University of Bridgeport with fields of specilization in the Near East and North Africa (with

389

particular emphasis on Palestinian Problems), U.S. Diplomatic History and International Relations. He is the author of <u>Mauritania</u> and <u>Historical Dictionary of Mauritania</u> and has contributed chapters in <u>Islam In Africa</u>, <u>Encyclopedia Americana</u> and several other publications. For his research, he received several grants and fellowships from the National Endowment for the Humanities, Fulbright Hayes, the Africa Service Institute and other organizations. At present he serves as the President of the AAUP University of Bridgeport Chapter.

JESSE LEVITT, professor of Modern Languages with specialization in French literature and Romance linguistics, has taught at the University of Bridgeport since 1965. Previously, he had taught at Washington State University and worked as a foreign broadcast translator for the Federal Government. Dr. Levitt's publications include the <u>Grammaire des Grammaires of Girault-Duvivier, a Study of 19th century French Grammar</u> (Mouton, the Hague, 1968). Mr. Levitt has been editor of the periodical <u>Geolinguistics</u> and of <u>Geolinguistic Perspectives</u> (University Press of America, 1985), and has published some 35 articles on French and general linguistics and on onomastics.

WESLEY MENZEL is a professor of Education, teaching pre-service and in-service Science teachers. His background, training and early work experience have been in Agriculture and Science Education. "Food and Agriculture for a world community" is a senior course given by him and it focuses on soil conservation, hunger, food systems and the Business of Agriculture.

ROBERT J. NASH, a Professor of Education (ethics and philosophy) at the University of Vermont, is author of more than sixty journal articles, book chapters, and monographs, including a recent article entitled "Where There Is No Vision, The People Perish: A Nation At Risk."

ALBERT J. SCHMIDT is the Arnold Bernhard Professor of History and Professor Law in the University of Bridgeport School of Law. He has written in both History and Law. His book on the Architecture and Planning of classical Moscow will be published this year by the American Philosophical society.

CHARLES J. STOKES, the Charles Anderson Dana Professor of Economics at the University of Bridgeport, is an author of many books in economics, including Economics for Managers (McGraw-Hill, 1979) and Housing Market Performance in the U.S. (Paeger, 1976). Stokes has also contributed to many learned and technical journals. Formerly an economic columnist for the "Christian Science Monitor", Stokes continues to serve as columnist for several local, regional and national newspapers and magazines. One article, his now famous "Theory of Slums" in Land economics (June 1962), has been re-published several times in foreign languages and continues to be referenced in many standard works on third world urban problems.

T. MATHAI THOMAS is Acting Chairman of the Department of Education at the University of Bridgeport. He has taught courses in Education as well as in Sociology, Psychology, Philosophy and Peace Studies. Now he serves as the Chairman of the Society for Educational Reconstruction and is active in a few other professional organizations. His books include: Images of Man (1974), Kerala Immigrants in America (1948) and Global Images of Peace and Education (edited 1987). He is on the Board of Examiners for the Ph.D. Thesis at the Madras University and Kerala University, India. Last year he was a Visiting Faculty member at Yale University.

CHARLES C. WEST is a Stephen Colwell Professor of Christian Ethics at the Princeton Theological Seminary. He is the author of several books, including Ethics, Violence and Revolution, The Power to be Humans, Communism and the Theologians and Perspectives on South Africa. He has made significant contributions to the World Council of Churches and to ecumenical efforts in general. His writings provide new perspectives and understanding on society and social issues of our times.